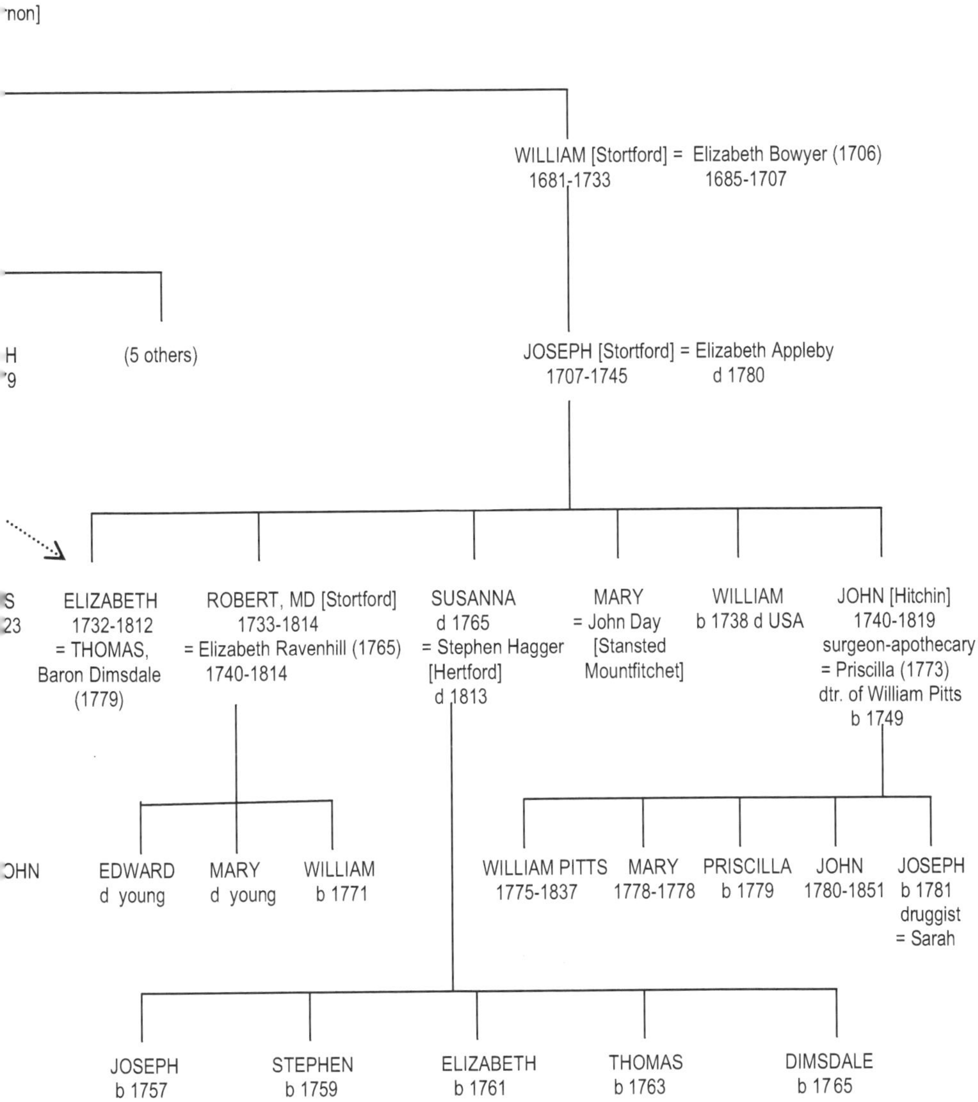

·non]
WILLIAM [Stortford] = Elizabeth Bowyer (1706)
1681-1733 1685-1707
H
'9
(5 others)
JOSEPH [Stortford] = Elizabeth Appleby
1707-1745 d 1780
S
23
ELIZABETH
1732-1812
= THOMAS,
Baron Dimsdale
(1779)
ROBERT, MD [Stortford]
1733-1814
= Elizabeth Ravenhill (1765)
1740-1814
SUSANNA
d 1765
= Stephen Hagger
[Hertford]
d 1813
MARY
= John Day
[Stansted
Mountfitchet]
WILLIAM
b 1738 d USA
JOHN [Hitchin]
1740-1819
surgeon-apothecary
= Priscilla (1773)
dtr. of William Pitts
b 1749
OHN
EDWARD
d young
MARY
d young
WILLIAM
b 1771
WILLIAM PITTS
1775-1837
MARY
1778-1778
PRISCILLA
b 1779
JOHN
1780-1851
JOSEPH
b 1781
druggist
= Sarah
JOSEPH
b 1757
STEPHEN
b 1759
ELIZABETH
b 1761
THOMAS
b 1763
DIMSDALE
b 1765

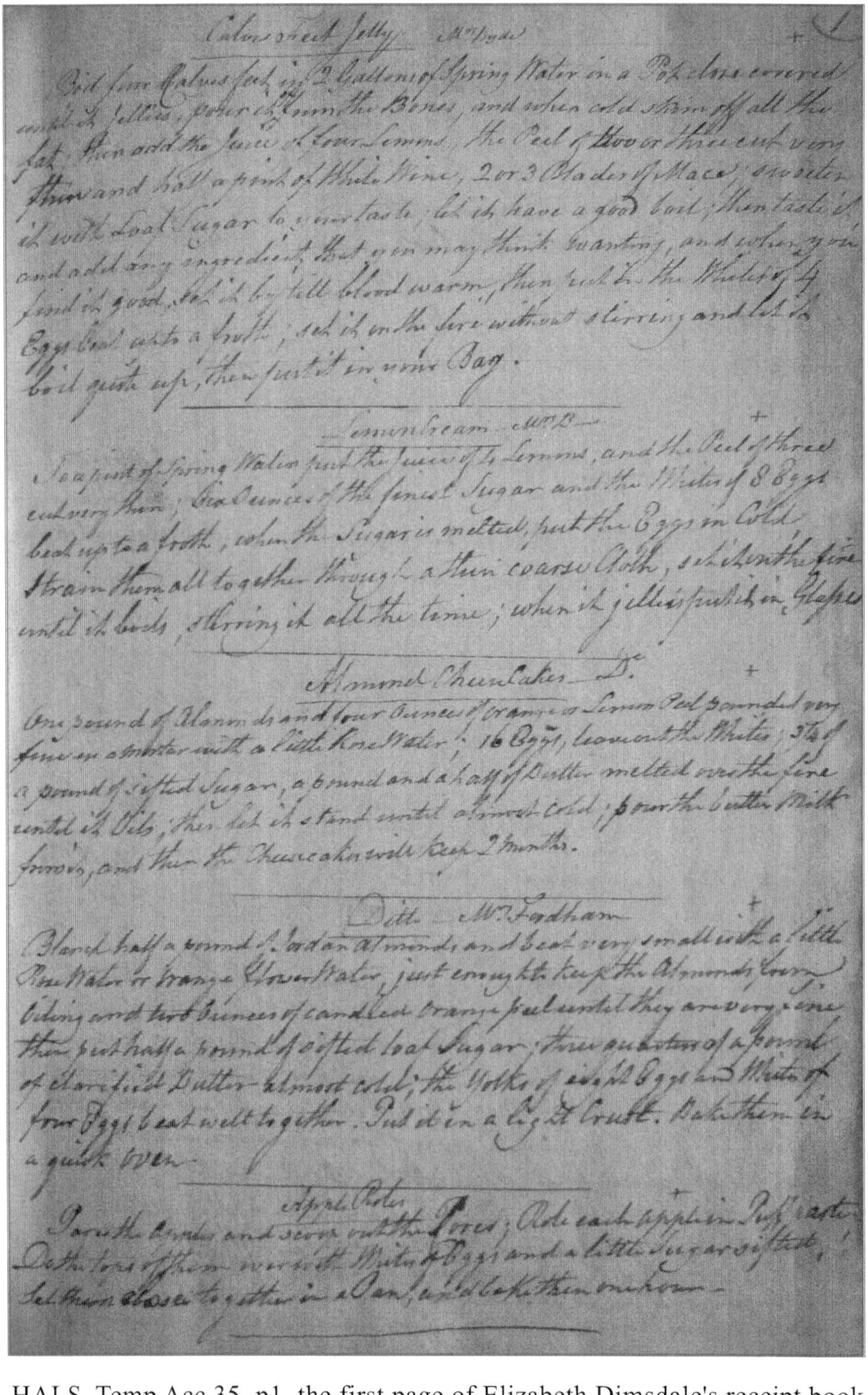

1

Calves Feet Jelly Mrs Dyde

Boil four Calves feet in 2 Gallons of Spring Water in a Pot close covered until it jellies, pour it from the Bones, and when cold skim off all the fat, then add the Juice of four Lemons, the Peel of two or three cut very thin and half a pint of White Wine, 2 or 3 Blades of Mace, sweeten it with Loaf Sugar to your taste, let it have a good boil; then taste it and add any ingredient that you may think wanting, and when you find it good set it by till blood warm, then put in the Whites of 4 Eggs beat into a froth; set it on the fire without stirring and let it boil quite up, then put it in your Bag.

Lemon Cream Mrs D

To a pint of Spring Water put the Juice of 4 Lemons, and the Peel of three cut very thin; six Ounces of the finest Sugar and the Whites of 8 Eggs beat up to a froth, when the Sugar is melted, put the Eggs in Cold. Strain them all together through a thin coarse Cloth, set it on the fire until it boils, stirring it all the time; when it jellies put it in Glasses

Almond Cheesecakes D.

One pound of Almonds and four Ounces of Orange or Lemon Peel pounded very fine in a mortar with a little Rose Water; 16 Eggs, leave out the Whites 3 4; a pound of sifted Sugar, a pound and a half of Butter melted over the fire until it boils, then let it stand until almost cold; pour the Butter Milk from it, and then the Cheesecakes will keep 2 months.

Ditto Mrs Fordham

Blanch half a pound of Jordan Almonds and beat very small with a little Rose Water or Orange Flower Water, just enough to keep the Almonds from oiling and two Ounces of candied Orange peel until they are very fine then put half a pound of sifted loaf Sugar, three quarters of a pound of clarified Butter almost cold, the Yolks of eight Eggs and Whites of four Eggs beat well together. Put it in a light Crust. Bake them in a quick oven

Apple Poles

Pare the Apples and scoop out the Cores; Role each apple in Puff paste. Dab the tops of them over with White of Eggs and a little Sugar sifted, set them close together in a Pan, and bake them in an oven.

HALS, Temp Acc 35, p1, the first page of Elizabeth Dimsdale's receipt book

Hertfordshire Record Publications Volume 28

THE RECEIPT BOOK OF

BARONESS ELIZABETH DIMSDALE, c1800

Edited by Heather Falvey

Hertfordshire Record Society

Volume for the membership year
2012/13

Hertfordshire Record Society

ISBN 978-0-9565111-1-9

Printed and bound in the UK
by Stephen Austin Ltd
Caxton Hill, Hertford, England

Contents

Illustrations

Acknowledgements

First and foremost, thanks are due to Mr Robert Dimsdale for allowing the Society to publish this fascinating manuscript belonging to his family. It was particularly kind of him to deposit it as a temporary accession at Hertfordshire Archives and Local Studies (Temp Acc 35) and also to allow the ever-helpful staff there to copy the whole book so that I could work on the transcript at home and only trek across the county to view the original when I had a stack of queries to resolve. Robert has been a mine of information about the family, supplying transcripts or copies of numerous private documents and being unfailingly polite when answering my many questions.

Although interested in the subject, and a competent cook, I have no expertise in the history of food or of cookery books and so have relied heavily on the work of culinary historians as well as my own research skills. Gilly Lehman's study *The British Housewife: Cookery Books, Cooking and Society in eighteenth-century Britain* provided a solid background on cookery books and cooking in the eighteenth-century and drew my attention to the receipt book of Elizabeth Raper of Thorley: that Elizabeth had a fleeting Dimsdale connection. Particular thanks go to Tom Jaine of Prospect Books, a small but marvellous publishing house specialising not only in facsimile cookery books but also in new books on the history of food and cooking. He came to my rescue on several occasions when words for the Glossary seemed untraceable. Thanks also to Sue Flood, General Editor (and County Archivist) for all her help and advice; to Martin Hagger for providing detailed information about the family of Susanna, Elizabeth's sister, thus enabling me to clear some rather muddied waters; to Anita Pond for designing the jacket; to Jean Riddell for identifying some of Elizabeth's contacts; and to Jane Walker for the family tree.

Some of the receipts have only vague quantities or have ingredients now impossible to find, others can be followed fairly easily and I have tried a few; however, the Hertfordshire Record Society accepts absolutely no responsibility for the consequences if you choose to try out any of them.

Abbreviations

Cross, *An English Lady*	A G Cross, ed, *An English Lady at the Court of Catherine the Great* (Cambridge, 1989)
DFA	Dimsdale family archive (private)
ED	Elizabeth Dimsdale
ERO	Essex Record Office (Chelmsford)
Glasse, *Art of Cookery*	(Hannah Glasse), *The Art of Cookery made plain and easy* (London, 1747; paperback facsimile edition, Totnes, 2004).
HALS	Hertfordshire Archives and Local Studies (Hertford)
HRS	Hertfordshire Record Society
Lehmann, *British Housewife*	Gilly Lehmann, *The British Housewife: Cookery Books, Cooking and Society in eighteenth-century Britain* (Totnes, 2003)
Nott, *Cook's*	John Nott, *Cook's and Confectioner's Dictionary* (London, 1726; reprinted with a glossary by E David, London, 1980)
ODNB	*Oxford Dictionary of National Biography* (online version)
OED	*Oxford English Dictionary* (online version)
Raffald, *Experienced English Housekeeper*	Elizabeth Raffald, *The Experienced English Housekeeper* (Manchester, 1769), edited by Ann Bagnall, with an Introduction by Roy Shipperbottom (Lewes, 1997)
Smith, *Compleat Housewife*	(E) Smith, *The Compleat Housewife: or, Accomplished Gentlewoman's Companion* (16th edition, London, 1758; facsimile, Oxford, 1983)
TNA	The National Archives (Kew)
VCH Herts, III	W Page, ed, *The Victoria History of the Counties of England: Hertfordshire*, vol III (London, 1912)

Introduction

Some time after 1800, when she was in her late sixties or early seventies, Baroness Elizabeth Dimsdale copied almost 700 receipts (recipes) and more than 80 housekeeping tips into a parchment-bound book. Whereas previously the manuscript transcribed and published here has been referred to as a 'commonplace book', such works generally comprise 'passages or matters to be especially remembered or referred to'.[1] Rather than a repository of memorable passages, this book is a well-stocked store-cupboard of recipes and household preparations; we have therefore chosen to describe it as a 'receipt book'.

At the top of roughly a quarter of the items Elizabeth indicated their provenance: some had been given by friends and acquaintances in Hertfordshire society; others came from donors who cannot now be identified due to her tendency to use initials rather than names; others had been gleaned from published works ranging from medical treatises to scientific journals. Many of the receipts have the same title as those published in numerous printed cookery books that were in circulation during the later eighteenth century, but their ingredients and methods differed; a handful, however, are recorded verbatim from such sources, indicating that she, and her acquaintances, were collectors, or at least readers, of such publications. Some of the receipts are of foreign origin given by acquaintances of her late husband; many, no doubt, had been handed down through the family.

The order in which she entered them in her book is entirely random - she did not sort them by type - although there is some grouping according to donor. Rather than analysing these receipts for their culinary merits and what they indicate regarding the development of cooking and dining in the late eighteenth century, the purpose of this introduction is to consider who Elizabeth was and what can be discovered about the contents of her book.

Elizabeth Dimsdale and her immediate family

The Dimsdales were, and still are, a well-known Hertfordshire family. Lionel Munby has demonstrated how between the 1630s and 1780s no fewer than fourteen related Dimsdales were medical men, of whom at least seven were practising Quakers. He notes that 'The descendants of Robert Dimsdale, barber-alehouse keeper of Hoddesdon, include one baronet, one knight, and three MPs,

---

[1] *OED*, 'common-place book'.

two of whom were barons of the Russian Empire'.[2] The family was also involved in banking: by 1769 the bank of Dimsdale, Archer and Byde was in existence.

Elizabeth Dimsdale was born on 29 April 1732 at Bishops Stortford.[3] She was the eldest child of Joseph Dimsdale, a surgeon, and his wife, Elizabeth (née Appleby). She had three brothers, Robert, William and John, and two sisters, Mary and Susanna.[4] Joseph was twice-over the first cousin of Thomas Dimsdale, later the famous smallpox inoculator, their fathers having married sisters. (See the family tree in the endpapers.) Little is known about Elizabeth's early life, except that her father died in early 1745, when she was only 14 years old. In his will, made on 27 January 1744/5,[5] he bequeathed her his farm called Parkers, in Takeley (Essex), then in the occupation of Widow Fenney, and also £50 from his other lands in Hertfordshire and Essex. Since they were under age at the time of their father's death, he appointed his wife guardian of all of their children and of the lands granted to their daughter Elizabeth and their son Robert. Joseph also left Robert 'all my Books of Physick and Instruments of Surgery and Mathematicks and all my Stills and Mortars', clearly expecting him to follow in his footsteps and become a medical practitioner; which he did. Joseph's executors were his wife and his cousin, Thomas.

Elizabeth seems to have been quite close to her sister Susanna, who married Stephen Hagger of Hertford, a Quaker miller at Sele Mill, which he rented from Thomas, first Baron Dimsdale. In his will Hagger described himself as a 'mealman'.[6] On various occasions he acted on behalf of Thomas in business and land transactions.[7] Susanna and Stephen had five children, and Elizabeth was in attendance at the births of their first son, Joseph, in 1757, and of their

---

[2] Lionel Munby, 'True Quakers? The Dimsdale family and the rise of the medical profession 1600-1800', in Lionel Munby, *The Common People are not Nothing: Conflict in Religion and Politics in Hertfordshire 1575-1780* (Hatfield, 1995), quotation from p155.

[3] Family tree held in DFA.

[4] The dates of birth of her sisters have been reported inconsistently and cannot be ascertained.

[5] TNA, PROB11/737/441, will of Joseph Dimsdale, surgeon, of Bishops Stortford, probate granted 18 February 1744/5.

[6] TNA, PROB11/1556/240, will and codicils of Stephen Hagger, mealman, of Hertford, probate granted 5 May 1814.

[7] See, for example, HALS, D/EHx/T3.

fourth son and fifth child, Dimsdale, on 11 December 1765.[8] Susanna died the following day and on 16 December was buried in the 'Friends' Burying Ground' at Bishops Stortford.[9] Elizabeth was originally named as one of Stephen's four executors but she did not act in that capacity as she predeceased him. In her will, she made bequests to Stephen, to his surviving children and to two of his grandchildren.[10]

As we shall see, Elizabeth was also close to her youngest brother, John, who, in adulthood, lived in Hitchin and was married to Priscilla, née Pitts. John Dimsdale was a surgeon or surgeon-apothecary.[11] Although not qualified as a medical doctor, he was sometimes addressed as such. Of twelve extant letters between him and Thomas and/or Elizabeth and another correspondent (Samuel Scott - a Hertford Quaker), three are addressed to him as Surgeon, one as Dr and four as Mr. That he supplied many prescriptions is indicated by the bills he sent to Hitchin Priory for treatment of various members of the Radcliffe family, their servants and their horses and hounds between 1768 and 1779.[12] He and Thomas compared notes on how cases should be treated. Indeed, judging by one of Thomas's letters, John must have considered accompanying Thomas to Russia in 1768 and Thomas also suggested to him that it would be worth his (John's) while to go to northern Europe on his own account.[13]

Elizabeth and her husband seem to have had far less contact with her eldest brother, Robert, who was a qualified doctor. He was concerned with the foundation of the Benevolent Medical Society for the United Counties of Essex and Hertford. The first meeting took place in 1786 and a fund was set up for the relief and benefit of widows and orphans of physicians, surgeons and apothecaries in the two counties. These persons were 'exposed to numerous sources of infection and suffer(ed) premature death frequently thereby and the

[8] TNA, RG6/1337, Society of Friends' Registers, Notes and Certificates of Births, Marriages and Burials, Bedfordshire and Hertfordshire, register of Monthly Meeting of Hertford, Births, p24. The births of all five children are recorded on the same page.
[9] TNA, RG6/1337, register of Monthly Meeting of Hertford, Burials, p236.
[10] See Appendix III, will of Elizabeth Dimsdale.
[11] Information in this paragraph has been taken from various letters in the DFA archive and from Dimsdale deposits at Friends House, Euston Road; see also Munby, 'True Quakers?'.
[12] See, for example, HALS, DE/R/F211/13 (1776); F212/12 (1779); and various items in the DFA.
[13] DFA, TD B7.

fair prospects of a family suddenly blasted and a painful reverse presented to persons well brought up, but thus cut off from future resources'.[14] Dr Robert was the chairman of the Society and Baron Thomas its treasurer from 1787 until his death. Little is known of Elizabeth's sister Mary, except that she married John Day of Stansted Mountfitchet (Essex); or of her brother William, who died in America.

For much of her life, from a fairly young age, Elizabeth lived with Thomas and his family as a kind of housekeeper. Thomas was born on 29 May 1712 in Theydon Garnon (Essex), the fourth son and sixth of the eight children of John Dimsdale, surgeon, and his wife Susanna (née Bowyer).[15] Most of Thomas's siblings died young, only he and his brothers Robert and Joseph living beyond 25 years of age. Their father was a member of the Society of Friends and their grandfather, Robert Dimsdale, had accompanied William Penn to America in 1684. As already noted, many of the Dimsdales were medical men: Thomas was first apprenticed as a surgeon to his father in Theydon Garnon and then studied at St Thomas's Hospital, London, under Joshua Symons and John Girle. According to his obituary in the *Monthly Magazine* entitled 'Memoirs of Baron Dimsdale', Thomas 'was greatly respected by both of these gentlemen, for his close application in the prosecution of his studies'.[16] He began practising medicine at Hertford in 1734.

In 1739 he married Mary, only daughter of Nathaniel Brassey of Roxford, near Hertford, banker and MP for Hertford Borough from 1734 to 1761.[17] The Brasseys were not Quakers and since Quakers were forbidden to marry outside the Society the marriage brought Thomas into conflict with the Friends at Hertford. The detailed record in the local Minute Book reveals the unbending attitude of the Friends and also Thomas's desire to maintain his Quaker connection.[18] Mary died childless in 1744. In 1745 Thomas offered his services

---

[14] Essex Record Office, D/Z 15/1, Minutes of the Benevolent Medical Society for the United Counties of Essex and Hertford, front page.
[15] This section on Thomas is adapted from the *ODNB* entry for him and supplemented with material from the DFA, except where otherwise noted (T E Kebbel, 'Dimsdale, Thomas (1712–1800)', revised Andrea Rusnock).
[16] 'Memoirs of Baron Dimsdale', *Monthly Magazine, or, British Register* (1 July 1801), pp511-13.
[17] Munby, 'True Quakers?', p161.
[18] HALS, NQ2/1A/15, Hertford Monthly Meeting Minutes, 1728-1741. The exchanges are recounted in full in Munby, 'True Quakers?', pp161-2.

to the duke of Cumberland to assist the physicians and surgeons in the army.[19] He accompanied the English army to Carlisle, on the surrender of which he returned to Hertford.

In 1746 he married Ann Iles, daughter of John Iles, and a relative of his first wife; they had eight sons and two daughters.[20] At about the time of his marriage he inherited a fortune from Lady Susanna Dimsdale, widow of Sir John of Hertford, and so initially he retired from his profession. However, with the increasing size of his family, in 1761, at the age of 49, he resumed practice and took his degree as a physician from King's College, Aberdeen.

He began to specialise in the treatment of smallpox and became well-known as an inoculator. This inoculation treatment, which entailed infecting a patient with smallpox, preceded vaccination with cowpox by many years.[21] In 1767 he published *The Present Method of Inoculating for the Small-Pox*, which proved popular, going through six editions in five years and being translated into several foreign languages. In this work, Thomas described a safer, less invasive inoculation procedure, which had first been pioneered by Daniel Sutton. He also described at great length various cases of patients whom he had inoculated, detailing their symptoms and recovery from the process. In 1768 he was invited to St Petersburg by Catherine the Great to inoculate herself and her son, the Grand Duke Paul.[22] Thomas was accompanied and assisted by his son, Nathaniel, then a medical student in Edinburgh. The empress was obviously confident in Thomas's good practices; indeed, she clearly had far more

---

[19] 'Memoirs of Baron Dimsdale'.

[20] Just after Ann's death, Thomas wrote: 'We had 10 children born alive & several miscarriages – 3 dyed infants – 7 were living at the time of their mother's death' (DFA, TD D1). The identities of the children have been reported variously in different sources. The names and dates used in this volume are those given in the pedigree prepared in December 1965 for Mr Thomas Edward Dimsdale by Rodney Dennys, herald of the Royal College of Arms and Rouge Croix Poursuivant.

[21] See, for example, P Razzell, *The Conquest of Smallpox: The Impact of Inoculation on Smallpox Mortality in Eighteenth Century Britain* (London, 1977).

[22] For accounts of Thomas's and Nathaniel's visits to Russia and of Thomas's inoculation techniques, see I M Graham, 'Two Hertfordshire Doctors', *East Herts Archaeological Society Transactions*, XIII, part 1 (1950-51), pp44, 46-54; W J Bishop, 'Thomas Dimsdale, MD, FRS (1712-1800) and the inoculation of Catherine the Great of Russia', *Annals of Medical History*, IV, 4 (July 1932), pp311-38; P H Clendenning, 'Dr Thomas Dimsdale and Smallpox Inoculation in Russia', *Journal of the History of Medicine and Allied Sciences*, XXVIII, 2 (April 1973), pp109-25.

confidence in him than in any Russian practitioners. She could not, however, answer for the confidence of her subjects, and so allegedly had relays of post-horses prepared for him for an instant, rapid escape in case of disaster. Fortunately both she and her son recovered successfully from their inoculation. Within a few weeks of this, Thomas recorded that he had inoculated more than 140 Russian nobles with 'better success than I ever had with the same number in England and all are perfectly well'.[23] Thomas and Nathaniel were lavishly rewarded not only by the imperial family but also by the Russian nobility. Both father and son were created Barons of the Russian Empire. Thomas received a sum of £10,000, with an annuity of £500, and £2,000 for his expenses. The empress presented him with miniatures, set in diamonds, of herself and her son, and granted him an addition to his family arms in the form of a wing of the black eagle of Russia. On his return to England, in 1769 Thomas was made a Fellow of the Royal Society.[24] Back in Hertford, he continued to inoculate famous and ordinary people alike. In 1774 Omiah, the 'noble savage' brought back from Tahiti by Captain Furneaux, was sent to him for inoculation.[25] According to Thomas, the king 'ordered Omiah to be placed under my Care to be inoculated … it was thought absolutely necessary to have him inoculated'. Thomas had opened a 'house of reception' which was a nursing home for such patients before and after inoculation.

During this time Elizabeth was living with Thomas and his family, but she did not remain in Hertford continuously. From 3 July to 7 September 1776 she went on 'A Tour from Dover to Paris' in the company of a Colonel Sharpe and his niece Miss Sharpe. She kept a detailed record of this journey, in which she shows herself to be an astute observer of people and places; with the benefit of hindsight, it is clear that her observations on society in pre-Revolutionary France are particularly percipient.[26] Two letters exchanged between Elizabeth

[23] DFA, TD B6, letter from Dr Thomas Dimsdale to Henry Nicols, 3 December 1768.
[24] Munby, 'True Quakers?', p163.
[25] The Dimsdale family archive contains a manuscript book (hereafter, Family MS book) into which Elizabeth copied various items including 'Some Anecdotes respecting Omiah who came from Otaheite written by Baron Dimsdale'. Omiah, a Tahitian, arrived in England on Captain Furneaux's ship in 1774 and returned with Cook on the *Resolution* in 1777. He was an object of fascination to London's high society, meeting with such figures as Mrs Thrale, Fanny Burney and Samuel Johnson. He also had his portrait painted by Joshua Reynolds. To the proto-Romantic thinkers, he represented the noble savage, a man untainted and uncorrupted by 'modern' European society.
[26] Her account of 'A Tour from Dover to Paris, 1776' occupies 63 pages (Family MS book, pp33-95).

and Thomas while she was in Paris have survived. Elizabeth's letter, dated 31 July 1776, opened with her concerns about the health of Thomas's wife.[27] She expressed herself 'extremely glad to find my Cousin continues mending & hope the next account will be that she is got down stairs & likewise that you are all well which will give me great pleasure'. She then recounted various sights on their journey to Paris and her observations on the capital itself. 'In regard to Paris I am rather disappointed, tho I have not seen much of it at present Miss Sharpe has hired a Coach as her own Coach will not do here & it is like the Lord Chancell[o]rs Coach with the sides glass I have been out with her in it to the Mercers & the Coachman has a fine large bag wig, really it surprises me not a little to see how everybody is dresst & powderd…'. They were going to 'Marlow' [Marly] to 'see the King dine in publick, indeed we are to see every thing that is worth notice'. However, the party's servants were complaining about the beds. She closed by asking Thomas 'give my Duty to my Mother & kind love to my Cousin & all Relations'. Less than a week later, on 11 August, Thomas replied with a chatty letter. The main section is reproduced in full as it provides interesting insights into the family's activities and welfare.[28]

> We were all extremely glad to hear a good Acc[oun]t of the health of your whole Party & entertained with the amusements that you have already met with, tho I expect they are only the prelude to far greater of which we expect a full acc[oun]t on your return I wish it was possible to have a view of you just when you are dressed to wait on the King the Headdress & Rouge which I hope you now wear to appear like other Mortals would be matter of entertainment. I have a good Acc[oun]t to give of your Cousins health which has mended fast of late insomuch as to spare me to take a journey to Leeds which will occasion an absence of at least 10 Days.[29] All the rest of us very well But you will be sorry to hear that your old favorite Jack has been shot for Madness.[30] He was by all acc[oun]ts most dangerously & violently seized & we think it a great happiness that none of the Children or family were bit & I think it was well that neither you or I who have been foolishly fond of him were in the Way. In respect to home news I can only say that my Bro[ther] has taken Miss Marlbrough[s] House & is about to commence Housekeeper again.

[27] DFA, TD D14.
[28] DFA, TD D8.
[29] The health of his wife Ann.
[30] A pet dog.

In his postscript, Thomas noted 'I saw the Hitchin Family lately I think Y[ou]r Brother[31] better the rest well - but there has been & indeed still is a bad fever in Hitchin for which Y[ou]r Nephew[32] & his Nurse are now living at Rocksley' (Roxley, near Willian).

While in Paris Elizabeth visited the Abbé L'Epayes, who had invented a method for teaching those deaf and dumb from birth, and recorded detailed observations on his lessons.[33] She also was driven past the Bastille some 13 years before it was stormed and having briefly described its exterior, she observed 'We did not continue long looking at this miserable place, for the dreadful stories we had heard of People being confined there, made such an Impression on our Minds, that we were very glad to leave it'.[34]

She made several comments on the food in France, some complimentary, others not. At Villeneuve:

> a dirty looking Girl after laying the Cloth came in with something dangling on her Arm which she laid on the Table, Curiosity led me to a near inspection, when behold it was a loaf of Bread made in a compleat circle, with a round for the Arm to go in. the same Person soon after brought a Dish of Mutton Chops, which she unfortunately let slip off the Dish on the floor, but they were very soon replaced after blowing off the dirt, and put upon the Table.[35]

In Paris, however, things were better:

> In regard to our living at the Hotel we had no reason to complain, as our dinners were always one or two plain Dishes, the rest in the French Stile, and great plenty of fine Fruit and Ice every Day, the Peaches and Melons I thought good, at Breakfast we had French Rolls and good Butter, which used to come up in Ice, but they never put any Salt in their Butter.[36]

On their way back to Calais, they passed through the small town of Souchet

---

[31] John.
[32] William Pitts Dimsdale, son of John and Priscilla, was only 1 year old at this time.
[33] Family MS Book, pp56-57.
[34] Family MS Book, p58.
[35] Family MS Book, p46.
[36] Family MS Book, p73.

> where we stopped to Change Horses, the Inhabitants were assembled to celebrate the Village Festival; All was Life Joy and Harmony; not a discontented Face to be seen, nor would they suffer us to pass without a Taste of their Festive Cake, and tho but little better than common Bread, yet the Chearfulness and Goodwill with which it was given, made me think it the best that I had ever eaten of.[37]

From the letters exchanged between Thomas and Elizabeth in 1776 it is clear that Thomas's wife Ann was not in good health and she died less than three years later, on 9 March 1779. She was buried at the Friends' burial ground at Bishops Stortford.[38] Just under eight months later, on 3 November 1779, Thomas and Elizabeth were married.[39] Thomas and Ann's youngest son, also Thomas, recorded the marriage somewhat wryly: 'He then married his third wife, Elizabeth Dimsdale, who had resided in the family most of her life, at an advanced time of life, of course had not any children by her'.[40] Shortly after their marriage Thomas wrote to Elizabeth's brother, John, and it is clear from this letter that there was genuine affection between the newly-weds.[41]

> I must now address you by a new Name that of Dear Brother & just say that we are got to Hertford & should be glad to see you & Sister when it may suit you to spend a Day with us not as a matter of form but when quite convenient. The desire I had to make sure of a Companion for Life of the Person I esteemed the most of any one in the World & the certainty of its being agreeable to my whole Family were my inducements & I hope as reasonable as a Man at my Time of Life can give - The reason for its being precipitated I dare say your Sister has informed you & I have now the additional satisfaction of assuring you that, as expected, every one of your Cousins have assured me that they are perfectly well pleased with the Event. The Spare Rib you was so kind to send was eat twice by the D[octo]r his Wife[42] & we two & agreed to be some of the finest meat of the kind we ever tasted.

---

[37] Family MS Book, p96.
[38] On 20 March 1779 her husband Thomas recorded the manner her death, her deathbed wishes and her burial. (DFA, Thomas Dimsdale junior's memoranda).
[39] The event was reported in *The Gentleman's Magazine* (Arthur Jones, ed, *Hertfordshire as recorded in* The Gentleman's Magazine (Hatfield, 1993), p157).
[40] DFA, Thomas Dimsdale junior's memoranda.
[41] DFA, TD D5.
[42] Perhaps Elizabeth's brother Robert and his wife, also Elizabeth.

In his letter Thomas refers to, but does not explain 'The reason for its being precipitated'. His son's wry comment indicates that this was no shot-gun wedding, so it seems likely that the reason for its speed was simply that the couple wished it so.

In 1780 Thomas stood for election as Member of Parliament for Hertford: he came top of the poll, above William Baker, and defeating John Calvert.[43] His actions during his parliamentary career were largely dictated by his Quaker beliefs and his integrity was recognised. 'He owes his seat entirely to the good opinion entertained of him by his electors, amongst whom he is an old and favourite resident. Oratory is not one of his talents, but it is believed, however, that he will ... vote upon every subject from the unbiased influence of his principles and conviction.'[44]

Less than eighteen months after their marriage, Thomas and Elizabeth travelled together to Russia. Thomas had been summoned to inoculate Catherine the Great's grandsons, the Grand Dukes Alexander and Constantine. Elizabeth kept a journal of their travels, beginning at Dover on 21 June 1781 and returning just over six months later, on 30 November.[45] She described not only the places, buildings and countryside that they passed en route to, and back from, St Petersburg, but also their assorted modes of transport, and the food that they ate. At Ghent, they had 'an excellent Dinner served up at half past two'.[46] The cost per head was 'three Skellings', about 'One and Ninepence English'. The first course was 'Soup, Bouille Beef. A fine dish of Peas and what they call Des Herbes'; the second course consisted of 'a Ragou of Sweetbreads,[47] a Fowl, a roast Duck and salted Tongue'; afterwards there was 'a good Desert [*sic*] of Strawberries, Cherries, and Biscuits'. She was an acute observer of the various

---

[43] L B Namier and J Brooke, eds, *The House of Commons, 1754-1790*, vol. II, *Members A-J*, pp325-326, p325.

[44] *The English Chronicle*, 1781, quoted in Namier and Brooke, *House of Commons, 1754-1790*, II, *Members A-J*, p325.

[45] The *ODNB* entry for Thomas Dimsdale states erroneously that the second visit to Russia took place in 1784 (Kebbel, 'Dimsdale, Thomas (1712–1800)', revised Rusnock). Elizabeth's journal has been published in Cross, *An English Lady*. Cross states that Thomas and Elizabeth were married in early 1781 and that the journey was made 'within months of their marriage' (p11), but this was not the case, since they were married in November 1779.

[46] Cross, *An English Lady*, p19.

[47] Elizabeth entered two receipts for 'Bouille Beef' and one for 'Ragoued Sweetbread' in her book; here in Chapter IV.

peoples, whether of high or low status, and their clothing, employment and activities. For example, she noted that Russian merchants and tradesmen seldom kept books of accounts as many could not read or write, and were 'unacquainted with the knowledge of Figures'; however, 'Their manner of reckoning is by Machine with Several Rows of Wires, upon which Beads are strung of different colours'. Having outlined how the abacus worked, she noted 'I bought one of these Machines as I admired it much, and brought it home with me'.[48] She also described in detail the huge imperial summer palace of Tsarskoe Selo, its grounds and her presentation there to the empress.[49]

An observant traveller, she was fascinated by the differences between English and Russian life, in particular the consequences of the extremely cold winter weather. Interestingly, she appreciated the nutritional benefits of freezing food. An English lady living in Russia had informed her that

> good Housewifes about the end of October kill their Poultry, and keep them packed up with a layer of Snow between them and take them out for use as Occasion requires: by this means they save the nourishment of the Animal several Months. Veal frozen at Archangel and brought to St Petersburg, is esteemed the finest they have nor can it be distinguished at the Table from that which is fresh killed being equally juicy ...[50]

Perhaps unsurprisingly, she made a number of other observations regarding Russian food and medicinal remedies. The contents of ants' nests were much sought after, although they 'are certainly a larger kind of Ants, and the Anthills considerably larger than any we have in England.[51] 'The Vinegar', wrote Elizabeth, 'is very curious, and I thought very good, not unlike distilled Vinegar, all the Russians prefer it to any other it is made from Ants'. She then described how it was produced: 'a Pitcher is placed in the Centre of the Nest which the Ants crawl into, when there is sufficient number of them in the Pitcher boiling Water is poured on them and it is stopped close and stands all night, the next

---

48 Cross, *An English Lady*, p45.
49 Cross, *An English Lady*, Chapter 3, 'Tsarskoe Selo'. See also the slightly mischievous account of her presentation to the Empress given by James Walker in *Paramythia* (London, 1821), quoted in Cross, *An English Lady*, p12.
50 Cross, *An English Lady*, p45.
51 This and the following paragraphs on ants' nests are taken from Cross, *An English Lady*, p68. The receipts for vinegar collected by Elizabeth are in Chapter XV - there is not one for 'Ant Vinegar'.

morning the whole is filtered off for use'. But this was not the only useful product from ants' nests:

> I was farther informed of a great Curiosity and Vertue in the Ants nest, which is the Oil of Ants; this is found at the bottom of the nest in a Bladder, and is reckoned very effectual in bruises or sprains and very scarce owing to the difficulty of procuring the Bladder whole, as few people know how to get it, tho' it is to be found in every Nest.[52]

Furthermore an English acquaintance in Russia had 'collected a great number of Ants eggs in the Summer, and dried them in an Oven to feed her Turkeys in the Winter, which she found answered extremely well, and the Turkeys soon got fat with them'.[53]

Elizabeth described how the empress dined at one o'clock, the food being served on silver dishes carried by soldiers first to Catherine and then to the Dimsdales and other guests. Elizabeth discovered that the cost of their 'Table' (ie board) was 90 roubles a day, which was about £18 sterling.[54] Every day they had a dinner 'not inferior' to the following:

> Soup, Fish, Boiled Chicken & Cauliflower,
> Roast leg of Mutton or Beef with Potatoes over it,
> A small dish with a Forequarter of Lamb roasted
> Duck, Fowl, and two Snipes (all in one Dish)
> Fine piece of Hamburgh Beef,[55]
> Cuttlets and Sausages,
> Hash Duck and stewed Mushrooms
> Cray fish. Apple Puffs[56]
> Seven dishes in the Desert [*sic*]. Oranges, Apples, Pears,
> Cherries, Macaroons,[57] Biscuits, Stewed Pippens, and
> Parmesan Cheese.

---

[52] Elizabeth's receipts for salves and ointments are in Chapter XVIII - there are none for 'Oil of Ants'.

[53] Chapter XV includes several ways to fatten fowl, but not this one.

[54] Cross, *An English Lady*, pp68-9.

[55] In Chapter XIII, Potting and collaring meat, there is a receipt for 'Hamburg Pickle', a brine in which to pickle meat.

[56] There are receipts for puffs in Chapters V and VI, but none for 'Apple Puffs'.

[57] In Chapter XI, Cakes, there are several receipts for 'Macaroons' and 'Macaroon Biscuits'.

There was also always a hot supper of seven or nine dishes. She commented that the 'House Lamb I thought very extraordinary they kill them so young, for really a Leg was not larger than the Leg of a Goose, and esteemed a very great Rarity'.

Elizabeth enjoyed a variety of Russian fish, including 'Sterlet', which was 'shaped not unlike a Sturgeon, and its mouth was very different from any fish I ever saw near its throat'.[58] This was 'a most delicious Fish, … by far the best Fish I ever tasted', and she especially liked it cold in jelly. There was also Shaddock which was 'in great plenty, very like our Cod, but I think not so good'. She had two kinds of Salmon Trout but thought Sturgeon 'an indifferent coarse Fish'. Crayfish were plentiful and 'the largest I ever saw'; however, the Russians had 'no Lobsters or Oysters except they are sent from England'.[59] She was also fascinated by the numerous hot houses, one of which was 800 feet long. The fruit reared therein included water melons, peaches and nectarines.[60] She was surprised by the 'very great plenty of exceeding fine China Oranges' which she had ascertained were not native to Russia.

Once or twice while Elizabeth and Thomas were there, the empress suffered from 'very slight Indispositions'.[61] Thomas was consulted and he advised her to take some 'white Wine Whey' before going to bed.[62] Since no-one at court knew how to make it, Catherine told the baron 'if he would see it made, she would take it'. Elizabeth described how later that evening a courtier called on them, followed by a footman carrying a gold saucepan and a basketful of excellent wines from which Thomas should choose one that he thought 'proper to make the Whey with'. Elizabeth, rather than Thomas, made the whey and he took it to the Empress to drink. She 'asked him whether he saw it made, which he assured her he did, then she immediately took it and drank it'. As Elizabeth astutely observed, this was placing 'a very great Confidence in the Baron'. She

[58] A sterlet is 'A small species of sturgeon, *Acipenser ruthenus*, found in Russia' (*OED*).
[59] Cross, *An English Lady*, p69.
[60] Cross, *An English Lady*, p71. Nectarines were being grown in England from the early seventeenth century onwards (*OED*). In 1715 in Datchworth peaches and nectarines were recorded as tithes at harvest (Jane Walker, (ed), *Datchworth Tithe Accounts* (HRS vol XXV), p29).
[61] Cross, *An English Lady*, pp69-70.
[62] 'Wine whey' was a medicinal drink made from wine and milk.

modestly noted that she made the whey three times and that on the last occasion Catherine's apothecary came to see it made.[63]

Elizabeth and Thomas left St Petersburg on 15 October 1781 and began their homeward journey, which was beset by bad weather. They finally arrived at Dover on 30 November.[64] Thomas was almost 70 when they returned from Russia. He was re-elected to parliament in April 1784 but did not stand again in 1790, being succeeded by his son Nathaniel.[65]

From surviving family letters and papers, it is clear that from their return to England until Thomas's death nearly 19 years later, Elizabeth and her husband lived mostly at Cowbridge House, Hertford, but also stayed in Bath and London from time to time. Although rather reclusive, they were not without visitors. For example, in the 1790s they welcomed scientist Jan Ingen Housz to their home in Hertford, and in 1790 he stayed with them at Bath.[66] Another friend was Dr John Carr, who as well as being master at the grammar school in Hertford taught English to Russian students billeted in the town. Dr Carr wrote humorous verses, such as the following, about Elizabeth, entitled 'On a Gold Ring for Priscilla Dimsdale's Aunt':

> As Gold is said to clear the eyes,
> Your Gift, Sir, I am bound to prize.
> But for her Aunt an added Ring,
> Priscilla says, is not the thing.
> Presents, as she pretends to reason,
> Should be adapted to the season
>
> Of Times and Seasons let her prate,
> I meddle not in the debate;
> For with this sprightly Niece of mine
> All Competition I decline,
> Thinking this Ring, that prompts her Wit,

---

[63] A receipt for 'Whey' is recorded in the receipt book. In her journal Elizabeth does not record the ingredients added to the wine; her receipt uses white wine, milk, orange juice, lump sugar and boiling water.
[64] In Hanover on 16 November Elizabeth stopped her journal, noting, 'I caught a very bad cold which prevented my continuing my Journal' (Cross, *An English Lady*, p93).
[65] Namier and Brooke, *House of Commons*, II, *1754-1790*, p326.
[66] N Beale and E Beale, *Echoes of Ingen Housz* (Salisbury, 2011), *passim.*

May her young finger better fit.[67]

Thomas lost the sight of one eye and became virtually blind in the other in 1783, but it is alleged that a cataract operation in 1784 was successful and his sight in that eye remained good until the day he died.[68] He continued to practise medicine from time to time, often freely, although he was paid £21 for inoculating the two children of the second Viscount Palmerston in May 1787;[69] and in the 1780s and 1790s he inoculated the ten children of Walter Spencer-Stanhope MP of Cannon Hall in Yorkshire.[70] In Hertford he was still busy inoculating. A local landowner and MP, William Baker, a political opponent of Thomas and a supporter of the third duke of Portland, wrote to the duke as late as 1792 complaining that 'the two Barons, for the sake of their Parliamentary interest in the town, are disposed to attend many of the inferior families gratuitously'.[71]

That all of Thomas's children may not have been on the best of terms with Elizabeth is suggested by a letter that Thomas wrote to them towards the end of his life urging them to recognise her merits. After explaining that the bequests set out in his will reflected, and compensated for, the value of the benefits that they had received individually during his lifetime, he added: 'I earnestly recommend you all to pay the most Affectionate regard to my dear Wife whose prudent and loving concern for mine and your happiness has contributed to my own & your happiness and as I believe also to the improvement of my

---

[67] HALS, D/EX 363/Z2. The verse must date from before 1800 as the Baron is mentioned elsewhere on the same paper. Priscilla was the daughter of Elizabeth's brother John. Carr prefaced the verses with the comment 'Pray forgive me for adding some nonsense, which came into my head yesterday after what I saw and heard at the house of the Baroness'.

[68] The cataract operation, performed by Baron Wenzell, is mentioned in various obituaries for Thomas but it cannot be substantiated (See, for example, 'Memoirs of Baron Dimsdale', p513).

[69] B Connell, *Portrait of a Whig Peer* (London, 1957), p169.

[70] He inoculated ten Stanhope children, the last in 1796 (A M W Stirling (ed), *The Letter-Bag of Lady Elizabeth Spencer-Stanhope* (online version; Project Gutenberg ref 7253). All the inoculations were in February, March or April and so may have happened at Bath. It is possible that Nathaniel was the inoculator but Thomas is the more likely as he and Stanhope were MPs together when the first child was born in 1784. This was perhaps an exception for an old friend and colleague

[71] University of Nottingham Library, PwF 230/1, letter from William Baker to the third Duke of Portland, 8 November 1792.

property'.[72] Thomas died at Hertford on 30 December 1800, aged 88, and was buried in the Quaker burial ground at Stortford on 6 January 1801.[73]

Elizabeth continued to live at Cowbridge House and perhaps sometime soon after Thomas's death began compiling her receipt book.[74] Her last will and testament, written on 2 September 1808, has two 'codicils', one of which is dated 17 November 1803 and is apparently an earlier will, although the probate court treated it as a codicil.[75] All three documents disclose a close kinship network amongst her own relatives: she made various bequests to the husband, children and grandchildren of her deceased sister Susanna; to her brother Robert and his son William; and to her brother John, his wife Priscilla and their children.[76] Evidently Elizabeth considered some of Thomas's bequests unfair, despite the explanation that he gave in the letter mentioned above. In particular, she wanted his plate to pass to his daughter Ann because it appeared to her (Elizabeth) 'rather a hardship she was excluded from having any of the other plate of her late father'. Ann lived with Elizabeth at Cowbridge House and continued to live there until her own death in 1832, after which a detailed inventory of the contents of the house was drawn up.[77] Elizabeth wrote the second codicil in June 1812, in which she made monetary bequests to her cook (£5), and also to two named servants, Betty Squires, her maidservant, (£20), and the housemaid Mary Warren (£5). She stated that Mary was the servant of her sister, presumably meaning her sister-in-law, Priscilla. Since Elizabeth made these bequests less than four months before she died, it seems likely Mary had been sent over from Hitchin as extra help for her. Elizabeth died on 16 October and was buried at Bishops Stortford, near her beloved husband.

---

[72] DFA, TD D2. His very detailed will is TNA, PROB 11/1352/110, probate granted 17 January 1801.

[73] Several obituaries and accounts of his life were published (See, for example, 'Memoirs of Baron Dimsdale'; 'Memoirs of the Hon. Baron Dimsdale', *European Magazine and London Review*, 42 (1802), pp83-7).

[74] The book's watermark can be dated to 1800.

[75] TNA, PROB11/1538/279, will and codicils of Elizabeth Dimsdale, dated 2 September 1808, 17 November 1803 and 21 June 1812, probate granted 11 November 1812. A full transcript is given as Appendix III.

[76] Since there are no bequests to her sister Mary, her husband John or any children they may have had, it seems likely that they predeceased Elizabeth.

[77] HALS, DE/D/1172, inventory of household goods at Cowbridge House, Hertford, late Miss Ann Dimsdale's. Her will is TNA, PROB11/1801/465, probate granted 29 June 1832.

The provenance of Elizabeth Dimsdale's receipts

Named and traced donors

Of the 770 receipts and housekeeping hints collected in the book (not allowing for duplicates, of which there are several), 219 record the name of the person from whom Elizabeth acquired the receipt. Of the remaining 551 doubtless some were created, or at least adapted, by Elizabeth and some had been handed down through the extensive family network, but as no earlier family receipt book has survived this has been impossible to verify. Nevertheless, it has been possible to trace the origins of a number of the unattributed receipts. This section examines some of the sources that have been identified for the receipts, one of which has particular implications for the dating of the book.

Firstly, although in some cases Elizabeth gave the name of the receipt's donor, in others she gave only their initials. Some of these initialled donors can be linked with names spelled out elsewhere in the book. Of the donors themselves, some have been identified firmly, others rather more tentatively. These people are listed alphabetically, with some biographical details, in Appendix II. Some donors were from various Hertfordshire families; others had residences in the county, such as the Duchess of Ancaster; others were acquaintances from elsewhere; yet others were family members, such as the baron himself, or Elizabeth's brother John Dimsdale, his wife Priscilla and their daughter, also Priscilla, or more distant relatives such as Mrs Calvert of Albury.

Given the medical connections of the family it is perhaps surprising that there is not a single medicine or palliative – folk or otherwise – in the compilation. Elizabeth did include a receipt for 'Pomade Divine' (a salve for bruises or a sore breast), and just a handful of possets and gruels for invalids.[78] Upon consideration, this omission is not as strange as it first appears. There would be little reason for her to record medicines and remedies when many of the male members of the family were doctors, surgeon-apothecaries or druggists who were able to supply her, and the rest of the family, with the finished articles.[79]

---

78 Household preparations are in Chapter XVIII; possets and gruels in Chapter XIV.

79 Robert Dimsdale has recently found a note by Sir John Pringle stating that the Dimsdales used a particular prescription for three generations in Essex and Hertfordshire; they also used prescriptions known to 'countrymen' (presumably, country folk) (Royal College of Physicians of Edinburgh: Pringle MSS). There are no surviving copies of the medical prescriptions allegedly published by Robert Dimsdale for his friends before he left for New Jersey in 1683.

Some of the receipts use ingredients that are no longer available and research has shown that certain ingredients or additions indicate the age of a receipt. For example, 'sippets' - a garnish of small sops of fried or toasted bread - were often found in seventeenth-century receipts but were used far less frequently in those originating in the eighteenth.[80] This would suggest that the receipts recorded by Elizabeth where a garnish of sippets is added had come down from an earlier period.[81] Others, however, are more recent concoctions, such as those using potatoes as the main ingredient, of which Elizabeth collected several.

Potato receipts

Two kinds of potato had been brought back to England by Sir Francis Drake: 'Virginia' potatoes and 'Spanish', ie sweet, potatoes.[82] It is clear from receipts that throughout the seventeenth century both were regarded as a speciality food and in most cases they could be used interchangeably. Virginia potatoes were introduced into Ireland probably no later than 1588 but it was a long time before they became common in England, beginning in Lancashire in the 1680s.[83] They spread more widely during the first half of the eighteenth century and their popularity grew when cereal crops failed. Initially, however, they were the food of the poor. As the starch content of Virginia potatoes became known, boiled, mashed potatoes were used as a foundation for puddings. Published in 1744, *Adam's Luxury and Eve's Cookery* set out numerous ways in which potatoes might be eaten.[84] In 1796 H Kirkpatrick published a pamphlet advocating the potato, with advice on growing and a few receipts. It was aimed at prosperous southerners. In Lancashire 'Potatoes are the chief maintenance of the lower classes of people here and almost the sole food of children. They are also in great estimation amongst persons of higher rank, and there is rarely an entertainment at which they have not a place at the table'.[85] The potato is a rare example of a food stuff moving upwards through the social scale rather than

---

[80] Lehmann, *British Housewife*, p276.
[81] See: A Matelot ([p124]; now pp8-9); To stew Carp ([p47]; p9); To stew Carp ([p137]; pp9-10); Lobster Ragoued ([p109]; p11); Inky Pinky ([p50]; p33); Oyster Sausages ([p150; p110).
[82] C A Wilson, *Food and Drink in Britain* (London, 1973; pbk edn, 1991), pp217-18. See also R N Salman, *The History and Social Influence of the Potato* (Cambridge, 1949).
[83] Lehmann, *British Housewife*, p158.
[84] See examples from this publication in Wilson, *Food and Drink in Britain*, p219.
[85] H Kirkpatrick, *An account of the manner in which potatoes are cultivated and preserved, and the uses to which they are applied in the counties of Lancaster and Chester* (Warrington, 1796), pp2-3.

downwards. Kirkpatrick gives instructions for boiling and roasting potatoes and a recipe for potato pie, which comprised beef steaks and onions with some water, covered in sliced potatoes, and baked for two hours. The receipt for the modern 'Cottage Pie' (minced cooked beef, covered with mashed potato) is 'by many persons esteemed a palatable and certainly may be made a very frugal dish. A small dish of this sort sometimes finds a corner on genteel tables at supper'.[86]

As well as receipts that include potatoes in the ingredients, Elizabeth has receipts for 'Potatoe Cream' ([p32]; p86), 'Potatoe Pastry' ([p89]; p46), 'Crust of Pastry without flour' ([p83]; p46), 'Potatoe Bread' ([p112]; p102) and two for 'Potatoe Pudding'([pp81, 138]; pp59, 60).[87] These use potatoes in the ways advocated by Kirkpatrick: in the potato bread and puddings they replace cereal flour; the 'potato pastry' is actually a meat pie with mashed potato instead of pastry; the 'crust of pastry without flour' is made with sieved, boiled potato instead of flour. The potato cream receipt is more unusual in that it uses potato starch as a thickener, the resultant cream being like a custard.[88] Elizabeth recorded a receipt for 'Irish Macani' ([p81]; pp108-109), from 'Lord O'.[89] This savoury dish, unsurprisingly, has potato as its main ingredient but she expresses her frustration as the amount of potatoes was not specified by the donor: 'as the quantity of Potatoes is not mentioned this must be ascertained by trial'. 'Lord O' also supplied a receipt for 'Souflée Pudding' ([p82]; p62), which, like the potato cream, used potato starch as a thickener in this rich soufflé. Finally at the end of the receipt for 'Beignets a l'Allemande' ([p31]; p108), which are mashed potato savouries rolled in breadcrumbs and then deep-fried, Elizabeth notes that if minced or forced meat were used instead of potato, they would be called 'Croquettes'.

---

[86] Kirkpatrick, *An account*, p38.

[87] Glasse, *Art of Cookery*, has several receipts for potatoes, including four for potato pudding and one for potato cake (pp98, 105); five for various ways to cook potatoes (pp98, 99).

[88] None of the other receipt books that I have consulted, neither (originally) manuscript nor printed, include a receipt for potato cream. Kirkpatrick explains how to make potato starch from the sediment that forms in the water in which grated potatoes have been boiled (Kirkpatrick, *An account*, p39).

[89] Perhaps John Fitzpatrick, second earl of Upper Ossory (1745-1818), who was elected MP for Bedfordshire in 1774 and was Lord Lieutenant of Bedfordshire; one of his homes was at Ampthill (Beds) (Matthew Kilburn, 'Fitzpatrick, Anne, countess of Upper Ossory (1737/8–1804)', *ODNB*).

Foreign receipts
As well as potato receipts from Ireland, there are a number of other foreign receipts. Several are marked 'French' or 'French Receipt': some of these may have been collected by Elizabeth during her visit to France during 1776, when she and the baron travelled to and from Russia in 1781, or during their trip together to Paris in 1782.[90] Furthermore, some of her French receipts were given by named donors and there were many cookery books containing French receipts in circulation in the late eighteenth century from which some may have been gathered.

There are also several receipts for curry and 'India Pickle'. Again there were many in circulation, and several of the receipts given here have different donors; two, one for curry and one for curry soup, were noted as originating in 'Mirzapore', a town in British India, now in Bangladesh. One of the receipts calls for 'curry powder' ([p125]; p44) and at the bottom of that entry are given the name and address in London of a supplier of curry powder.[91] Interestingly, the earliest dated reference to 'curry powder' in the *OED* is 1810.

Not surprisingly there are a handful of Russian receipts, most of which, perhaps relate to pickling cucumbers. One ([p169]; p145), entitled 'Russia Cucumbers' came from 'Smirnove'. This was Iakov Ivanovich Smirnov (1754-1840), Ukrainian chaplain to the Russian Church in London from 1782 to 1837; he was also a diplomat and agricultural specialist. He knew the baron and Elizabeth well.[92]

Another Russian receipt was collected from a printed source, probably in the baron's possession. Elizabeth recorded the receipt for 'Russian salted Cucumbers' (pp145-146), against which she notes: 'For this an other [*sic*] Articles, see Philosophical Transactions for 1778 Part 2nd'. This issue of the *Philosophical Transactions of the Royal Society* contained a paper entitled 'Part of a Letter from Matthew Guthrie, MD, of Petersburgh to Dr Priestley, FRS, on the antiseptic Regimen of the Natives of Russia', read on 30 April 1778.[93] As

---

[90] DFA, TD B15 is entitled 'Menue pour Le 13. Juin 1782' . It is a manuscript version of an extensive menu from a French restaurant or hotel listing dishes and prices.
[91] See note to that receipt.
[92] A G Cross, *By the Banks of the Thames. Russians in Eighteenth-Century Britain* (Newtonville, Mass, 1980), *passim*.
[93] *Philosophical Transactions of the Royal Society*, 68 (1778), pp622-36; the method for salting cucumbers is on p632.

well as 'The manner of preparing the Russian salted cucumbers', Guthrie included receipts for various qualities of 'quass' ('a liquor which not only serves them for drink but also as sauce for a number of dishes'); 'The manner of making the Russian rye bread'; how to make a porridge from fermented oat-meal bran, which in Scotland, he said, was called 'sooins'; and also methods for drying horseradish and preserving turnips. These, presumably, are the 'other Articles' referred to by Elizabeth. Matthew Guthrie (1743-1807) was one of the numerous British doctors practising in Russia, living there continuously from 1770 until his death, having visited briefly in 1769. His scholarly and scientific interests went far beyond medicine and he contributed many papers to scholarly journals. For example, he became involved with questions of quarantine and plague prevention and in 1781 published a paper on the topic in *Medical and Philosophical Commentaries*.[94] In her account of her trip to Russia with Thomas, Elizabeth records meeting Guthrie.[95]

The receipt of Sir Charles Knowles, 'To cure Beef or Pork to keep many Years to be red & Juicy' ([p1[illegible]6]; p116), could have come to Elizabeth in one of two ways. As Sir Charles, a naval officer, was chief of the surveying branch of the Russian navy from 1770 to 1774,[96] he *may* have been an acquaintance of the baron, although their paths would not have crossed in Russia. However, his receipt also occurs in various printed books, for example, on pp289-90 of the ninth edition of John Farley's *London art of cookery*.[97]

Ingen Housz

The foreigner who donated the receipt for 'Nectar' ([p53]; p130) was far more than just an acquaintance - he was a family friend and regular visitor to the Dimsdales' various homes. Dr Jan Ingen Housz's 'Nectar' is a fermented drink made from raisins, lemons, sugar and water which apparently 'will ferment much and is best put into Stone Bottles. Glass Bottles being more liable to break'. Thomas Dimsdale's long friendship with Ingen Housz (rendered

---

[94] See, for example, 'Guthrie, Matthew (1743-1807)', *ODNB*; A. G. Cross, *By the banks of the Neva: chapters from the lives and careers of the British in eighteenth-century Russia* (Cambridge, 1997), *passim*.

[95] Cross, *An English Lady*, p83. Guthrie gave Elizabeth information concerning the population sizes of St Petersburg and Moscow.

[96] 'Knowles, Sir Charles (d.1777)', *ODNB*.

[97] John Farley, *The London art of cookery. and housekeeper's complete assistant* … (9th edition, London, 1800). Several historians have pointed out that 'John Farley' was a pseudonym for Richard Johnson; see, for example, Lehmann, *British Housewife*, p416.

'Ingenhouz' by Elizabeth) lasted from 1768 until Ingen Housz's death in 1799.[98] Elizabeth, who lived at Hertford Priory with Thomas and his second wife Ann from an early age, may even have been there when Dimsdale and Ingen Housz together carried out inoculations at Little Berkhamsted in early 1768, but after she became Thomas's wife she certainly met him on many occasions. He probably stayed at their house in Red Lion Square, London; in 1790 he stayed with the Dimsdales at Bath; and he is known to have visited them at Hertford in 1791, 1792, 1793, 1795 and 1796, usually staying in July and August, and sometimes in September. Nathaniel Dimsdale assisted him with experiments in the garden at Cowbridge House in 1795 and 1796.[99]

Some (undated) comments by Ingen Housz have survived concerning methods for preserving fruit that were followed at 'Baron Dimsdale'. As these obviously refer to methods advocated by the lady of the house, they are worth quoting in full here, especially as only one of the three is recorded in her receipt book.[100]

> Currents are to be preserved in the same way as goesberries, but at Baron Dimsdale they always put them in the bottle without water; and leave open the bottle during the whole time it is heating in the kettle. They cork the bottel the next day.[101]
>
> At Baron Dimsdale they preserve Damsons by boiling them with Syrop, without smalling them. They put them in a pot to cool. When cooled they cover them with an oiled paper, upon which they pour melted mutton sued[*sic*], which being hardened prevents the air coming at it.[102]
>
> In some houses they preserve Damsons in the same way as goesberries.

---

[98] Beale and Beale, *Echoes of Ingen Housz*, *passim*.

[99] The plan of Cowbridge House on this volume's dust jacket shows the vegetable garden, which was probably the scene of Ingen Housz's manuring experiments, with which Nathaniel assisted.

[100] The methods are recorded in Ingen Housz's papers, a transcript of which was supplied by Norman and Elaine Beale to Mr Robert Dimsdale.

[101] This Dimsdale method for preserving currants is recorded in Elizabeth's book as 'To preserve Currants' ([p42]; p75).

[102] There is no such receipt in Elizabeth's book. There are four receipts for damsons or bullaces, but these are for damson, bullace or plum cheese (See Chapter VIII).

To preserve goesberries the whole year

Fill a strong bottle having a large mouth with goesberries of that kind that have a tender skin. Place the bottle open in a kettle full of cold water with some straw or hay under it to prevent the bottle tutching the bottom; heat the water till the berries are swelled and become soft but not to boiling. Take out the bottle, and when cooled cork it well and seal the cork with melted rosin. Let it stand up right in a cool place. When the goesberries are to be used, some of the uppermost must first be taken out as they are commonly mouldy. All the remainder must be employed at once.

Other people fill the bottle with water when the goesberry are in it. They put the bottle in a kettel with cold water till the berries are swelled and soft, but not to the boiling point of the water in the kettel. When the bottel is cooled, it is to be corked and sealed. Some of the liquor is to be put in the tart.

Some cork the bottle in the first method, before they place it in the kittel full of water. NB Miss ?Jope of Hertford told me, that the method of filling the bottle with water seldom or never fails, but the cook of Baron Dimsdale never puts water in the bottle.[103]

From printed cookery books

During the course of researching the receipts in Elizabeth's book, it has become clear that she had access to various late-eighteenth-century printed cookery books, for several of the receipts have been taken almost verbatim from some of them. These have been noted in the footnotes.[104] For example, 'Rasberry Fritters' ([p95]; p60) is almost the same as Elizabeth Raffald's 'To make Raspberry Fritters'.[105] The only difference being that Mrs Raffald specifies *two* Naples biscuits and closes with the instruction: 'Lay round them green and yellow sweetmeats and serve them up'. She comments 'They are a pretty corner dish for either dinner or supper'. Elizabeth Dimsdale's receipt for 'Mushroom liquor and Powder' ([p32]; p138) is almost the same as that given by E Smith.[106]

---

[103] There are no gooseberry receipts in the book.

[104] It would, of course, be impossible to compare all of Elizabeth's receipts with all of those in the massive number of printed cookery books in circulation. The following are the main ones that have been consulted: Glasse, *Art of Cookery*; Nott, *Cook's*; Raffald, *Experienced English Housekeeper*; Smith, *Compleat Housewife*.

[105] Raffald, *Experienced English Housekeeper*, p90.

[106] Smith, *Compleat Housewife*, p86.

Similarly, the instructions 'To take out Iron Moulds' ([p171]; p157) are almost word-for-word Hannah Glasse's 'To take ironmoulds out of linen'.[107]

Same titles, different receipts

Even just a cursory glance through the numerous surviving eighteenth century cookery books - whether manuscript, manuscript now published, or printed - recognizes that many receipts had the same or similar titles. There are at least two points to be noted about this. Firstly, receipts were openly plagiarized and so the 'original' receipt might appear either in manuscript or in print many times, either in exactly the same form or with very slight amendments.[108] Secondly, many receipts had the same or similar titles but different ingredients and/or methods.[109] Elizabeth's receipts are no exception, with many falling into these two categories; indeed, within her book not only have some receipts been duplicated but also others have the same, or similar, titles and different ingredients and/or methods. To illustrate the point regarding different receipts with the same title, one example will suffice: that of 'Cracknells', which were a kind of biscuit. Elizabeth's receipt and method are as follows:

> Add one pound of Butter to a quart of Flour, half a Nutmeg grated, The Yolks of 4 Eggs beat with 4 Spoonsful of Rose Water. Put the Nutmegs and Eggs with the flour, and wet it into a Stiff Paste with cold Water. Then roll in the Butter, and make them into shapes. Put them in a Kettle of boiling Water. When they swim take them out with a skimmer, and put them into cold Water. When hard, lay them out to dry, and bake them on Tin Plates. ([p133]; p93)

Neither the ingredients nor the method of the receipt 'To make Cracknels' published by Elizabeth Moxon in 1764 bear comparison. She wrote:

> Take half a pound of fine flour, half a pound of sugar, two ounces of butter, two eggs, and a few carraway seeds; (you must beat and sift the sugar) then put it to your flour and work it to paste; roll them as thin as

107 Glasse, *Art of Cookery*, p168.

108 Jennifer Stead has analysed the receipts published by Hannah Glasse and identified those lifted from other writers. See Stead, 'Tables of Corresponding Recipes', in Glasse, *Art of Cookery*, pp.xxxi-xxxiii.

109 The variations in similarly titled receipts became very obvious when searching for possible sources for Elizabeth Dimsdale's receipts in the books listed above.

> you can, and cut them out with queen cake tins, lie them on papers and bake them in a slow oven. They are proper to eat with chocolate.[110]

E Smith's receipt 'To make little Cracknels' is different again. Amongst the main ingredients are flour, dried lemon and orange peel, coriander seeds and eggs. Unlike Elizabeth Dimsdale, Smith does not drop pieces of the mixture in boiling water prior to baking; furthermore, Smith's biscuits are baked in a very hot oven, whereas Moxon's 'slow oven' means a low temperature.[111]

From scientific books and journals

Elizabeth Dimsdale took a handful of her receipts and household tips from scientific books and journals. Mention has already been made of Dr Guthrie's Russian receipts reported in the second issue in 1778 of *Philosophical Transactions of the Royal Society*. Elizabeth also copied out 'The Test of Dr Hardy on the Colic of Poitu' ([p161]; pp165-166). This is a method for testing for the adulteration of food with lead. James Hardy noted that leaded cider was not only the cause of Devonshire colic, but also of the gout. He published a detailed paper thereon in 1778, noting that the original test was prepared by a Doctor De Haen and giving De Haen's Latin text in a footnote.[112]

Whereas it is probable that the baron owned a copy of Hardy's paper and issues of *Philosophical Transactions*, three of the other scientific items recorded by Elizabeth were not published until after his death. Perhaps these were in the possession of her brothers John or Robert, or of her step-son Nathaniel, all of whom were medical men. In February 1803 the *Monthly Magazine* published a receipt for making milk-white paint, which had previously been published in the French magazine *Annales des Artes*. In 'To make a Milk White Paint' ([p167]; p161) Elizabeth reproduced the receipt word for word, apart from one error, writing 'Spanish White three *Ounces*' instead of 'Spanish White three *pounds*' -

---

[110] E Moxon, *English Houswifry* (1764 edition; web edition by eBooks@Adelaide), receipt 245.

[111] Smith, *Compleat Housewife*, pp178-9.

[112] James Hardy, *A candid examination of what has been advanced on the colic of Poitou and Devonshire, with remarks on the most probable and experiments intended to ascertain the true causes of the gout. By James Hardy, M D Of Barnstaple, Devonshire* (London, 1778). The test is on pp44-45.

which would have made quite difference to the effectiveness of the paint.[113] It is clear that the *Monthly Magazine* was her source for this method of making white paint because the next receipt in her original book was another household tip that appeared on the same page of that magazine. This was Brugnatelli's method for converting rancid oil to wax ([p167]; p166).[114] Again, the method is reproduced verbatim, except that Elizabeth substituted 'rectified spirits of wine' for 'alcohol', which is the same ingredient. Since she copied out both of these receipts, it can be stated without doubt that the receipts on pages 167 onwards in her book were entered during or after February 1803. Thus, while it is likely that many of the receipts were collected during her time as 'housekeeper', some, including the two published in the *Monthly Magazine*, were collected after her husband's death.

The last item in her book is a method for preventing a disagreeable taste in cream or butter, under which she notes her source as 'Curwen's hints'. In 1808 J C Curwen published *Hints on the Economy of Feeding Stock, and Bettering the Condition of the Poor*.[115] In the chapter 'On supplying Milk for the Poor', the footnote to page 144 explains how to prevent that disagreeable taste. Elizabeth has copied it virtually word-for-word. And so we know the date of the last receipt written in the book and therefore can state confidently that it was not until at least 1808 that Elizabeth added her final entry.

The nature of Elizabeth Dimsdale's receipt book

Unlike many earlier manuscript receipt books, Elizabeth's was not compiled so that it could be handed down through directly successive generations for she had no children of her own. In her will she made bequests to several of Thomas's children and to her nephews and nieces, but although she bequeathed several other manuscript books, she did not mention her receipt book at all. Her nephew, Dr William Dimsdale, was to have 'my Journal to and from Russia in a black box and all that is in it, my book of pictures of the Russian People in the Russian Empire, and the five volumes of the Account of Russia'; her nephew,

---

[113] The receipt for making milk-white paint, first published in *Annales des Artes*, was reproduced in the *Monthly Magazine, or, British Register* (1 February 1803), p65, column 2, in the section entitled 'Literary and Philosophical Intelligence'.

[114] Luigi Valentino Brugnatelli (1761-1818) pharmacist, inventor and publisher. His method for converting rancid oil to wax was reported in column 1 on p65 of the *Monthly Magazine* (1 February 1803).

[115] J C Curwen, *Hints on the Economy of Feeding Stock, and Bettering the Condition of the Poor* (London, 1808).

Joseph Dimsdale, 'my book of old letters of my great grandfather and grandmother'; his brother, John, 'one of my books to make it equal between John and Joseph'; her niece, Elizabeth Hagger ,'one of my large bibles'; and Elizabeth's sister-in-law, Priscilla Dimsdale, because she had requested it, 'my manuscript book which ... contains serious religious Anecdotes'.[116]

Neither Elizabeth herself nor her receipt book can be neatly categorised. Although written up in the 1800s, the receipts were collected during the preceding decades, yet exactly when is impossible to pin down. Many were collected during her time as 'housekeeper' for Thomas and his wife Ann, although she probably continued to collect receipts when she herself was the lady of the house; indeed some can be dated to after Thomas's death and as noted above the last one entered can be dated confidently to 1808.

Manuscript books containing receipts for remedies, confectioneries and cookery survive from about the middle of the sixteenth century.[117] The owners, if not the writers, of such books were aristocratic ladies and those from the wealthy gentry. Initially the majority of receipts were for remedies and confectionery as elite ladies were less likely to be interested in cookery. Using the example of Lady Elinor Fettiplace, Gilly Lehmann has demonstrated that receipts were collected from a variety of sources: some were family prescriptions from earlier generations and others were obtained from various friends; Elinor Fettiplace also owned at least one printed book that contained receipts.[118] Although the printing of cookery books began in the early sixteenth century, production really took off in the 1650s, when eight new titles and 25 reprints were published.[119] Lehmann's analysis of the manuscript collection of receipts compiled by Rebecca Price (1660-1740) shows that collectors like Rebecca copied printed receipts into their books as well as those passed on by hand.[120] This is an interesting illustration of the way in which receipts quite literally circulated, since the contents of printed receipt books were first set down as individual

---

[116] TNA, PROB11/1538/ 279. However, the receipt book is known to have been handed down through several generations of John's family and was passed to Thomas's descendant, Mr Thomas Edward Dimsdale, before Sir John Dimsdale died in 1978.
[117] Lehmann, *British Housewife*, p33.
[118] Lehmann, *British Housewife*, p33; see also Hilary Spurling, *Elinor Fettiplace's Receipt Book* (Harmondsworth, 1986).
[119] Lehmann, *British Housewife*, p383, Appendix I: Cookery book production by decade.
[120] Lehmann, *British Housewife*, p47. Rebecca Price's manuscript cookery receipts have been published in Madeleine Masson, (ed), *The Compleat Cook* (London, 1974).

manuscript receipts. As Lehmann comments, 'printed cookery books simply reproduced on a large scale the established mode of transmission of new receipts. Exchanges between manuscript and print were not entirely in one direction, and each enriched the other'.[121]

The social status of those who kept manuscript receipt books changed gradually over time. Lehmann has noted that by the Restoration 'the vogue for collecting receipts from one's friends and writing their illustrious names against the titles of the receipts had passed amongst the aristocracy, as these named receipts had now flooded the market in printed books'.[122] Just as printed receipts had shared the 'secrets' of aristocratic kitchens, so collecting receipts moved lower down the social scale. Various manuscript collections by gentry women have survived from the eighteenth century but there is a shift in emphasis over time, with later books devoting more space to household hints and hobbies than to cookery and confectionery.[123] Lehmann has suggested that by this time it was to women lower down the social scale that manuscript collections devoted *entirely* to cookery belonged, giving the example of Elizabeth Raper, the daughter of an East India Company merchant.[124]

Elizabeth Grant, neé Raper (d.1778)

It is probable that Elizabeth Dimsdale knew of Elizabeth Raper, even if they were not acquainted. The latter was the only child and heir of John Raper and his wife, Elizabeth, daughter of William Hale of Twyford House, Thorley (near Bishops Stortford).[125] Elizabeth Raper and her parents lived at Twyford House. Her father's eldest brother, Matthew, had inherited Thorley Hall (and the manor of Thorley) from his father. The two brothers were near neighbours in Thorley

---

[121] Lehmann, *British Housewife*, p47. Today both kinds of books are highly sought-after collectors' items. See, for example, the range of manuscript receipt books and printed books from the collections of Stanley J Seger sold at Sotheby's (London) on 15 July 2010. These books are described and illustrated in the 120-page catalogue, *Books for Cooks*, published by Sotheby's to accompany the sale.

[122] Lehmann, *British Housewife*, p72.

[123] Lehmann cites as an example the book of Caroline Lybbe Powys (BL Add MS 42173, begun in 1762 and added to until the 1790s). Of the 143 receipts, 40 are for cookery, 13 for preserves, pickles and drinks, 37 for medicines and cosmetics, and 53 for household hints and hobbies.

[124] Lehmann, *British Housewife*, p72.

[125] See *VCH Herts*, III, pp374, 375.

and both were merchants in the East India Company, trading with China.[126] In 1762 Elizabeth married William Grant MD of Rothiemurchus, Inverness-shire, and after their marriage they lived in Lyme Street, London, where Dr Grant had established his practice.[127] So in fact, *contra* Lehmann, she was not far below gentry status.

Elizabeth wrote out a manuscript book of receipts and also kept a journal. In 1924 a transcript of all of the former and some of the latter was published by her great-grandson Bartle Grant.[128] According to Grant, 'Miss Raper was a noted housewife and cook; she kept house for her father and mother, ordering the meals, looking after the linen, etc., and these receipts, clearly worded and well condensed testify to her practical knowledge of cookery'. The book of 101 receipts is inscribed 'Rothiemurchus: 1770' and it seems likely that the receipts were written or copied out while she stayed there on a visit after her marriage and 'left there "for the good of the house"'.[129] The book remained in her husband's family home, and 22 receipts and remedies were subsequently added in another hand.[130]

According to her diary entries, prior to her marriage, Elizabeth had a number of admirers, one of whom was a member of the Dimsdale family. On 30 April 1760, she 'met Dr Dimsdale in the lane' at Thorley. Later she and her friend, Mistress Parsons, 'went into the pastor [?*pasture*] where were the Dr and Mrs King, the Dr very much my humble servant and all that egad. Chatted very sociably, some significant squeezes from the Dr'.[131] On 26 May, she was 'Up before 7, dressed and to Stortford before 8 to B[rea]kf[as]t with Mrs Dimsdale. The Dr not up till some time after we got there. B[rea]kf[as]t over we walked in the garden, the lover very pensive, kept close to me, sighed, squeezed and sighed again; his mother looked very arch but said not a word'. The friendship

---

[126] Bartle Grant, ed, *The Receipt Book of Elizabeth Raper, and a portion of her Cipher Journal, written 1756-1770 and never before printed* (London, 1924), pp2-3.
[127] Grant, *Receipt Book*, p35.
[128] Both Thorley Hall and Thorley manor eventually passed to Elizabeth Raper's son John Peter Grant (b.1774) and Twyford House to her daughter Elizabeth Grant, their mother having died shortly after the latter's birth in 1778 (*VCH Herts*, III, p375; Grant, *Receipt Book*, pp36-7).
[129] Grant, *Receipt Book*, p2.
[130] Grant surmised that as many of the additional receipts were for medical remedies they had been added by her husband (Grant, *Receipt Book*, p76).
[131] Grant, *Receipt Book*, p21.

continued, Elizabeth referring to the doctor as 'Liver' in her journal. On 26 June, he sent her some tame partridges which she kept in a partridge house; she recorded showing them to him on 25 September; however, after October 1760 he was not mentioned again in the journal. It seems most likely that 'Dr Dimsdale' was Robert, the eldest of 'our' Elizabeth's three brothers (b1733). (See the family tree.) By 1760 their mother had been widowed for 16 years. Five years later, in 1765, Robert married Elizabeth Ravenhill.

There is no indication in Elizabeth Dimsdale's receipt book that any of them had been acquired from Elizabeth Raper. Many of the receipts in their two books have the same or very similar titles but since this is a feature of all manuscript (and printed) receipt books of the period this is scarcely surprising.[132] There are, however, two receipts that should be mentioned particularly. Firstly, on page 5 of Elizabeth Dimsdale's book, there is a receipt for 'Orange Wine' against which is written the donor's name of 'Leaper'. Although the second half of the word is not particularly legible, the first three letters are definitely 'Lea', thus its provenance was not 'Raper'. Furthermore, the receipt for 'Orange Wine' in Elizabeth Raper's book (p82) comes in the section of receipts added later by someone else. Secondly, on page 61, Elizabeth Raper has a receipt entitled 'Crocant Past', which is a sweet pastry made with 12 ounces of flour, 6 ounces of fine sugar, 4 large spoonsful of fine oil and enough water to make the paste 'a proper stiffness'. Having combined the ingredients, the cook is instructed to 'Roll it out and sheet the pan and bake the past as soon as you can, but rub the pan with a piece of fresh butter before you put the past on, move the crust as soon as baked before it's taken out of the oven, because it you don't it will stick fast to your pan'. Elizabeth Dimsdale ([p159]; p46) has a receipt entitled 'Crust for a Crocant', which simply gives the ingredients (Six Ounces of Flour, 1½ ounces of Butter, 2 Ounces of Fine Sugar) but with no method, just the laconic comment 'For a small dish'. 'Crocant', or more correctly 'Croquant', was a French sweet pastry, often containing ground almonds. Receipts for three different kinds of 'Croquantes' are given in Clermont's translation of the French cookery writer Menon.[133] None of the most popular contemporary English

---

[132] Compare, for example, the following receipts in Elizabeth Raper's book with those of a similar name transcribed in this book: 'Oxford Sausages' (p72), 'Walnut Catchup' (p67), 'To pickle Oysters' (p51), 'Dutch Blancmanger' (p62).

[133] See, for example, Menon, trans. B Clermont, *The Professed Cook: Or the Modern Art of Cookery, Pastry and Confectionary, Made Plain and Easy. ...*, vol 2 (2nd edition, London, 1769), pp406-8, 'Croquantes à la d'Estrées', 'Croquante en Caramel' and 'Croquante de Pâtes d'Amandes'.

printed receipt books consulted for this Introduction included receipts for 'Croquant', but here it is appearing in two manuscript receipt books by Hertfordshire collectors. Perhaps the two Elizabeths knew a French cook, or had access to some French cookery books or to French receipts in translation? Maybe Elizabeth Dimsdale acquired hers during her travels?

Printed receipt books

Lehmann has discussed at length the nature of printed eighteenth century cookery books and the readership at whom they were aimed. One of many developments was publication by women, many of whom were themselves housekeepers or cooks. Initially they were anonymous, for example, when E Smith's *Compleat Housewife* appeared in 1727 only the author's initials were on the title page.[134] Similarly, it was not until the fourth edition of Hannah Glasse's *Art of Cookery*, published in 1751, that her name, in the form of her signature, appeared on the title page; prior to that the book had simply been authored 'By a Lady'.[135] However, by the 1750s 'women were putting their names to their works and boasting of their long experience as cooks and housekeepers' to emphasise that their receipts had been tried and tested.[136] Similarly, the professionalism of these cooks and housekeepers is apparent in their cookery books.[137] Mrs Elizabeth Raffald, née Whitaker, author of *The Experienced Housekeeper*, is a remarkable example of this.[138] In 1760 she took up the position of housekeeper to Sir Peter and Lady Elizabeth Warburton at Arley Hall, Cheshire, where she remained until shortly after her marriage in March 1763.[139] She and her husband, John, moved to Manchester, where she occupied a shop in Fennel Street, whence she sold, amongst other things, 'Yorkshire Hams, Tongues, Newcastle salmon, potted meats, portable soups (sticky glue-like tablets to which hot water was added), sweetmeats, lemon preserve, and

---

[134] Although the author is sometimes referred to as Eliza Smith, the name 'Eliza' never appears in any editions of E Smith's book. See Lehmann, *British Housewife*, p451; and also G Yost, 'The Compleat Housewife or Accomplish'd gentlewoman's Companion: A Bibliographical Study', *William and Mary College Quarterly*, 18 (4) (October 1938), pp419-35, p427.

[135] Glasse, *Art of Cookery*. The modern edition published by Prospect Books includes additional recipes from the fifth edition with a biographical introduction, bibliography, glossary and notes.

[136] Lehmann, *British Housewife*, p61.

[137] Lehmann, *British Housewife*, p137.

[138] Raffald, *Experienced English Housekeeper*. The modern edition has been edited by Ann Bagnall and has an Introduction by Roy Shipperbottom.

[139] Raffald, *Experienced English Housekeeper*, pp.viii-ix.

mushroom ketchup'.[140] Her husband came from a family of market-gardeners, and their gardens were situated only 200 yards from Fennel Street. She ran several other business activities, including a register office (where servants seeking work were introduced to employers seeking servants) and the compilation of a Manchester Directory listing local merchants and businesses. Between their marriage in 1763 and September 1774, she gave birth to six daughters. And she also wrote her book. Although she had left Arley Hall in 1763, it is clear that she maintained links with the Warburton family.[141] Indeed, she dedicated her book to Lady Elizabeth.

Lehmann has emphasised that over time ladies became removed from the kitchen and that by the eighteenth century they were certainly not cooking themselves but were purchasing printed books for their cooks and housekeepers to use.[142] Owners of these printed books are hard to identify. Wills and inventories rarely give itemised lists of books: they are usually lumped together with a single valuation.[143] Although, as noted above, it has not been possible to undertake a detailed analysis of the provenance of Elizabeth Dimsdale's receipts, it is clear that some have been taken from printed books. Since she was wealthy and educated, and clearly interested in collecting receipts, it seems highly likely that she would have possessed some printed cookery books. However, there is little definite proof apart from the handful of receipts in her book that can be identified in published works.

In 1832 a detailed inventory and valuation was made of the contents of Cowbridge House, following the death of Elizabeth's step-daughter, Ann. This document includes an extensive list of some 2,500 books that were in the library and on various other bookshelves in the house at that time.[144] The baron, Ann's father, had bequeathed his books equally between his five sons, all of whom predeceased their sister. Ann inherited books from several of her brothers as they died, and in her will she left them to her executors to divide between her nephews Thomas Robert and Charles John 'as fairly as it can be done by

---

140 Raffald, *Experienced English Housekeeper*, p.x.
141 For example, the Arley accounts show her being paid 14s 2d for sturgeon in 1770 (Raffald, *Experienced English Housekeeper*, p.xii).
142 Lehmann, *British Housewife*, pp68-9.
143 See, for example, Lorna Weatherill, *Consumer Behaviour and Material Culture in Britain 1660-1760* (1996 edition), pp7-13, 207, cited in Lehmann, *British Housewife*, p62.
144 HALS, DE/D/1172.

valuation and by lot ...'. Frustratingly, but perhaps unsurprisingly, this long list of books does not include a single cookery book.

Testing the receipts

Elizabeth's position as housekeeper introduced her to menu planning and the need for a wide variety of receipts to ring the changes in the household's diet. As will be discussed below, the housekeeper's role was not that of a 'hands-on' cook. Her receipt book is not a working cookery book, i.e. it is fair copy rather than a book splattered with fat, flour or other ingredients, but there is plenty of evidence that Elizabeth, or her cook, had used the receipts. Some are marked 'Ex[cellent]'. In other receipts Elizabeth made various comments indicating that either she, or her cook, had queried the ingredients or the method; she subsequently suggested adjustments or alterations. These particular receipts are very illuminating as they show Elizabeth's interest in the workings of the receipts that had been given to her.[145]

For example, after the receipt for Mandam ([p111]; p142), a sauce containing finely chopped cucumber, seasoned with chopped onions, cayenne pepper and salt, to which is added one spoonful of Madeira Wine and one of Water, and two of Vinegar, she noted 'Better <u>without</u> Water'. Following a receipt for 'India Pickle' ([p160]; p149) which is the pickling liquid for the equivalent of 'piccalilli', noticing the absence of turmeric, which she knew was usually used in such receipts, she has noted '*Quere* if Turmerick should not be included'. Perhaps mindful of the strong smell, against the ingredients of a liquid to destroy bugs in beds ([p174]; p162) in which *half a pound* of camphor is added to one pint of spirit of turpentine and one pint of spirit of wine, she has noted 'que[ry] if not one ounce'. At least one receipt simply did not work: at the end of a receipt that claimed to increase the amount of bread produced from a certain quantity of flour by using bran liquor (liquid produced when bran is boiled in water and then strained) instead of plain water ([p83]; p99), she noted '<u>This did not answer</u>'. Finally, on occasion she was stumped by the method given in a receipt: one of the instructions in the receipt 'To preserve and Candy Orange & Lemon Peel' ([p44]; pp.79-80) is to boil the peels 'until the Sugar is at a casting height'. Elizabeth has underlined these last two words and then noted '*que*' What does this mean'. In fact this was one stage in the range of recognized descriptions of the state of heated sugar.[146]

---

[145] If she had concocted these particular receipts, she would not have needed to query the methods or ingredients in the fair copy.

[146] See Glossary under 'casting height'.

The role of the housekeeper
'By the last decades of the eighteenth century, in an ideally-run home with a full complement of servants, the housekeeper had assumed the role of the housewife of the early years of the century [...].'[147] This included the supervision of lower servants and sometimes even teaching various aspects of cookery. The shift in responsibilities was reflected in the contents of the printed cookery books of the period. The compiler of *The Ladies' Library* (1790)[148] described in detail the role of the housekeeper. By this time, of course, Elizabeth was no longer 'a kind of housekeeper' but was the lady of the house: she and Thomas were living quietly together mostly at Cowbridge House in Hertford, occasionally staying in London or Bath. Nevertheless it is useful to set out here the housekeeper's expected duties in order to demonstrate their wide variety and also the way in which an 'entertainment'[149] should be managed in such a household.[150]

The housekeeper must:

- be well acquainted with the business of a cook and confectioner, before she can be duly qualified for her own
- know how to order and keep a good economy throughout the whole family
- ... keep a good understanding with the cook and other inferior servants, by supplying them regularly with all necessaries ...
- provide good servants for the kitchen, and to change them, and tradesmen also, whenever they are found unfit for their business or negligent with it ...
- bargain with all tradesmen whatever, who supply the family with eatables[151]

For an entertainment she should:

---

[147] Lehmann, *British Housewife*, p76.

[148] *The ladies' library: or, encyclopedia of female knowledge, in every branch of domestic economy: comprehending, in alphabetical arrangement, distinct treatises on every practical subject ... In which is included a vast fund of miscellaneous information, ... In two volumes ...*, vol 2 (London, 1790), pp61-64, 'House-keeper'.

[149] The modern equivalent is a dinner party.

[150] The various points are quoted in full except where ... indicates otherwise.

[151] Here details are given on how to deal with the butcher, the poulterer, the cheesemonger, purveyors of fish, fruit and herbs, the grocer, chandler and oilman. All kitchen furniture likewise falls under her care.

- be able to form the plan of an entertainment, to draw up a bill of fare, and to order the courses for every different table
- know what is most liked of all sorts of entries [*sic*], soups, roast dishes, and side ones, otherwise it will be impossible for her to make a bill of fare as it ought to be. … again, some skill in the cook and confectioner's arts is requisite, unless she will be always asking advice of them
- take her precautions accordingly, inquiring of the butcher, poulterer, &c, what they have by them, that she may provide the best of every thing
- be informed of the number of guests, in order to lay to the table in a proper manner; and order the dishes so that no two of the same sort may be near one another; for, besides that this has an ill appearance, it might confine some of the company to what they do not like
- form a regular plan of the whole entertainment, and make a draught of each course, as well as the desert [*sic*]; ranging every one in its proper place, observing well the sizes of the dishes and what they are to contain; and if the family servants are not sufficient, she will call in assistance [those] on whom she can depend, that every thing may be done in good order …
- the form of the table ought likewise to be considered, in order for ranging of the plates and dishes in such a manner, that every person may come at what he likes, and that the waiters may not be forced to disturb the company, in serving or taking away; a circumstance that is shocking, and yet this happens but too often, for want of taking proper care beforehand
- As an ill-attended or ill-served table is always a cause of censure on the master or the family, she must never fail to have the table covered in good time, and see every thing in readiness and well arranged before the company is announced; and whoever of the servants waits at table, will inform her when any thing is found fault with, and also what gave satisfaction, that she may avoid future errors, and continue to please
- When the last course is served up, she must prepare to range the desert [*sic*] in the manner in which it is to be served; and then go to the kitchen to see what is come from table; and if any articles will serve another time, they ought to be taken care of, and locked up, the rest given to the servants

Although most housekeepers would not often be expected to provide an 'entertainment', as the above instructions indicate, they would need to know how the courses should be laid out. In *The Experienced English Housekeeper*,

Elizabeth Raffald provides 'Directions for a Grand Table'.[152] Her recommended bill of fare has 25 dishes per course although she does not wish to 'confine any Lady to such a particular number of dishes'. The key is for the dishes to be in season and so most could be 'got without much difficulty'. No two dishes are to be the same. She provides two copper-plate diagrams of the first and second course of a typical entertainment in January, showing the various dishes placed in a symmetrical arrangement according to their type. The centre-piece of the first course is 'Mock Turtle' and of the second 'Transparent pudding cover'd with a Silver Web'.[153] She does not provide an engraving for a third course or a cold collation 'for that generally consists of things extravagant' and her purpose in the whole book is to 'join economy with neatness and elegance, being sensible what valuable qualifications these are in a housekeeper or cook'.[154] She does, however, set out 'a dessert of sweetmeats' which 'will make a pretty appearance after the cloth is drawn and be entertaining to the company'.[155] This winter series of desserts, which like the other course has to have 25 dishes, has five different ices for the middle 'either to be served upon a frame or without', dried and fresh fruit, fruits preserved in brandy, nuts and olives.

Elizabeth Dimsdale's book is simply a collection of receipts. There are no bills of fare and only a few indications regarding the course for which a particular dish should be served or where it should be set on the table. For example, following the receipt 'To stew Beef' ([p67]; p33) which uses either 6 or 8 lbs of beef, she has noted 'Eight pounds make a hansome bottom Dish, and five or six pounds for a side Dish'. Similarly, at the end of the receipt for 'College Pudding' ([p79]; p56), she has noted 'Half this quantity is sufficient for a side Dish'. Likewise, the timing of the preparation of 'Lemon Cheese' ([p94]; pp82-83) depends on when it will be served: 'If it is for dinner it should be made over Night; if for supper in the Morning'.

The original book and the transcript presented here

Although now quite rare, manuscript receipt books, such as that compiled by Elizabeth Dimsdale, with their wide-ranging contents taken from a variety of sources, both personal and printed, were not unusual in earlier centuries. This

---

[152] Raffald, *Experienced English Housekeeper*, p193.

[153] Raffald, *Experienced English Housekeeper*, pp194-5. She gives two receipts for 'A Transparent Pudding' (pp84, 97); the latter is a calves' foot jelly layered with raisins, almonds and candied lemon.

[154] Raffald, *Experienced English Housekeeper*, pp2-3.

[155] Raffald, *Experienced English Housekeeper*, p193.

particular book does, however, possess a distinguishing feature: the sheer volume of receipts contained therein. Elizabeth Raper's manuscript book contains 123 receipts in total, of which 22 had been added in a different hand;[156] the Totteridge receipt book transcribed by the O'Donoghues contains 133;[157] the manuscript book of Caroline Lybbe Powys has 143;[158] that found by Beverley Nichols has 154;[159] Margaretta Acworth's book has about 350;[160] Rebecca Price's has 556.[161] With 770 receipts and housekeeping tips Elizabeth Dimsdale's book has by far the most entries. Perhaps the explanation for this huge difference is that she collected them over a long period of time, continuing until she was in her mid-70s. Probably she had kept the receipts in various books or loose leafs and eventually decided to transfer them all into one book. Exactly when she compiled the book is unknown but given that the paper in the book is watermarked 1800, it is clear that she did not start to write in the book itself until sometime in, or just after, 1800. She did not enter the receipts in any particular order but she did continue to add to them until 1808, as demonstrated by the inclusion of Curwen's method for preventing a disagreeable taste in milk.[162]

As noted previously, the book was not a working book. There are no floury handprints anywhere. Perhaps its compilation was a means by which Elizabeth kept herself occupied during her widowhood. The book, covered in parchment, measures 32.5 cm (12¾") by 20.5 cm (8") by 3.5cm (1¼"). It has no inscription. Without any preface or preamble, page 1 commences with a receipt for 'Calves Feet Jelly' from Mrs Byde. In general there are four or five receipts per page. Pages 1 to 170 have been numbered manually by Elizabeth and the vast majority of the receipts therein are culinary; next come 154 blank pages, on several of which is a watermark comprising the figure of Britannia inside an orb,

---

[156] Grant, *Receipt Book.*

[157] V F O'Donoghue and P N O'Donoghue, eds, *Georgian Cookery; Recipes and Remedies from 18th century Totteridge* (New Barnet, 2007).

[158] The original is BL: Add MS 42,173; the receipts are counted in Lehmann, *British Housewife*, p73, n42.

[159] D Rhodes, (ed), *In an Eighteenth Century Kitchen: A Receipt Book of Cookery 1698* (London, 1968).

[160] The original is TNA, C107/108; the receipts are counted in Lehmann, *British Housewife*, p73; extracts have been published in F Prochaska and A Prochaska, (eds), *Margaretta Acworth's Georgina Cookery Book* (London, 1987).

[161] Masson, ed, *Compleat Cook* comprises Rebecca Price's manuscript cookery receipts.

[162] The last receipt is taken from Curwen, *Hints on the Economy of Feeding Stock*, p144 (See also p.xxxii above).

with a crown above; the following 12 pages (which have been numbered 171 to 182 by the editor) contain mostly housekeeping hints. Elizabeth compiled an index of the receipts on pages 1 to 170, beginning it on the front endpapers and continuing on the left-hand page opposite page 1. After the housekeeping hints are 33 blank pages and then the rest of the index is on the next three pages. The final page is blank, with the watermark clearly visible.

To give this published transcript structure and clarity it was decided to reorder the receipts and household hints into thematic chapters so that the reader could appreciate the wide range of items without being overwhelmed by variety on every page.[163] For the record, the original order of the receipts, with their page numbers, has been set out in Appendix I. The popular but authoritative book by Elizabeth Raffald, *The Experienced English Housekeeper*, has been used as a model for the various chapter headings. The first edition of 1769 was reprinted in 1997. By the judgement of the modern editor, Ann Bagnall, in that reprinting four receipts were moved from where Mrs Raffald had placed them to the chapters in which the modern editor thought they ought to be.

> ... two fritter recipes which were in chapter V have now joined the other fritters in Chapter VI, and those for Lemon Pickle and for Browning - both so important to Elizabeth Raffald as English answers to expensively made cullis[164] - are moved from Chapter I (Soups) where they hardly make their point, and look as though they were printed there as an after-thought; they are now in Chapter IV (Made Dishes), where they clearly belong.[165]

Gilly Lehmann has subsequently pointed out that Mrs Raffald had in fact placed the latter two receipts exactly where she meant them to be. She gave no receipt for 'cullis', a notoriously expensive French ingredient, because 'I have found by Experience, that Lemon Pickle and Browning answers both for Beauty and

[163] This practice was also adopted by the editors of the receipt book of Elizabeth Serrell of Wells (Somerset), a much shorter book than Elizabeth Dimsdale's, containing just 66 items. See A Baines and J Imray, (eds), *Elizabeth Serrell of Wells, Her Recipes and Remedies: An Eighteenth Century Kitchen Commonplace Book* (Wells, 1986).
[164] 'Cullis' is an Anglicization of the French word 'coulis', 'a preparation for thickening soups and stews' (Glasse, *Art of Cookery*, 'Glossary', p182).
[165] Raffald, *Experienced English Housekeeper*, Editor's Note, pvi.

Taste (at a trifling Expence) better than Cullis, which is extravagant'.[166] Lehmann explains that Mrs Raffald placed these two substitute preparations at the beginning of her book 'just as French authors placed basic broths and cullises at the beginning of theirs'.[167]

The editor of this current volume claims no experience in such matters, but has tried to assign receipts to the various chapter headings in Mrs Raffald's book, with the few exceptions that are noted below. Hopefully the allocations make sense and there are no glaring errors. Elizabeth Dimsdale gives no receipt for 'Browning' although she uses brown gravy in several receipts. The ingredients and method in her receipt for 'Lemon Pickle' are different from those of Mrs Raffald; nevertheless it has been placed at the beginning of Chapter I here.[168] In fact she used lemon pickle only once in any of the receipts: that for 'Veal Ragout' ([p59]; p40).

'Puffs' have presented a problem regarding categorisation. In Mrs Raffald's book, there are three kinds of puffs: 'Curd Puffs', baked and resembling the filling of a modern baked cheesecake, are in Chapter X (Creams, Custards and Cheesecakes);[169] 'Lemon Puffs', 'Chocolate Puffs' and 'Almond Puffs', similar to meringues, baked in the oven, are in Chapter XI (Cakes);[170] and 'German Puffs', similar to fritters, being deep-fried in boiling lard, are in Chapter V (Pies).[171] Fritters themselves, on the other hand, are to be found in Chapter VI (Puddings).[172] Elizabeth Dimsdale has a receipt for 'German Puffs' but these are nothing like those of Mrs Raffald, resembling the latter's 'Curd Puffs', and so have been put with the Cheesecakes in Chapter X. It is Elizabeth's various recipes for 'Spanish Puffs' that are very similar to Mrs Raffald's 'German Puffs' both in ingredients and method; accordingly, these have been put in Chapter V. The receipt for 'Termin Puffs', which contain flour and are baked in the oven, has been placed in Chapter VI (Puddings).

---

[166] Quoted in Lehmann, *British Housewife*, p248; this quotation from Mrs Raffald is from the original volume; the spelling and punctuation has been modernized in the reprint (p3).
[167] Lehmann, *British Housewife*, p248.
[168] The provenance of the 'Lemon Pickle' receipt is given as 'Madam de la Combe'. It has not been possible to trace this donor with a French name.
[169] Raffald, *Experienced English Housekeeper*, p132.
[170] Raffald, *Experienced English Housekeeper*, pp140-1.
[171] Raffald, *Experienced English Housekeeper*, p80.
[172] Raffald, *Experienced English Housekeeper*, pp89- 90.

Elizabeth has entered some of the receipts twice, which is scarcely surprising considering the sheer volume of receipts. In the transcript that follows, duplicates (and any minor variations) are noted but only printed once; where receipts have the same name but different ingredients and/or methods, both versions have, of course, been reproduced.

In a letter written in 1853, Elizabeth's niece Priscilla stated that her aunt had had a copy made of her journal documenting her journey to Russia with her husband, explaining that Elizabeth had destroyed the original 'as it was feared it might in those days get into print in some way or other'.[173] Fortunately Elizabeth's receipt book did not suffer the same fate; hopefully she would have been pleased that it has now got into print 'in some way or other'.

[173] Cross, *An English Lady*, p17, letter dated 5 July 1853. Priscilla said that the person who had made the copy of the journal was 'named Jeeves - a Brother of the Maiden Ladies who lived nearly opposite to my Cottage at Hertford'. A receipt for 'Ginger Bread' ([pp7, 73]; p95) was supplied by 'Jeeves'.

Editorial conventions and notes

+ *	sign/comment added by ED against some receipts
Ex	extended to Ex[cellent]
underlining	retained where used by ED
{…}	brackets used by ED
~~word~~	word deleted by ED
~~*illegible*~~	illegible deletion
\word/	word inserted by ED
[*sic*]	as written by ED
[*sic*; *recte* ...]	as written by ED; likely correction
[?…]	possible word (original unclear)
[letter]	letter(s) inserted to correct spelling
[p]	page number in the original (placed next to title of receipt)
Mrs	has not been expanded to Mistress but should be understood
'minuite'	ED's spelling for 'minute'

name of donor of receipt has been added where 'ditto' in original

capitals remain as in the original manuscript

some punctuation has been added to aid the reader

Sizes of ingredients, weights and measures used by ED

Culinary research has shown that some ingredients used in eighteenth-century cookery were smaller than today, such as nutmegs, eggs and poultry.[174] Jennifer Stead has noted that the 'large hen's egg' used by Hannah Glasse would have been the equivalent of a small egg today. Both Stead and Jane Grigson have noted that since quantities of seasonings given for poultry dishes appear insufficient, eighteenth-century poultry was probably smaller.[175]

Furthermore, there is the vexed question of the size of 'a spoonful'. Elizabeth Dimsdale uses the following quantities: spoonful, teaspoonful, large teaspoonful, tablespoonful and meatspoonful. Stead carried out various tests concerning measurements of ingredients given by Glasse using modern measuring spoons and an eighteenth-century teaspoon with a deep bowl. She found that 'a large teaspoonful' (her deep-bowled spoon heaped) was the equivalent of a modern UK standard level tablespoon. Concluding that teaspoon measures were often bigger, she suggests that eighteenth-century receipts calling for a teaspoonful meant a tea-measuring spoon rather than a tea-stirring spoon.[176] Karen Hess has suggested that 'a spoonful' was somewhere between one and two modern tablespoonsful.[177]

Elizabeth Dimsdale also gives capacities by cups and glasses: 'a small Tea Cup full of grated Cheese' (in 'Irish Macani'); 'Vinegar {about a Tea Cup Full}' (in 'To stew Cabbage'); a 'Breakfast cup' of breadcrumbs (in 'Panada'); and a 'Wine glass full of water' (in 'Paté Royale'). The sizes of these receptacles would have been known to contemporaries following the receipt.

Space does not permit a discussion of the vicissitudes of the history of the standardisation of weights and measures in Britain.[178] Suffice it to say that it was not until 1824 that the Imperial Weights and Measures Act 'revolutionized British metrology', repealing as it did all previous statutes, ordinances, decrees, orders-in-council and assizes.[179] This being the case, the capacities and volumes

---

[174] Stead, 'Quizzing Glasse', p.xxix-xx.
[175] Stead, 'Quizzing Glasse', p.xxix.
[176] Ibid.
[177] Hess, *Martha Washington's Booke of Cookery*, p517.
[178] See, for example, Zupko, *British Weights and Measures: A History from Antiquity to the Seventeenth Century* (Wisconsin, 1977).
[179] Zupko, *British weights and measures*, p97.

given in ED's receipts, which were gleaned from all manner of sources, were not necessarily standard with each other, and they were not imperial measures. In particular, it must be remembered that before 1824 the pint was equivalent to 16 fluid ounces, which is what the American pint was in ED's time and still is. Therefore, liquid measures given in the receipts are generally smaller than today's equivalents. Listed below are the measures found in the receipts.

Weights mentioned

drachm: one-sixteenth of an ounce ('To stew Lampreys or Eels' calls for 'about a drachm of Mace')

ounce (oz): contained 16 drachms

pound (lb): contained 16 ounces (approx 0.45 kg)

stone: contained 14 pounds

hundred, hundredweight (cwt): contained 112 pounds (approx 50.8 kg) ('Clara wine' requires 'a quarter of a hundred of fine powdered Sugar'; and 'To cure Beef or Pork …' says 'to every hundredweight of Beef …')

Dry goods volumes mentioned

peck: one-quarter of a bushel

bushel: contained 4 pecks (56 lbs) (approx 27 kg). (In 'A considerable Increase by making Bread with Bran Water', when giving the quantities needed to produce this 'increase', ED says 'For a sack of 5 Bushels or 280 Pounds [of flour] …', confirming that one bushel contained 56 lbs)

Liquid measures mentioned

fluid dram: ('Sansparolli' requires '2 drams of Musk')

fluid ounce: contained 8 fluid drams

gill: one-quarter of pint

pint: 16 fluid ounces

gallon [ale measure]: measured 282 cubic inches (Cowslip Wine requires '8 Gallons of Water {Ale Measure}')

hogshead [ale measure]: contained 51 gallons (In the receipt 'To recover Beer that is Flat', the first instruction is 'Take four Gallons out of a Hogshead')

gallon [wine measure]: measured 231 cubic inches (One of the receipts for Currant Wine yields '20 Gallons Wine Measure')

hogshead [wine measure]: contained 63 gallons (One of the receipts for Raisin wine specifies 'a Hogshead of Water {Wine Measure}')

THE RECEIPT BOOK OF

BARONESS ELIZABETH DIMSDALE, c1800

Chapter I: Soups

[p164] Lemon Pickle[1] Madame De la Combe
A dozen Lemons squeezed, a little of the Peel,[2] 2 Anchovies; A good quantity of Pepper Corns, Mace, Cloves, and Nutmegs, a Handful of Horse-radish, and the same of Shalots. Let it boil, and bottle it for use.

[p87] To make Solid Broth
Take four Knuckles of Veal, wash them clean, and boil them in 10 or 12 Quarts of Water, until they become a strong Jelly; Then strain the Broth off, and let it stand until it is cold. If there is any scum, take it off; then put it either in a Silver or China Dish and set it over a Pan of boiling Water over a clear Fire; stir it occasionally a little, until it becomes quite thick; Then put it in small Pots, and let it stand until it is cold.

[p3; p35] Crays fish or Lobster Soup (Daubignée)[3] +
Cleanse them and boil them in Water with Salt and Spice. Pull the ~~feet~~ \Claws/ and Tails, and fry them; Break the rest of them in a Stone Mortar; season them with savoury Spice and an Onion, grated Bread, hard Eggs, and sweet herbs, likewise some good Broth. Strain and put to it some scalded parsley, a few Mushrooms, the feet & tails and a french Role.

[p33] Curry Soup Mirzapore[4]
Make some very rich Chicken broth with a couple of Fowls \which you/ will ~~you~~ boil until they fall to pieces, and all the flesh comes from the bones. Then pass it through a Cloth squeezing it very hard, and get all the goodness out of the Fowls. Let this cool. Take another Fowl which you will cut up as for a fricassee, put to it a little Onion, Garlick, Turmeric, Coriander Seeds, Salt, red Pepper and

---

[1] See Introduction, 'The order of the receipts', for the placement of this receipt.
[2] Mrs Raffald used Lemon Pickle in white and brown sauces. Her receipt is very different, being based on dried quarters of lemons. These, together with various spices, are covered in boiling white wine vinegar, allowed to stand for 3 months, strained, fined, refined and bottled. She commented: 'It is very good for fish sauce and made dishes, a teaspoonful is enough for white, and two for brown sauce for a fowl. It is a most useful pickle and gives a pleasant flavour' (Raffald, *Experienced English Housekeeper*, p42).
[3] The receipt on [p35] (Cray Fish or Lobster Soup) does not give the donor's name.
[4] Mirzapore was a town of British India (now in Bangladesh), in the province and 50 miles east south east of the city of Allahabad, and 30 miles west by south of Benares, on the right bank of the Ganges.

a Bay Leaf. Add just Water enough to boil a Fowl a little while, then put it all into the broth you first made. Stir in also a little Rice boiled dry and let the whole act gently for about half an hour. Serve it up all together. The Broth must be heated again before you add the rest to it.

NB this would be equally good, if the Broth was made with Veal.

[p3; p35] Egg Soup[5] (Daubignée) +
Make a good Veal Broth; Take Chervil, Sorrel and Cabbage Lettuce; Blanche them. 10 Yolks of Eggs to be beat up with Cream. When put in the Soup and on the fire, keep stirring it, taking care it does not boil.

Add 8 poached Eggs, and thin crusts of Bread when you serve up.

[p4] Gravy Soup (Daubigny) +
Six pound of Gravy Beef. Boil four pounds to strong Broth. The other two pounds draw to gravy with a piece of Bacon, and a great many sweet herbs and Onions and all sorts of Roots. Try a Savoy, a Lettuce, and slice a Cucumber.

[p139] Gravy Soup
Draw the Beef as if making Pease Soup, and add a proper quantity of Water.

Some clarify with White of Eggs.

[p59] Hessian Soup
Take Seven pints of Water, One pint of split Pease, one Pound of Lean Beef cut in small pieces, three quarters of a Pound of Potatoes, 3 Ounces of ground Rice, two heads of Celery and three Leeks, or Onions. Season it with Pepper and Salt and some dried Mint to the Palate, boil all together until reduced to 5 Pints. Strain it through a Cullender.

A little Apple and a little Brandy may be added.

[p21] Pease Soup
One quart of Pease, three pounds of Beef, a head of Celery, Turnips, Onions, Parsley, Thyme to your taste; Boil it three hours. Add one spoonful of whole Pepper. Strain it through a Sieve. Put it in a Saucepan, Boil it 10 Minuites. Mix a little dried Mint with it.

[p12] Brown Pea Soup + Basset
About three pounds of Gravy Beef, draw it in a Stew Pan with a piece of Butter; 2 or 3 Onions sliced; 2 small turnips and one Currant [*sic*; *recte* Carrot] sliced.

---

[5] Receipt on [p35] says 'for 10 persons'; no donor is named.

Let it be thoroughly drawn for about one hour, then pour it into a Pint of split Pease which have been boiling in about 5 quarts of Water {Water and all} and ½ or ¾ of a pound of Neck end of fresh Pork. Let them all stew well together until of a proper thickness; then rub the whole through a Cullender, and send it to Table with fine Bread.

[p114] Brown Pea Soup B D Cook
About 3 pounds of Beef, and half a pound of pickled Pork {Bacon makes it taste of smoke} a handful of white Pepper, 2 Onions, a pint and a half of split pease; six quarts of Water. Let them stew down 3 hours; put not any salt in until the last, and very little is wanted. Fry some Bread in Butter, then cut dices. Put it in your Tureen with a very little dried Mint. Some spinage boiled in Water by itself, put in the Tureen. You should put in two hearts of Celery at first with the Meat whole; and when it has boiled one hour & a half, or until it is tender, take it out and put it in the Tureen, after it is cut in thin slices. When the Soup is ready to serve up; strain it into the Tureen, and take particular care when it is strained, that there is not any Fat in it.

[p134] Brown Pea Soup
About 6 pounds of Gravy Beef, 3 pints of Split Pease, 2 or 3 heads of Celery, 6 Anchovies, 2 Onions, a handful of Mint, put them in three Gallons of Water. Boil all together until the Meat is boiled to rags, then strain through a Sieve.

[p14] Green Pea Soup, without Meat or Water *
Take six or eight Cucumbers pared, scooped and cut thick, 8 or 10 Coss Lettuces, 5 Onions, and a handful of Parsley picked, some White Beat Leaves and a little Chervil, if you chuse. Put these into a Stew Pot with better than a quarter of a Pound of Butter, some Pepper and Salt; Stew all slowly till the Juice is out of the Herbs. Have ready boiled a Pint of old Pease, Strain the liquor from the Herbs and squeeze the Old Pease through a Sieve into the Liquor. Then boil tender by themselves 4 or 5 Cucumbers, pared, scooped, and cut into quarters, two or three Cabbage Lettuces cut; these and a Pint of young Pease put to the Liquor and let them stew slowly until enough.

When the first Herbs are stewing, if you find there will not be Liquor enough, add some more Coss Lettuces and Cucumbers.

[p80] Root Soup
Make some strong Beef Broth; Take some Carrots, Celery, Onions and Turnips, clean them well and peel them into a Saucepan without Water, only a small piece of Butter, and a crust of Bread fried: Cover and sweat them. Then rub

them though a tammy soup strainer, and put them into the Broth with a little Sorrel and Cayenne Pepper.

[p147] Scotch Broth

A quart of green Pease, four Cabbage Lettuces, two Dozen of Onions, if very young, cut small; put them down with the Pease; let them stew together at least one hour, then pour in boiling Broth, made of Beef, Mutton, Veal or Chicken, or a mixture of them. The Broth must be light and seasoned high with whole Pepper & Salt.

You may add Artichoke bottoms, Turnips and Carrots.

The stewing the Lettuce and Roots well should be particularly attended to, and Veal gives it an excellent Flavour.

[p65] To make a Soup French Receipt

Take about 3 pounds of lean Beef, a very small piece of Liver. Put them in the Pot, and pour boiling Water on them. Then put the Pot before the Fire and let it boil until it is perfectly scummed & free from Fat. Let it stand before the Fire, and stew by slow degrees: put in some Salt, Carrots, Turnips, some Parsley, Celery and a little Pepper; and about two hours after, put in a Cabbage cut in quarters.

To make the Soup good, it ought to be at the fire 4 hours or 4 hours & a half, and after it had been once boiled and scummed, it must stew by very slow degrees. All the Vegetables, except the Cabbage should be put in about 2 hours after the Soup is began, and the Cabbage should not be put in until half an hour before it is served.

[p90] To make a Soup

Pour peeled Onions cut round the thickness of half a Crown, flour and fry them in six ounces of Butter until they are brown, then put three pints of broth or boiling Water, pepper and salt to you taste, with some thin slices of Bread, boil it a proper thickness, and serve it up.

[p77] Soup a la Reine Miss H' (?Hatton) see page 81

Make a good gravy Soup; then take a pint and a half of good Cream, just simmered and put in just before it is served up.

[p81] Soup a la Reine See page 77

Make a good gravy Soup, and then take a pint and half or a quart of rich Cream just simmered, and put it in just before you sent [*sic*] it up.

[p3; p34] Soup Cressé[6] Daubignée +
Put into a stew pan a quarter of a pound of Butter, half a pound of Ham, six Carrots, six Turnips, three Celery Roots, one Onion. Cut all into slices, and let it stew over a slow fire about two hours and a half, stirring it from time to time to prevent burning. After that take a handful of Crumbs of Bread, and cut them into little square bits. These you will fry and join with the above, also a pint of gravy or broth. Let it stew half an hour more or longer, if required: The whole must be quite tender and soft as a sop. Then force it through a french flannel, and keep it warm to garnish the Mitonage or Soup.

The Mitonage must be made as follows. Take the leaves of three or Four Lettuces, a good handful of Sorrel; wash these well, and cut them in large pieces; Stew it down about ten Minuites with a little Butter; then wet it with two pints of Broth. Let it boil a Moment with some Fried Bread, & when you are ready to dish up, put the Porrage over this Mitonage with two pinches of powdered Sugar & Salt.

This Soup should be of the thickness of Cream and the Colour of a Guinea.[7]

[p21] Soup Cressé
Six Turnips, four Carrots, 4 Onions, one Leak [*sic*]. Cut them very thin, fry them in butter until they are of a good colour, then wet them with broth or gravy made savory. Let them stew until they are tender, then press it through a Sieve, boil it again and skim it.

The Broth to \be/ added according to the quantity of Soup wanted.

[p105] Soup meagre with Pease
Two quarts of Pease, two quarts of Water; When the Pease are boiled, strain them, and mash them well; take a pint of Milk, Spinage, beat, Leaks & Celery, shred them and boil them well. Thicken with Flour. When the herbs begin to boil, season it with Pepper and Salt. When almost boiled, put into it two Ounces of Butter.

[p21] Turnips Soup
Slice five Turnips, three Onions with a piece of Butter into a Stew-Pan; cover it close, and let it stew half an hour; then add as much good Beef broth as you want Soup, add a little Mace, and some white Pepper Corns. Let it stew two

---

[6] No donor named in receipt on p34.
[7] Receipt on [p34] has 'the Colour of Gold'.

hours. Add a piece of Bread to thicken it, then rubb it through a Sieve, and add half a Pint of Cream.

[p8] Turtle Soup Ex[cellent] Mrs Wright +
A pint of strong Beef and Veal Broth, the Juice of two Lemons, the peel of half a Lemon shred as fine as possible; a large Onion entirely mashed; some sweet Herbs tied in a piece of Linen to keep them from swimming about. A little Salt, a tea spoonful of Chian Pepper. All these Ingredients are stewed together until the meat is quite tender, which will be in about one hour and a half, if done gently. When the Soup is finished add a teacup full of Madeira or to your taste. When it is put in the Dish, the Yolks of hard Eggs and forced Meat Balls with some Chopped Oysters. They should all be swimming in the Liquor.

A Bone of Ham or some Veal Bones are a great addition. The Brains not to be put in.

[p15] Vegetable Soup without Meat or Water * Ex[cellent]
Take 4 Cucumbers, 6 Lettuce, 10 Onions and a handful of Parsley, Thyme, 6 Carrots, 6 Turnips, a stick or two of Celery, two ounces of Butter. Stew all slowly until the Juice is out. Strain the Liquor from the Herbs: Have ready one Pint of Old Pease boiled, squeeze them through a sieve into the Liquor. Add lastly a small quantity, at pleasure, of young Pease, and if it is preferred a Lettuce or two; add them to the Liquor and stew slowly until enough. Add Pepper & Salt.

[p3 ; p35] White Soup[8] (Daubignée) +
Boil half a pound of Rice very Tender in Milk and Water, then add to it two quarts of good Veal Broth and Herbs, also a french Roll. Stew it well, season it, serve it up with a Forced Chicken in the middle.

[p93] White Soup Mrs C'
A Knuckle of Veal, wash it well, then put it in a Pot with six Quarts of Water, let it boil and skim it. Then put in a few Cloves, and Mace, some white Pepper and a whole Onion. It will take four hours to boil. Then strain it into a Pan, and be careful in skimming off all the fat. Put it in the Pot again with a quarter of a pound of Vermicelli; half a pint of Cream, The whites of two Eggs finely beaten, and a head of Cellery. Let it boil half an hour.

When you send it to Table, cut the crust off a French Role, and toast it of a fine brown, and put it in your Tureen whole.

---

[8] No donor named in receipt on [p35].

[p114] A la Reine Vermicelli or White Soup B D Cook

A Knuckle of Veal; 2 pounds of the thick end of the Loin of Mutton without the fat. Stew it quite down with an Onion and a blade of Mace. Add about 5 quarts of Water, or enough to cover the Meat. Stew it 3½ hours, and make it the day before you use it; and remove all the fat and sediment at the bottom. Then put it in a Stew-pan with a quart of Cream. When it is well mixed and smooth, put in a little of the Liquor, and beat it until it is as thick and like Cream; Then put it in your soup with a little Cayenne Pepper; A quarter of a pound of Almonds should be blanched, and then beat very Fine with a little Cream. Mix it well with your Soup, and strain it through a coarse Cloth. Then put in an Ounce of Vermicelli. Make some Forced Meat Balls, and just boil up your Soup. Then add a little Salt to your taste; but do not set it in the Fire after adding the Salt, as it is apt to curdle it.

You should boil some spinage in Water by itself and give it 2 or 3 Chops. Then put it in the Tureen and pour the Soup upon it. The forced Meat Balls will be best boiled in a Water by themselves, and add them to the Tureen of Soup. 5 Minuites will boil them. Little or no pepper should be put in, as it makes it of a dust Colour.

Chapter II: Fish[9]

[p160] To boil Fish firm
When the Water boils, add as much Salt as will make the Water support an Egg. Then put in the Fish while the Water is boiling.

No vinegar should be added.

[p67] To make a Matelote
Carp may be stewed in the way I am going to describe; But the ingredients are proper for a small dish of flat Fish.

If you stew Carp take more Ingredients, and let it stew longer in proportion to the size of your Fish.

Put a slice of Butter in your Stew-Pan, shake it and stir it over the fire untill the Butter is of a fine Brown, but take it off occasionally least it should turn black.

Then shred two small onions very Fine, and put them in with a good spoonful of Red Wine. Put in your Fish, shake them up in it, and then put in a small Glass of Hot Water, two pinches of powdered Cloves, the same quantity of pepper, and a little Salt to your Taste; a little Thyme and Bay Leaf, and about half a quarter of a pound of Raisins. Stir it frequently, and let it stew up on a very slow Fire until your Fish is done enough, with the Stew Pan covered close up.

They will require to stew at least a quarter of an Hour.

In this dish the Wine maybe omitted, and a small spoonful of Vinegar used in its place.

[p124] A Matelot
Cut Carp and Eels into hansome pieces. Season them with Pepper and Salt to the taste; then put them into Port Wine and Water, equal quantities, but not more than just enough to stew them All, also four or five thin slices of Ham or Bacon, a bunch of Parsley, Thyme and sweet Marjoram; three Cloves and some Lemon slices. Stew the Fish slowly, and when enough, take it out and strain the Liquor, and have ready half a pound of burnt Butter to thicken the Sauce. Then put in Mushrooms and Capers to heat, and put the Fish in again if you have not kept it

[9] Sauces for different types of fish are given at the beginning of the chapter. Mrs Raffald includes collared, potted and pickled fish in this chapter rather than in Chapter XIII, Potting and Collaring; accordingly, ED's receipts for potting fish are included here.

very hot while you thicken the Sauce. Have some small Onions boiled tender to put in the Dish, and put the Sauce over the Fish, and Fill the Dish Full.

Not any Sauce is sent to Table but what is in the Dish.

Any fish may do, but should make a part of them.

Toasted sippets round the Dish.

[p106] Water Souchy[10]

Boil the fish in Water enough to cover it. Put a little Salt, have a good handful of Parsley roots cut in their fillets, put them into a Stew-pan. After the Fish is enough done, drain the Water through a Hair Sieve over the Parsley roots. Let it boil until tender. Then have a few leaves of Parsley scalded and put to it. Serve the fish up in a deep dish with the Liquor over them.

[p47] To stew Carp

The Fish being scaled, gut them and cut them in pieces. Put them in a large sauce-pan with a quart of Red Wine, a little Vinegar {half a pint} a bundle of Herbs, spice of all sorts, an Anchovy, several small whole Onions. Cover them close, and let them stew about a quarter of an Hour; then add the Blood you washed out and a piece of butter rolled in flour.

Serve them up hot with little sippets of fried Bread round the Dish.

[p134] To stew Carp

Take a Carp; Suppose of nine pound weight, cleanse, scale and dry it. Then half fry it of a clear brown in Beef dripping or Suet. Have ready two quarts of Gravy made with three pounds of Beef, a little Pepper, Salt, 3 middle sized onions, Lemon, Thyme, and a very little Cayenne Pepper. The Beef should be drawn before the Water is added. Stew the fish in the Gravy one hour or one hour and a half until three parts done, stirring the Gravy often to keep it always moist. Then add about a quarter of a Pint of Red Wine {a little Mushroom Catchup} about 2 Tablespoonsful, a little of the Liquor of pickled oysters. Just before it is dished up thicken it with a piece of Butter, about the size of a Walnut rolled in Flour, a little Nutmeg and a small quantity of Lemon Juice.

[p137] To stew Carp

Take a brace of live Carp, scale and gut them; put them in a Stew-pan with a pint of Beef gravy, half a pint of red Wine; an Onion stuck with Cloves, 3 Anchovies, Pepper, Salt and Mace at pleasure, a bunch of sweet Herbs, 2 or 3 Bay Leaves. It must nearly cover them; Cover it close, let it stew gently; put

---

[10] Glasse has a similar receipt 'Water-Sokey' (*Art of Cookery*, p90).

them in a dish with Sippets of fried bread. Strain the Sauce, thicken it over the Fire with burnt butter, pour it over the Fish. Garnish with barberries, Lemon slices &c.

[p15] To stew Eels +

Cut the Eels in small pieces, fry them of a nice ~~colour~~ Yellow; have some rich gravy well seasoned with Essence of Anchovies, thicken the sauce with crusts of bread, or Rice flower, & the flowers [*sic*] should be put in the last thing, just before the Eels.

A little essence of Lemon is a good addition.

[p69] To stew Lampreys or Eels

Clean them well, dry them in a Cloth, take half a Nutmeg, about a drachm of Mace, three or four Cloves not beat very fine and a little Pepper and Salt. Rub a little on the outside and inside of the Lampreys, then roll them round, and put them into a Stew-pan. Put to them half a Pint of Red Wine with the same quantity of rough Cyder and Water, there should not be quite enough to cover them. Put to them a sprigg or two of Lemon Thyme and Savory, a few Pepper Corns, 2 or 3 Blades of Mace, and a little Lemon Peel. Let them stew gently until they are tender. When they are about half done, put in 2 or 3 anchovies. They will take about 2 or 3 hours in stewing. When quite done, thicken the liquor with a good slice of Butter, a little flour, & squeeze in a quarter of a Seville Orange.

[p26] To Stew Flounders Sir E Hulse

An hour before your stew them, put in an equal quantity of Elder Vinegar \&/ White Wine, Slice an onion and put in an anchovy, a bit of Thyme, a little Pepper & Salt. Stew all together, then take out your Fish, and thicken the Sauce with Butter.

[p10] Haddocks like Pigs Head +

Cut them down the Belly; take out the Back Bone; strew a little Pepper, Salt and sweet Herbs in the inside. Turn the tail into the Mouth. Put them in a Pewter Plate; wet them over with the Yolks of an Egg; a few fine Crusts of Bread, and set them as near the fire as you can. When dry and hard, taste them with a little Butter. They will take two hours, and when you serve them up, put the sauce in the Dish, but do not pour it over them. Use Oyster sauce.

[p139] To dress Ling
Put it in cold Water on the \first/ Morning of ~~the~~ \two whole/ day\s/ before it is intended to be dressed; change the Water on the second day; change it again on the day it is to be dressed for luke-warm water, scrubbing it thoroughly and let it soak then until about one hour before dinner; in which remaining time it will be boiled enough.

[p143] To dress Ling
Put the Fish in lukewarm Water early in the morning; let it remain in it until early the next morning; then take it out of the Water, scrub it well with a brush, and scrape it quite clean. Then soak it a short time in cold Water, and then put it in the fish Kettle, and let it simmer over the fire. The Water is to be changed 3 or 4 times before it is ready for dinner, by pouring out the Water, and putting the Fish into fresh cold Water. It is to simmer only the whole time excepting the last 10 Minuites before it is taken up; during which time it is to boil.

Garnish with Egg and Egg Sauce.

[p84] To make a Fricassee of Lobsters M N
Boil the Lobsters as for eating; cut the Tails in halves. Take out the Claws, have a Stew-pan ready; put into it half a pint of Cream, and a quarter of a pound of butter; keep stirring them together all the time, or they will be greasy. Put your Lobsters in with a little dried Mace, and a little Salt; Set them on the fire to heat and them dish them up.

[p109] Lobster Ragoued
Take a boiled Lobster, slice it, take some strong Veal or Mutton broth, one Anchovy and a piece of Butter of the size of a small Walnut rolled in flour, half a spoonful of Ketchup, a few Pepper Corns. Boil all these together before you put in the Lobster, then put it in, make it thoroughly hot and serve it up.

Garnish the Dish with toasted Sippits.

[p28] To stew Lobsters with Pease
Take the inside of two Lobsters of a middling size, and boil in very Salt water. One pint of Green Pease, three Cucumbers dried, the hearts of two Cabbage Lettuce cut small; an onion, twelve grains of white Pepper, a quarter of a pound of fresh butter & a Glass of Water. Let the Pease, the Butter and the Herbs be boiled for half an Hour over a slow fire; then put in the Lobsters cut small, and then boil the whole gently for another half hour. Put in a little Salt to you're taste.

[p150] A Ragout of Oysters
Open 20 large Oysters, take them out of their liquor. Save the Liquor and dip the oysters in a Batter made as follows: Two Eggs; beat well, a little Lemon Peel grated, a little Nutmeg grated, a very little Parsley chopped fine; beat all together with a little Flower. Have ready some butter or dripping in a Stew-Pan. When it boils dip in your Oysters one by one into the Batter and fry them of a fine brown. Then take them out, and put them in a dish before the fire.[11] Then take a clean pan and have half a pint of good gravy ready, add three spoonsful of oyster Liquor, one spoonful of White Wine; a little bit of butter rolled in Flower. Stir all together, let it boil up. Then put in the oysters & when the Sauce is of a good thickness, dish them up.

[p136] Salmon Caveach M[is]s C[la]y
Cut it in pieces; about three Inches broad; fry it and let it lay until it is cold, then put it into a Jar. Mix a tea Cup full of Sweet Oil with as much Vinegar as will cover the Fish. In this pickle put ground black Pepper, and salt sufficient to make it high.

As you put the Fish into the Jar, you may slice an onion or two and mix with it; also some blades of Mace and whole Pepper.

[p123] Soals a la Cartolette
Take three Soals, Fry them crisp in Hogs lard, then make them brown. Take half a pint of gravy, half a pint of White Wine, a blade or two of Mace, Salt, a few Truffles and a Lobster cut in square pieces, Two or three Anchovies, one Onion; put into a Saucepan with the fish and boil awhile. Then put them in the Dish with the Sauce over them. Garnish with thin Slices of Lemon.

[p113] Stewed Soals
About half fry them. Then take them out and put them in a Stew-pan. Stew them in rich gravy with a little Red Wine, and a bit of Lemon Peel, an Onion, a Few cloves and Horse-radish cut in small bits. Stew them about two hours. The slower the better. There is not any occasion for Flower to thicken the Gravy, as the richness of the Soals will do it sufficiently.

[p134] To dress Sounds and Tongues
Soak them in the Morning; clean them well, and pick off the skins.

---

[11] To here, almost the same as Glasse, 'A Ragoo of Oysters' (*Art of Cookery*, p56).

[p170] Baked Herrings or Sprats

Wash and drain without wiping them; season with Allspice in Fine Powder, salt, and a few whole Cloves; lay them in a Pan with plenty of Black Pepper, an onion, and a few Bay Leaves.

Add half vinegar and half small Beer, enough to cover them. Put Paper over the Pan, and bake in a slow Oven. NB Gut, but do not open them.

[p170] Stewed Sprats[12]

Suppose six dozen. To be stewed in a Stew Pan. Pepper and Salt sprinkled between every Layer, and Pepper Corns and a few Cloves added, with some Bay Leaf. Let them be covered with good Vinegar, then to simmer gently for about three quarters of an hour; and afterwards put into an Earthen Pan.

[p70] Carp Sauce

Take a quarter of a pint of strong Beef gravy, one Anchovy, a Spoonful of Catchup, a little Mace, whole Pepper and Salt; one Onion, a little Oyster or Mushroom liquor, with Lemon Juice and red Wine to your Taste. Boil them all together and strain. Then add half a pound of Butter, and when it is melted put in a quarter of a Pound more well flowered to thicken it. A little of the Butter must be burnt, and put in to colour the Sauce.

[p27] Cold Sauce for Fish or Flesh

Take a quart of Verjuice, put it in a Jug; then take Jamaica Pepper whole, some sliced Ginger, Mace, a few Cloves, some Lemon Peel, Horseradish sliced, some sweet herbs, six Eschalots peeled and eight Anchovies: Two or three spoonsful of shred Capers. Put them into a clean linen Bag, and put the Bag into your Verjuice. Stop the jug close for use.

A spoonful cold or mixed with melted butter {as Soy} is very good.

[p25] Dutch Fish Sauce

Thicken melted Butter with the Yolk of an Egg; Put a spoonful of Vinegar to it.

[p18; p116] Dutch Sauce for Cod or Pike[13] Mr Y Thomas

A small stick of Horseradish scraped with half a pint of Water and a Cup of Vinegar, and three Cloves with a little Mace. Boil it half an Hour, then strain it:

---

[12] In the original manuscript after this receipt there are 154 blank pages, the final written pages contain mostly housekeeping hints and some remedies. These now comprise Chapter XVIII.

[13] No donor named in receipt on [p116].

Mix your Butter with a little Flower: Melt your Butter in the Liquor with the Yolks of two Eggs well beat, and then pour your Butter into the Eggs. Stir it together.

[p27] Dutch sauce for boiled Turbot or any Flat Fish
Three or four spoonsful of Vinegar boiled for some Minuites with three or four blades of Mace. Then take it off the Fire, and put to it better than a quarter of a pound of Butter; the Yolks of 2 or 3 Eggs well beaten. Shake this until the butter is ~~quite~~ well melted, but do not set it on the fire after the Eggs and Butter are put in. Serve it up without taking out the Mace. It should be of the thickness of boiled Custard.

[p78] Fish Sauce Miss H' (?Hatton)
Take a pound of Butter, put three Spoonsful of gravy or Water, and one of Vinegar; The Yolks of two eggs well beaten and four Anchovies chopped small and a Bay Leaf, a whole Onion, and a little beaten Pepper, a little Nutmeg; Keep it stirring over the fire until it is melted very thick; then squeeze in the Juice of a Lemon and serve it up.

You may add to it Shrimps, Oysters or Lobsters cut small. But it is very good without.

[p103] Fish Sauce
A quarter of a Pound of Anchovies. Half a pint of Vinegar. An Onion stuck with Cloves; A stick of Horseradish. Half a pint of Port wine boiled together until the Anchovies are dissolved. Then strain through a Sieve. When cold, add half a pint of Catchup.

[p135] Sauce for Fish or Flesh
Put a quart of Verjuice in a Jug. Take whole Jamaica Pepper, some sliced Ginger, some Mace, a Few Cloves, some Lemon Peel, Horse-radish sliced, some sweet herbs, 6 Shalots peeled and 8 Anchovies, 2 or 3 spoonsful of shred Capers. Put all these in a linen Bag, and put the Bag in the Verjuice. Stop close the Jug & keep it for use. Mix it with any Sauce.

[p15] A rich gravy for Lampreys +
First make a rich gravy, add Pepper, Salt and Onion, and equal quantities of red Wine, Cyder and Water.

[p26] Lobster sauce Mrs Trail
When the Meat is taken out of the Lobster, crack the Shells and put a little Water to them, and let them simmer over the fire for an hour, then strain it through a sieve, and to two spoonsful of this Water put four spoonsful of White gravy and three spoonsful of White Wine; one large Anchovie, or 1½ of small; A very little beaten Mace, all ~~boiled~~ these put together in the fire must be boiled; thicken your sauce with flower and butter to your taste. It will take near ¾ of a pound of butter. Take the spawn and dry it; beat it, and put as much as you like to colour it. At the last put in your chopped Lobster, and let it have one boil up.

When you make shrimp sauce; boil the shrimps as the Lobster and make the sauce the same way.

[p10] Oyster Sauce
Make it in the usual way, and grate some [*illegible deletion*] Crumbs of Bread fine; it thickens and makes it smooth.

[p27] The Sussex Sauce for Carp & Tench
A quarter of an Ounce of black Pepper, 2 Ounces of Anchovies, Cloves, mace, Thyme, Lemon Peel, Horseradish, an Onion sliced and a little Parsley, a small quantity of each, simmer all together in half a Pint of Water for three or four hours, then strain it, and add a quarter of a pint of red Wine and simmer it; then thicken it with flour and butter.

[p62] To Collar Eels
Take the largest Eels you can get, skin & split them down the Belly, take out the Bones, season them with a little Mace, Nutmeg and Salt. Begin at the Tail and roll them up very tight; bind them up in a little coarse Incle, boil it in Salt and Water, a few Bay Leaves, a little whole Pepper and a little Vinegar. It will take up an hour or longer boiling according to the size of your roll; when it is boiled you must tie it, and hang it up until it is cold; then put it into the Liquor it was boiled in and Keep it for use.

If your Eels are small you may roll 2 or 3 of them together.

[p105] To Collar Eels
Take a large Eel, Skin and bone it; then take beaten Cloves, Mace, Nutmeg, a little Pepper and Salt, one handful of thyme and Winter Savory, mix all together, and strew it on the inside of the Eel. Then roll it up hard and tie it with Tape. Then take Vinegar and Water, as much as will cover the Eel. Let it boil until you can run a straw through, then take it out, and when the Liquor is cold, put them together.

[p62] To pot Eels like Lampreys
Gut and wash your Eels clean, but do not skin them, leave the heads on; these with all sorts of spice {a little Cayenne Pepper} put ~~them~~ into a Pot and clarify a sufficient quantity of Butter to cover them. When you think them baked enough, take them out of the Pot, drain them, and clarify as much more butter as with the original will be sufficient to cover them for use.

[p4] To Pot Lobsters Daubigny +
Pick the Lobsters clean; Cut them with a Knife, but not fine. Season them with pepper and Salt. Put a quarter of a pound of butter to a pint of Lobster, and mix the Lobster and Butter together, but d'ont melt the butter. Press it down close in the Pots; Cover it with Pepper, and put it into the Oven, and as soon as you take it out press the Meat close again. Let it stand until cold; then Pour clarified Butter over it.

[p94] To pickle Oysters Mrs C'
To a quart of Oysters, add a pint of Vinegar, a little Lemon Peel, about a spoonful of whole White Peppers, some Mace, a little Salt; let them just boil up; then strain them from the Liquor, and let them both stand until they are cold. Then put them together, and they will be fit for use

[p129] To pickle Oysters +
To a quart of Oysters put a pint of Vinegar, a little Lemon Peel; about a spoonful of whole White Pepper, some Mace, a little Salt, let them just boil up; then strain them from the Liquor, and let both stand until cold, then put them together, and they will be fit for use.

[p139] To pickle Oysters
Take large Oysters, open them as clean as possible, and take care not to cut them; save the Liquor and wash therein every oyster singly to prevent their being gritty, then strain the Liquor through a Fine Muslin Bag or Cloth. Put the oysters and Liquor together in a sauce Pan and put it over the fire, and let them simmer seven minuites. Then take them off and add a little Horseradish sliced, a little whole Pepper, Jamaica Pepper and Mace, and a little Salt to a quart of Oysters, a pint of White Wine Vinegar, which must be put in before the oysters are set on the fire.

[p140] Pickle Oysters {Mrs L}
Take 50 Oysters, wash them in their own Liquor two or three times, strain each time. Put not any Water to them if the Oysters are Fine; their own Liquor being

sufficient. Let them just boil; then take them & strain the Liquor again. Put Mace, white whole Pepper, very little ground Pepper. When it is well boiled, add a spoonful of Vinegar. Pour it on the Oysters boiling.

[p142] To collar Salmon

Wipe the Salmon until it does not leave a stain in the Cloth. To 15 pounds of Salmon add one ounce of black Pepper well beaten and half a pound of common Salt. Let it lay all night, then tie it very tight with matting. Then take half an Ounce of Pepper bruised and half a pound of Salt; 2 Quarts of Vinegar and three Quarts of Water. Put the Salmon in the liquor when it boils, and let it boil ¾ of an hour. Separate the Salmon from the liquor, and let each be perfectly cold before they are put together.

[p31] To pickle Salmon

After the fish is boiled take it out of the Water, which Water must be boiled again with Salt, Vinegar white Pepper and two or three Cloves. When cold pour it over the Fish.

This a very savry Dish.

Chapter III: Roasting and Boiling (including sauces)

[p173] Meat

All Fresh Meat should be put into the Water boiling.

And Salt Meats to cold Water, unless it should not be sufficiently salted, then put it in when the Water is hot, as it strike in the Salt.

[p173] Chickens, Veal and Lamb

Are whiter for being boiled in a Cloth with some Milk in the Water.

[p56] A Brown Hash of Chicken &c

Take a Lump of Butter, shake it over the fire in a Stew Pan until it is brown. Put in some Water {or a little Soup} a pinch of Pepper, Salt and Powder of Cloves with an Onion cut small and a little Thyme and Bay Leaf; then put in the Chicken, cover it up, and let it stew until it is thoroughly warm.

[p147] Stewed Chickens

The Chickens used, to be thoroughly washed and skinned. Cut them in joints, and put them on in cold Water with a little parsley. When it is well boiled and the broth good, put in two Eggs well beat and give it one boil to make the broth clear.

A piece of Mutton, Veal or Lamb is a good addition.

[p145] Fowls roasted the Scotch way

Put two large Fowls to roast, and under them some Eggs {both Yolks & Whites} broke in a pewter dish, taking care they do not run into the other, but are kept separate. Baste the Fowls in the common Way with Butter. The Gravy from the Fowls drop on the Eggs, which should be moved round by turns towards the Fire; and when the Fowls are done, they are to be sent to Table in the same pewter Dish {if clean}. The fowls being laid in the middle, and the Eggs round them.

[p109] To boil a Ham

Having put your Ham into a Copper or large Pot, let the Water be ~~boiled~~ heated so slowly that it may be at least three hours before it boils, ~~after which an hour and a half~~, after which and [*sic*] hour and a half will boil a small and two hours a large Ham. You must constan[t]ly skim the Liquor.

[p121] To boil a Ham
After it is properly soaked, roll it up in clean Hay, and boil it thus wrapped up. The rind must be rubbed with a clean Flannel when taken out of the Pot.

[p17] To Baste a Hare +
Cut a Rasher of Bacon, fold it in a piece of Paper twisted at each end, light the Papers and hold it in a pair of Tongs, and baste the Hare with it.

[p19] Dunstable Larks
8 Larks for our Supper at Dunstable. They were all on one Spit which was small, and designed for that purpose. They were laid very close to a brisk fire and turned very briskly; In about ~~10~~ 2 Minu~~i~~tes they were flowerd, after about as much more time they were basted with a great deal of Butter, so as to keep quite a stream pouring on them at the same time. They were turned as quick as possible, so that they were quite covered with a very thick froth. In this manner they were roasted for about 4 Minuites; and then the Cook with a Dish full of very fine grated Bread strewed them over by handfulls, holding the Dish under to catch what Bread did not stick. Being removed a little way from the fire, they were then laid close, and in about a Minute the same was repeated, so as to get as many Crumbs to stick as possible. They were then laid near the fire again, and turned carefully and slowly, sometimes backwards, sometimes forwards, but very steadily: This took up about 5 Minuites more; So that I judge they were about 10 Minuites a doing by a very brisk fire, and lying almost so close as to touch the Bar~~r~~s. When the Crums were brown they were taken up and laid in two Rows in the Dish, and the four that were not separated stuck close together by the strength of the Cement of the Crums and Butter. They were done extreemly nice.

They were not more that 10 Minuites at the fire.

[p31] Hashed Mutton
Put an Onion into some Gravy with some pepper and Salt, a little Catchup; thicken it with a little flower; boil it for a few Minuites, take out the Onion, put in the Mutton cut thin, and any gravy that may have run from it, a little Garlick Vinegar, just simmer it up, shaking it until it is thoroughly hot, but do not let it boil, for that makes all hashes hard. Garnish with Pickles:

If you [have] no gravy boil the mutton bones with an Onion or a Clove or two, a bit of Lemon peel, a bunch of sweet herbs and a Few pepper Corns. Strain it.

[p58] A Brown Hash of Mutton, Beef or Hare &c French Receipt
Mince the Meat as small as possible, and shred some Shalots very fine, and mix among it. Put a Lump of Butter in a Stew Pan with a very little fat. When it is melted fry some toasted Bread in it to put round the Hash. Then put the Meat into the Butter in the Pan. Pour some hot Water upon it and mix it together. Put in part of a Sage and Bay Leaf, and a small sprig of Thyme, and some Parsley shred very fine. A little Pepper, Salt & powder of Cloves, and a very little Vinegar. Put in these whilst it is stewing over the fire, and before you serve it up, Pick out the Sage and other Leaves.

[p36] Boiled Pigeons
Stuff them with sweet Herbs, chopped Bacon, grated bread, butter spice and the Yolk of an Egg; tie them at both ends and boil them. Garnish with slices of Bacon, or pickled Pork and stewed Lettuce or any Vegetable you like.

[p13] To roast Sparib of Pork +
A short time before it is taken off the Spit rub it over with Yolk of Eggs, and them shake over it some Captains' Biscuits finely powderd.

[p145] Tongue and Udder[14]
If the tongue and Udder are to be dressed on Thursday, put them in Salt on Saturday. Boil them nearly enough to eat; then take them out of the Pot, and stick the thick end of the Tongue with a Few Cloves, and put it and the Udder in a Dutch Oven, so as to be of a nice brown.

Send them to table in one or two dishes or one if you prefer it, with good Gravy, and Currant Jelly sauce.

[p109] To boil a Tongue
A dried Tongue should be boiled three hours; having been First soaked in Water for a Night. But a tongue fresh from the Pickle should not be put in until the Water boils, and it will be done in two hours.

[p92] Venison to dress B D Cook
Spit it; then rub it over with the Yolk of an Egg; then butter a Sheet of writing paper, and cover it over; on that part put a Sheet of White brown Paper [*sic*], and tie it tight with a Pack-thread & baste it with Milk.

Allow Four pounds to an hour.

---

[14] Raffald's 'To boil a Tongue' is very similar; the accompanying currant jelly is sliced rather than a sauce (*Experienced English Housekeeper*, p35).

Sauces

[p7] Bread Sauce + [*in both margins:* III] [*left margin:* 2°]

To a pint of Water put half a large Onion and half a Meat Spoonful of pepper Corns, boil them together \till [*blank*]/ strain it and put to the liquor grated bread enough to thicken it: three spoonsful of cream, a lump of butter the size of an Egg and a little Salt. Boil it well.

[p20] Bread Sauce {Cock [*or* Cook] Crawford}

Take 20 Pepper Corns, 8 onions peeled and washed, One Pint of Milk; boil these together until it comes to half a Pint; then strain it through a Sieve. Add a piece of Butter the size of a Walnut, and bread to make it a proper thickness. Boil these together until soft enough to work through a Sieve. Then add a little more butter and cream, and serve it up.

[p110] Celery Sauce

Take a large bunch of Celery wash and pare it very clean from the green part. Cut it in small pieces; boil it gently in a little Water, until it is tender; then add a little beaten Mace, Nutmeg, Pepper and Salt, thickened with a piece of butter rolled in flour, and a quarter of a pint of Cream. Boil it up, and pour it in the Dish.

[p135] Essence[15]

A Knuckle of Veal, half a pound of Ham, some sweet Herbs in 3 Gallons of Water, to be stewed down to a quart until of the consistence of Glue. When to be used place it near the fire and it will dissolve, but not any Water is to be added. Brush the Chops over with ~~illeg~~ this to glaze them.

[p25] Sauce for boiled Fowls Mrs M

Chop some Anchovies, add a little cold Water, Mace, Salt and Pepper and a little Lemon Peel, then mix a small piece of butter with flour, melt it, stirring it all the time; then add a spoonful or two of Cream.

The Liver is to be chopped fine with Parsley, and added to the Sauce, before it is put into the dish.

[p18] Sauce for Boiled Fowls Mrs Harvey + [*in both margins:* III]

The Yolks of two Eggs, a little Cream, and a very small quantity of Catchup. It must be set on the fire, and stirred till of a proper consistance and thickness. The Eggs should be well beat before they are added to the Cream.

---

[15] An essential(!) base for sauces in French cuisine (Lehmann, *British Housewife*, p276).

[p92; p160] Sauce for Boiled Fowl[16] Mrs C'
A quarter of a pint of Cream with a little bit of butter and a little Flour, and two or three Spoonsful of Lemon Ketchup.

To make the Ketchup: Cut 4 or 5 Lemons without Spots into quarters, throw some Salt over them; then put them into a Jar, and let them stand before the Fire, but not too close, two days; then boil some of the best Vinegar with some Nutmegs, Cloves, Mace and Ginger, and white Pepper. Pour it on the Lemons boiling hot, keep it close covered; it will be fit for use in a little time.

[p121] Sauce for cold Fowl or Game
Chop a middling sized Onion fine; the same quantity of Parsley chopped fine, one spoonful of Vinegar, two spoonsful of Oil. The ingredients are to be well mixed together, and poured over the cold Fowls cut in pieces.

[p133] A good Sweet Sauce for boiled Mutton &c
A quarter of a pint of Broth the Mutton was boiled in; add 4 Spoonsful of Pickle and Capers or Samphire; set it on the Fire to boil; then add a Carrot which had been first boiled tender, and 4 spoonsful of Capers or Samphire shred. Put this in the Liquor, when it boils stir in 4 Ounces of Butter, and shake a little flour; sweeten it, and put it over the Meat.

[p27] To Fry Cucumbers for Mutton Sauce
Brown some Butter in a Pan, and cut the Cucumbers in slices, drain the Water from them; then fry them brown; Put them in a Saucepan with a little ~~sauce~~ \salt/ and pepper, and a piece of an onion, some Gravy. Stew them together and squeeze on a little Lemon Juice; shake them and put them under the Mutton.

{Rackets Savory Dish}[17]

[p2] Pauvre Sauce[18] +
Chop four Shalots very fine with a little Parsley; mix them well together, and add two table Spoonsful of Vinegar; An Anchovy cut small or Anchovy liquor {if you have not any Anchovies} to your taste. Add a little Carrouch, Chian, and Salt.

If no Carrouch use Walnut pickle.

---

[16] The receipt on [p160] gives only the first two lines and no donor.
[17] It has not been possible to identify 'Rackets'.
[18] This and the next two receipts are versions of 'Poivrade Sauce'. Note the mangling of the spelling as the receipt is passed around.

[p92; p103] Poverroy Sauce[19]
Four Shallots chopped fine; put them in half a Gill of ~~Brandy~~ Gravy, a little Pepper and Salt and a spoonful of Vinegar.

or

Six Shalots {large ones} chop very fine, put them in a sauce Pan with two spoonsful of Vinigar and two of White Wine. Boil them for a Minuite or two.

[p104] A good Sauce
Six Shalots {large ones} chopped very fine; Put these in a Sauce Pan with two Spoonsful of vinegar and two of White Wine. Boil them for a Minuite or two.

[p164] Sauce Piquante for roast Veal &c
Take a lump of Butter, shake it in a Stew Pan until it is quite brown. Then put into it 6 small Shalots cut fine, a large spoonful of Vinegar, a lump of dripping, 2 pinches of pepper, and powder of Cloves, a little Thyme and part of a Bay Leaf and Sage, a little Salt if the dripping is not quite salted. Pour in some hot Water, or Soup is better; let it boil a little. Drain all the Fat from the Meat, and pour this Sauce over it.

[p50] Sauce Piquants [*sic*]
Moisten Mustard with Olive Oil, and the Yolk of one Egg; and add Vinegar, shallots, an Anchovy, Pepper and salt.

This Sauce is good either Hot or Cold. If used with cold Fowl, Pork &c a few herbs chopped small, and added to it will be found a great improvement.

[p49] Sauce Robert Mrs S
Put a small quantity of Butter and a spoonful of flour in a Saucepan. Colour it over a slow fire. When it is of a good Colour, add three large Onions cut very fine, and a sufficient quantity of butter to make the Onion boil. Moisten it with a little Broth. Skim the fat from the sauce, and let it boil half an hour. When it is served up add salt, pepper, mustard, and a small quantity of Vinegar to your taste.

The flour at first \should/ be well browned of a cinnamon Colour.

This sauce is excellent for fresh Pork, Pigs feet, or Turkey's legs broiled.

---

[19] The receipt on [p103] (Poverry Sauce) only has the first two lines.

[p103] Shalot Sauce for Roast Fowl
Six Shalots chopped fine; put them in a Saucepan with a gill of gravy; a spoonful of Vinegar; some Pepper and Salt, stew them for a minuite; then pour them in your Dish or sauce Boats.

[p102] A standing Sauce for a Kitchen
A quart of Red or White wine in a glazed Jar; the Juice of two large Lemons; five large Anchovies, some whole Jamaica Pepper, sliced Ginger, Mace, a few Cloves, a little Lemon Peel, Horseradish sliced; some sweet Herbs, 6 Shalots, 2 spoonsful of Capers with their Liquor. Put all in a linen Bag, and put it into the Wine. Stop it close and set the Jar in a Kettle of Water. It must boil one hour, and be kept in a warm place.

A spoonful or two of the Liquor is good in any Sauce.

Chapter IV: Made Dishes[20]

Mock turtle

[p2] Mock Turtle +

Take a Calfs Head, scall [*sic*] off the hair; When cleaned, cut the horny part into thin slices with as little of the lean as possible; put a few chopped Oysters to the Brains; Then have ready between a quart and three pints of strong Veal gravy or Mutton with a quart of Madeira Wine, a large teaspoonful of Chian Pepper. Batter a large Onion, and the peel of half a Lemon chopped very fine, a little Sauce and the juice of two large Lemons and some sweet herbs sliced very fine. Stew all these together until the Meat is tender, which will be in about one hour and a half. Then have ready a Turtles Back Shell lined with a paste of flour and Water, which must be set in the Oven to harden. Then put the ingredients into the shell, and put it into the Oven to brown. Garnish with Yolks of Eggs, boiled hard and some forced Meat Balls.

Two Cows heels and a Calfs foot dressed the same way, make a good Dish.

[p9] Mock Turtle +

Parboil the Head untill the white Meat is as tender as you like; then cut off the horny part, and stew it tender in fine rich Gravy. Then put in your white Meat with a little Salt, a little sweet Herbs cut fine, a large Onion ~~cut~~ \chopped/ fine, a few Oysters cut small, 3 or 4 Lemons, three quarters of Madeira Wine; forced Meat Balls and Yolks of Eggs boiled hard. Beat up the Brains and mix with the Gravy and as much Cayenne Pepper as you like.

Do not add the Eggs and Balls untill it is ready for serving up.

[p132; p156] Mock Turtle[21] see page 156

Let the Hair be scalded of a Calves-head as clean as that of a Pig. Then boil it whole for a ¼ of an hour. Afterwards cut the horny part into thin slices with the lean that is tender, and the Brains must be added after they are chopped; when this is put into a stew pan add a quart or three pints according to the size of the Head of strong Mutton or Veal Broth, a pint of Madeira \Wine/ with the Juice of two Lemons and the peel of one shred as Fine as possible, a large Onion entirely mashed; some sweet herbs cut exceeding small, a little Salt, and a whole Tea

[20] The contents of this chapter, which include curries, are listed in order of the main ingredient. Mrs Raffald commences Chapter III with receipts for Mock Turtle, so ED's Mock Turtle receipts have been placed first here.

[21] The receipt on [p156] is headed 'See page 132'.

spoonful of Cayenne Pepper. All these must be stewed together until the Meat is quite tender, which will be in about one hour and a half. When it is put in the Dish, the Yolks of hard Eggs and Forced Meat balls should be laid on the surface.

This will keep good a Week or ten days.

Chopped oysters are by some thought an improvement.

NB the Brains & sweet Herbs may be left out.

[pp98-99; p158] Mrs Clapham's Mock Turtle

Parboil the Head until the white Meat is as tender as you like, then cut off the horny part, and stew it tender in fine rich Gravy. Then put in your white Meat, with a little Salt, a little sweet Herbs cut fine, a large Onion chopped fine; a few Oysters chopped small, 3 or 4 Lemons; three quarters of Madeira Wine, Forced Meat Balls and Yolks of Eggs boiled hard: Beat up the Brains and mix with the Gravy, and as much Cayenne Pepper as you think will do.

Do not add the Eggs and Balls until it is ready to serve up.

Heads, Tripe, etc

[p69] To make Brawn

Take a Pig's face, feet and ears &c rub them with Salt-petre, let them be salted, in common Salt, three days; then boil them very tender; Have ready a wooden Mould proper for Brawn {an old Seive will do} let it stand in a Pewter plate, and put a Cloth in the Mould, or you will find it difficult to get the Brawn out. When it is boiled and quite hot, take out all the Bones, and then take the different pieces as you judge best, and place them in the Mould alternately fat and lean; take care to put pieces of skin outside. Press it down afterward as close as possible, and let it remain under the weights for one Night. Take it out of the Mould and keep it in a pickle made of Salt and Water, and a handful of Bran and a little Vinegar. This Pickle should \be/ boiled, and the Brawn should not be put in until it is cold again. The Pickle should be made fresh every 3 or 4 days.

A couple of ox feet are good ingredients.

[p28] To roast a Calfs Head

The Head being nicely washed and picked, take out the Brains and Tongue: Make a large quantity of Forced Meat with Veal and Suet well seasoned; Fill the whole ~~with the~~ Head with it. Skewer it and tie it on the Spit. One hour and half will roast it. Beat up the Brains with a little Sage and Parsley finely shred, a little Salt and the Yolks of 2 or 3 Eggs. Boil and Blanche the tongue, cut it in large slices & fry it and the Brains; and also some Forced Meat in Balls, and some slices of Bacon.

The sauce is made with strong Broth, with Oysters, Mushrooms, Capers and a little white Wine thickned with Butter and Flower.

[pp100-101] To bake a Calves Head
Take a head clean picked, washed and dried in a Cloth; spread it in a Dish, the flesh side upwards, strew on it Cloves, Mace, Salt and Nutmeg with a few sweet herbs shred fine {such as parsley, Lemon thyme, Winter Savory and a very small quantity of knotted Marjoram} then flour it thick, and lay on small lumps of Butter placed pretty thick, all over it. Have ready two Anchovies chopped fine; one or two Onions stuck with a few Cloves, a small bunch of herbs, half a Lemon Peel, a Gill of strong White Wine {not sweet} as much Water; mix these together, and put into the Dish with half the Brains; the other half should be sliced, well floured, and fried a pale brown for garnish;

When the Head is baked, which with a proper heat will be in an hour and a quarter, or perhaps less if not very large and thick; When done take the baked Brains \mashed fine/ and liquor from the Dish into a Saucepan and some butter well flowered, and boil all together, until it thickens to a smooth Sauce. After which quicken it with the juice of Lemon to your taste, and pour into the dish under the Head.

It may be served up with Mushrooms, Forced Meats, Oysters, Truffles or what you please; But rashers of fine Bacon and the Fried Brains should not be omitted. A few leaves of sweet Basil is a good addition.

[pp28-29] To hash a Calves Head
Boil the Head almost enough, then cut it in half; the finest half Scotch and st[r]ew it over with grated Bread, and a little Parsly shred fine, set it before the fire to brown, and baste it with butter; cut the other Half and the tongue in thin slices as big as a crown piece, have some strong gravy ready, and put it in the Saucepan with the Head; An Anchovy washed and boned; the Head and Tail cut off; a piece of onion, two or three Cloves, two Blades of Mace just bruised and put in a Bag; then put in a little flower, and set it to stew. When it is enough add the Yolk of four Eggs Well beaten with two Spoonsful of White Wine and some grated Nutmeg, & stir it in your hash, until it is thick enough; then lay your broiled Head in the Middle and your hash round it. Garnish the Dish with forced Balls and small slices of Bacon.

If you thicken with Trouffles and Morells simmer them in 2 or 3 Spoonsful of Water for a few Minuites, then put them with the Liquor into the Sauce.

[p29] To Hash a Calves Head White
Boil half a Calves Head ~~Meat~~ in Milk and Water; cut it in slices when cold, Flour it and put it in a Stew Pan with some Veal gravy, a little beaten Mace and Salt, and a few Morelles, a few Artichoke bottoms parboiled, a few Oysters with the beards taken off, stew in a good piece of Butter rolled in Flour; put in the liquor; the Yolks of two Eggs well beat; half a pint of cream; stir all together until it is of a good thickness, and just before it is taken up, put in some fresh or some pickled Mushrooms; if Fresh they must be simmered in two or three Spoonsful of Water; garnish with forced Meat, and the Brains Fried.

[p29] Garnish for a Calves Head
Beat up the Brains with a little Lemon Peel cut fine, a little Nutmeg grated, a little Mace beaten; a little Thyme shred small, a little Parsley, the Yolk of an Egg. If you use the whole Brains take the Yolk of two Eggs. Have ready some dripping boiling in a Stew Pan: Fry it in little Cakes of the size of a Crown piece.

[pp54-55] Calves Head Brawn Ex[cellent]
Take the Head with the Skin on, split it nearly in two, lay it flat on the dresser, and take out all the Bones quite clean. Let it lay in a Pan of cold Water until the next morning, when it must be washed in warm Water several times to take out the Blood; then spread it open on a Cloth to dry, chop sweet herbs of all sorts, Lemon peel, half a Nutmeg & Cloves and Mace made very fine, pepper and Salt, being all well mixed together, strew them over the inside of the Head; then roll it very tight and bind it with six Yards of Tape, as tight as possible, then roll it in a Cloth over the Tape, and tie it at the ends & middle. Put it in a Kettle of cold Water with the Bones, and a handful of Salt & pepper, about one pint of Vinegar, and all sorts of Herbs, Onions & Celery. Let it stew gently six hours, but not boil; then take it out of the Kettle, lay it in a dish; but do not take off the Cloth until next morning. The pickle it was stewed in should, when cold, then poured the next morning over it through a Strainer; but it must be quite cold when poured on the Head.

The pickle must be boiled up fresh twice in every Week. The Brains are not used. The Tongue must be taken out and parboiled to take off the Skin, when it must with the Ears, being also boiled, be rolled together, and put in the small end of the Head, to make it nearly of equal size to the other end.

[p30] Calves Liver Stewed
Lard the Liver and put it into a stew pan with some Salt, whole Peppers, a bundle of sweet herbs, an onion and a blade of Mace; let it stew until tender,

then take it up and Cover it to Keep hot, st[r]ain the Liquor it was stewed in, skim off the fat, thicken it with a piece of butter rolled in flour, and pour it over the Liver.

[p142] To stew Ox Cheek
After the Cheek has been well soaked in Water for 2 or 3 ~~days~~ \hours/; let it be well cleaned, then stew it until tender with a Knuckle of Veal. Strain off the Liquor and clear off the fat. Put the Broth into the Pot with the Cheek again; take a quarter of a pound of Butter, or Gravy; Lemon, thyme, one Onion; some Flour rolled up with Butter, ~~or Gravy, Lemon, thyme~~ to make it of a proper thickness. Season it with Cayenne Pepper and Salt. Add half a Lemon and Forced Meat Balls.

[p102] Ox Palates Baked[22]
When you salt a Tongue cut off the Root, and take some Ox Palates: Wash them clean; cut them into 6 or 7 pieces. Put them into an Earthen Pot, just cover them with Water; Put in a Bladder [*sic*; *recte* Blade] or two of Mace; 12 whole Pepper Corns, 3 or 4 Cloves; a little Bundle of Sweet herbs, a small onion, half a spoonful of raspings. Cover it close with brown Paper, and let it be well baked. When out of the Oven, season it with Salt to your Palate.

[p115] Ragoued Sweetbread
Take a sweetbread; lard it thick with bacon and roast it; It will take an hour with a good fire. Then take a raw Sweetbread cut it in slices, cut very thin; rub it over with the Yolk of an Egg, sprinkle a little Pepper and Salt, grate a little Lemon Peel and a very little Mace. They [*sic*; *recte* Then] fry them in good dripping or Hogs Lard, lay them to the Fire to dry. Then put them in a Stew-pan with a little good Gravy made with Veal and Beef and an Onion and whole Pepper in it. Use no more gravy than will just cover the fried Sweetbread, which should lay in the middle of the Dish. It will take ½ an hour to do in the Stew-Pan slowly.

[p107] White Sauce for a Fricassee
Make some broth of Veal, a little Pepper, Mace and a little Cream. Thicken it with a piece of Butter rubbed in flour.

---

[22] Almost the same as Glasse's 'Ox Pallat Baked' (*Art of Cookery*, p60).

[p127; p10] An excellent Fricassee of Tripe[23]
Cut the Tripe in pieces, and stew it down very tender with a quart of good strong Broth. If for a large Dish, Your Broth made with Beef and Mutton well seasoned with Pepper, Salt, a Faggot of sweet Herbs, and parsley and two Onions. After your Tripe is stewed down, take out of that liquor and put it into a Tasser,[24] that you design to shake it up in. Take the fat off from your Broth, and then put about a Pint or rather less of it into the Tasser with the Yolk of Eggs beat well; better than half a pint of Cream, a little Nutmeg grated; half a Dozen Cloves, 2 Blades of Mace; a little Butter dipt in Flower, and shake it up together over a clear Fire. Put in the juice of half a Lemon, and two Spoonsful of White Wine if you like it. Take care it does not turn. When thick and well relished to your Taste, dish it. There should also be put in about a Gill of Mushroom Buttons.[25]

[p32] To fricassee Tripe
Let it be very white, cut it in small pieces, put it into some boiled Gravy with a little cream, and a bit of butter mixed with flour. Stir it until the butter is melted, add a little White Wine, Lemon peel grated, chopped parsley, pepper and Salt, pickled Mushrooms or Lemon Juice. S[h]ake all together, stew it a little.

Skirts eat well broiled, and make an excellent Pye.

[p144] To stew Tripe brown Mrs M'w
Take a pound and half of gravy Beef, put to it a little Pepper, Mace & Mix with three pints of Water. Let if simmer one hour and half over a slow Fire until it is reduced to about one quart. Then take ⅔rds of a Tripe and cut into pieces about half an Inch broad and two long, taking out most of the Fat. Then put to it 25 or 26 small Onions whole; then throw it into the Stew-pan, and throw the Gravy warm over it, and let it stew about ~~half~~ an hour and half, then thicken the Gravy with Flour and butter & a table spoonful of Mustard. Then stew if half an hour more. NB The Gravy must be brown.

Beef

[p30] Alamode Beef
Take the Rump and bone it, throw it in a Pan ~~*illegible*~~, with bacon and butter; then add to it two quarts of gravy drawn with bacon and herbs, put in an Onion or two stuck with Cloves, a little Pepper, and let it stew together 3 hours and turn it sometimes. Keep it close covered, strain off the Liquor, and skim off the

---

[23] Receipt on [p10] is entitled 'Bath Receipt for Fricaseeing Tripe'.
[24] Receipt on [p10] has 'Vessel' but on p127 it is definitely 'Tasser'.
[25] Last sentence on [p10] reads: 'Pickled Mushrooms may be preferable to Wine'.

fat: Then put the Liquor and Beef together and a quarter of an ounce of Mushroom powder, some Trouffles and Morrels blanc[h]ed, put these to the Beef and let it stew another hour. A little butter and flour to thicken the Sauce, and a little Lemon Juice to your taste.

[pp56-57] Boeuf a la Mode French Receipt
Take a piece of Lean Beef, without any Bone and just large enough to fill the Pot you intend baking it in. Lard it all over with shreds of fat Bacon rolled in seasoning. For a pound & quarter of Beef, take two or three small pieces of the rind of Bacon and lay in the bottom of the Pot, and two large Onions cut in pieces; About 4 pinches of Pepper, 3 of Powder of Cloves and a little Salt: Then lay in the Beef: Put some thin slices of fat Bacon upon it and then another seasoning as before of Pepper, powder of Cloves and Salt. Pour in about half a Tumbler full of hot Water; put in a small lump of Butter, half a Bay Leaf and a little sprig of Thyme. Cover up the Pot. Take some Bread paste, wet it, and lay all round the Edge of the Pot when it closes, to prevent the steam from getting out.

It may be eat hot or Cold from the Oven; or it may be kept in the House several days and will be equally good: But in that case it must never be opened until it is wanted, and should be heated again in an Oven, or set by the fire {still close covered} and shook sometime untill it is heated.

NB The Bacon should not be much salted, and even then it must be several times washed.

[p101] Bouillée Beef {B D Cook}
Put a piece of Brisket Beef {the thick part} in a saucepan of Cold Water, just enough to cure [?*recte* cover] it {about 10 o'Clock} with a little Salt, and when it begins to boil to add Celery, Turnips, half a dozen Onions, as many Carrots, a bunch of sweet Herbs, a little whole Pepper tied up in a Rag. Let it stew; not boil; about half past 3, then skim it well, and take the Beef out, and strain the Soup which is served up in a Tureen with a little Turnip, Carrots, Celery and Toasted bread; and the Bouillée is put in a Dish with Gravy made of the Soup, thickened with butter and Flower {taking care it does not look greasy} and some fine chopped Carrots, and sliced pickled Cucumbers, or french Beans, are to be preferred. These being all chopped fine, and poured over the dish make it look fine.

[p151] Bouille Beef
Put about 5 or 6 pounds of the middle part of the Briscuit of Beef into a Gallon of cold Water. Set it over the fire, and stew it slowly on a gentle boil, or simmer

for about 4 or 5 hours, or until it is made very tender. Some cut Carrots and two large Onions or 5 or 6 small ones, one Turnip if large, if small 2, 4 Cloves and a bundle of Parsley and Thyme are also to be put in at First with the Beef. When the Bouillée is quite enough, it is to be taken out of the Soup; and the Soup is to be strained through a fine Sieve. If the Soup after straining is not thought fine enough, a piece of lean Beef is to be put in, and it must boil sometime longer. After straining it through a Sieve, the fat must be taken quite off the Top of it. Then it is to be cleaned with the Whites of two Eggs, and the Shells are to be used also.

The Soup is served up in a Tureen by itself and the Bouillée in a Dish. The Sauce for the Bouillée is a nice thick Gravy made with lean Beef, to which a little Pepper, and Salt should be added. When the Gravy is quite prepared add some scooped Carrots and Turnips; they being first boiled tender in their scooped shape by themselves and put in the gravy, and a little sliced pickled Cucumbers. These are mixed with the Gravy when it is made, and poured over the Bouillée in a dish. Be very careful that there is not any Fat in the Gravy, and that it does not look greasy.

[p113] Cuckow and Sauce B D Cook

Three pounds of Beef, 2 pounds of Scragg of Veal, five quarts and a pint of Water, a handful of White Pepper, two Onions; stew it quite down, which will take 2½ hours. Then strain it through a sieve, and put it in the Pan again. Take two handsful of Spinage, a handful of Beet leaves; cut them about the size of your Thumb. Take 5 heads of Celery cut in thick slices; Ten Potatoes, pare, slice and quarter them in 4 pieces, an Ounce of Salt Fish skinned, then pull[ed] in small pieces, a quarter of a pound of Bacon, cut in thin slices. The Soup is to be boiled up after the Meat and strained from it. Take off the Fat and put all the other things in while it is hot, they will otherwise turn yellow. When all things are put in, stew the Soup an hour and half slowly.

You should have boiled rice in a plate to eat with it.

[p149] Boeuf a la Daube

Bone a rump of Beef; the smaller and thicker of Meat the better. Take out all the Suet, which is underneath. Lard it with Bacon covered with sweet Herbs and a little Allspice. When it is larded tie it up tight both across and along ways with Tape {which will keep it in proper shape}. Then put the Bones with it in a Stew Pan in about two quarts of Water. Cover it down close. The sooner it is put on in the morning the better, and let it stew until dinner time {supposing it 4 o'clock}. Put in with it about one Turnip, some Onions, a bunch of sweet herbs and a Carrot or two. The Beef should be put in a Stew-pan on a Strainer that it may not break in lifting it out. A little before dinner take out the Beef on the strainer; Cover it up before the fire. Skim the Gravy clear of fat. Thicken it with a good quantity of Carrot and Turnip cut quite small, a little Flour and Butter, and pour it on the Beef.

[p50] Inky Pinky Mrs K'
Boil Carrots and cut them in slices and lay them in a Stew Pan with some slices of Roast Beef {the inside is preferable} a large Onion and strong Gravy and let it boil. Then add a very little Vinegar; thicken it with Butter rolled in Flour. Take out the Onion and serve it hot with toasted Sippets.

[p67; p60] To stew Beef[26] Miss C[la]y
Take six or eight pounds of the thick part of a Brisket of Beef, set it on the Fire, with rather more Water than will Cover it; put in a little Salt, skim it carefully; then add a good quantity of whole Pepper, three large onions and Carrots cut in slices & two Turneps. Let it stew gently about 5 hours; have ready some Carrots cut in different figures, boiled by themselves. Take up some of the gravy from the Beef, clear it from the fat, and mix it with a little Beef Gravy, that has also been strained, put the Carrots into it, and add a good quantity of pickled Girkins, Mangoes, Capers, & Colliflowers.[27] Put it in a Saucepan, and make it hot, and pour the whole over the Beef; then take up carefully, or it will break into pieces.

Eight pounds make a hansome \bottom/ Dish, and five or six pounds for a side Dish.

[p136] Stewed Beef Stakes Mrs P'r
Take rump Stakes, beat them, fry them a little, draw a little Gravy. Season with Cloves, Mace, Pepper and Salt. Beat the Spices very fine. Stew them half an hour in the Gravy.

Fowl etc
[p97] Chicken with Rice B
Four spoonsful of rice, blanch it in Water, then put it in a Stew-pan with fine strong Broth; two onions stuck with Cloves, a blade of Mace and a piece of lean Ham. Stew it very tender, Just before you dish it, add near half a pint of thick Cream.

Your Fowls must be stewed in rich Broth this poured over them. You may add Cayenne Pepper.

---

[26] Receipt on [p60] has no donor.
[27] Receipt on [p60] has: 'add a good quantity of pickled girkins and others'.

[p10] Rice for boiled Chickens +
Put a quarter of a Pound of Rice after it is well washed and picked in a small Stew Pan, and put to it a quart or rather more of Water, which may half fill the Stew Pan. Let it stew slowly untill it is quite dry which will take near two hours: Do not stir it, and if you add any Water while it is doing, it softens and spoils it.

[p51] To dress a Cold Fowl Mrs K'
Cut it up and beat two Eggs, grate in a little Nutmeg & a little Salt, some chopped Parsley, and crumbs of bread; beat all well together. Dip each piece of Fowl in it, and have some dripping hot in a Pan; fry them a good Brown. Have a little good gravy ready; thicken it with a little flour, and add a spoonful of Ketchup. Put the fry in a dish, and pour the sauce over it.

If you please you may add Mushrooms; and Garnish with Lemon.

[p140] To dress a Duncan Fowl[28]
Take a Full grown Fowl and string the legs, bruise the Liver fine. Boil two Eggs hard; bruise the yolks and add to the Liver and one Anchovy chopped very fine; a little Cayenne Pepper, black Pepper, Nutmeg and Salt, Lemon Peel, Shalots, Parsley, Lemon, thyme, Marjoram, two Ounces of Fresh Butter; one Teaspoonful of Flour. Mix all well together in a Ball; put it in the body of the Fowl, sew up each end of the Fowl, tye it up. Let the Pot boil & put the Fowl in, and let it boil one hour. Brown some butter in the Stew pan and Flower the Fowl, and brown it all over in the Stew pan. Make some good gravy and a little melted Butter.

[p47] A Daube
The Fowl or Turkey being picked and trussed as for boiling, cut some small pieces of Bacon fat, roll them in pepper, salt, cut Parsley, Chalots and sives; Lard the Bird with them: Then put it in a Stew pan, just big enough to hold it with a pint of White Wine, some Gravy, a few Carrots, Turnips, some Onions, a bunch of Pot herbs, pepper and Salt. Let it stew very gently. When it is done, take it out of the Stew-pan. Then strain the liquor, and put it in a Dish to cool. As soon as it jelly's cover the Fowl or Turkey with it.

---

[28] 'Duncan Fowl' cannot be identified. 'Dorking fowl' were a breed of poultry characterized by a long square form, and possessing 5 toes (*OED*) (first recorded mention 1840). 'Dun-birds, also known as 'Duncur', were wild ducks - the pochard or red-headed duck, *Fuligula ferina*; also, locally (Essex), the Scaup Duck, *Fuligula marila* (*OED*). Tom Jaine says this is not obviously a duck recipe (personal communication).

Eat it either hot or Cold; But if you cut it hot, you must not let it stand to cool and jelly.

[p25] Fowl a la Tartare
Split the Fowl; rub it in Butter and sweet Herbs, pepper it, and broil it.

[p35] Pigeons
Take savory forced Meat, and roll it out like Paste, put it in a flat Pan. Then lay ~~it~~ in thin slices of Bacon, Pigeons sliced, sweetbreds, tops of Asparagus, Mushrooms, Yolks of hard Eggs, Cockcombs and the tender end of [*blank*] Palates boiled, blanc[h]ed and sliced. Cover them with another layer of forced Meat as for a Pye. Bake it, turn it onto a Dish, pour Gravy on it.

[p35] Pigeons en Compôte
Truss, lard and force them, season them and stew them in strong Broth, make for them a Ragout, and garnish them with anything you like.

[p16] Stewed Pigeons Mrs Harvey *
Take four Pigeons and stuff them; flat the Breast Bones, and dress them as for baking, drudge them over with a little flour and half roast them; then put them into a Stew Pan with as much brown gravy as will cover them and let them stew until done enough.

The Brown Gravy is to be made of the Giblets of the Pigeons and a little Meat added, an onion and a few Cloves; and when the Pigeons are nearly done enough, add a little red Wine and thicken the Gravy with a little Butter and Flour.

Forced meat
[p29] To make Forced Meat
Take half a pound of Veal and half a pound of Suet, cut fine and beat in a Marble Mortar or Wooden Bowl; a few sweet herbs fine, a little Mace dried and beat fine, a small Nutmeg grated, a little Lemon peel cut very fine and a little Pepper and Salt. The Yolk of two Eggs. Mix all well together, and roll it in round Balls and roll them in flour. Fry them for brown sauce. Roll them for white sauce. A few Minuites a[re] enough.

[p87] To make Forced Meat
Half a pound of Lean Veal, as much Beef, Suet, a quarter of the Peel of a Lemon sliced Fine. Beat this in a Mortar to a fine Paste, then Season them with Nutmeg, Mace, Salt and a little Pepper, and the Yolk of two Eggs, Half a Role grated.

Beat them altogether, then roll them into Balls, and put them into boiling Water; give them 3 or 4 boils, take them out and fry them brown.

Hare, rabbit etc

[p70] To Cabbage a Hare

Cut the Hare into small pieces; put a little more Water than will cover it; Season it with Cloves, Mace, Pepper, Salt, half a dozen large Onions, a little Thyme, and two Anchovies. The Hare must not be washed, and the Blood should be saved and stewed with it. Stew the things together until the Hare is tender, then strain it from the Liquor. Stew some Cabbage and Spinage an hour in the liquor with a quarter of a pound of burnt Butter. Put in the Hare just to warm, and then serve it.

The spinage and burnt Butter may be omitted, and some gravy added instead of them. A piece of fat Bacon should be sent in a separate Dish.

[p144] A White Fricassee of Rabbits

Take two Rabbits, cut them into pieces. Then put them into a small Stew-pan, barely cover them with a little weak broth, put to it a blade of Mace, a blade of Cinnamon, and some whole white pepper, a little Thyme, Parsley and a small Onion. Then let it stew over the fire until the Meat is tender; then take it off and strain the Liquor through a Sieve. Skim off the fat, wipe the Meat with a clean Cloth; then put it all together into a clean Stew-pan, and place it over the fire. When it boils take it off; put to it 2 Yolks of Eggs, and a quarter of a Pint of Cream. Then put it to the Rabbits with a quarter of a pound of Fresh Butter mixed with Flour to make it of a proper ~~consistence~~ thickness. Put in it a small quantity of Juice of Lemons and Salt to your taste.

NB after the Cream is put in it, it must be shook about until it is thoroughly done; but must not boil.

Mutton

[p17] A Grilled Breast of Mutton +

Take a part of a Breast of Mutton and boil it very tender; It may be boiled in Soup and either used immediately after, or kept till you have occasion for it.

Take a Dish, fill it with Soup; put in about 10 small Shalots cut very fine, a large spoonful and a half of Vinegar, about two pinches of Pepper and two of Cloves, and rasp in a little crust of Bread. Take the boiled Mutton and put it in a Gridiron over the Stove until it is well heated & take care to turn it and do it equally on both sides. Then lay it in the Dish with the Sauce, cover it up and sit it by the fire or over a Stove, until it is quite hot.

If you have not any Soup, put some Warm Water, a lump of Sugar and a little Salt as a substitute for it.

[pp58-59] A Harrico of Mutton French Receipt
Take a Neck or Loin of Mutton, and cut it into small steaks before you begin your sauce. Put a Lump of Butter in a Stewpan with a Spoonful of flour. Stir it over the fire until it is a dark brown, but take care it does not get black; then put in a basinfull of boiling Water; two pinches of Powder of Cloves, and the same of Pepper & Salt; about eight little onions, put in whole and some sprigs of thyme & a Bay Leaf. Then put in the Mutton, cover it close, and when it has stewed a little time skim off the Fat, and then put a good plate of Turnips and Carrots cut in small pieces. Keep the Stew Pan close covered, and let it stew very slowly for about 4 Hours.

[p90] Harico of Mutton Mrs C'n (?Champion)
Take a small boned Neck of Mutton, or Loin; cut off the fat, and cut it into Steaks. Season them well with pepper and Salt; flower them and fry them of a good brown; drain them from the Fat and pour them into a Stew-pan, with strong broth enough to cover them, with some Parsley and other Herbs; have ready some small Onions boiled in Milk until they are tender and some Turnips and Carrots cut into dice ready boiled; pour them into the Stew-pan when the Mutton is half done and let them stew all together, when done add a little Ketchup.

[p110] Harico of Mutton
Take a Neck of Mutton and cut it in pieces; then cut off all the Fat and the Chine Bones, then beat it with the Cleaver until it is quite ~~soft~~ flat and flour it. Fry it until it is brown, then take some strong Gravy, put it in the Stew-pan with the Mutton, with some thyme, an onion stuck full of Cloves, and some white Pepper. Salt it to your taste. Let it stew until very tender, which it will be in about 3 hours. Then take a piece of butter and Flower, brown it and strain the Liquor [*blot*][29] it. Then take the Turnips and Carrots cut in the form of dice boiled some time before, stir all together & serve it up.

[p57] Mutton D'Etruffe Madame la Combe
Take about half a Leg of Mutton, and lard it all over with small pieces of fat Bacon rolled in Seasoning. The seasoning must be made with Powder of Cloves, Pepper and Salt, and a little Thyme, well mixed together. Lay a Lump of Sugar

[29] This short word is illegible: perhaps 'over'?

on the bottom of a deep \Stew/ Pan, cut a piece of the fat of Bacon into very thin slices and lay round it all over the bottom of the Stew Pan. Cut a carrot small and lay in it, and cut about 20 or more little Onions into it: Put in a good pinch of Pepper, Salt and Powder of Cloves, with a small sprig of Thyme and part of a Bay Leaf and two Tumblers full of boiling Water: Then put in the Mutton: Cover it close up, let it boil thoroughly; then Cover the fire with ashes; let it stew very slowly for about 5 Hours. Turn the Mutton frequently and always Keep the Stew Pan close covered.

If you Find it necessary you may add a little more Water when the Mutton is half done.

For a whole Leg of Mutton of course double the quantity of ingredients will be wanted.

[p93] Ragout of Neck or Breast of Mutton Mrs C'
Cut into Steakes, season it with Pepper, Salt, Sweet Herbs, and Crumbs of Bread and the Yolk of an Egg. Fry them in Butter, make a Pint of Beef Gravy, put in it Cloves, Onion, Anchovies and Catchup. Thicken it with flower and Butter. Put the gravy in the Dish, then lay the Steaks in a Cloth.

[p147] To stew a Leg of Mutton
Rub a Leg of Mutton over with Jamaica Pepper; then stuff it at the Top of the Bone with a Clove or two of Garlick. Put it into a Pot with three large Onions, a piece of Lemon Peel, a bundle of Sweet Herbs, a piece of fat bacon, and a little Salt. Cover it down close with a wet Cloth round the edge of the Cover, that no steam may get out. Set it over a very slow Fire. When it is enough {which will be when quite Tender} take it up and lay in the Dish. Take all the fat of the Gravy. Put to it ½ a pint of red Wine, the Juice of a small Lemon and some Morrells. Thicken the Sauce as you like.

Veal

[pp25-26] Fricandeau Mrs M
A slice of Fillet of Veal about the thickness of 4 or 5 Inches, cut it into two pieces, take off the Skin, then lard it. Brown some Butter & fry the Veal; then add Pepper, Salt, Cloves, Onions, Lemon peel: Let the whole stew three hours over a slow Fire with little or no Water. Then strain the Gravy through a Sieve and mix it with Sorrel: Put this in a dish, and lay the Veal over it.

Pick a good quantity of Sorrel, and wash it clean; then put it in a Stew Pan with a piece of Butter, a little Pepper and Salt. Let it stew over a slow Fire without any Water, and when sufficiently stewed, thicken it with the Yolks of two or three Eggs.

[p159] Hodge Podge {B' D}
Make it with a scragg or Knuckle of Veal, or a scragg of Mutton. Put it on the fire with Water enough to make it a strong Broth and when it has boiled to be pretty good, put in the best end of the Mutton cut in thin Chops, and cut off some of the Fat; and put in with them some Greens, young Carrots and Turnips, Lettuce. Green Pease are a good addition. When the Chops are very tender serve it up, and be very careful to skim off the fat.

[p51] Italian Savory Cake Mrs K'
Two pounds of Leg of Veal, beat it in a Mortar with one pound of Beef Suet: Beat with it two Rusks soaked in Milk; a little Lemon Peel seasoned with Pepper, Salt and ~~Mustard~~ Nutmeg. Mix up with the Yolks of 2 Eggs; flower your Hands and roll the Veal &c into Balls or Roles, or in one Cake: then fry them. Lastly stew them in a little Veal Gravy, thickned with Rusks, and serve up.

[p113] Ragout of Veal
Half roast a fillet of Veal, lard it over with Bacon excepting the Fat; put in stuffing as for roasting. When about half done, take it up, put it in a Stew-pan with gravy enough to do it sufficiently, so as just to cover it that it may not grow dry. Put in with it a bunch of Sweet Herbs, a few Oysters, an Anchovy or two, let it stew from morning until dinner. The slower the stewing the better. Then strain the gravy from the Herbs, thicken it and pour it over the Veal.

Serve it up with a Few pickled Mushrooms, some truffles and Morels stewed in a little Water or Gravy of the Veal and add to the Gravy in the Dish, when it is served up.

[p56] A Ragout of Veal A small Dish French Receipt
Take about 3 pounds of a Breast of Veal; Chop it in small pieces or Steakes, put a tolerable large piece of Butter in a stew Pan, with a Spoonful or two of Flower. Stir it over the fire until it is of a dark brown, but do not let it get black; then put in as much boiling Water as you think will Cover the Meat; Stir it together and then put in the Veal. Put in three pinches of Pepper, the same of Powder of Cloves, & a little Salt with half a Bay Leaf and a little sprig of thyme. Put in eight or ten small pieces of the fat of Bacon {well washed to take out the Salt} and about 6 large Onions cut in halves or quarters. Set it on the fire at least 3 hours before you want it. Let it boil at first and stew fast for almost one hour, & then cover the fire, and let it stew very slowly. Keep the Stew Pan close covered, and be attentive to stir it frequently.

[p59] Veal Ragout French Receipt
Take about 3 pounds of Veal Steaks cut from the Loin, boil them until they are tender; then take them out of the Saucepan; beat up the whole of one Egg; do the Steaks entirely over with it; then strew Crumbs of Bread over them as thick as the Egg will let them stick, fry them in butter until they are very brown. Have ready some good Beef gravy, with a little Lemon pickle; a little Ketchup and Lemon Juice, thicken it properly; put it in the Dish first, and then the Veal. The Veal will do exactly the same as if it had been dressed before.

The remainder of a Fillet makes a better dish than Steaks.

[p105] To Stew a Breast of Veal
Take a breast of Veal, cut it in pieces and fry it until it is enough; Then take some strong Broth made with more Veal; put it in a Stew Pan with seasoning of Spice and Lemon peel; let it boil, then put in the fried Meat, and let it stew sometime. Then add some Oysters with the Liquor thickened with Flour. Put some white Wine, and when stewed enough put it into your Dish with Forced Meat Balls made of Veal Suet, sweet herbs; Season and beat it well together. Then beat an Egg and mix with it; roll it into Balls with Flour; they must be fried brown and put all together.

[p13] To stew a Breast of Veal +
Cut off both ends – boil them for Gravy – raise up the Skin part, stuff it with forced Meat made of part of the Sweetbread, a few Bread crums, a little Beef Suet, two Eggs, Pepper, Salt, and a little Nutmeg, skewer this down under the Skin. Drudge the Veal with flower, tie it up in a Cloth, and boil it in Milk and Water. Serve it up with a Sauce poured over it, made of a little Gravy, about 12 Oysters, a few pickled Mushrooms, a bit of Lemon peel and Juice, thickned with flour and butter; over all lay a sweetbread, sliced & fried. Garnish the dish with Lemon, Pickles and Mushrooms.

It may be boiled almost enough, and then grilled in a dutch Oven if agreable with or without Sweet herbs strewed over it; or grilled only like a Calfs head after being boiled.

[p78] To stew Veal Miss H' (?Hatton)
Cut some Slices of Leg of Veal in pieces of the size of half a Crown; take a bunch of sweet Herbs, a large piece of Mace, and some salt; put these to as much Water as will cover the Veal. When it boils, put it in the Veal & let it stew two hours; then take out the Veal, dip a piece of butter in flour and put into the liquor; let it boil a little, and pour it through a fine strainer to the Meat in the Dish.

[p30] White Collops
Cut your Veal thin and beat it, take a little Butter in a stew pan, and pass them off quick, and take them up in a Plate, cover them and do not let them grow hard, put the parings of the Veal and the Bone into a Pan with a little Water, let it boil, strain it and let it settle; then take the white gravy and thicken it with a little flour, and when it has boiled, put in the collops and serve them with forced Meat balls, which must be boiled. You will add a little Cream, white Pepper and salt, a little Lemon Juice, or pickled Mushrooms, a few scaled Oysters, cocks Combs, artichoke bottoms, or anything you like.

[pp57-58] Veal White French Receipt
Take a small part of Leg of Veal. Put it in a good sized Stew-pan with a Lump of Butter, and a little flour over it. Shake the Veal about in it until the Butter is melted. Then half fill the Stew-pan with Hot Water. Cut in a small Lump of fat Bacon in very little Shreds, put in two small onions, two pinches of Pepper and a little pinc[h]e of Salt, let it Stew by degrees on a slow fire for at least 6 Hours, and let the stew pan be close covered up. But take care to turn the Veal, and shake it frequently. When it is time to serve it, Mix and beat the Yolks of two Eggs in about half a Cup of Milk or Cream. Then take the Veal out of the stew pan, and lay it in a Dish; leave a little of the Liquor the Veal had been stewed in, in the Pan, and put your Eggs and Milk, about half a spoonful of Vinegar into it. Give it one stir, or shake over the fire, but take care it does not boil; then pour this Liquor over the Veal, and serve it up.

A Fricassee of Chicken may be done in the same way, but will not require more than one hour and a half.

Never finish any White Dish until the moment you want it, for if you set it to the fire, it will be spoiled. If any accident obliges it to be Kept hot a little time; set it in a Stew Pan, or Pot filled with boiling Water, and cover it close.

Take care that all the White is taken from the Yolk of the Egg, when you put it on, and always stir the sauce the same way. The Salt should be washed from the Bacon.

[p81] To make Veal Olives
Take 8 or 10 pieces of Veal, the same as for Scotch Collops. Wash them over with Eggs; then season them, and lay over them a little forced Meat. Role them up and roast them.

Make a Ragout sauce, and garnish the Dish with slices of orange.

[p166] Veal Steaks in papers Madame de la Combe
Cut the Steaks small, put them into squares of writing Paper, with some Salt, Pepper, Parsley, Mushrooms, Shalots, all minced very Fine, and a little Butter. Put the Paper over the Steaks, but let the ends come out: Butter the Paper on the outside. Let them broil over a slow Fire on the Gridiron, and put a Sheet of buttered Paper under the Steaks.

Serve them with the Paper on them.

[p169] Minced Veal under the brown raised up Mrs Kennett
The Veal is roasted in the usual manner, and then the brown raised up and the Meat cut from the bones, and minced with Cream, pepper & Salt, and the heads of the smallest Asparagus boiled & mixed with it, and the brown laid nicely over it again.

Curry

[p2] Currie +
A large Onion, cut small; fry it in two Ounces of Butter, and a very small piece of Garlick with it; fry it until it is all dissolved; add a teacup of Water. Then take three quarters of a pound of Veal, cut it, in small ~~pieces~~ slices, wash it and flower it well. Put a table Spoonfull of Curry Powder in to the Onions, and half a Tea Spoonfull of Black Pepper and a little Salt; then add about a pint of Water, shake all together in a stew Pan. Next put the Meat in, and let it stew gently about one hour, and squeeze in the juice of half a Lemon before it is dished.

[p2] Preparation of the Rice for Ditto (Currie) +
Simmer the Rice in several different Waters, which makes it curl & let it drain on a Sieve. It should not boil in the different Waters.

[p33] Curry Mirzapore[30]
Cut up the Fowl or meat into small pieces, put to it 2 Ounces of Butter, a little Onion or Garlick; about a desert spoon full of Curry Powder, some Salt and red Pepper to your taste. Mix all well together, then let it simmer gently for about half an hour. After that pour half a pint of Warm Water over it, and let it stew for half an hour longer.

If the Curry is made of brown Meat, if will take much longer stewing. Take care to let it do very gently.

---

[30] See note to Curry Soup in Chapter I.

Wash and boil your Rice in Hot Water. For every pound of Rice take one quart of Water. When it is tender enough, pour off the Water, cover it close and dry it over a gentle fire.

[p79] To make a Curry Miss H' (? Hatton)
One table spoonful of Coriander Seed, half a Tea Spoonful of White Cumming Seed, a quarter of a Tea Spoonful of Founigreak Seeds to be parched over a gentle fire with care not to burn it, and then pound it. One tea spoonful of Turmarick, one of Pepper and one of Salt to be added. Having your Fowl cut up, rub the powder on each peice until you have used two spoonsful. Have a good \deal/ of butter in your Stew-pan and a sliced Onion; fry it a fine brown and as it drys, put a little broth or gravy, add a little Cayenne Pepper and the Juice of half a Lemon.

[p80] To make Curry \page 79/ E H from Mrs Davies
[*This receipt has been crossed through.*]
One Tablespoonful of Coriander Seed; half a Teaspoonful of Coriander Seed.

[p157] To make a Pillow,[31] the Indian Way
Take three pounds of Rice, wash it when picked very clean; put it in a Cullender; let it drain very dry; take ¾ of a pound of butter, and put it in a pan over a very slow fire until it melts. Then put in the Rice, and cover it very close, that it may keep the Steam in; add a little Salt, some whole Pepper, six blades of Mace and a Few Cloves. A little Water should be put in to keep it from burning. Then stir it up very often, and let it stew until the Rice is soft.

Boil two Fowls and a fine piece of Bacon of about 2 lb weight; Cut the Bacon into two pieces, lay it in the Dish with the Fowls. Cover it over with the Rice, and garnish it with about 6 hard Eggs and 12 Onions fried whole and very brown.

This is the true Indian way.

[p157] To boil Rice
Put two quarts of Water to a Pint of Rice; let it boil until it appears enough; then throw in a spoonful of Salt, and turn it out into a Cullender. Then let it stand about 5 Minuites before the fire to dry, and serve it up in a Dish by itself. Dish it up and send to Table.

---

[31] ie pilau

[pp157-158] A Currey {the Indian Way}
Take two small chickens, and skin them \as/ for a Fricassee. Wash them clean and stew them in about a quart of Water for about 5 Minuites. Then strain off the liquor, and put the Chickens in a clear Dish. Take three large onions, chop them small and fry them in about two Ounces of Butter. Then put in the Chickens and fry them together until they are brown. Take a ¼ of an Ounce of Turmeric, a large spoonful of Ginger and beaten pepper together, and a little salt to your palate; strew these ingredients over the Chickens while frying; then pour in the liquor and let it stew about ½ an hour, then add ¼ of a Pint of Cream, and the Juice of 2 Lemons and serve it up.

[p125] A Currie
Cut one or more Fowls as for a Fricassee, strew flour over it. Fry butter in it, but <u>not</u> hard or brown them. Add as much Water as will stew it, with 5 or 6 Bay Leaves, a large Onion Cut, and a Table spoonful and half of Currie Powder.[32] Mix together, cover up and stew until tender. Serve it up, taking out the Bay Leaves.

Fish, Mutton or Veal does the same way, but if Fat, it should not be Fried. If you chuse it tart, add the Juice of a Lemon.

Currie Powder is bought at Mr ?Bonjorman's in a Court opposite the India House.[33]

[p138] To make Curry stuff[34] {Mrs C'}
Two teacups Full of Coriander Seed; one Cup of Black Pepper; one Cup of Cummin Seed; half a Cup of Mustard Seed; double this quantity of Rice, 2 or 3 pieces of Turmerick. Put a frying Pan on the Fire; when thoroughly hot, roast the Rice brown, let it be pounded or ground fine. Then roast the Pepper and Coriander Seed crisp, pound and grind them together, roast the Cummin and

---

[32] See Glossary regarding the *OED*'s first dated reference to 'curry powder'.
[33] Neither the name of the seller nor the location of his shop are particularly legible in the original. However, John Roque's map of London, first published in 1747 and reproduced in *A to Z of Georgian London*, indicates a possible site: in Section 13, square Ca, on the south-west of the junction of Leadenhall Street and Lime Street, is a large unnamed building to the south of which is a yard labelled 'India House Yard' and to the west of which is a lane and a building labelled 'East Indian House'. In section 15, square Dc of Richard Horwood's 1813 map of London, reproduced in the A-*Z of Regency London*, the large building itself is called India House. East India House was in Leadenhall Street. It was rebuilt in 1726, enlarged in 1799 and demolished in 1862; new premises for Lloyd's were built on the site (Weinreb and Hibbert, p250).
[34] A receipt for curry powder.

Mustard Seed together and pound or grind them also, roast some Turmeric and Capiscum together and grind them or sift them until of a fine powder.

Russian dish

[p19] A Russian Dish – Chee

Take a small piece of Bacon or pickled Pork, about one pound of Beef cut in small pieces; four Cabages sliced, 8 or 10 onions, a large handful of Parsley picked from the Stalks, and near a quarter of a Pint of Vinegar and half a Pint of Grists. Salt and Pepper to your Taste. Let it stew slowly for ~~two~~ \three/ hours. It should be kept covered with Water.

Pork is better than Bacon. Put the Vinegar in last.

Chapter V: Pies (including pastry)

[p38] Biscuit Crusts for Tarts
Rub three Ounces of good Butter with a pound of fine Flour, until they are very well mixed; then add two ounces of Loaf Sugar finely Powdered; the Yolks of two Eggs beat up with as much Water as will make it into a Paste, mix it well, roll it out thin, then cover your tarts, and with a feather do them over with the White of the Eggs beat to a froth, sift sugar finely powdered over them.

[p159] Crust for a Crocant[35]
Six Ounces of Flour; 1½ ounces of Butter, 2 Ounces of Fine Sugar. For a small dish.

[p83] Crust of Pastry without flour Mrs Clitherow
Boil four pounds of Potatoes and mash them with a little Butter. Take two pounds of ground Rice, scald it for five Minuites and let it drain in a sieve until cold. Then mix the Potatoes and Rice together, and work them well into a Paste with the Yolk of 3 or 4 Eggs, and a handful of fine Sugar pounded, and a few grains of Salt. Let it settle half an hour, and make tarts or pastry in the usual way of common pastry.

[p89] Potatoe Pastry
Take two Tea spoonsful of ground pepper and one of Salt, either agreable to your taste; then sprinkle the Pepper and Salt over the Steakes, lay them in the Dish, pouring about half a pint of good gravy over them; then put on the Top Lid, boil one Gallon of Potatoes, mash them with one Ounce of butter and milk enough to make them of a proper consistence. Lay the Potatoes on the Tin pressed close, making them lay higher in the Middle.

There should be little fat with the Beef or Mutton to prevent it being greasy.

[p106; p153] Paste for Tarts[36]
One pound of Flour, one pound of Butter, a quarter of a pound of fine Sugar, three Eggs, but only two Whites, that will wet the Paste. Flake your Butter with

[35] See Introduction (p.xxxvi) for another version of 'Crocant Paste' and for a discussion of the two receipts.
[36] Receipt on [p153] is entitled 'Fine paste for Tarts'.

Flour, but <u>not</u> to rub it in. The other White of the Egg with fine sugar will wet the lids of the Tarts. This must be done in Patty Pans.

[p120] A short Paste for Tarts
Take a pound of flour, ¾ of a pound of Butter, rub all very small, add 3 spoonsful of Loaf Sugar beat and sifted, beat the Yolks of 4 Eggs well, add a spoonful or two of Rose Water, work them into a paste. Roll them thin. Ice them over and bake in a slow Oven.

[p135] A short Crust Mrs P'r
8 Ounces of Flour, 7 of Butter, rub it well in until it is in small Crumbs; then add about a Table spoonful of Water, or just enough to wet it. Then make it into a Lump and beat it with a rolling Pin. Then roll in any manner you chuse.

[p14] Sugar Crust for Tarts * Ex[cellent]
Rub in half a pound of butter with a pound of Flour, one Yolk of an Egg beat with a little Water; put in a handful of sifted \loaf/ Sugar and knead them together. To ice the Tarts, beat the White of an Egg to a froth, and a little Loaf Sugar.

Set the Tarts in an Oven for a short time, take them out, ice them, and put them again into the Oven.

[p117] Sugar Crust
Rub in half a pound of Butter into a pound of Flour, one Yolk of an Egg beat with a little Water, and put in a handful of sifted \Loaf/ Sugar. Only knead it to make it mix. Add water enough to make a paste.

[p1] Apple Roles +
Pare the Apples and scrap[e] out the Cores; Role each Apple in Puff paste; Do the tops of them over with Whites of Eggs and a little Sugar sifted, Set them close together in a Pan, and bake them one hour.

[p5] Spanish Puffs[37] + Ex[cellent]
A pint of Milk, put into a Saucepan with a little Salt; when it boils stir in a little flour, untill it is as thick as a hasty pudding. Continue to stir it on the fire, untill it is quite thick; Then put it in a Mortar, and pound it untill it is quite smooth.

---

[37] See Introduction, p.xlv, regarding the placing of the next three receipts. Raffald had a very similar receipt 'To make *German* Puffs' (*Experienced English Housekeeper*, p80). She concluded with the comment 'It is a proper corner dish for dinner or supper'.

Then break in two Eggs, and keep pounding them together untill they are quite mixed. A little Brandy, Nutmeg \& sugar/ is then added[,] then take some Hogs lard, let it be quite hot and put it in the Pan, and drop a Tea Spoonful of the Batter in it at a time thus forming small Balls. When brown, turn them; fill the Pan with them, keeping them separate; lastly put them on a sieve to drain, and strew a little powdered Sugar over them.

[p49] Spanish Puffs Byd
Take a pint of Milk; boil it, stir it in [*sic*] as much flower as will make it as thick as a Hasty Pudding. Beat it in a Mortar until no Lumps are to be seen. Then add six Eggs, a little sugar, & a little salt to your taste. Let it stand one hour; then fry them as you do Fritters in Hogs lard.

see folio 5. Excel[lent]

[p108] Spanish Puffs
Half a pint of Milk, a bit of Butter about the size of a Walnut, put it on the fire, let it boil, then stir ~~it~~ in some Flour until it is a thick pudding, and will leave the Pan. Then take it out and let it cool. When cold put it in a Marble Mortar, then beat it well with a wooden Pestle. Then break in one Egg and beat it again & continue beating until you have used Four [eggs]. Put in only two Whites. You may beat for 10 Minuites between every Egg. When it is enough it will be a good thick batter.

Then have ready some good boiling lard in a Frying Pan. Take a large silver Skewer, and drop as much as will go through the hole of it, and when of a Fine brown serve them up with grated Sugar over them. Take care to have a good deal of lard in the Pan.

[p33] Gravy for Fish Pyes
Best Wine, best Vinegar, Oyster liquor, Anchovies and drawn Butter; When the Pies are baked; pour it in hot.

[p33] Gravy for Meat Pies
Red Wine, Gravy, Oyster Liquor, two or three Anchovies, a bunch of sweet Herbs and an Onion. Boil this up and thicken with brown Butter; then pour it into your Pye when you take it out of the Oven.

[p136] Seasoning for Meat Pies and Sauce Mrs P'r
One Ounce of Ginger and of Pepper, ½ an Ounce of Cinnamon, Cloves and Nutmeg each, & 6 Ounces of Salt, mix them Well & keep them dry.

It is a great addition to all Meat Pies & brown Sauce.

[pp65-66] A Duck Pye
Take the Liver and all the inside of the Duck which is fit to eat; wash it well; take a slice of the Fat of Bacon, a little Veal and a few Shalots; mince them all very small together; and with a little Thyme and Bay Leaf cut small, and a seasoning of Pepper and Salt, put it in the inside of the Duck. Lard the Duck all over with a little Shred of fat Bacon, rolled in seasoning. Take such a quantity of Flour, as you think will make paste enough to go round a Duck. Lay the flour on a paste Board, put two Yolks and one white of an Egg into the middle of it. Break almost a pound of Butter very small into the Flour; put as much Water as is necessary to mix it, and mix it very lightly and touch it as little as possible.

Roll out a piece of this Paste out very thin, lay it on a Dish; then lay a thin slice or two of Fat Bacon on it, and afterwards the Duck with the Breast downwards, and then another thin slice of Bacon upon the Duck. Lay a thin Crust upon the Top, and then another this Crust upon that.

Turn up the bottom Crust nearly round the Duck, lay the Top Crust over it, and join them together until it forms an Oval standing Pye to the shape of the Duck; but touch the crust as little as possible. Crimp and ornament the Pye all over with little Irons for that purpose. Make a hole in the Top of the Pye, roll a thin piece of Paste, and put in like a Chimney and then roll up a piece of Card and put inside of it.

Have a Cark [*recte* Cork] ready the size of the Chimney and cork it up the moment the Pye is taken out of the Oven, and do not take out the Cork and Card until the Pye is quite cold. About one hour and a half in a quick oven will bake it.

Make a seasoning of Salt, Pepper and a little Thyme, Bay Leaf and shallot. All the Bacon with which the Duck is larded must be dipped in it, and as the Duck should be covered in every part with sliced Bacon; that side of the Bacon which it is next to it, must also be dipped in it. If the Bacon is much Salted, it must be well washed to get out the Salt.

[p115] French Pye B D Cook
Make some good Puff Crust; then cut some slices of Bacon as thin as possible, and if you let it lie in some boiling Water to take out the Salt, it will be better: Lay at the bottom of the Dish the Bacon, then Chickens, Ox Palates, sweetbreads sliced, and Oysters; small pieces of Veal and Beef are a good addition. Between every layer, add a little Pepper, Salt & Mace and some slices of Bacon; and on the Top of the Pye, add hard Eggs, forced Meat Balls, and strew a little Sweet Herbs. Fill the Dish with as much nice Gravy made From Veal or Mutton as it will hold.

You must boil the ox Palates near two hours before they will peel. The Chicken and sweetbread or any of the other things must not be boiled, unless you do it to Keep them.

Add Asparagus cut in small pieces, and layed [*sic*] them between every layer makes the Pye much more nice.

If the Dish is not very deep have some gravy to put in just before it is served up.

[p96] Lemon Pies B
One pound of Suet chopped fine; one pound of Currants, well picked; one pound of Fine Loaf Sugar. Two Lemon rinds pared, boiled, and then beat very Fine in a Mortar. Then squeeze the juice of your Lemons {without the pulp} into the mixture with four spoonsful of red Port.

[p154] Lemon Pies
Take three Lemons cut them in two; squeeze out the Juice. Boil the pieces in plenty of Water until quite tender; then with a Spoon scoop out the pulp – throw that away – pound the rind fine in a Mortar. Add to them equal quantities of lump Sugar in powder, double the quantity of Suet; as many Currants as are agreable and Lemon Juice also.

Some add a little Apple and some a Few stoned Raisins chopped, no Spice, a Full quarter of a Pint of Brandy {and some add a little Red Port} also a small quantity of Salt.

[p59] Lemon minced Pies
Take one Lemon, grate off the Yellow part, cut through the middle and squeeze out the Juice; then boil the inner skin free of the Pulp a long time; chop it very small & put to it the Juice and the grated coat; one quarter of a pound of Suet chopt very Fine, one quarter of a pound of Sugar; the same of Currants.

This quantity will make 7 Pies.

[p73] Lemon Minced Pies
Take four large Lemons, squeeze the Juice on a Pound of fine powder Sugar; Then boil the peels in several Waters until they are quite tender. Chop them fine; add 12 Ounces of Mutton suet chopped very fine, and one pound of Currants; Mix them well with the Sugar and juice, and fill the Pies.

[p91] Meat Mince Pies Mrs C'n (?Champion)
Two pounds of Beef parboiled, four pounds of Suet, two pounds of common Sugar, four pounds of Currants, half an Ounce of beaten Cinnamon, half an

Ounce of Cloves, the same of Mace, two Nutmegs, the juice of four Lemons, the rind of one Lemon as thinly pared as possible and finely chopped, half a pint of White Wine, the same of Brandy, half a Spoonful of Salt, some Citron, Half a candied Lemon peel, the same of Orange peel.

If raisins to be added, half a pound is sufficient.

[p9] Mince Pies + Mrs P' Beng[e]o Hall
Three pounds of Suet; one pound of raw Meat chopped together; Three pound of Raisons stoned and chopped, one dozen of large Apples, Six pounds of Currants, ¾ of a pound of Sugar, one Nutmeg, a little Cloves and Mace, one ounce of Salt, the rind of two Lemons; the Juice of 6 Lemons, a pint of White wine, half a pint of Brandy. Put in what sweatmeats you please

[p97] Mince Pies B
One pound of Apples, three quarters of a pound of Suet chopped fine, a pound of Sugar, a pound of Currants, a Seville Orange, or if small use two; the juice of one Lemon, a Nutmeg, a little Mace and Cloves {about half a quarter of an Ounce of both together, or according to Palate} half a Glass of White Wine, about the same quantity of Brandy; the rind of a Lemon grated, and what sweetmeats you please.

[p14] Minced Pyes Ex[cellent] + Cowell
A penny Role grated, a pound of Lemons whole, a pound of Plumbs chopped, a pound of Sugar. Squeeze the Juice out of the Lemons, and boil the Pulp until it will beat in a Mortar; it must be boiled in several Waters to take out the bitter. Mix them well together.

[p131] Minced Pyes Mrs B'd
Two pounds of Raw Meat, 6 pounds of Suet, chop them together very fine, 12 large Apples, 3 pounds of raisins stoned and chopped, 6 pound of Currants washed and picked; a pound of powder vinegar, 2 oz of salt; the rind of three Lemons grated, two Nutmegs grated, of Mace and Cloves a quarter of an oz. Mix all together, then put a quart of Sack, the Juice of 12 Lemons; a quarter of a pint of Brandy, put it in a Pot. It will Keep three Months.

You may add Orange, Lemons, Citron when you make your Pies.

[p124] Partridge Pye
Take a Partridge boiled or roasted. Mince the Meat very small, take 2 Ounces of lean Bacon, boil it and put it in a Marble Mortar and beat it very fine. Mix them,

and season to your palate with Pepper, Salt and a little Shalot and make Forced Meat.

One Partridge is enough to season three [other partridges]. The Bodies must be Filled whole and put into a Pye and baked. Eggs boiled hard and cut into quarters are put in the Pye.

[p145] Sea Pye

About 3 pounds of Rump or Edge Bone of Beef in slices, put it in a Saucepan, then upon a layer of new Sea or Captains' Biscuits {they must be new} lay a large Fowl cut in quarter, then Salt, ground Pepper, Cayenne, a good deal of Onion sliced, then put on some Biscuits which are to collect the fat, that will rise to the Top. Then pour in Water enough to cover the whole. The lid of the Saucepan should be covered as close as possible {with a Cloth if necessary}. To stew very gently 4 hours or until tender. Take the Biscuits out of the Saucepan with a skimmer, and send the whole to Table in the order they are in the Saucepan, except the Top Biscuits which may be greasy. Put it in a deep Stew-dish. But do not take in quite all the Gravy.

[p104] Welch Pyes Mrs Fordham

A pound of Beef Suet; cut it very fine; a pound of Apples chopped fine, a pound of Currants, a pound of Sugar; then add Cinnamon, Cloves, Mace, Nutmeg, Lemon peel cut Fine; mix them well together. Bake them half an hour; put them in an Earthen Pan, and cover them close.

They will Keep half a Year.

Chapter VI: Puddings[38]

[p167] To answer the purpose of an Egg in a Pudding
Two table spoonsful of Snow Water mixed in a Flower pudding will answer the purpose of an Egg and make it as light.

[p141] Almond Pudding
Half a pound of Almonds blanched, beat them in a Mortar with a Spoonful of Cream. Then to a quart of Cream or Milk put 8 Eggs beaten with a little Wine; ½ a pound of Sugar, one Nutmeg and a little Cinnamon; ¼ of a pound of grated Naples Biscuit. Mix all well together; pour it in the Dish with paste about the edges of the Dish & some sweetmeats. Stick some blanched Almonds cut in slices at top. It should be set over the Fire.

[p136] Princess Amelia's Pudding Mrs P'r
Six Eggs, only Four Whites; a Pint of Cream; the inside of a Roll grated, 3 large Apples made into Sauce. When cold mix all together with half a pound of melted Butter. Add half an Ounce of Citron and candied Lemon peel cut thin. Sugar, Nutmeg and Lemon Peel to your taste. Butter the Cups they are baked in.

[p48] A Dish of Apples and Rice Byd
Boil a pint of Rice in some Milk until it is done, add a little Nutmeg, and when boiled enough to eat tender, place it in a Dish, leaving a hollow place in the middle for the Apples. Keep the Rice dry, so that it may not run about the Dish. Pare your Apples the same as for sauce, and stew them in a little Water with a little Sugar, and when done put it in the middle of the Rice. Then set it in a warm Oven half an Hour before Dinner. If it is not brown enough when taken out, the Salamander should be used.

[pp59-60] An Ommelette a la Pomme
Take eight Eggs {both Yolks and Whites} beat them up together, and fry them in a Stew-Pan with a large Lump of Butter, shake and stir them about constantly to prevent them from sticking to the Pan until they are of a nice brown, take 7 or 8 good sized Apples, cut them small & Stew them until they are tender in butter, Sugar and a little Water, lay the Apple in your dish, and them turn the Ommelette out of the Pan upon it; but do it very carefully and without breaking the Egg, and let the side that was next the Pan be uppermost.

---

[38] Puddings in this chapter include both sweet and savoury ones.

[p74] Apple Pudding
Take some large Apples {about a dozen} simmer them over a slow fire until they are soft; take out the Pulp and rub them through a Hair seive. Take a pound of the bruised Apples and 8 Eggs Yolk & Whites of Eggs: Beat the Eggs for a quarter of an Hour. Half a pound of Butter melted with flour, a little Rose Water. Sweeten it with Loaf Sugar to your taste and beat it all well together. Put a thin Puff Paste in your Dish and about an Hour & a quarter in a slow Oven will bake it.

You may add about half an Ounce of Candied Peel.

[p77] Baked Apple Pudding Miss H' (?Hatton)
Take Apples according to the size of the Pudding, boil them well and while they are baking stir a piece of butter in them, if a large pudding put a tea Cup of Brandy in. When it is cold put in the Yolk of 4 Eggs. Put a Crust at the bottom of the dish and bake it.

[p116] Baked Apple Pudding
Take ¾ of a pound of sharp Apples; scald or roast and pulp them. 8 Eggs, only 4 Whites, the Juice of two Lemons and the rind grated, ¼ of a pound of Sugar, single refined, six Ounces of Butter carefully melted without either Flower or Water. Mix them together. Lay a thin puff paste at the bottom of the Dish. Bake it in a slow Oven, and not in a deep Dish.

[p142] Baked Pudding
The best way in all Puddings that are to be turned out of the Dish, is to butter a sheet of writing Paper, and lay it at the bottom of the Dish.

[p123; p148] A fine Baked Pudding
Take two penny white Loaves, grate them, put to them a pint of cold Milk seasoned with Nutmeg, Mace, Cloves and a handful of Sugar; a 1½ lb of Beef Suet shred Fine, a pound of Currants, 8 Eggs, well mixed with a Glass of Mountain. Butter the Dish, and Bake it.

[p8] Bath Puddings +
Take half a pound of Bread grated; half a pound of Butter melted in half a pint of Milk; six Eggs, a little Nutmeg, and Loaf Sugar to your taste, and a little Ratafie or Brandy: Put it in Cups, a quarter of an hour in a quick Oven will bake it.

[p109] Baked Bread Pudding
The Crum of a penny Loaf, cut it in thin slices; about a quart of new Milk boiled and poured out hot. Stir it in half a pound of Butter while it is hot, six Eggs, leaving out three Whites, a little Nutmeg & Cinnamon, some Salt, some Candied Orange Peel cut small. Sweeten it as you like. Butter the Dish and bake it enough to stiffen it.

[p95] To make a quaking Bread Pudding
Take a Pint of good Milk; boil a Laurel Leaf in it; and if you chuse a ~~*illeg*~~ \bit/ of Cinnamon, & then beat three Eggs, whites and all. Pour the Milk scalding hot on the eggs, and set it over a slow fire to thicken: as it is over the fire shake in four spoonsful of grated Bread with a little Sugar, and when it is thickened as the bread does not fall to the bottom, have ready a bason buttered and put the Pudding into it. Fifteen Minuites will boil it; If it is too much boiled it will fall, else it will be as light as it can be carried to Table.

[p37] Bushbridge Puddings[39]
A Pint of Cream, one Ounce of Butter melted in it; Mix it with the flour and thin as for Pancakes; four Eggs, leave out the White of One; beat them well with one Spoonful of Rose Water. Grate in a little Nutmeg, Wine and Sugar to your taste. Put it in large Tea Cups well buttered in the inside; Bake them ¾ of an Hour in a quick Oven. Turn them out just as you serve them; pour some Wine, melted Butter and Sugar in the Dish.

[p37] Carrot Pudding
Boil a large Carrot and grate it fine. Pass it through a Sieve & put to it 8 Yolks and 4 Whites of Eggs. Beat them very well, add a little grated Bread. Some Nutmeg, Sugar and a spoonful of Sack and half a pint of Cream, Make it as thick as a boiled Custard and put paste about the Dish.

[p7] Colledge Puddings +
Three Sponge Biscuits, 4 Yolks of Eggs, half a candied Orange, half a candied Lemon, half a pound of Veal Suet, half a pound of Raisins, half a Nutmeg, the crumb of a penny Role, a Glass of Brandy, a little powderd Sugar. Make them into long Roles and fry them. The Sauce, Butter, Brandy, White Wine made thick.

---

[39] Perhaps a reference to the village of Bushbridge, near Godalming (Surrey), or to Robert Barker (c.1732-1789), created 1st baronet of Bushbridge in 1781, army officer in the East India Company and then MP (biography in *ODNB*).

[p79] College Pudding Miss H' (?Hatton)
Take four penny Loaves and grate them, one pound of Beef Suet minced very small, one pound of Currants and some Nutmeg grated, mix all these well together, then wet them with a spoonful of Cream & nine Eggs; Then rub them round or into what form you please. Melt a pound of Butter and put into a Dish and put the Pudding in and set it over a Charcoal fire. Keep them covered for a little time after they are first set on. When they boil and look brown, turn them; and when they look brown all over, they are enough.

The sauce should be butter and sugar, and a little Mountain Wine.

Half this quantity is sufficient for a side Dish.

[p68; p166] Cream Fritters[40] {French}
Put into a Stew-pan a quarter of a Pint of Cream, a quarter of a pint of Milk, a very little salt, a pinch of rasped Lemon Peel; let it boil until it is reduced to one half. Afterwards put in three Table Spoonsfull of Flour, which should be mixed with the Cream over the fire, and stir it until it is very thick. Take it from the fire, roll it out to the thickness of half a Crown piece; Cut it into the shape of a Lozenge, fry it, and then strew Sugar over it, and brown it with a hot fire shovel.

[p109] Curd Puffs
Rub 4 spoonsful of Cheese curd through a Hair Sieve; add to it four spoonsful of Flour, Two Eggs, one white, a little Nutmeg and Sugar to your taste. Mix all well together. Drop them into a Pan. Fry them like ~~*illeg*~~ Fritters.

Sauce: White Wine and Sugar.

[p158] Custard Pudding
Take a pint of Cream or New Milk; add to it 6 Eggs well beat, Whites \&/ all; 2 Spoonsful of flour, half a Nutmeg grated and a little Rose Water. Sugar to your taste. Butter a Cloth, and put it in when the Water boils. Boil it half an hour.

Melt butter for a sauce.

[p168] Custard Pudding Mrs D[imsdale] of Hitchin
2 Spoonsful of Flour, 2 Eggs, one spoonful of Sugar, a pint of Milk and a little Cinnamon, but better a little Lemon peel boiled in it; mix together while the Milk is warm; to be boiled three quarters of an hour. To thicken the Milk and Flour over the Fire; then add the Eggs &c &c

---

[40] Donor of receipt on [p166] is Madame de la Combe.

[p37] Farly Newhavens Receipt for Dutch Puddings[41]
A Pint of Cream, let it boil and then put in half a Pound of Butter and a little Mace, stir the whole together, and add a quarter of a Pound of Flower beat into six Eggs leaving out four Pound [*sic*] of the Whites, bake them in little Pans ¾ of an Hour. The Sauce Butter, Wine and Sugar.

[p73] Firmity
Let the Wheat be well threshed until it is free of Husk. Then to every quart of Wheat put two quarts of Water, and let it either boil or bake for about 5 hours. Boil a quart of the Wheat when thus prepared in two Quarts of good Milk. Thicken it with flower & Eggs. Sweeten it to your taste, and put in a few Currants.

The Wheat will keep several days.

[p61] Hunting Pudding
Take eight Eggs beat well, half a pound of Suet chopped very Fine, half a pound of Currants, half a pound of Raisins stoned and chopped; A penny Loaf grated, some Nutmeg and Sugar to your taste and half a Glass of Brandy. This pudding will take four hours boiling.

[p6] Imperials * Exc[ellent]
Steep three Spoonsful of fine flour in half a pint of Cream, and five Eggs, Whites and Yolks. Add to it three or four Ratafie Cakes, Lemon peel rasped, and orange flour Water and Sugar to your taste; put it in the fire for half an hour, stirring it round all the time. When it is enough done, let it cool; when cold cut it into small pieces, like buttons, and shape them round; beat up two Eggs with cream, and dip the fritters into it. Fry them of a fine Colour; then glaze them with Sugar & a Salamander.

[p11] Lemon Pudding +
The Yolks of 10 Eggs; four of the whites well beaten; the Peel of 2 Lemons grated, or rather half a peel more, the juice of 2 Lemons, ¼ of a pound of Loaf Sugar; Mix all well together just before it is set in the Oven; stir into it ¾ of a pound of Butter, melted thick. Cover the bottom of the Dish and around the Dish with Puff Paste. Let it bake one hour.

---

[41] There is no receipt for 'Dutch puddings' in the various editions of Farly's *London art of cookery*. I have not found any other receipts for Dutch puddings nor any referring to 'Newhaven'.

[p61] Lemon Pudding
Grate the outside rind of two Lemons, add to it the Juice of one Lemon, take eight Eggs, beat up half a pound of butter melted, half a pound of Loaf Sugar, mix all well together; then lay a thin puff paste in a dish; An Hour will bake it.

[p35] A light Pudding
Five Eggs, two spoonsful of flour; a Pint of Milk, to boil one hour.

[p71] A light Pudding
A Pint of Cream, 8 Eggs, leave out 2 of the Whites, One spoonfull of flour, and a little Salt; mix all well together & boil it.

You must have sweet sauce.

[p23] Little Puddings in Cups
Take half a pint of Cream, two Ounces of flower, 3 Eggs, leaving out two of the Whites, and mix them together with one Ounce of Melted Butter. Loaf Sugar to your taste, and a little White Wine put into the Cups. They will bake in 10 Minuites.

[p153] To make Mays Puddings
Take a quart of Cream, and stir as much fine flour in it, as will make it almost as thick as a Pancake. Then beat well the Yolks of 7 Eggs and 2 Whites and put them together, and let them be well stirred. Put in Salt to your taste, but not until you are ready to bake. Then let the oven be very hot, and bake them in China Cups well buttered, they must stand ¾ of an hour.

If you chuse you may make a boiled Pudding of the same only a little more flower in it, to put in the middle of the Dish with the baked ones round about it, and some drawn butter under it.

[p159] Millet Pudding
Half a pound of Butter, two Tea Cups full of Millet. Mix it well in your Dish. Then add 2 Quarts of Milk, a quarter of \pound of/ Sugar, a little Nutmeg, and bake it.

[p26] Orange Pudding
Take the Peel of three Seville Oranges, boil them tender in a large stew-pan of Water; Beat them well in a Mortar; add to them 4 Savoy Biscuits, 5 Ounces of Butter; the juice of one ~~Lemon~~ \Orange/, Sugar to your taste, the Yolk of three Eggs and the White of one. Make a Puff Paste for the bottom of the Dish to slip out, and some Paste across the Top.

[p74] Paté Royale[42]
Take a Wine Glass full of Water, put it in a Stew-pan with a Lump of fresh Butter, let it boil a moment, and put in as much flower as the liquor will take, and make it into a paste. When it is cool put 4 Yolks and 2 Whites of eggs into the Paste. When it is well mixed and beat together, force it through a Machine for the purpose into the frying Pan & let it be fryed in Hogs lard or clarified Butter. Serve it hot & strew some powdered Sugar over it.

[p122] Plumb Pudding
Half a pound of Beef Suet; half a pound of Currants; half a pound of grated Bread, 4 Ounces of powdered Sugar, 6 Eggs, half a Nutmeg; some Orange Peel and Citron cut in small pieces. It will boil 2½ hours.

Pour melted Butter, Wine & Sugar over it.

[p125] Plumb Pudding as Mrs P'
One pound of Suet chopped fine, a pound of Raisins stoned, 8 Eggs, half the Whites, four Tablespoonsful of Flour, 2 of Sugar, ¼ of a lb of Citron, one Nutmeg, 16 Cloves, 2 blades of Mace, some China Orange Peel, fine; one Glass of Brandy, and as much Cream and Milk as will make it of a proper thickness – about a TeaCup full is enough. To be boiled 4 or 5 Hours.

[p101] Plumb Pudding without Eggs Lady Gould
Half a pound of Currants, half a pound of Raisins, one pound of Flour, one Pint of Milk, one pennyworth of Treacle, a very little Suet shred fine; a little Nutmeg. Boil it well, as it requires more boiling than a Pudding with Eggs.

[p97] A Rich Plumb Pudding B
A pound of Beef suet, half a pound of flower, half a pound of Raisins stoned, half a pound of Currants, a little Bread grated, eight Eggs and a little Brandy. Butter the Cloth. It will take four hours to boil.

Send it to Table with Wine Sauce.

[p81] Potatoe Pudding
2 Pounds of Potatoes grated, three Eggs, one Pint of Milk and two Ounces of Moist Sugar. Beat them well together and bake them.

---

[42] A receipt for fritters.

[p138] Potatoe Pudding
To a pound and a quarter of well boiled Potatoes beat fine in a marble Mortar, add half a pound of Potatoes [*sic*], and half a pound of Sugar. Then drop in 6 Eggs, one at a time into it, and rub them all well together in the Mortar, when well mixed, grease the Dish, and send it to a brisk Oven. ½ an hour will bake it. The Ingredients should be mixed while the Potatoes are warm, and the Top of a light brown.

[p133] Puffs to fry instead of Fritters
Take a pint of Milk, and mix as much Flower as will make it a hasty Pudding. Take care to mix it with a little Milk first, & more by degrees; that when you set it on the Fire to thicken it may not go lumpy. Pour it out to cool, and add to it three Eggs, a little Salt and Sugar. Beat all in a Mortar. Fry them in good Lard over a quick fire. They should be dropped small, and will be round.

[p95] Rasberry Fritters[43]
Grate Naples Biscuits, pour over them half a Gill of boiling Cream; When it is almost cold, beat the Yolk of 4 Eggs to a Strong Froth. Beat the biscuits a little, then beat both together enceedingly [*sic*] well. Put to it two Ounces of Sugar, and as much juice of Rasberry as will make it of a pretty Pink Colour and give it a proper sharpness. Drop them into a Pan of boiling Lard; the size of a Walnut.

When you dish them up, stick bits of Citron in some, and blanc[h]ed Almonds cut lengthways in others.[44]

[p95] Rice Fritters Mrs C'
Wash some rice in 5 or 6 Waters, and dry it very well before the Fire; then beat it in a Mortar very fine. You must have at least an Ounce of it. Then put it in a Saucepan; Just wet it with Milk, and when it is quite incorporated with it, add another Pint of Milk. Set the whole over a Stove, or a very low Fire, and take care to keep it always moving. Put in a little Sugar, and some candied Lemon Peel grated. Keep it over the fire until it is almost come to the thickness of a Fine Paste: Flour a Piel [?*recte*, Peel], pour it on and spread it broad with a rolling Pin. When it is quite cold, cut it into small pieces, taking care that they do not stick one to the other. Flour your hands, and roll up the fritters hansomely & fry them.

---

43 Almost the same as Raffald's 'To make Raspberry Fritters' (*Experienced English Housekeeper*, p90). She specifies *two* Naples biscuits.

44 Raffald's final instruction is: 'Lay round them green and yellow sweetmeats and serve them up'. She comments 'They are a pretty corner dish for either dinner or supper'.

When you serve them up, pour a little Orange Flower Water over them, and add Sugar.

[p73] German Rice Milk
Take a quarter of a pound of Rice, 2 quarts of Milk, a quarter of a pound of Sugar grated, with the rind of one Lemon, and mix it with the Yolk of 8 Eggs. First boil the Rice with a little Milk, and put in the rest by degrees. When the rice has boiled one hour, it must be mixed with the Eggs and Sugar; then poured into a Bowl and set to cool.

[p61] Ground Rice Pudding
Boil four spoonsful of ground Rice in a Pint of good Milk, add to it two spoonsful of melted Butter and 5 Eggs with a little grated Lemon peel, mix it well together and sweeten it to your taste. Three quarters of an hour will boil it.

[p77; p80] Rice Omelet Miss H' (?Hatton)[45]
A quarter of a pound of Rice, boil it in new Milk until it is like a hasty Pudding, then put it in a dish to cool, when quite cold cut it in 8 quarters [*sic*]. Make a boiled Custard thick, and when you have laid the pieces in a China Dish, pour the Custard upon it, and lay on every piece Rasberry Jam or Currant Jelly, with a large piece in the middle.[46]

[p2] Rice Pudding +
Boil a Pint of Milk in two Ounces of Rice until it is soft; Then add one ounce of Currants, and the Yolks of three Eggs stirred in while it is warm; Boil the whole together half an hour, take it off, turn it out of the Bason, and send it up with some sifted Sugar.

[p84] Rice Pudding
Two Ounces of Rice, three Eggs, a Pint and quarter of Milk. Sugar to your taste. Wine sauce.

[p72] Sago Pudding
Boil 4 Ounces of Sago in a quart of Cream or good Milk untill soft; When Cold put in 6 Eggs {omitting 3 Whites} well beat, 3 Spoonsful of White Wine, half a

---

[45] Receipt on [p80] has no donor.
[46] Receipt on [p80] ends: 'and on every quarter put a lump of Rasberry Jam or Currant Jelly. The largest Lump in the middle'.

Nutmeg, and a little Bread Grated; Sweeten it to your taste. Make this quantity into 3 Puddings. A little more than half an hour will boil them.

Make sweet sauce.

[p148] Sago Pudding
Take 2 Ounces of Sago, boil it in a quart of Milk until it is reduced to a pint. Then add the Yolks 4 Eggs with the Whites of only 2. The Crumb of 2 Roles, 3 Spoonsful of Mountain Wine, a little Sugar and half a Nutmeg. Boil them in three Basons about one hour.

[p108] Semolina Pudding Mrs M'y
Two Ounces of Semolina to be boiled and stirred over a slow fire to the consistence of a Custard. Take it off the fire and add a piece of Butter as large as a Walnut. Add two Eggs, leaving out the White of one. One Ounce and a half of lump Sugar in powder, and the peel of half a Lemon or less according to your liking. Mix all these together. To be boiled and baked as Rice Pudding.

[p82] To make a six hours Pudding
Take a pound of Raisins of the Sun, and Stone them and a pound of Beef Suet cut small; beat 6 Eggs well together, one Nutmeg grated and three spoonsful of flower, 3 spoonsful of Cream. Salt it to your taste. Mix them all together and tie them close in a Cloth and Keep it boiling six Hours.

You may, if you please, mix Wine and Sugar with your butter.

[p82] Souflée Pudding Lord O
To three table spoons-ful of Potatoe Starch, add one pint of Cream, ¼ of a pound of fresh butter, a little Cinnamon and Lemon Peel, with white Sugar to your taste. Put all on the fire until it becomes a thick Custard; then add the yolks of 14 Eggs, with the Whites whipped to a very thick consistence, a Glass of Brandy, and a little orange flower Water. Three quarters of an hour will bake it, and it must be served up in what it is baked in & immediately from the Oven.

[p145] Suet Pudding {Mrs G C}
In making a Suet pudding, the Suet should be well worked together with the flour with the hand, as in mixing Butter with Flower in making of Paste, and a little powdered Ginger will make the pudding lighter; and when cut at Table to break in pieces.

A very small quantity of Ginger is recommended in making Pye Crust; also in the Crust of an Apple pudding, which should be puff paste.

[p118] Lady Sunderlands Puddings[47]
A Pint of Cream, eight Eggs leaving out 3 Whites, five spoonsful of Flour, and half a small Nutmeg. When they are going to the Oven, butter small Basons; fill them half Full; bake them half an hour, grate some sugar over them.

For Sauce, melted Butter, Wine and Sugar. When baked turn them out of the Basons, and pour some of the Sauce over them.

[p154] A Tansey
One pint of Cream; ½ a pound of Biscuits, a pint of spinage Juice with a little Tansey; A small handful of Sorrel; the Juice of half a Seville Orange; a little Mountain Wine; 12 Eggs {beat only half the Whites} sweeten it to your taste; Strain in the Eggs and set it over the Fire; Keep stirring it until it thickens; when cold put it in a Dish. A little baking will do; turn it out on a Plate with a ¼ of an Orange round it.

[p123] A common Tansey pudding
A pint of Cream, a pint of Juice, 16 Eggs, the Whites of 8. Just thicken it over the fire and bake it.

[p11] Termin Puffs +
Beat two Eggs and beat them with half a pint of Cream, a little Sugar, half a Nutmeg grated, 2 Spoonsfull of flower, and one Ounce of butter melted without Water; beat all well together, and let it stand 3 or 4 Hours; then butter and flower your Cups, and pour in your Batter; bake them three quarters of an hour in a quick Oven; Turn them out of the Cups and serve them hot, melt butter with your Sugar and white Wine for Sauce.

[p116] A Twopenny Pudding
Mix two spoonsful of flour with a little Cold Milk \to the thickness of Butter. Boil a pint of Milk/ and put to it boiling hot. When it is a little cool put in four Eggs, a little Salt, half a spoonful of Sugar and the rind of a Lemon. 1¼ Hour boils it. Let the pot boil when you put it in. Sauce: Wine with Butter.

---

[47] This receipt circulating in print by at least the 1780s. The version here is exactly the same as that printed in John Farley, *The London art of cookery, and housekeeper's complete assistant. On a new plan. Made Plain and Easy to the Understanding of every Housekeeper, Cook, and Servant in the Kingdom* ... (6th edition, London, 1789), p203. It does not appear in the earlier editions of Farley's book. The same receipt is also in Charlotte Mason, *The ladies' assistant for regulating and supplying the table; Being a complete system of cookery, &c* .... (6th edition, London, 1787), p381.

[p120] White Pot Mr W'd
Take two large Table spoonsful of Flour. Stir it by degrees into 3 Pints of Milk, boil it until it is as thick as pap. Pour it into a deep Pan, intended to be use in baking, and cut into it half a pound of fresh Butter. Stir all together. Break into it 9 Eggs, both Yolks and Whites, a Nutmeg grated, a Pint of warm Water, Lisbon Sugar to your taste.[48] Add three pints of Milk, if it will fill the Pan; if not, add more.[49] Stir well together, send it to the Oven. It takes 3 or 4 hours in baking.

The best way of determining the quantity of Milk is by filling the Pan 3 parts full. The rest of the Ingredients will, when added, fill it quite. It shrinks in baking.

[p76] To make White Puddings Miss Hatton
Take half a pound of biscuit; break it into a Bason; pour a pint of boiling Cream over it, cover it close and put in the Yolk of [*blank*] eggs, a little spice, suet and some slices of Orange or Lemon Peel, with some Currants.[50]

---

[48] 'White Pot' was usually a form of 'Bread and Butter Pudding' (Lehmann, *British Housekeeper*, p232). See, for example, Glasse's 'A White-Pot' (*Art of Cookery*, p79). Perhaps ED has missed out some breadcrumbs from this receipt?
[49] This is not an additional 3 pints of milk but a comment regarding the original quantity of milk boiled and thickened with flour at the beginning.
[50] This receipt resembles 'Bread and Butter Pudding'.

Chapter VII: Table Decorations[51]

[p1; p91] Calves Feet Jelly Mrs Byde[52] +
Boil four Calves feet in 2 Gallons of Spring Water in a Pot close covered until it Jellies, pour it \off/ from the Bones, and when cold skim off all the fat; then add the Juice of four Lemons, the Peel of two or three cut very ~~fine~~ \thin/ and half a pint of White Wine, 2 or 3 Blades of Mace; sweeten it with Loaf Sugar to your taste; let it have a good boil; then taste it, and add any ingredients that you may think wanting, and when you find it good, set it by till blood warm,[53] then put in the Whites of 4 Eggs beat up to a froth; set it on the fire without stirring and let it boil quite up, then put it in your Bag.

[p126] Flummery Mrs C't Albury
Beat two Ounces of Almonds very fine and tye them up in a piece of Muslin & boil in a quart of new Milk with a Tea cup full of Rose Water, and an Ounce of the finest Isinglass, pulled into very small pieces. Boil it until the Isinglass is dissolved. When it is almost done, put in an Ounce & half of fine Sugar. Strain it through a Muslin in Cups, and when cold, stick them with Almonds.

[p72] Almond Flummery
Take a pint of Spring Water, and put to it 1 oz of Hartshorn. Let it boil until the Hartshorn is consumed. Then strain it through a flannel bag upon some Lemon Peel finely shred, and let it stand until stiff. Then beat 30 Jordan Almonds with some Orange flower Water. Strain it into your Jelly. Dissolve it over the fire; Strain it into a Dish, and when cold, stick it with almonds quartered.

[p39] Dutch Flummery
A Ounce and half of Isinglass boiled in a pint of Water until dissolved, a little White Wine to your taste; the Yolk of Four Eggs well beat, the Juice of two Lemons, the Rind of one, mix it well, and set it on the fire, Keep stirring it until it boils, then strain it into Moulds.

---

[51] Mrs Raffald's Chapter VII includes savoury jellies and jellies that were specifically used as table decorations; fruit jellies are in Chapter VIII, Preserving. The same distinction has been attempted here.
[52] Both receipts are credited to Mrs Byde.
[53] Receipt on [p91] has 'milk warm'.

[p124] A floating Island
½ a pound of roasted apples, ¼ of a pound of Sugar, the juice of 2 Lemons, the whites of 3 Eggs. Beat all together with a wooden spoon or wisk until it is a high froth. Put some Cream in the dish and add \to/ the rest.

[p137] Blanc Mange
Take a quart of new Milk, put into it one Ounce of Isinglass, a Bay Leaf, a piece of cinnamon, 2 Spoonsful of Rose Water. Let it simmer slowly over the fire a quarter of an hour in a well tinned saucepan. Sweeten it to your taste, and strain it through a lawn Sieve. Let it be almost cold, take off the Scum, and put it into Moulds. Wet them with a little Rose Water before you put through [*sic*] the Blanc Mange in.

Before it is quite cold, if you like it, add a little White Wine.

[p137] Dutch Blanc Mange
Two Ounces of Isinglass to a quart of Water boiled away to half, add a bit of Cinnamon, a little Mace, and a few Cloves. Beat up 6 Yolks of Eggs, 3 Gills of Mountain; one Gill of Rose Water and a quarter of a pound of Sugar. The juice of two Lemons. Boil the rind of one with the Isinglass. When the Isinglass is reduced to a Pint add the other Ingredients, and let it boil together for a minuite. Strain it; Wet the Glasses before you Fill them.

[p90] Manche Blanche Mrs C' (?Champion)
Four Eggs, a pint of Cream, a spoonful of ground Rice, one laurel Leaf, beat them together, sweeten it to your taste; let it boil until it thickens, then put into [*no more*]

[p121] To Colour Jellies
for white Colour use Almonds, pounded and strained
yellow, put in some Yolks of Eggs, or Saffron steeped in the Jelly and squeezed
red, some Juice of red Beet
grey, Cochineal
purple, purple rensale or powdered Violet
green, juice of Beet or Spinage, which should be boiled

[p6] A Jelly Mrs Hads[le]y Exc[ellent] +
Four pints of strong Jelly: One pint of Wine {Beer Measure} Ten large Lemons; rub some lumps of Sugar on the rinds of three Lemons. The rinds of two cut for the Jelly to drop on. The Whites of six Eggs well beat with the Shells; Boil all together about twenty Minuites, add Sugar to your taste.

[p15] Apple Jelly +
Take 8 Apples, put to them one pint of Water, set them on the fire to boil twenty minuites. Dissolve one Ounce of Isinglass in a pint of Water. Strain the Juice from the Apples, add to it the Isinglass with the Juice of 2 Lemons and the Rind of one. Sugar to your taste. Take a little Cochineal and put it in a Bag; set it on the fire.[54] When it begins to look red take out the Cochineal; let it stand until almost Cold, then put it in the Moulds.

D'ont make it too red, only to be just coloured.

[p129; p159] Lemon Jelly Mrs B'[55]
To About a pint of spring Water, put the Juice of six Lemons, and the rind of three pared very thin; sweeten with the finest Loaf Sugar[56] to your Taste. Beat the Whites of 8 Eggs; and when the Sugar is melted put all together and strain it hard through a strong thin Cloth. Then set it on a quick Charcoal Fire in a silver Saucepan and Keep it stirring until it boils; then put it in Glasses.

[p9] Orange Jelly * Mrs ?Mosely
Take twelve China and three Seville Oranges, grate the Peel of three of the China ones, and squeeze out the Juice of all through a lawn sieve, a pound of treble refined Sugar with about half a pint of Water; boil it to a candyheight, and have Isinglass enough to make it stiff ready clarified. Then put all together and boil and scum it a few Minuites, then put it in a Bason; stir it about a little, and let it stand till it is cool enough to push in the Moulds you intend.

It is better made the day before it is intended to be used.

[p24] Orange Jelly Mrs H'
Dissolve full two Ounces of pulled Isinglass in a pint of Water; pare your China Oranges very thin; squeeze the Juice of 8 China Oranges, of 4 Seville Oranges and of 4 Lemons: Add six Ounces of Loaf Sugar to the Juice of the Fruits, and mix it and the Peel of the Orange with Isinglass Jelly; Boil all together, and strain it through a lawn sieve. The Jelly may be made into any Form.

The making Cups of the oranges, and pouring the Jelly into them are hansome for Table.

---

[54] ie put the bag containing the Cochineal into the liquid and put the liquid over the fire.
[55] Receipt on [p159] has no donor.
[56] Receipt on [p159] simply says 'with fine Sugar'.

[p36] Orange Jelly
12 China Oranges, 3 Seville Oranges, 3 Lemons. The paring of one Lemon grated, 2 Ounces of Isinglass, one pound of fine Sugar. Boil it together and strain it. When quite cold, put it into the Mould.

[p97] Dutch Syllabubs B
Half a pint of Mountain Wine; the same quantity of Cream, half a Lemon squeezed and half the rind grated. Sugar it to your taste. Whisk it up and Fill your Glasses almost to the Top with the liquid. Then put the froth upon that.

[p100] Everlasting Syllabubs B D
A quart of good Cream, a pint of Rhenish Wine, half a pint of Sack, the rind of 3 Lemons grated, and the Lemon Squeezed; ¾ of a pound of fine Sugar. Whisk it well for half an hour and put it in the Glasses.

[p36] Lemon Syllabub
One Quart of Cream, a Pint of strong White Wine and the Juice of one Lemon. The Peel of two grated; Sugar to your taste. Beat this with a Whisk until it comes to a Froth. As the Froth rises, put it into your Glasses. Let them stand a Night to clear.

[p89] Solid Syllaboobs Mrs Champion
Two large Lemons, grate off the rind, squeeze the Juice and take out the Seeds, put it to a pint of White Wine, and near half a pound of fine powdered Sugar, and a quart of thick Cream: Whip it all together with a whisk untill it is as thick as paste, put it in your Glass, let it stand a Night.

Twill Keep a Week.

[p92] To make very fine Syllabup
A Quart and half a Pint of Cream, a pint and half of White Wine, three Lemons, near a pound of double refined Sugar {beat & sifted}. Put it to your Cream; grate off the yellow rind of the 3 Lemons & put that in, and squeeze the juice of the Lemons into the Wine, and add that to the Cream. Then beat all to a Whisk half an Hour. Then take it up with a Spoon and fill the Glasses.

It keeps good 9 or 10 days, and is best three or four days old.

Chapter VIII: Preserving[57]

[p130] To Clarify Sugar Mrs B'
Your Sugar should be broke into large Lumps, and just dip your Sugar into clear Water. Then put the Sugar in a Silver Saucepan, and let it stand until melted. Set it over the fire, and let it boil as fast as it can. Skim it until clear.

[p46] Currant Jelly
Put the Currants over the fire until they boil. Then put them into a Sieve and let them drain. Take an equal quantity of Juice and of clarified sugar, boil it until it jellys. Keep it well skimmed, then put it into Pots.

[p64] Currant Jelly
Pick your Currants from the Stalks, and put them in an Earthen Pot. Set it in Water over the fire, and let them boil until the liquor runs from them. Then put to 3 pints of Juice 2 pounds of Sugar. Let it boil until it Jellies. Take the scum clear off and put it into Pots.

[p155] Currant Jelly
To a pound of stripped Currants add ¾ of a pound of the best Sugar. Boil them 20 Minuites very fast. Then strain through a Hair Sieve.

[pp91-92; p11] Harslern [*recte* Hartshorn] Jelly[58] Mrs Byde[59]
Take three pints of strong Jelly, one pint of Lisbon, six Ounces of Juice of Lemons, a quarter of a pound of fine Sugar; the Whites of eight Eggs well beaten, mix all together, set on the fire just to boil a little until the Egg is hard, and the Liquor looks curdled, then pour it through a Jelly Bag, put the first that runs, back again, until it runs clear, then let it run on the paring of one Lemon, but only the Yellow part, then put it into Glasses for use.

If the Weather is cold, let it run through the Bag near the Fire.

---

[57] As in *The Experienced English Housekeeper*, the receipts for jellies, jams, cheeses, marmalades and preserves have been separated out.
[58] John Nott, H22, is 'To make Hartshorn Jelly'. The ingredients and method are similar, except that his first instruction is how to make 'strong jelly', ED's first ingredient. He says: 'Boil half a Pound of Hartshorn in three Quarts of Water, over a gentle Fire, 'till it becomes a Jelly; if you take out a little in a Spoon to cool, and it hangs upon the Spoon, it is enough, strain it from the Hartshorn while it is hot.'
[59] Receipt on p11 has no donor.

[p152] Hartshorn Jelly
Take 6 Ounces of it, put it in a Stone Pot with a quart and half a pint of spring Water; stop it very close, and boil it 5 hours, then strain it through a Jelly bag, until it is very clear. Then put to it the Juice of 2 Lemons and half a pound of double refined Sugar.

[p24] Lemon Jelly Mrs M'
The Juice of 6 Lemons; the Whites of six Eggs; half a pint of Spring Water, sweeten it to your taste. Mix all well together, strain the liquor through a Muslin; Boil it in a slow fire. As soon as it thickens it is enough.

[p169] Lemon Jelly
Pare six Lemons, and put their rinds into a quart of Water near boiling hot, let them stand half an hour; then pour off the Liquor, and put to it the Juice of the Lemons with Sugar to your taste: Then beat the whites of 3 or 4 Eggs very well, and put to them about six spoonsful of the Lemonade, with a quarter of a pint of Brandy: Put it upon the fire in a small Vessel, and let it boil up; then take it off the Fire, and put it to the rest of the Liquor, and give it one good stir, and put it through a Jelly Bag until it becomes clear.

[p98] Orange or Lemon Syrup
To a pint of juice add a pound of the best double refined Sugar; let them boil together a quarter of an Hour, and continue skimming it as it boils. When the syrup is cold, bottle it for use.

[p129] Apricot Jam
Your apricots, which for this Purpose need not be the best, should be stoned and cut in slices. But you should First weigh your Apricots & for every pound, allow 14 Ounces of double refined Sugar which should be broke in Lumps: Each Lump should be dipped in Water and then put into a Silver Saucepan, and made to boil as fast as possible; skimming it until it is quite clean. Then put in your apricots, and Keep them boiling, the faster the better, until they are enough, which you may know by their being quite clear. Then put into your Glasses, or Pots while warm.

[p40] Conserve of Quinces
Cut away the rinds, cores and seeds. The[n] cut the fruits in small pieces to the weight of Four pounds; boil them until soft, and then put to them three pounds of sugar; boil it to a consistance.

This is excellent to recover lost Appetite.

[p155] Rasberry Jam
A pound of Rasberries, ¾ of a pint of Currants Juice, a pound and half of the best Sugar well powdered. Wash the Rasberries well, then put in the Juice and Sugar, and boil all together. Scum it well until you see it will jelly, then set it by.

The infusion is made after this manner. Strip the Currants. To a quart of picked Currants put half a pint of Water, boil it until you observe all the Currants are broken; then run it through a Jelly Bag.

[p66] Bullace or Damson Cheese
Take the Bullace and bake them; When they are baked rub them thro' a hair Sieve and measure the Pulp. To every Pint of it, there must be a pound of Sugar with a little Water, and boil it to a Candy. Then put in the Pulp and boil it to a Jelly.

[p99] Bullace Cheese
Put the Bullaces in an earthen Pot, and set them in an Oven until these become Pulp; then force them through a hair Sieve with a Spoon, measure the Pulp; to every pint add a pound of Sugar; then set it on the fire, and boil two hours.

Damson Cheese is made the same way; only use ¾ of a pound of Sugar to a Pint of Pulp.

[p156] Damson Cheese
Weigh the Damsons, put them in a Pan and set them in an Oven to be thoroughly baked; then pulp them through a warm sieve. To every four pounds when sent to the Oven, add one Pound of Sugar. Stir it into the Juice; boil it up quick until it is thick. Put it into Gallipots and it should cut, when cold, like Marmalade.

[p158] Plumb Cheese
Take Damsons, put them in a Jug covered close in a kettle of Water over the fire, until they are quite tender. Then work the pulp through a Sieve with a Spoon. Put it in a Pan over the fire while it leaves the Pan clean; then let stand until it is cold. To a pound of Pulp put ¾ of a pound of Sugar beat and sifted. Then, beat it for two hours with a wooden spoon. Then put it in paper Coffins, and dry it in a stove.

[p45] Apple Marmalade
Boil some Apples {Rennets} whole in Water, just until they become a little soft; then plunge them into cold Water to get off the Skin. Take the Pulp which you pass through a Sieve, pressing it hard. Put that which you have passed through

the Sieve into a preserving Pan on the fire to dry it a little, and let it remain until it becomes quite thick: Then take it off, and put it into a Dish. Take the same weight of Sugar as of Marmalade, clarify it, and boil it to a strong syrup. Then put the apples into it and mix them with a Wooden Spoon. Put it again on the fire, only to warm it, stirring it constantly. When it is near boiling, take it off: When nearly cold put it into Pots.

[p45] Orange Marmalade
Take three pound of Seville Oranges and the same weight of fine sugar. Cut the oranges in two, or squeeze out all the Juice & Pulp. Boil the Peel in five or six Waters {they must all be hot except the first} when they are tender and not bitter, put out the pieces with a fork and cut the Peel in ~~narrow~~ long, ~~thin~~ \narrow/ pieces. Strain the juice of two more oranges to them and put peels, juice and sugar in the preserving Pan. When almost boiled enough, squeeze in the juice of two Lemons.

[p24] Orange Sweetmeat Mrs M't
Take any quantity of Seville Oranges, pare them very thin; boil the rind tender, changing the Water two to three times, then cut it in shreds; squeeze the juice out, and clear the Pulp from the Skin and Seeds. Then mix all together, and to every pound of orange add ¾ of a pound of Sugar, and Boil it to a proper consistence.

[p45] Peach Marmalade
Peel the Peaches, and slice them, Pound the sugar, sift it, and add to a pound of fruit ¾ of a pound of sugar. Put the sugar and Fruit together, and let them stand a Night: Then boil them to a proper consistence.

The Marmalade gets stiff by Keeping.

[p45] Quince Marmalade
Take Quince liquor, and of every pint a pound of fine sugar. Then take the Quinces, pare and slice them, and put in as many as the liquor will cover. Boil them to a Jelly when they will turn red.

Keep the skellet close covered.

[p129] Red Marmalade (Mrs B')
Grate the worst of your Quinces, and squeeze them, and let them stand all Night to settle. Next day, pare, quarter, and core the best of your Quinces into a large Pan of Water. To every pound of Quinces, put half a pint of the expressed Juice and three quarters of a pound Sugar. Set them in you preserving Pan over a slow

fire for three hours; or until you think them of a good Colour. Then break them and add about a quarter of a pound [*sic*] of Juice, and a Lump or two of Sugar to your taste, after which let them boil pretty fast until they are thick enough. Do not put them into Pots or Glasses until almost Cold.

[p128] For preserving Apricots
You must remember that the Fruits be not quite ripe, and the finest and clearest should be carefully picked out for preserving wet in Glasses and drying. Those that are not so nice will do very well for Jam.

[pp41-42] To preserve Apricots
Take out the stones of ~~four~~ \24/ large Apricots; pare them and cover them with a pound and a half of fine powdered Sugar, let them stand six or seven hours; then set them on a slow fire, boil them until they are tender and clear. If any are clear before the rest take them out and put them in again. When they are all become clear, let them stand with Paper close on them untill the next day, then take a strong codling jelly and boil a quarter of it with two pounds of Sugar. Make the Apricots scalding hot, pour the Jelly on them, boil them very gently together, and when the Apricots rise in the Jelly, put them into Pots.

[p42] To preserve Green Apricots
Gather them before the stones are hard, wet them and lay them on a Coarse Cloth, put to them three or four handfuls of Salt, rub them until they are smooth; then put them in scalding Water, and put them on the fire until they are ready to boil. Take them off again, let them stand until they are almost cold; repeat this 2 or 3 times then cover them close. When they look green boil them until tender: After which take their weight of sugar and to every pound of Sugar put half a Pint of Water, and make a Syrup; let this stand until near Cold; then put in the Apricots and let them boil until they are clear. Warm the Syrup every day until it is pretty thick.

[p129] To preserve Apricots in Syrup Mrs B'
You are to proceed in the same manner as you do to dry them, only observe you must have one pound of Sugar to one pound of Apricots, and as you pare them, you should cut some in halves, and some in Quarters. When these are boiled enough, that is, until they look clear, and are tender; you should immediately take them out of the syrup with a Spoon, and put them into Glasses. The syrup should then be strained through a piece of fine Muslin, and the Glasses filled therewith.

[p41] To preserve Barberries
A pound of Barberries picked from the stalks; put them into two quart Pots, and set them in a Pot full of hot Water to stew them, after that strain them and add a pound of Sugar and a pint of Rose Water, boil them together a little; then take half a pound of the best clusters of Barberries you can get and dip them in the Syrup while it is boiling. Take out the Barberries and let the Syrup boil until it is thick; when cold put them into Pots with the Syrup.

[p73] To preserve Barberries
Take full ripe Barberries, and strip them from the Stalk; take their weight in Sugar, and as much Water as will wet your Sugar, give it a boil and skim it, Then put in your Barberries; let them boil until they look clean, and your syrup thick; put them into Pots, and when they are cold, cover them up with a Paper dipped in Brandy.

[p128] Cherries Wet Mrs B'
Pick your Cherries {Carnation} are best, but Kentish will do. Stone them. To every Pound put 14 Ounces of Sugar, sifted very fine & let them stand until the Sugar is melted. Then set them on the Fire to boil until they are clean; then set them by until they are cold, & put them into Glasses.

[p41] To preserve Cherries
Pick them and take out the Stones; put to every pound of Cherries a quarter of a pint of the Juice of White Currants passed through a Jelly Bag and the weight of both Liquor and Cherries of the best Sugar; sift the Sugar and sprinkle it as you put it into the preserving Pan, boil and scum it until the Cherries look clear. Then put them into Pots.

[p6] To preserve Cherries, Currants, Plumbs or other Fruit for Tarts +
Put the fruits you wish to preserve into stone Jars or wide mouthed Bottles. To every quart put a quarter of a pound of Lump Sugar finely sifted; put the Sugar on the top; Tie Bladders over them very close, and set them in a Saucepan of cold Water upon a slow fire. When the Sugar is all melted the Syrup rises above the fruits {which is seen through the bladder} take the Jars or Bottles out of the Water. When they are quite cold, tie a piece of ~~bladder over~~ Leather over the Bladder, and keep them in a dry cool place.

[p110] To preserve Codlings
Codlings full grown and nicely picked; put them in spring Water covered with Vine Leaves over a slow fire. Take care they are free from cracks, then take

them out. Keep the Water after ~~warming~~ \running/ it through a Sieve to take the leaves from it; then boil it up with a Lump of Alum, and when the Water and Codlings are cold, put them up in an Earthen Jar. Seal them to keep them from the Air.

Some omit the Alum & Vine Leaves.

[p42] To preserve Currants

Put a layer of Currants and a layer of Sugar in a fat Dish or Pan, boil them until all the Syrup is pretty thick; scum them as they boil, then take them off the fire and when cold put them into your Pots.

[pp177-178] To preserve Oranges whole or in Halves B D

Open them, take out the seeds, and press the Juice out with a spoon {which will be little} as the Oranges should not be broken. Rub a knife over the outside of the oranges to press out the Oil, or they will not be tender. Next lay them in Water several days. Afterwards boil them until tender. ~~Then lay them in Water several days~~. They should then be well dried, and lastly put in a rich Syrup.

It is uncertain whether a little of the Juice was added to the Syrup.

[p42] To preserve Quinces, White or Red

Core and pare the Quinces. Those you would have White put into a pail of Water for two or three hours. Then take as much Sugar as they weigh; wet it and boil it a little. After that put in the Quinces, and let them boil as fast as they can until tender and clear. Then take them out and boil the Syrrup a little higher. When cold put the Quinces and Syrrup into Pots. Those you would have red, put [*blank*] and dry into the Sugar & let them boil gently {being close covered} until they are red. The[y] must <u>not</u> be put into Cold Water.

[p41] To preserve Rasberries

Take the juice of Red and White Rasberries. If you can procure not any of the latter, take half codling Jelly. Put \a [?]pint/ and a half of juice to two pound of Sugar; boil and scum them, then put in ¾ of a pound of large rasberries, boil them very fast until they are a Jelly and clear; but do not take them off the fire for a quarter of an hour, after they have begun to boil fast. Then put them into Pots, the rasberries first, then the Jelly strained from the seeds; this you will not put to the Rasberries until they begin to cool. Stir them that they may not all lie at the Top of the Pot.

[p50] To preserve Strawberries whole

Gather the Strawberries with the Stalks, or before they are too ripe, lay them on large Dishes, that they may be separate. Sift fine, double their quantity of double refined Sugar; strew it over them. Let them stand whilst you take a few other Strawberries and press them in a Jar with double their weight of Sugar; Tie them down and put the Jar into a Pot of boiling Water to drawn[*sic*] out the Juice; then strain them through a Muslin Cloth into the preserving Pan. Boil and skim them well, and when quite cold put the Whole Strawberries in, and set them on the fire until they are about Milk warm. Take them off and let them stand until cold: Put them on again, and let them get a little warmer and then cool them. You must repeat this several times until they look clear.

Be careful not to let them boil up, as that would take up the stalks, and make them too soft. The Person who does this must not hurry in doing them, as they are very delicate & readily soiled.

Chapter IX: Drying and Candying

[p127] To make clear Cakes[60] Mrs B'
When you have drawn your Juice, boil it at least three quarters of an hour or until it is about half wasted. To a pint of Juice add ¾ of a pound of Sugar in Lumps; stir it until it is melted. Then set it in the fire to be hot; but not boil; then put it in Glasses, and let it stand until it will turn out.

[p44] To Candy Apricots, Pears, Plumbs &c
Cut the Fruit in half, then put sugar upon it and bake it in a gentle Oven close stopped. Let them stand half an hour, then lay them singly on Glass Plates to dry, and sift a little powdered Sugar over them.

[p44] To candy Cherries
Take them before they are ripe, stone them, and pour clarified sugar boiling upon them.

[pp43-44] To dry Apricots
Take four dozen and a half of apricots, Stone and pare them; Cover them with four pounds of sugar finely powdered, putting Sugar on them as you pare them, and the remainder when they are all pared. Let them lie four or five hours until the Sugar is almost dissolved: then set them on a slow fire until it is quite melted. Boil them gently as they grow tender, take them out and put them on an Earthen Plate until all are tender enough: Then put all in together and let them boil a little more. Put a Paper close upon them and let them stand a day or two. Then make them very hot but not to the degree of boiling, and put the Paper on as before. Let them stand two days more, and put them on earthen Plates in a Stove with as little Syrup as possible; turn them every day until dry. Scrape off the syrup as you turn them. Put paper close to them, and lay them up before they are too dry.

Or you may let the syrup candy a little, lay the Fruit in it, give it a heat, then turn them, give them another heat and the next day lay them out on Glasses to dry.

---

[60] ED does not specify the type of fruit to be used; the receipt appears to make a kind of fruit jelly. In Raffald's receipt 'To make Currant Clear Cake' (*Experienced English Housekeeper*, p120) once the fruit and sugar mixture has jellied, it is cut into rounds which are then dried.

[p128] To dry Apricots

To one pound of Apricots, ¾ of a pound of double refined Sugar sifted very fine. Stone them and pare very thin, and as you pare them put them in the preserving Pan, but st\r/ew the Sugar over them. Let them stand until some of the Sugar is dissolved into a Syrup. Then set them over a slow Fire, and let them simmer a little at First, and Keep them turning until they look clear and are tender; then take them off, and let them stand in the Syrup three or four days. You should remember to crack all the Stones, and take out the Kernells, which should be boiled a while in some Water to blanch them, and take away part of the bitterness. These Kernells should be boiled with the Apricots in the Syrup about half the time. A Pewter Dish should be set over a Chaffing Dish of Coals, and while it is warm, should be wiped with a clean Cloth until no more blackness comes off.

Your Apricots should then be taken out with as little of the Syrup as you can, and laid one by one in the Dish, observing to lay the halves on one another as well matched as you can, and a Kernell between each. The Dish should then be taken off the Coals and they should be set by, and every day be shifted to a Fresh Dish warmed in the same manner; and if the Weather should be very damp, it will be of service to let them stand a little while on the Coals. They must be treated in this manner until they are dry; but if there should be any sunshine, to let them have the advantage of it as much as possible.

[p43] To dry Cherries

Stone them and to every ten pound of Cherries put three pound of Sugar finely powdered. Shake them well together and put them on the fire until the sugar is well melted: Then boil them a little and let them stand in an Earthen Pan until the following day: Then make them scalding hot, and when they are cold again, lay them on Sieves: then put them into a gentle Oven, and let them stand in it all night. After that, turn them, and put them in again. When they are dry, keep them very close in a Box without any Paper between them.

Your oven must not be hotter than when you draw out small Bread or Pyes.

[p127] To dry Cherries

To every pound of Cherries put half a Pound of Sugar sifted very Fine. Stone the Cherries, and as you do them, sprinkle the Sugar to melt them. Then set them on the fire, and let them simmer a little at first; then let them boil one hour, or until you think they are enough; Then set them in a Pan until next day, and then put them in a coarse Hair Sieve & let them stand until the Syrup drains from them, then spread them on a Sieve to dry.

[p43] To dry Plumbs

Weigh the Plumbs and for each pound of Plumbs take a pound of Loaf Sugar. Scald the Plumbs, take out the stones, and peel off the Skins; Lay them on a dry Cloth. Then wet the sugar a little, and put it on the fire; keep stirring it one way, until it boils to Sugar again. Take some of this sugar, and put it in the bottom of the preserving Pans and lay the Plumbs upon it: Strew the rest of the Sugar upon them. Let it stand until it is melted, then make it scalding hot {but do not let it boil} twice a day. When the syrup is very thick, lay the Plumbs on the Glasses to dry. Keep them always warm, sifting a little Sugar over them until almost dry. Wet the stones in the Syrup and dry them with Sugar. Put them into the Plumbs and when quite dry, put them in boxes with Paper between.

[p23] Fruit Cakes

Five pound of Apples pared and cut small; five pound of Plumbs stoned, two pounds of Sugar. Put them in a Pot, a layer of each alternate, and let it be well baked. Mash it altogether as you would mix Marmalade. Spread it on Tins, and set it in the Oven until quite dry. Cut it out as you like.

[p22] Fruit Paste

To a pound and a quarter of fruit, add ¾ of a pound of fine Sugar in fine Powder. Stew the apples until very soft, half a Lemon, a little Peel grated, boil it until it becomes a stiff Paste. Put it into shallow Dishes.

[p39] To preserve Green Leaves

Take little Leaves of a Pear Tree; keep them close stopped in a hot scalding pale Verjuice and Water; then give them one boil in some Syrrup and lay them between two Glasses to dry, smooth and cut them in the shape of apricot or any other Leaf, and stick them in your Apricots, Cherries, or plumbs close up as Natural as you can.

Apricot leaves will not bear greening being too tender.

Take care always to gather your Leaves with good stalks.

[p44] To preserve and Candy Orange & Lemon Peel

Cut the Oranges or Lemons in half, take the Pulp out of them, and lay the Peels three days in clear Water changing it once or twice in a day. Then boil them in three ~~different~~ \several/ Waters until they are tender. Afterwards take half a pound of good Sugar, clarify it, put one pound of the Peels into it, and boil them until the Sugar is a full Syrup. Let is [*sic*] cool and put it away in Pots. When you wish to candy them, take them out of the Syrup, wash them clear from it in warm Water, and dry them with a Cloth. Then make a new Syrup for them and boil it to a good height \manus Christi/. Put the Peels into it, and boil them until the Sugar is at a <u>casting height</u>. *que' What does this mean.*[61] Afterwards take them off the fire, and Keep stirring them until the syrup begins to Cool. Take the Peels out, and when cold, they will be candied White & clear for use.

[61] See Glossary under casting height. Near the beginning of a receipt book complied during the period 1700-1760 was recorded the following information: 'To know when sugar is boiled to a Manus Christie Heighte'; 'When boiled to a candy height'; and 'When boiled to a casting height' (Rhodes (ed), *In an Eighteenth Century Kitchen*, p8).

Chapter X: Cheesecakes, Creams, Custards

[p20] French Butter
Take 2 Ounces and a half of Isinglass boiled for 10 Minuites in half a Pint of Water. Then add a pint of White Wine, the Juice of two Lemons & a half, a little Saffron to Colour it, Sugar to your taste. D'ont boil it after the addition of Wine, Lemon, & Sugar, for it will then look thick. Strain it through Muslin.

[p116] French Butter
One Ounce and half of Isinglass to a Pint of White Wine. Four spoonsful of Water; the juice of 4 Lemons; Sugar to your taste. Boil altogether for an hour; then strain it and stir it until almost Cold.

Put it in any shape you chuse to turn it out, and send to Table. Dip the things it is put in, in Cold Water, and do not wipe them dry and they will turn out clean. Add a little saffron.

[p107] French Cheese
Take a pint of Milk and boil it; beat four eggs well with one Glass of White Wine; sweeten it to your taste. Stir it into the boiling Milk until it turns to a Curd, and then strain it through a Sieve, and put the Curd in a Net until cold; then turn it out in your dish, and beat up a little Cream with Sugar and one small piece of Cinnamon.

[p141] Cheese Cakes
Take the curd of about two quarts of Milk, a little grated Nutmeg, a quarter of a pound of Butter; 2 Ounces of Sugar, 5 Ounces of Carraway Seeds, 3 Eggs. Use the Paste at the bottom, and Edge the Pans.

[p141] Cheese Cakes ~~*illeg*~~ Mrs B very good
To A Pound & half of Cheese Curd add 10 Ounces of butter. Beat both in a Mortar to a paste; then add ¼ pound of Almond beat with a little Orange Flower Water; a pound of Sugar, 8 Eggs {leave out half the Whites} a little beaten, Mace, a little Cream. Beat all well together ¼ of an Hour; bake in a puff paste, in a quick Oven.

[p78] Cheese Cakes Miss H' (?Hatton)
Take the Curd of Milk, rub it through a Sieve with a little Butter and one Egg; take the White out, beat them well together with a little Nutmeg, Sugar, Brandy & Currants.

[p106] Plain Cheese Cakes
One Gallon of Milk, set it, then put it in a Cloth and let it drain, then beat the Curd well with a rolling Pin, put in it six Ounces of Butter. The Yolk of Eggs [*quantity not given*] and one White, 3 Ounces of Almonds blanched and beat; Sweeten it with \Sack and/ Sugar as you please. Let the Milk be warm, and two or three spoonsful of Rennet will do.

[p1] Almond CheeseCakes Mrs Byde +
One pound of Almonds and four Ounces of Orange or Lemon Peel pounded very fine in a Mortar with a little Rose Water; 16 Eggs, leave out the Whites; ¾ of a pound of sifted Sugar, a pound and a half of Butter melted over the fire until it Oils; then let it stand until almost cold; Pour the butter Milk from it, and then the Cheesecakes will keep 2 Months.

[p1; p117] Almond CheeseCakes Mrs Fordham[62] +
Blanch half a pound of Jordan Almonds and beat very small with a little Rose Water or orange flower Water, just enough to keep the Almonds from Oiling and two Ounces of candied Orange peel until they are very fine, then put half a pound of sifted loaf Sugar; three quarters of a pound of clarified Butter almost cold; the Yolks of eight Eggs and Whites of four Eggs beat well together. Put it in a light Crust. Bake them in a quick oven.

[p99] Almond Cheese Cakes {B}
Four Ounces of Almonds blanched, and beat with a little Rose Water, four Ounces of fine Sugar; six ounces of butter clarified, four Eggs leaving out two Whites. Beat all well in a Mortar, and bake them in Patties with Crust at bottom.

[p64; p74] Apple Cheese cakes
Half a pound of Apples pared and grated. The peel of two Lemons, and the Juice of one, 6 Eggs, one of the Whites omitted. Half a pound of Butter clarified, and half a pound of Butter [*sic*; *recte* sugar] sifted.

[p94] Lemon Cheese Mrs C'
A quart of thick Cream, add to it the Juice of two Lemons; both large, a little of the Peel pared thin, as much Sugar as will sweeten it, and a spoonful of Orange Flower Water. Whip all these together until solid. Then lay a Napkin in the bottom of a small hair sieve, raised a little on one side. Let it stand all Night; then tye the Napkin to make it round.

---

[62] Both receipts are credited to Mrs Fordham.

When you turn it on the Dish, Garnish it with Rasbery and Currant Jelly.

If it is for dinner it should be made over Night; if for supper in the Morning.

[p60; p68] Lemon Cheese Cakes Miss Clay[63]
Boil very tender the Peel of two large Lemons, and pound it in a Mortar with a quarter of a Pound of Loaf Sugar; the Yolks of 6 Eggs, half a pound of fresh Butter, and a little Curd beat fine, pound and mix together, lay a puff paste in the Patty Pans; fill them half full and bake them.

Orange Cheese Cakes are done in the same way, except that you boil the peel in two or three Waters, to take out the bitter taste.

[p100] Lemon Cheese Cakes B D
Grate the rind of 4 Lemons, squeeze the Juice upon them, & let it stand to steep all night; then put four Ounces of fine Sugar; 2 Ounces of melted Butter thick; three Eggs leaving out one White, a little Nutmeg, and two spoonsful of White Wine, put them in Patty Pans with Crust.

Orange Cheese Cakes are made the same way, only the rind and juice of two Oranges to two Lemons.

[p141] Lemon Cheese Cakes
Boil the peel of two large ~~Almonds~~ \Lemons/ until tender, then pound it well in a Mortar with a ¼ of a pound of loaf Sugar; the Yolk of 6 Eggs and ½ a pound of fresh Butter, and the Juice of half a Lemon. Pound and mix well all together. Add a little Mountain Wine. Paste at the bottom of the Patty Pans, and they should be Filled half Full.

Orange Cheese Cakes are made the same way; but to take out the bitterness boil in 2 or 3 Waters.

[p153] Orange Cheese Cakes
Take half a pound of Almonds blanched, and beat with Rose Water, ½ a pound of Sugar beaten and sifted, ¾ of a pound of Butter melted and almost cold, 8 Yolks of Eggs, 4 Whites well beaten, the Peel of half a large Orange boiled very tender, and the bitterness almost boiled out. Beat well in a Mortar all together, and put it in a light Crust.

---

[63] Receipt on [p68] has no donor; the heading says 'See page 60 – the same'.

[p38] To make abundance of Cream
Take a skimming Dish full of the Top of the Milk; add to it four spoonsful of powdered Sugar and a very little good Rennet, then stir it together that it may thicken a little; then set it in a warm place, and a great deal of Cream will arrive in an hours time.

[p106] Whip Cream
Half a pint of Sack; half a pint of Cream, the juice of two Lemons, or a little Milk, as much Sugar as will sweeten it to your taste. Use a Chocolate Mill to Froth it.

[p79] Barley Cream
Take french Barley picked and washed very clean, half a quarter of a Pound, boil it in Water until it is very soft, and the Water clean; then strain the Barley & put near a quart of Cream to it; boil them well together with a blade of Mace & a Clove or two, stirring it often; add the White of an Egg well beat with two spoonsful of Rose Water; sweeten it to your taste.

[p104] To make a Cream of Codlings
First scald your Codlings and peel off the Skin; then scrape the Pulp from the Cores and strain them with a little Sugar and Rose Water; then lay the Pulp of [the] Codlings in the middle of the Dish and Cream round it.

[p46] To make cream of any sort of Fruit
Take either Currants, Mulberries, Rasberries, Strawberries &c or other Juice Fruits; sprinkle them with Rose Water. Press out the Juice through a Cloth and draw the Milk from the Cow onto it: sweeten this with a little sugar, then beat it up with a Wisk until it froths and it will be excellent.

Instead of Milk you may mix Water with the Juice, and cool it like Wine in Tea or Cold Water. This makes a very pleasant beverage in Summer.

[p1] Lemon Cream Mrs Byde +
To a pint of Spring Water put the Juice of 4 Lemons, and the Peel of three cut very thin; six Ounces of the finest Sugar and the Whites of 8 Eggs beat up to a froth, when the Sugar is melted, put the Eggs in Cold, Strain them all together through a thin coarse Cloth, set it on the fire until it boils, stirring it all the time; when it jellies put it in Glasses.

[p37] Lemon Cream
A Pint and a half of Water. The Juice of three Lemons; shred the Peels very small and steep them in the Liquor 2 hours before you make the Jelly. Shake it well together, and strain it through a hair sieve. Then take the Yolks of 2 and the Whites of ~~three~~ \4/ Eggs, and as much fine Sugar as you like. Stir all together; then set them on the fire in a Dish, stirring it cautiously, until it is of the thickness of Cream.

A little Ambergrease maybe added {if approved of} with the Sugar.

[p153] Lemon Cream
Take a quart of Cream, boil it, then set it to cool with a little piece of Lemon peel in it, stir some time that it does not cream at the Top. Then squeeze the juice of two or three Lemons into a deep Glass with as much fine Sugar in powder as you think will sweeten it. Stir it well together until the Sugar is dissolved. When the Cream is cold, pour it into the Glasses to the Lemon and Sugar, lifting your hand high to make it froth.

You should make it a day before you use it.

[p167; p72] Lemon Cream {without Cream} Madame de la Combe[64]
Take the rinds of two large Lemons, put it into a pint of boiling Water. Let it stand close covered, half an hour. Then put to it the juice of three ~~large~~ Lemons, and Sugar to your taste. Take your Eggs, leaving out the Yolks, beat them well, put them to the Juice; then stir it over a gentle fire, stirring it until it thickens, but it must not boil. Strain it through a fine Hair Sieve[65] into a Bason, and then fill your Glasses.

[p100] Raw Lemon Cream {B}
The juice of three large Lemons, sweeten it, and put it in the Glasses you send it to the Table in. Take a pint of Cream, make it as warm as Milk from the Cow, put it in a Tea pot, and hold it very high, and pour it on the Lemon Juice in the Glasses.

It is best done some hours before you want it.

[p51] Lemon Sallad Mrs K
Grate the Peel of a Lemon, and squeeze the juice into a Dish; sweeten a pint of Cream; boil it and pour it hot upon the Lemon, and let it stand to be cold without stirring it. If you chuse, some sweetmeats may be strewed over it.

---

[64] Receipt on [p72] has no donor.
[65] Receipt on [p72] has 'a Fine lawn sieve'.

[p36] Potatoe Cream
A spoonful of Potatoe starch, one Gallon of new Milk, six Yolks of Eggs, let it cool. Then add the six Whites beat to a Froth, and mix the whole together. Bake it in an Oven, but first powder it over with fine Sugar to give it a Colour. You must put a little Salt & Sugar with the Potatoe Flour when you boil it.

[p7] Rhenish Cream +
The peel of two Lemons, 2 ounces of Isinglass, half a pound of Lump Sugar, the Yolk of five Eggs, a pint of White Wine. Mix them together, let them simmer over a slow fire; strain through a sieve; let it stand till nearly cold & then put it into a Mould.

[p71] Renish Cream
Take two Ounces of Isinglass, boil it in a pint of Water and strain it. Add the juice of two Lemons, and the rind of one, with half a pint of White Wine; boil them together with Loaf Sugar to your Taste. Then take the yolks of 6 Eggs very well beat; Pour them in gently, constantly stirring it and be careful not to let it boil. Pour it into a Bason, and continue to stir it constantly until it is almost cold; then put it into the Moulds.

[p100] Sago Cream
Two ~~\tea/~~ spoonsful of Sago; boil it in two Waters, straining the Water from it. Then add half a pint of Milk, boil it until it is tender and the Milk wasted. Then add a pint of Cream, a blade of Mace, a small piece of Lemon Peel, sweeten it to your taste, and boil it until it is thick.

[p37] Steeple Cream
A quart of rich Cream, boil it over Night, and set it by in a Pan the next morning, put in Fine Sugar to your taste, a quarter of a Pint of Mountain. Take a large Lemon, pare it, put the Peel into the Pan, and with a Whisk, beat it ~~all~~ one way; as it gets thick put it in the bottom of the Sieve, until you send it to Table.

[p77] Burnt Cream Miss H' (?Hatton)
A quart of Cream; boil it with a piece of Lemon Peel and very fine bitter Almonds beat fine; sweeten it to your taste, take the Yolk of 8 Eggs well beat; have ready the dish you serve it up in. Set it over a Pan of boiling Water. Put it on a Stove, mix your Eggs & Cream together; pour it into the Dish. Let it stand until it is as thick as Custard; then grate some fine Sugar over it. Have ready a hot iron to hold over it until it is as brown as you like.

[p165] Burnt Cream
Take a pint and half of new Milk, and the Yolks of 6 Eggs; beat the Eggs up very well with a spoonful of flour. When the Milk has boiled put in the Eggs, and stir it <u>constantly</u> over the fire until it thickens; Stir it only one way. Sweeten to your taste with lump Sugar. Do not let it boil after the Eggs are in. When you have taken it from the Fire, put in a large spoonful of Orange Flower Water. Pour it in a dish or deep Plate, and let it stand until it is quite cold. Then strew some powdered Sugar all over it. Heat a Salamander or a fire Shovel red hot & burn the Sugar with it, until it is of a nice brown all over.

NB The Sugar must not be strewed over the Cream until the moment before it is burnt, and the fire shovel must be held over it so close as to touch it.

[p165] Burnt Cream another way Madame de la Combe
Take 6 Yolks of Eggs free from the Whites. Stir them in the Pan with a little flour. Then pour in the Milk by degrees and mix it well. Set it on rather a quick fire, and stir it constantly until it is as thick as very good Cream. Sweeten it to your taste, and take it from the fire before you put in the Orange flower Water. Set it to cool, and proceed as before.

[p40] Custards or burnt Cream
One pint of good Cream, boil it over a slow fire; then take the Yolks of two Eggs, beat them well, mix them with Four spoonsful of good Milk. Add Sugar to your taste, boil this; then put it into your dish, grate a good quantity of fine Sugar over it. Have your Salamander very hot and brown your Cream with it.

[pp110-111] Boiled Custard
Put a quart of Milk in the fire with a small bit of Cinnemon & Mace, a few bitter Almonds {about 12 pounded} or 12 Apricot Kernels. When boiled strain it, and then put immediately to it moderately warm nine Eggs, only one white, being first well beat and strained. Then add a spoonful of Mountain Wine. Stir it gently over the fire to prevent it curdling, even to almost boiling. Stir it the whole time until of a proper thickness until it seems to hang at the bottom of the Sauce-pan. Then take it off and when about half cool, put it in Cups.

[p118] Boiled Custard Mrs B
Set a pint of Milk and four Bay-leaves over the fire; boil them until properly flavored. In the mean time beat the Yolks of 4 or 5 Eggs well. Stir into it a Tea Spoon\ful/ of Flour, first mixed with a little cold Milk; then stir them into the Milk over the Fire, boil it up only once. Then take it off, and continue stirring it until cool. Sweeten to your taste.

[p18] A Custard Mrs Wright Ex[cellent]
Boil a pint and a half of Milk with an Ounce of bitter Almonds blanched and pounded; then beat the Yolks of 4 Eggs, and one Tea Spoonful of Flour together. Mix them first with a little Cold Milk, then put them to the warm Milk, and boil it up. Keep stirring it one way while it is boiling & a little time after it is off the fire. It must boil gently.

[p61] Custards Miss C[la]y
Half a pint of Cream, put in a Saucepan over a slow Fire. You may add a little Cinnamon, or Nutmeg, or a Few Almonds beat fine according to your taste, and a little Lemon Peel cut very thin. Beat up the Yolk of 5 Eggs with a spoonful of Rose Water put in, as soon as the Cream boils up. Mix it thoroughly by pouring it quick from the Bason to the Saucepan and back again several times. Sweeten it to your taste and let it thicken over the Fire, but be careful it does not boil.

It may \be/ flavored with anything you like {oranges flour water} which should not then be put in, until the Custard is taken from the Fire; and the Spice or Almond should then be omitted.

[p71] Créme a Petit Pots: Baked Custards French
Take 9 Yolks and one White of an Egg; beat them and put them into a deep Dish or Stew-Pan. Take a pint and a half of New Milk; Boil it and then pour it into the dish with your Eggs constantly stirring them while you pour them in. Sweeten it to your taste with pounded Lump Sugar, and put in two large spoonsful of Orange Flower Water: Then put it into little Cups and bake it in a Baine Marie viz: Take a stew-Pan with some boiling Water, and put the Cups in it & set it on the Stove. Put a Cover on the Stew pan, that fits very close, and lay some fire upon it. Let the Cups stay in until the Custards are quite stiff and set into them. Do not put too much Water in the Pan, for if it comes more than half way up the side of the Cups, it will of course boil in and spoil them.

[p75] A Triffle Miss Hatton
Lay some Cake or Biscuit at the bottom of your Dish, put Brandy sufficient to soak it, make a Custard and pour upon it; Whip a thick Syllabub & put on the Top.

[p96] Triffle {B}
Take Macaroons {pick off the Papers} and Ratafie & Savoy Biscuits. Lay them in a deep Dish until the bottom is covered. Then add in as much Sack as will soak them. Then make a Custard {half Milk and half Cream} when it is a little cool, pour it over it, and fill it to the Brim of the Dish. When cold make a Whip

Syllabub, and froth it over the Custard, raising it as high as you can. Garnish it with Currant Jelly.

[p74] To make German Puffs[66]

Take a pint of Milk, 6 Eggs, leaving out 3 of the Whites and two Ounces of sweet Almonds blanc[h]ed, and beat well in a quarter of a pound of fresh butter, and one spoonful of flour. Mix these Ingredients well together, and sweeten it with Loaf Sugar to your taste. Let your Cups be only half full and bake them half an hour in a slow Oven.

Send them to Table with white Wine, Butter and Sugar.

[66] See Introduction (p.xlv) for the explanation for the placing of this receipt.

Chapter XI: Cakes, Biscuits and Bread

[p94] A Cimmon [*sic*] Cake Mrs C'
One pound ¾ of Flour, one quarter of a Ounce of all Spice; half a pound of Sugar mixed in with the Flour; half a pound of Butter melted in three Quarters of a pint of Milk; half a pint of Yeast and 4 Eggs.

[p7; p53] A very good plain Cake Hads[le]y[67] +
Seven Ounces of Loaf Sugar, four Ounces of Flour well dried & Sifted, 4 Eggs; rub some of the Sugar on the outside of one Lemon. Melt the Sugar in a Table Spoonful of Water, and whilst it is hot put the Whites of the Eggs to it, and whisk it until it is light; then add the Yolks well beat; then the flour. An hour will bake it.

[p9] A light Cake Crawly: Hil: *
One pound of Loaf Sugar broke small, one tea Cup and a half of Water, 2 spoonsful of Rose Water; let them boil a quarter of an hour. Then pour it boiling hot on 12 Eggs beat, leaving out 2 Whites. Whisk it briskly for an hour at least. Then strew in gradually nine Ounces of flower well dried, just before it is put into the Oven. It should be put into the oven as soon as the whisking is finished.

[p122; p125] A Cake[68]
A quarter of a Pint of Water, sit it over the fire with ¾ of a pound of Sugar broke small. Let it just boil up, pour it into a Pot. Add the Yolks of 7 Eggs & the Whites of 5, strained before they are put to the Sugar and Water. Wisk it an hour, and stir in a pound and half of well dried flour. Put a paper in the Pan which must not be buttered. Bake ¾ of an hour.

[p68] A Gateau Fourré
Take between a quarter and half a pound of Butter; put it into a Stew-Pan over a slow Fire with about a quarter of a Pint of Milk; stir it constantly until it melts; put in the Yolks of 12 Eggs, and continue to stirr it over the Fire until it is hot, but do not let it boil. Then pour it over not quite a pound an [*sic*] half of Flour; Add about a spoonful of Yeast, and a very little Salt. Beat it up together with your hands with great Force, and for a very long time. Then put it into a Tin or Earthen Pan, and put it in an Oven, About two hours will bake it. As soon as it

---

[67] Both receipts have the same donor.
[68] Receipt on [p125] is entitled 'A very light Cake'; neither has a donor.

comes out of the Oven, take it out of the Tin, whilst it is hot: Cut it horizontally into three slices {it should be very light and full of holes} have half a pound of Fresh Butter ready melted and quite hot. Pour as much Butter into each slice of the Cake as it will hold, and strew a great deal of Lump Sugar upon it, enough to enter the Cake and sweeten. The Sugar should be in fine powder. Then pour three spoonsful of Orange Flour Water on to it. Lay the Cakes together again, and let the parts of it fit closely to each other, and set it until the next day to cool.

[p152] A Fine Plumb Cake
4 Pounds of fine Flower, dry it well in an Oven or before the fire; when dry beat it all fine. Then take two pounds of butter [and] a pint of Cream, scald the Cream and melt the butter in it. 3 pounds of Currants well dried, ½ a pound of Raisins stoned and minced very small, ¼ of a pound of Almonds blanched and beat with Rose Water, 8 Eggs {But half the Whites} they must be well beaten, put into them a Glass of Mountain Wine; a quart of Ale Yeast. With the flower mix some Cloves, Mace, Nutmegs and Cinnamon beat very fine, ½ a pound of White Sugar, mix all these Ingredients except the Currants. Let it be a little before the fire. When the Oven is ready mix the Currants carefully, that they may not be broken. Butter a Hoop and put it in.

You may put in Oranges or Lemon peel candied & Citron cut in small pieces.

[pp140-141] Plumb Cake
Four pounds of Flour, 7 pounds of Currants well dried, 2 pound of Butter. Rub the butter in the flower, ¾ of a pound of fine Sugar sifted, a Nutmeg and some Mace, ¾ of a pound of Almonds, gently beat with a few spoonsful of Orange Flower Water; a pound of Citron, Orange & Lemon Peel. Put these in the Flower, 10 Eggs, leaving out 3 Whites, a pint of Yeast, a pint of Cream, half a pint of Mountain Wine. Warm the Cream, and mix the Wine and yeast with it. Then mix all together and beat it well. For the Juice, the whites of three Eggs, a pound of Sugar, and a spoonful of Orange Flower Water. Beat it well.

[p123] Pound Cake
1¼ lb of Flour, ¾ of a lb of sugar, one pound of Butter, 10 Eggs, a small TeaCupfull of Brandy, 2 Ounces of sweet Almonds sliced, and a Few Carraway Seeds. Bake it in a quick Oven.

[p141] Pound Cake {without sugar}
Beat a pound of Fresh butter to a Cream; add 6 Eggs and one spoonful of Yeast. Beat all together. Half a pint of new Milk made warm. Then beat them together until of the consistence of thick Cream. Add one pound of fine Flower; one pound of Currants with some Lemon peel and Sweetmeats. When all is mixed together, let it stand at a proper distance from the fire with a Cloth over it for about 2 hours. Then butter the pan in which it is to be baked. Beat it up well before you put it in the Pan, then take care it is put into the Oven immediately.

[p151] A pound Cake[69]
A pound of Butter, beat it in an Earthen Pan until it is ~~*illeg*~~ \like/ fine thick Cream, then have ready 12 Eggs {half the Whites} beat them well with the Butter, a pound of flour well dried, and beat in it a pound of fine Sugar and a few Carraways. Beat it all well together with your hand for an hour, butter the [*blank*] and bake it in a quick oven.

You may for change put in a pound of Currants well washed and picked.

[p80] A Rice Cake E H
Two Ounces of ground Rice pounded and sifted very fine; 4 ounces of Sugar, four Ounces of Flour, the rind of 2 Lemons grated; two Eggs and a quarter of a pound of Butter.

[p153] A Seed Cake
Take one pound of flour, one pound of fine Sugar, half an Ounce of Carraway Seeds; mix them together, set it to the fire to dry the flower well. Then take one pound of butter, beat it until it comes to a Cream; twelve Eggs well beaten {half the Whites} put them to the Butter, then stir in the rest. Butter the Hoop. Take care in baking.

It will keep a Month.

[p158] Almond Wafers
Blanche half a pound of sweet Almonds, cut half of them in thin slices; Beat the other half in a Marble Mortar with their weight of Sugar, and wet it with the Whites of Eggs. Roll it out thin and put on the cut Almonds. Bake it in Tins, and cut it as soon as it comes out of the Oven, and bend on a rolling Pin.

---

[69] Almost the same as Glasse's 'To make a Pound Cake', including the closing comment about adding a pound of currants (*Art of Cookery*, p138).

[p117] Biscuits Mrs Fordham
Eight Eggs, whites included, are to be beat for one hour with a pound of good Loaf Sugar, finely sifted, until the Liquor is as thick as butter. Do not suffer the mixture to stand still; but immediately stir in a pound of the finest Flour by degrees, until the whole be well mixed. Then fill Patty Pans about half full, and bake them.

[p133] Cracknells
Add one pound of Butter to a quart of Flour, half a Nutmeg grated, The Yolks of 4 Eggs beat with 4 Spoonsful of Rose Water. Put the Nutmegs and Eggs with the flour, and wet it into a Stiff Paste with cold Water. Then roll in the Butter, and make them into shapes. Put them in a Kettle of boiling Water. When they swim take them out with a skimmer, and put them into cold Water. When hard, lay them out to dry, and bake them on Tin Plates.[70]

[p136] ~~**Little Cakes \hot/ for Tea**~~ page 12
~~A ¼ of a pound of Flour~~

[p12] Little Cakes {hot} for Tea +
Of Flour ¼ of a pound; of butter ~~the same quantity~~ \a proper quantity/. Mix and rub them finely together; then put in one Egg and one Spoonful of Yeast. Let the Paste be roled very thin & with a Wine Glass divide it into parts of the size you chuse. Bake them on Tin Plates.

[p39] Little Cakes
A pound of flour, a quarter of a pound of Butter, as much moist Sugar, rub the butter well in the flour, and put the Sugar into the Water you wet the flour with; strew in Carraway Seeds; roll this very thin; prick it to prevent its blistering and cut it in shapes; bake in a slow Oven.

[p73] Little Cakes
Half a pound of Butter beat to a Cream. Half a pound of Sugar sifted, 5 Eggs {leaving out one White} well beat: Half a pound of Currants, Orange Peel, Citron &c, and bake them on Tins.

[70] In Smith's receipt 'To make little Cracknels' the biscuits are not put into boiling water before being baked (*Compleat Housewife*, pp178-9).

[p93] Little Cakes From Mrs Hill of Pelham
Have ready a pound of Flour sifted very Fine, and a \pound/ of Fine Sugar sifted. The Yolks of eight Eggs, and Four Whites and beat them well, put to them a large Spoonful of Rose Water. Take a pound of Butter, and work it soft with your hands, then work it in with the Eggs, which being done, put the Sugar to it by degrees, and then the Flour in the same manner, beating it well all the time, and For half an hour after, until your Oven is quite ready, which must be of a very moderate heat.

If you would add Plumbs, you must have ready picked, washed and well rubbed in a Cloth, near a pound of Currants, which must be mixed well in, a Few at a time, and just before you put it in the Oven.

Instead of Currants some use an ounce of Carraway Seeds.

Let the tin pans you bake them in be buttered in order to make them turn out easy, and you must not fill them near full as they will rise very much. Less than an hour is time sufficient for baking it.

This quantity will make 10 or 14 Cakes.

[p91] Small Cakes Mrs Champion
Half a pound of Flour; half a pound of Sugar, six Eggs, half Whites, one spoonful of Orange Flower Water. Fill the Pans half full, they must be well buttered; a little time bakes them.

[p48] Small Tea Cakes Byd
One pound of Flour, two ounces of Butter, four ounces of sifted sugar, one Egg, a quarter of an Ounce of Carraway seeds, as much Milk as will make it fit to roll. Kneed it well together; role it as thin as you please; prick it all over; cut it out with a Drinking Glass. Lay them on Tins & bake them.

[p124] Dutch Biscuits
Two pounds of Flour, 6 Ounces of Butter, rub the Butter into the flower, not too fine. 3 Eggs, 2 large spoonsful of new Yeast, half a spoonful of Sugar, ¾ of a pint of Milk, make them into a paste. Let it stand by a gentle fire to rise. Make them into small loaves & bake up on Tin sheets. Bake them rather more than ¼ of an hour in an Oven Fit for Tarts.

When taken out, cut them in halves, and dry them on Tin Sheets in a slow Oven.

[p73; p7] Gingerbread Miss Jeeves[71]
Take half a pound of flower, three *\quer. one/* quarters of a pound of Butter, one quarter of a pound of Treacle, half *\quer.* ¼/ a pound of coarse Sugar; half an Ounce of Ginger pounded. First, melt the butter and pour it upon the Sugar and Ginger, then mix the Treacle well with it, and put in the flour by degrees, roll it about a quarter of an Inch thick. Cut it in large Cakes, and bake it until it is quite crisp in a cool oven.

[p159] Gingerbread
Take one pound ¾ of Flour, rub in half a pound of Butter; half a pound of Sugar, a large Nutmeg; one Ounce of Ginger; one pound of Treacle; one Ounce of Carraway Seeds. Wash the Pan well with warm Milk. Roll it out, not too thin. Bake it well and Keep it dry.

[p88] Ginger Bread Cakes Lady P
Take ½ a Pound of Flour, two Ounces of Butter without Salt, 2 Ounces of the best moist Sugar, mix them well together. Take a quarter of an Ounce of Flour of Ginger, a quarter of an Ounce of Allspice, 10 Cloves finely ground, a quarter of an Ounce of Orange Chips finely Powdered. Mix these well together; moisten the whole Composition with Molasses; Knead and work it well, Roll it into Cakes for baking. A quarter of an hour in a moderate Oven is sufficient to bake it.

[p38] Maccaroons
Beat a pound of Almonds very fine with rose Water; then take a pound of powdered Sugar and beat it with the Almonds with the Whites of 4 Eggs then lay them on Water [*recte* Wafer] Paper and Bake them in an Oven.

[p104] Maccaroons
Blanch two pounds of Almonds in scalding Water; put to them a ½ pound of sifted Loaf Sugar, pound them in a Stone Mortar with the Whites of 8 Eggs, a little Rose Water. Beat them until rather thicker than butter for Fritters, drop them on Wafers & bake them on Tins.

[p151] Macaroon Biscuits
One pound of Almonds, and beat fine; have ready one pound of fine Sugar beat fine and sifted, a little Rose Water; put all together, and beat it to a paste. Then

---

[71] Both receipts are attributed to Miss Jeeves. Only in the one on [p73] are the quantities of the ingredients queried.

add 4 or 5 Whites of Eggs. Stir it together, and dress it out on a Wafer Paper, dust it with Sugar to make an [*blank*] and bake them in a brisk Oven. When cold break the Wafer Paper from the sides, and put them in a deep Pan to keep moist.

[p165] Macaroon Biscuits Madame de la Combe
Take a pound of fine Sugar finely powdered, divide it into two Parts. Blanche 4 Ounces of sweet Almonds, and two of Bitter Almonds. Pound them in a Mortar until they are fine, mixing by degrees one half of the Sugar with them. Then take the Whites of two new laid Eggs, beat them to as high a froth as you can, and mix them together with a wooden Spoon; and be careful to stir it always one way. Then drop the Cakes with a Tea Spoon upon clean writing Paper, and bake them on Tins in a cool oven, after the Bread has been drawn. When they are brown they are enough. Do not take them off the Paper until they are thoroughly cold, and keep them in a dry Place.

[p48] Oatmeal Cakes Dr R
Put some Oatmeal in a Cup and make a hole in the middle; pour in Water until it is of the consistence of Paste; Add a little salt in mixing it. Let it stand a short time, but not to ferment. Then role it out into small round Cakes divided into quarters, and bake it in an Iron Case over the Fire.

[p40] Olivers Biscuits[72]
3 pound of fine Flower, ½ pint of small beer and yeast; take some warm Milk, put it to your Yeast, and lay it to Sponge, let it remain one hour. Then take a quarter of a pound of ~~Biscuits~~ Butter, and some warm Milk and mix with your Sponge and lay it to rise before the fire; then roll it out in thin Cakes and put them before the Fire; bake them in a slow Oven & put a little Salt to the Flour.

[72] This receipt and the next are for Bath Olivers. Legend has it that near the end of his life Dr Oliver confided the recipe for the Bath Oliver, a savoury biscuit invented for his patients, to his coachman Atkins, giving him at the same time £100 in money and ten sacks of the finest wheat flour. Atkins is said to have opened a shop in Green Street and acquired a large fortune. Although Atkins did not feature in Oliver's will, the story was told to successive generations of the Oliver family. Fortt & Son of Bath, who were manufacturing the biscuit in the 1960s, lost any documents relating to the origins of the recipe when their premises were bombed in 1941 (*ODNB*, 'Oliver, William (1695-1764)').

[p99] Dr Oliver's Biscuits
Two pounds of the finest Flour, thoroughly dried; Two spoonsful of light Yeast, mix it in a little warm milk; put it into the Flour; set it before the fire to rise. Melt a quarter of a pound of Butter in as much Milk as will make it into a stiff paste.

This quantity will make three dozen and a half of biscuits, which must be rolled out thin. Bake them on Tin Plates in a slow Oven.

[p79] Ratifee Cakes Miss H' (?Hatton)
One pound of double refined Sugar, beat it and sift it through a fine Sieve, then take a piece of Gum Dragon as big as a small Walnut, and work it into the sugar, wet it, and make it into a Stiff Paste with White of [*blank*] Eggs beat to a froth. Then take eight Ounces of Apricot Kernels, beat them, and put them into the Paste. Then beat the Paste well, and put it in a Marble Mortar, then roll it about a quarter of an Inch thick, and cut them into any form you please. Lay them on tins and bake them.

The Gum Dragon must be steeped in Water 24 hours before you use it, and worked through a Fine Sieve.

If you cannot get apricot Kernels, 3 Ounces of bitter Almonds will do.

[p8] Rutland Cakes * Miss Ha't
One pound three quarters of Flour, a quarter of a pound of Butter, the same of Sugar and one pint of Milk. Melt the butter in the Milk as warm as from the Cow, to which add two spoonsful of good ale yeast, three Eggs beaten in it with the rind of two Lemons grated, some Currants and Seeds.

[p36] Savoy Biscuits
Take 8 Eggs; separate the Whites from the Yolks, and beat the former until they are very high. Then put in the Yolks with a pound of Sugar, beat this for a quarter of an Hour; and when the Oven is ready put in one pound of Fine Flour, and just stir it until it is mixed. Lay the Biscuits on Paper ?fix them, Let the Oven be hot enough to bake them quick.

[p86] Little Seed Cakes
One pound of flower, six ounces of Butter, half a pound of Loaf Sugar, four Eggs well beat, a few Seeds and a little Lemon Peel. Mix the Sugar and flour, and work the butter well in, put in the Seeds and Lemon Peel, and with the Eggs work them to a paste. Bake them on a Tin, or rather a quick fire.

[p60] Sweet Cakes
Take a large Cup of Loaf Sugar finely powdered, and double the quantity of fine ~~Sugar~~ flour; rub in as much butter as it will take, and add to it the Yolk of an Egg, a few Carraway Seeds and a teaspoonful of Brandy, ~~let~~ roll it thin & cut out the Cakes with a glass. Bake them on a Tin.

[p108] Thin Cakes
Rub the size of an Egg of Butter in three Pints of Flour very fine, make a good hole in the Flour; put the Yolks and Whites of two Eggs and some cold new Milk and Salt. Mix it up to a paste; roll it out, and cut it into what form you please, and bake them on a Girdle. They must be as thin as a Crown.

[p23] Wafer Cakes
Half a pound of flower, half an Ounce of Sugar, half an Ounce of Butter melted in a little warm milk; one spoonful of Yeast & a few Carraway Seeds. Put the butter in last; When cool, mix it into a stiff paste, knead it well; Roll it as thin as possible & cut it with a Glass.

[p49] Water [*recte* Wafer] Cakes Byd
Two pounds of Flour, half a pound of Butter, half a pound of sugar, some Carraway Seeds, a small Coffee Cup of White Wine, two Eggs, half a pint of Cream. Rub the Butter into the flower, then mix all together and make a Paste. Role it thin, and cut it with the Top of a Wine Glass. Prick them or they will blister; Bake them in Tins.

[p177] To keep Yeast Mrs H'y
Boil one Potatoe in as little Water as possible, and one spoonful of Yeast and one of Flour. Beat all well together one hour. Set it by for use.

[p176] To take the bitter out of Yeast
Toast a piece of Bread quite brown, and put it in the Yeast and Water.

[p23] Bath Buns
To one pound of Flower add Seven Eggs well beaten, 4 Spoonsful of White Wine, a little Rose Water; 4 Spoonsful of Yeast; mix them well together, put the Mixture before the fire to rise; Then take a pound of Sugar pounded; half a pound of flour, and three quarters of a Pound of Carraway Comfits. Mix all well together, and make them into bunns; and put them on tin Plates. Strew the remaining quarter of a Pound of Carraway Comfits with a little Sugar upon them. Half an hour will bake them.

[p17] Buns Mrs Anderson Ex[cellent] +
Take a quarter of a Peck of Flower, ½ pound of Moist sugar, ½ pound of Butter, ½ an Ounce of Carraway Seeds; mix these well together, and then take 4 Eggs, Whites and Yolks, and two table Spoonsful of light Yeast; Beat the Eggs and Yeast together, and then put them into the flour and take Milk lukewarm, and make it of the stifness of light Bread, and then role it into Buns, and set them before the Fire, and let them stand for one hour; and when they are fit to put into the Oven, take the Yolk of one Egg and a little Milk, and rub them lightly over with these mixed. Five or six Minuites will bake them.

[p104] Buns
Three pound of Flour, three Eggs, six Ounces of Sugar, half a pound of butter melted with Milk; half a pint of Yeast, one Ounce of Carraway Seeds.

[p106] Carraway Bunns
Two quarters of Flour; one pound of Butter, Nutmeg and a little Mace, rub them lightly together; Four spoonsful of Yeast, a little Sack, Half a pint of Cream; One pound of rough Carraways and four Eggs.

[p83] A considerable Increase by making Bread with Bran Water
For a sack of 5 Bushels or 280 Pounds, boil 25 pounds of Bran in 88 Quarts of Water; this when strained will produce 54 Quarts of Bran liquor. Use this instead of plain Water to make the Dough with the usual quantity of Salt and Yeast. The Bread will weigh 25 pounds more than in the common way; be as white and more moist. The increase is equal in weight to the Bran or 1/15 more in the Bread. This did not answer.

[p84] Bread with Rice Mrs Gardiner
Boil a quarter of a pound of unground Rice until it is quite Soft, pour it on the back of a Sieve to drain it, and when cold mix it with three quarters of a pound of flour, a tea cup full of Yeast, a tea cup full of Milk and a small table Spoonful of ~~Yeast~~ Salt. Let it stand for three hours; then knead it up and roll it up in a handful of flower so as to make the outside dry enough to be put into the Oven. About an hour and a quarter will bake it.

It will weigh one pound 14 Ounces, and will keep eight days.

It should not be eat until it is two days old.

[p111] Dow Nuts[73] Mrs Fordham
A quarter of a Peck of Flower, a pound of moist Sugar, 10 Eggs {Yolks & Whites} one Nutmeg grated, ¾ of a pound of fresh Butter, a quarter of a pint of Yeast. First melt the Butter over the fire in Milk; skim the Butter off. Mix the Sugar and Nutmeg with the Flour, making a hole in it at Top. Strain the Eggs and Yeast mixed together through a Sieve into the Flour; then put the Butter skimmed off the Milk into it also, with as much of the Milk as is necessary to make it into a paste. Let it stand by the fire half an hour to rise, throwing a Cloth over it. Then roll it out thick or thin as you like, cutting it into Nuts with a jagging Iron. Throw them into some Hogs-lard almost boiling hot; if quite boiling they are likely to be black, and if it does not near boil, they will be greasy. Stir them about with a skimmer with holes. Take them out with it, put them in a Cullender but do not put the hot ones to the cold, or they will be then heavy.

The thinner the Paste is rolled, the lighter and more cri[s]p it will be.

A little Sugar should be first put to the yeast and a little Milk, and set it by the Fire an hour to rise.

[p125] To make Muffins
Take 2 pounds of fine Flour, put in a Pan before the Fire to warm. When it is warm, take 3 spoonsful of Fresh small Beer Yeast, mix it with a little warm ~~Yeast~~ Milk; then strain it through a Sieve in the middle of the Flour, and let it stand to rise for a quarter of an hour. Then mix it up, not too stiff, but light, and let it stand half an hour longer to rise. Bake them on a thin Plate of Iron or a Tile Stone.

[p91] French Bread
Take seven pounds of flower, a quart and half a pint of warm Water, put an Ounce and a half of Salt in it, then take a pint of small bear[*sic*] Yeast, mix it altogether; then make it into Dough, let it stand half an hour to rise. Weigh seven Ounces to a roll. Let them stand a quarter of an hour to rise. Put them in a very quick Oven, that they may bake 25 Minuites or less.

---

73 Michael Krondl, a New York-based food writer, suggests that the origin of the American doughnut may well lie in Hertfordshire (See *Herts Past & Present*, 3rd series, no. 21 (Spring 2013), p10). The earliest reference he has found is in William Hone, *The Year Book of Daily Recreation and Information* (1832), p796. Michael has confirmed that ED's receipt is the earliest so far identified (personal communication). It is unfortunate that neither Mrs Fordham, nor *her* source, can be traced (see Appendix II).

[p96] French Rolls
Six quarts of Flour; rub in the quantity of a Walnut of butter, three pints of Milk luke-warm, half a pint of small Beer Yeast with one Egg beat in it, and a little Salt. Strain them mixed together into the Flour, and work it up into a smooth Paste, let it stand before the fire a quarter of an hour to rise. Then make them into Roles. Less than an hour will bake them.

[p119] French Rolls
A pint of Milk with a quart of Water, half a pint of yeast, to be mixed with Flour of a proper thickness for Bread, to stand one hour after it is mixed. To be made into rolls which are baked in 20 Minuites.

[p132] French Roles
Four pounds of the best Lammas Flour; break two Eggs into a Bason, beat them well; take half a pint of Skimmed Milk and a pint & a half of warm Water; Mix it with your Yeast until it curdles, add to it a spoonful of Salt, then strain it through a Fine Sieve. Make a hole in your Flower, put in your Milk and Eggs, Yeast and Water. Mix it well but not too stiff. Let it lie until it rises; then Mould them not too big, and let them stand on raspins of Bread until they rise, put them in a quick Oven; Let them stand 20 Minuites.

[p46] Roles
Take more than a ¼ of a Peck of Flour, put it into a wide Pan, then take the whites of 3 Eggs well beat, as much Barm as you think will raise it, without making it bitter; Add warm Milk to make it up mixed with the above. Work it for a ¼ of an hour, until the Dough comes off your hands without sticking. Set it before the fire to rise half an hour: Make them up & put them in Paper Pans, let them stand a little time before you put them in the Oven. Half an hour will bake them in a quick Oven. When they are taken out, rasp them.

[p104] Short Roles
A quarter of a Peck of fine Flower; break into it ¾ of a pound of Fresh butter in small bits; put in some Salt, Sugar, beaten spice & Coriander Seed bruised, and a quarter of a Pint of Ale Yeast. When you have mingled them all well together, wrap it up in a warm Cloth to rise; and when the oven is ready make it into Rolls, prick them, bake and when you ~~cover~~ \draw/ them, cover them until they are cold, and make them into a paste with Canary and warm Milk.

[pp112-113] Potatoe Bread

Pare the Potatoes, put them into cold Water the day before they are baked and boil them over a moderate fire until well done and pour the Water from them and mash them with a Spoon. Set the Pan by the fireside covered close for a quarter of an hour to make them as dry as possible. Then turn them out into a Dish, and set them in an airy place all night. Weigh one part [of flour] in three of Potatoes. Mix the Flour and Potatoes together, and sift it through a coarse hair Sieve, take as much yeast as will make the same quantity of flour light, put two Eggs, beat it together with as much hot Water as will make it warm, and lay it to rise like other Bread.

[p23] Tops and Bottoms

Take four Pound of flower, three Ounces of Sugar, 5 Ounces of Butter, 4 Eggs well beat; A Pint of New Milk. Mix the Ingredients very well, set them before the fire to rise. Then Mould them in two parts in the form of a Loaf of Bread; but very small.

[p76] Wiggs[74] Miss Hatton

Take 3 pound of ~~Sugar~~ Flour, one of butter; melt it in as much Milk as you think it will make it very light, and full half a pint of all Yeast [*sic*; *recte* ale Yeast]; Put the Ale and Yeast [*sic*; *recte* ale yeast] into the flour, and stir it as you do for a Cake, then set it by the fire to rise for half an hour, then work in one pound of Sugar and one Ounce and a half of Carraway Seeds; then let it rise by the fire a little longer.

[74] Wigs were wedge-shaped buns of enriched bread that were eaten at breakfast, which, in the eighteenth century among the leisured classes was usually at about 10 o'clock (Lehmann, *British Housekeeper*, pp301-3).

Chapter XII: Little Savoury Dishes

[p115] To do Pigs Ears
Cut them in long slips, put them in the Stew-pan with a little White Gravy made very good with Veal, and about half a pint of good Cream; half an onion and a little White ~~Vinegar~~ Pepper and Salt. Then stew them about ½ an hour, or until you think they are tender enough. Then thicken it with butter and flour, and give it one boiling. Then take a little Parsley, not boiled, mince it fine \&/ put it in. Do not set it in the Fire after adding the parsley, which would spoil it.

[p12] To dress Hogs feet and Ears +
When nicely cleaned put them in a Pot with a Bay Leaf, a large Onion, and as much Water as will cover them. Season with Salt and a little Pepper, bake them with Household Bread. Keep them in this Pickle until you want them, then take them out and cut them in hansome pieces; fry them and take for sauce 3 spoonsful of the Pickle. Shake in some Flower, a piece of Butter, and a spoonful of Mustard. Lay the Ears in the middle, the Feet round, and pour the Sauce over.

[p149; p112] Calves Brains to dress B D Ck[75]
Three Yolks of Eggs, a handful of Crumbs of Bread, a little Salt & Pepper, beat up with the Calves brains. Put about half a spoonful of it into the frying Pan when it boils. Five Minuties will boil your forced Meat Balls.

[p55] Calves Feet
Take two Calves Feet, put them into a Pan with 2 Quarts of new Milk, add one Ounce of Isinglass, half a pound of Sugar, a little Nutmeg; tie a piece of brown Paper over it, and set it in a slow Oven three or Four hours. When taken out, strain the Liquor through a Sieve, and when Cold, take off the Fat quite clear.
This quantity will keep well 3 or 4 days.

[p107] To dress Calfs feet
Take four Calves feet and clean them well; then boil them quite tender, cut them in halves, and dip them in butter and fry them to a fine light brown. For sauce take a quarter of a pint of Vinegar, a table spoonful of mustard, a piece of Butter rolled in flour, and a little Salt. Keep the Sauce stirring until it boils; then pour it over the feet and serve it up.

[75] Receipt on [p112] has no donor.

[p40] Calves feet a la Sainte Manchoult[76]

Split them down the middle; tie them with twine, and put them into a Saucepan with some good broth, a spoonful of Hogs lard, a Glass of Brandy, some parsley, chives, 2 Cloves of Garlick, 3 Cloves, 2 Bay Leaves, Thyme, Bazil, Salt and bruised Pepper; let this stew over a very slow fire; When the feet is [*sic*] done and the sauce is nearly dried up to get half cold; then take them out of the sauce, and cover them with grated crums of Bread; strew lightly over some of the same grease over the Bread, then broil them carefully.

Cheese & cheese dishes

[p112] Loggerhead Cheese

Two pints of Cream, and 2 gallons of Milk warm from the Cow, and as much rennet as will turn it. Take the Whey from it and add a good deel [*sic*] of Salt; tie the Curd up in a Cheese Cloth, that the remainder of the Whey may run from it. Hang it up on a Nail, until it has substance enough to be put in a Net. Hang it in a Net until quite dry, 3 or 4 Months. After which when almost fit for use, lay it in an Earthen Pan covered up.

---

[76] This should be 'à la Sainte Menehout', a method of cooking meat that has been dipped in breadcrumbs. Sainte-Menehould is a district in the department of Marne, France, famous for its charcuterie, especially pigs' trotters. Alexandre Dumas, in *Le Grand Dictionnaire de Cuisine*, gives the origin of dishes 'à la Sainte Menehould' (quoted in Glasse, p197). 'One evening, following a great battle against the English, King Charles VII . . . came to lodge for the night in the little town of Sainte-Menehould, in which only five or six houses survived, the town having been burned. The king and his suite were dying of hunger. The ruined and ravaged countryside was lacking in everything. Finally, they managed to get hold of four pig's feet and three chickens. The king had with him no cook, male or female; so the wife of a poor edge-tool maker was charged with cooking the chickens. As for the pig's feet, there was nothing to do but put them on the grill. The good woman roasted the chickens, dipped them in beaten egg, rolled them in breadcrumbs with fines herbes, and then, after moistening them with a mustard sauce, served them to the king and his companions, who devoured the pig's feet entire and left only the bones of the chickens.' Massialot (pp83, 188, 192) gives recipes for chickens, pigeons and pigs-pettitoes à la Sainte Menehout; an alternative name was 'à la Mazarine'.

[p38] Rich Cheese
A pound and a half of old Cheshire Cheese; shave it very thin; then put it in a Mortar and add to it a quarter of an Ounce of Mace beat fine and sifted, half a pound of butter and a Glass of White Wine, mix and beat them together, and when perfectly incorporated put it in a pot. Cut it out occasionally in thin slices.

[p107; p150] A six Hour Cheese
Take a Napkin twice doubled in a pewter Soup Plate; pour into it a pint of very sweet Cream in the morning: Cover it over with the ends of the Napkin and put a Cullender over it. In the evening, turn it into a clean Napkin and plate, clip the edges round before you put it into the second Napkin.

If you chuse to eat it in hot Weather change the Napkin in three hours.[77]

[p4] Maccaroni (Daubigny) +
Take three Ounces of Maccaroni, put to it half a pint of Water or Broth, 2 or 3 bits of Suet, boil it till it begins to be tender, then take out the Suet, and if the Liquor is not quite wasted, pour it off. Put in three Ounces of rich Cheese, and as much Cream as it requires to stew it until it is dissolved. Pour it into a Dish, grate Cheese over it, and brown it with a Salamander.

[p88] To make Macaroni Miss Byron
3 Ounces of Macaroni boiled in a quart of Water: Strain off the Maccaroni; then add 3 Ounces of Parmesan Cheese, and one Ounce of Single Gloucester, one ounce of flour, 3 Tablespoonsful of Cream, double the quantity of Milk, a very little Veal Broth, and half an Ounce of Butter. Put them into a Stew Pan; boil it over a Stove until it comes to a proper thickness, and Salt it to your taste.

The Cheese must be grated very small.

[p96] To dress Macaroni Mrs C'
Put it into a Saucepan with Water enough to cover it, some Lemon Peel & a bit of Cinnamon. When it is tender add some Cream and Sugar. Take out the Lemon Peel and Cinnamon, and serve it up hot. It will take three hours steeping.

---

[77] The final line on [p150] reads: 'In hot Weather, if you chuse to eat it in 6 hours, change the Napkin in three hours'.

[p126] Macaroni Almacks[78]
Boil a little Macaroni until it is tender. Then rasp some Cheshire Cheese fine; boil a little thick Cream in a Stew-pan. When it boils put in the Cheese. Stir it over the Fire until it thickens. Put the Macaroni in the bottom of the Dish, and pour the Cheese over it. Have a Salamander ready to brown it.

[p168] Macaroni Mrs Kennett
Boil the Macaroni in Milk until it is soft, and then drain it through a sieve: some grated Cheese {Parmesan is the best} and some Cream must be put into a saucepan with a little pepper and salt, and a little butter, and made hot: The Macaroni is to be put into a dish and these ingredients poured over it. And a little dried Cheese grated on the top, and then burned with a Salamander.

[p5] Fondool {a Kind of Ramakin}
Six Table Spoonsful of grated Parmesan Cheese. The Yolk of three Eggs beat. The Whites whisked very hard by themselves. A Tea Cup full of whisked Cream.

The way to mix them

First the Yolks of the Eggs that are beat must be beat up with the Cheese; Then put the Cream that is whisked with it, and then mix the Whites of the Eggs, that are whisked very hard, all together; and put the whole into Papers, and bake them a quarter of an hour in a slow oven. They should be eaten quite hot when they will be very light.

[p26] Ramakins Mrs M
A quarter of a pint of Cream; the crumb of a half penny Role, Let it soak in the Cream; a quarter of a pound of Old mild Cheese, two Ounces of butter, which add to the Cheese grated, and put in a Stew Pan. Give it three turns over the fire. The Yolk of three Eggs well beat and the Whites whisked. Mix all together and

---

[78] This probably refers not to Almack's Assembly Rooms in King Street, St James's, but to Almack's Club, 50 Pall Mall, founded in 1762 by William Almack, who undertook to provide the members of his club with dinner, newspapers and gambling (Weinreb and Hibbert, p20). Apparently the most dedicated members of Almack's was a sophisticated set who called themselves 'Macaronis', a corruption of the Italian, 'maccherone', meaning a coxcomb. "They were exquisites who had travelled to Italy and prided themselves on the elegance of their dress and manners. At their insistence, macaroni was put on the menu at Almack's" (Anthony Lejeune, *White's: The First Three Hundred Years* at http://www.almacks.com/history-02.html [accessed 31/03/12]).

put in Patty Pans or Papers. A quarter of an hour will bake them in a Dutch Oven.

[p76] Ramakins Miss Hatton
Take half a pound of mild Cheshire Cheese, and a quarter of a pound of Butter, the Yolk of four Eggs. Pound it in a Mortar until it is quite fine and looks light; then beat it with a spoon, and make it as light as possible; have thin slices of Bread which must be fried in butter, and then spread them over with the Cheese and put them in the Dish they are designed to come to Table in. Have ready a hot salamander over them until you see they are done enough, look brown, and begin to rise.

[p96] To make Ramakins {B}
Grate of Cheshire Cheese and of Gloucester Cheese an equal quantity. Mix it with three Eggs quite smooth. Then cut a piece of Butter about the size of a large Walnut, and mix with your Ingredients, and as much Cream as will make it a Fine thick Batter. Then put it in small shapes. A few Minuites will bake it.

[p101] A Ramakin Mrs D[imsdale] of Hitchin
Take one Egg, and the weight of it in butter, with the weight of both in mild fat Gloucester Cheese shaved very thin, beat together in a Marble Morter. Having two Toats [*sic*; *recte* Toasts] ready, spread them with it, and have a Salamander or Dutch Oven ready to brown it. When of a proper Colour, cut them to pieces & send them to Table.

[p107] Ramakins Mrs M'rs
Half a pound of double Gloucester Cheese grated, three Eggs beat & a pound and half quarter of a pound [1⅛lb] of butter clarified, and a quarter of a pint of Cream mixed together. They are to be put into writing Paper doubled as small as Patty Pans, and to be baked for a quarter of an hour.

Other 'vegetarian' savoury dishes
[p112] Amlet B D's Cook
Break 8 or 10 Eggs, use both Yolks and Whites into a Pan, beat them well together, then shred in some parsley, and add a little piece of Butter, about an Ounce. Put a good piece of butter into a Stew-pan. Let it melt; then put in the mixture. Move it about and take care it does not burn. When enough on one side, turn it with a Knife and ~~add~~ do the other.

[p24] Omlet ?Wiltjie
Take 8 Eggs, break in a stew pan, add chopped Parsley, thyme, Chives and a few sweet herbs, pepper and salt and small pieces of Butter: Beat all these well together, and fry it over a quiet fire. For sauce: a little Gravy, Ham and Lemon, taken out when served up.

[p25] Omlet Orme
Ten Eggs, leaving out half the Whites, put them in a Pan; beat them well together: Chop ten or more young onions and a little Parsley, 3 Anchovies very finely chopped; add all these to the Eggs; Mix them well together, taste it, and if it is not relishing enough, add a little of the Liquor of Anchovies. Put a good piece of Butter in the frying Pan, let it boil, then put the Eggs in, and stir it all together.[79] Let it harden at bottom, but <u>not</u> at the Top; Double it, and put it in a dish with some Gravy.

When the Omlet is frying, take care to move it round the edge with a Knife; and when you can double it, it is done enough.

[p31] Beignets a l'Allemande
Take 8 Potatoes and boil them, pound them immediately in a Mortar with about one third of Butter, 3 Yolks of Eggs, a little Parsley and Chalot chopped very fine, season it with a little Pepper & Salt, then roll it up into little Balls of the size of a Green Gage Plumb, break two eggs into some crumbs of bread as for frying fish & dip the Balls into it to form a Crust round them, then fry them in boiling butter.

You may roll forced or minced Meat {as for Petit Pa't'es [Patties]}[80] instead of Potatoes, and do them with the Egg & Bread as above.

When they are made of Meat they are called <u>Croquettes</u>.

[p81] Irish Macani Lord O
Boil Potatoes as for mashing, then mash them fine.

Put a good lump of Butter with an Onion in a Tos pan. When just on the turn for browning, drudge in a little flour: stir it well up, and put a little good white Gravy to it when it boils, add a little Cream.

---

[79] The phrase 'the Eggs in, and stir it all together' has a line across the tops of the letters: as it would not make sense for this instruction to be crossed out, it is likely that the line is underlining 'Put a good piece of Butter in the frying pan'.

[80] See, for example, Glasse's receipt 'Petit Patties for Garnishing of dishes' (*Art of Cookery*, p60).

Add your Potatoes to this sauce with a small Tea Cup full of grated Cheese. Two minuites before you dish it, add the Yolks of two Eggs, beat up in two spoonsful of Cream; Season to your taste.

Parmesan Cheese is best, and as the quantity of Potatoes is not mentioned this must be ascertained by trial.

[p20] Panada[81]

Take of the Crumbs of Bread sliced very thin as much as will fill a Breakfast Cup, a blade of Mace and a Pint and half of Water. Boil them together until the Bread breaks without stirring the Liquor, or until the Liquor begins to appear curdled or smooth like Jelly. About a quarter of an Hour is sufficient. When taken add a little Sugar, Wine or Spice as agreable.

Sausages

[p105] Black Puddings

Scald some Milk; put it to some whole Oatmeal. Let it lie all night. One handful of Penny Royal, spice and Salt, Hogs Fat and as much Blood as will make it look thoroughly red.

[p10] Norwich Sausages *

4½ pound of the lean of a Loin of good Pork; 3¼ pounds of Bacon clear of Skin. Cut these in slices with a Knife, small and separately, then mix them together and chop them fine: Then add ⅛ of a bunce[*sic*] of ground Pepper; 2¼ Ounce of common Salt, ¼ of an Ounce of Mace fine and ¼ of an Ounce of Nutmeg or rather more, grated fine.

The Ingredients should be first mixed up well together; then sprinkled amongst the Meat, regularly and well. Then fill the Hog's Guts with it, but if stuffed too full they will be apt to burst in dressing.

[p122] Oxford Sausages

Take a Leg of Veal, cut out all the Bones, Gristle and Skin; and a Leg of Pork. To four pounds of Veal, add three pounds of Pork. Put in the fat of the Veal and three pound of Beef Suet, and some brown Sage chopped fine. Ten or twelve Eggs, mix them up with Salt and Pepper to your Taste. It must be pretty stiff. If you find they are too tender to fry, add a little grated Bread. Make the Pan quite hot before you put the Sausages in. You need not put in anything to fry them in.

---

[81] Raffald has a receipt for a savoury panada, with onion and peppercorns, but says 'You may use sugar and currants instead of onions and peppercorns if you please' (*Experienced English Housekeeper*, p148).

[p150] Oyster Sausages
Take some Meat either of Fresh Beef or Mutton, but take care it is tender and free from strings. Chop it as fine as for forced Meats, shred small. Season it with a little Allspice and Pepper to your taste. Then take a good quantity of oysters and clean them out of their Liquor. Shred them small and mix with the other ingredients. The Moisture of the Oysters will bind them enough together. Take care that they are Salt enough, and if necessary add some. Roll them into large Sausages, Flowering your hands as you roll them. Fry them in butter.

Dish them with sippets of toasted Bread.

[p28] Sausages
One pound of the lean and half a pound of \the/ fat \of/ Pork, half a pound of lean Suet all chopped very small. A small handful of Sage, grated Nutmeg, pepper and Salt to your taste. Beat the ingredients in a Mortar until fine.

[p86] Sausages
One pound and a half of fat Pork, and one pound of Lean. Lay a layer of each; then add half a handfull of beaten Black Pepper, a spoonfull of Suet, 3 Eggs, and a handful of grated Bread; the same quantity of shred Sage and the same of Marjoram. Let it stand one day mixed before it is put into the Skins; then hang them up to dry.

[p134] Sausages Lady G'd'
Two pounds of lean Pork, one pound of Veal, beat them well together with a rolling Pin. Add the weight of Meat in Beef Suet. Chop them together, add a handful of Sage cut Fine, pepper and Salt to your Taste. Mix all with 8 Eggs, half a Nutmeg. Being all well pounded and chopped. It may be used without putting in skins.

[p143] Sausages
1 leg of young Pork; cut off the lean, and shred it very small, leave not any of the Skin or Shreds. Take 2 pounds of Suet shred small; two handsful of red Sage, a little Pepper, Salt and Nutmeg; a small piece of Onion. Chop the Flesh and suet, and the rest together. When it is small enough, add the Yolks of 2 or 3 Eggs; mix all together and Form a Paste. Roll out as many pieces as you please in the Form of a common Sausage & fry them.

This paste will Keep a Fortnight.

Vegetables

[p134] To stew Cabbage

Brown a quarter of a pound of Butter, add a little Pepper, Salt and Vinegar {about a Tea Cup Full}, into these put some White Cabbage chopped as small as for Soup. Let it stew by the fire 2 or 3 hours, & just as you send it to Table add a little melted Butter. Stir it well together and particularly while it is stewing.

[p164] Colliflower to dress

Put a little Flour and Water into a Stew Pan, and when it is mixed, put in a lump of butter, the Yolk of an Egg, a little Pepper and Salt and a very little Vinegar. When the Colliflower is well boiled and the Water drained from it, break it small, lay it in a Dish, and pour the Sauce over it.

[p62] Stewed Cucumbers

Take some Cucumbers, pare, slice them, and cut into small pieces, and some Onions cut small and mix with them. Fry them brown with a little Butter, some strong Gravy, a little Catchup and a Glass of Red Port Wine.

[p107] To stew Cucumber Duchess of An[caste]r

Cut the Cucumbers, sprinkle them with Salt, wipe them dry, fry them in fresh butter until they are of a fine brown; put them in a good strong gravy with a Clove of Shallots and white pepper, or any other spice. When sufficiently stewed, thicken the sauce with flour and butter.

[p31] To stew Cucumber brown

Pare and slice them with a piece of onion; then put in a piece of butter in a frying Pan, and when it is hot put in your Cucumbers with flour on them; Stew them until they are brown; then take them out of the Pan, and put them into a saucePan with a little Sauce made of Broth or Gravy that is savory. When they are done, burn a piece of Butter in a Pan and when sufficiently burned, put in your Cucumber by degrees, and season with pepper & Salt.

[p30] French Beans stewed White

Boil them, put to them little Cream, gravy, pepper, salt, a bit of butter mixed with some flower. Boil the whole together.

[p31] French Beans done Brown

Do not split them but cut them in two, fry and drain them, Shake over a little flower; put to them some good gravy, an Onion, a little bruised Cloves, Chyan Pepper, Salt and some Catchup. Boil it up, shaking it. Take out the Onion.

[p54] To drop Caravansera French Beans
Cover them with Water and let them stew gently until quite tender. Then pour off the Water and put them into a Stewpan with gravy. Season them to your taste, and let them stand some time on the fire. They will take two or three hours in dressing.

[p164] French Beans
Put a lump of Butter into a Stew-pan, when melted, put in a small Onion shred very fine, and a little hot Water immediately put on it, or it will burn at the bottom of the Pan. When the Beans are boiled, and the Water quite drained from them, put them into the Butter; strew a little Pepper and Salt over them; add a little Milk and stir them constantly over the Fire. When they are thouroughly hot, and ready to serve up, mix the Yolks of two Eggs in a little Milk, and pour over the Beans, and shake them in it for a moment over the fire, but not to boil, or they will be spoiled.

About a ¼ of a pint of Milk is sufficient for the whole.

[p20] Stewed Mushrooms Cock [?Cook] Crawford
Clean them, let them soak for half an hour with a little Lemon-Juice squeezed in the Water. Put them in a Sieve to drain. Put a piece of Butter in the Pan, then throw in the Mushrooms, sprinkle a little Salt. Let them stew gently over a slow Fire for half an hour, ~~then take off~~, take them off, add half a pint of Milk, a piece of Butter rolled in flour, pepper and Salt to the taste. Put them on the fire to simmering.

[p32] Mushrooms stewed white
Wipe some large Buttons; boil them up quick in a little Water; put to them some Cream, a little butter mixed with flower; a very little Madeira, salt and Chyan Pepper and Nutmeg. You may add a little Lemon Juice.

[p30] Stew Pease
Take one good Cabbage Lettuce, cut it in two, put it in a stew Pan over a slow Charcoal fire. When the Water is a little Drawn from it put in your pease, and let them stew slowly, covering them close until they are sufficiently tender, and drawing the Liquor off if you find they produce too much. Thicken them with a little flower and Butter.

[p17] To make Pease boil Green
Add a little Pot ash to the Water.

[p46] Petits pois a la Bourgeoise[82]
Take as many Pease {Green} as will make a good Dish, wash them and put them in a Stew-pan with a piece of Butter, some Parsley and sives, and a Cabbage Lettuce split in 4. Let them stew in their own Liquor over a slow fire for an hour and a half. When they are tender and scarce any sauce remaining, put in a little sugar, very little salt and two Yolks of Eggs, beat up with some Cream, warm it, but do not let it boil.

Some leave out the Eggs and Cream, serving the Pease with their own Liquor, having them nearly dry.

[p88] A very good and cheap Vegetable Hodge Podge
Put half a pound of Scotch Barley into four quarts of Water. Let it boil gently between 2 and 3 hours {[or] overnight}. Cut some Carrots, Turnips, Onions, {or rather Leeks} and Celery into small pieces, and stew them with it until it is of a proper thickness. Put it in the fire the following Morning & cut some Savoy, Cabbages, Sprouts or other Grains [*sic*; *recte* Greens] into small pieces, fry them, and put them into the Stew with Pepper and Salt to your taste.

If a small piece of pickled Pork is added, it greatly improves it, or by using the Liquor in which Meat has been boiled, instead of Water.

[82] Glasse has 'To dress Veal a la Bourgoise', which includes a sauce made with egg yolks and a little gravy (*Art of Cookery*, p28).

Chapter XIII: Potting and Collaring

[p154] Collar Beef
Take a Flank of Beef, take off the inner Skin, wet it with red Wine {Claret}, Salt it with an Ounce of Salt Petre beat and Common Salt. Let it lay 24 hours, then shred some Savory and other sweet herbs very small and some Spice. Stew [*sic*; *recte* strew] it thick over the inside, roll it up very hard, bind it with Tape. Then put in a Pan with a pint of red Wine and bake it. If not tender when drawn, turn it and put it in the Oven and let it lye a little longer. Then take out the Liquor and let it drain until cold.

[p34] Hambed Beef
Take the lean part of a Buttock of Beef raw; rub it well with brown Sugar all over, and let it lay in a Pan or Tray 2 or 3 hours turning it ~~every day~~ \several times/.* Then roll it very strait in a coarse Cloth and put it in a Cheese press for 24 hours. After that hang it to dry in a chimney. When you boil it put it in a Cloth. When it is cold it will cut into Shivers.

* Salt it well with common Salt and Saltpetre and let it lie a fortnight, turning it every day.

[p161] Beef Hams
Take a leg of fat, but small Beef; Cut it in the form of a Ham. One Ounce of Bay Salt, an Ounce of Salt-Petre, a pound of Common Salt and a pound of coarse Sugar {this quantity does for 14 or 15 pound weight}. Rub it with the ingredients; turn it daily, and baste it well for one Month with the Pickle. Take it out, roll it in Bran or Saw Dust; then hang it in Wood Smoke for a Month. Next take it down and hang it in a dry place, not very hot. You may cut it in pieces and dress it in rashers, or when cold rasp it fine, and eat it as Dutch Beef.

A thick Briscuet of Beef may be done afterwards in the same Pickle. Let it lay one Month rubbing it daily with the same pickle, then boil it until tender. Hang it in a dry place. It eats well cold.

A shoulder of Mutton laid in this Pickle for a Week, and hung in Wood Smoke for a few days, and then boiled with Cabbage, is very good.

[p105] To pot Beef
Take a piece of the thick Flank or Stocking piece; cut it in Pieces & put it into pickle made with one Ounce of Salt-Petre and white Salt as will make the pickle strong to bear an Egg; let it lie 4 or 5 days; then put it in a pan to Bake. Put about half an Ounce of Pepper {Jamaica} beaten over it, but no liquor. When it

is well baked, put it in flakes, and press it close in a pot; skim off some of the fat, and mix with it to moisten; then pour over the rest of the Fat to cover it instead of Butter.

[p142] To rough Beef
To 20 pounds of Beef add one pound of common Salt, 2 Ounces of Salt-Petre; Warm them separately [by] the fire; then mix the Salt-petre with a handful of common Salt warm. Rub the Beef over by the fire until it is all well penetrated. Then mix the remains of the Salt with a pound of coarse Sugar and rub over the Beef. Then place it in the Cellar or cold place. The Brine will run in 2 or 3 days. Observe to turn it and rub the brine over it for nine days: Neglecting this will spoil the Meat if ever so well salted. Then take it out of the Pickle; wipe it dry with a coarse Cloth; and throw a handful of Flower over it; and hang it to dry in a room, where a constant fire is Kept.

[p120] To salt a Buttock of Beef in a Few hours Mrs D' H'
Take out the Bone and Kernels as clean as possible. Then tye it together tight with a small Cord. Having filled the Pan, which should hold a bushel of soft Water; lay it on Sticks, after having rubbed it moderately with common Salt. Then Cover it as thin as a Crown piece with a tenth part of Bay Salt, mixed with Common Salt. The Beef will be Fit to dress in 36 hours, turning it once or twice.

[p121] To salt Beef
Rub it well with Salt, but let the dish be tilted, so that the Meat may not soak in the Brine, which makes it hard; but it should be well rubbed with the Brine daily.

[p99] To salt Beef red Keyser [*or*, Kuper]
A Buttock of Beef of 60 lb is treated as follows. First rub it well over with common Salt. Let it remain for 24 hours. Then pour away what has drained from it, and rub it well over for sometime with full two Ounces of Cochineal finely powdered, and mixed well together with~~out~~ \about/ ½ or ¾ of a pound of coarse Sugar. After these have been thoroughly rubbed in the Beef {and worked into the holes if you like to have it stuffed after you have boiled it} rub in some common Salt, and strew it over at Top; perhaps about a Pound of Salt more or less according as you like for Saltness; let it remain 5 or 6 days or a week: And it will not be amiss to rub it twice in a day. Put it in a Copper of Water pretty hot, not quite boiling and let it do slowly. It will take 6 hours.

It cuts quite red and is not Salt.

[p34] Beef Scarlet
Take a Brisket rub it over with half a pound of bay Salt & a little White salt mixed. Put it in a pan; turn it every day for four days, it will be red. Boil it four hours and serve it with Savoy, or any other Vegetables. Garnish with Parsley.

[p81] The Peak Receipt
Take a round of Beef of about 20 pounds; Salt it with a quarter of a pound of Saltpetre at first, and then with as much common Salt as will make a brine for it. It must be turned in the Brine every day for 10 days. Then take some Bacon and cut it into square pieces, and season them with Cloves and Mace pounded Fine. You are to stuff the Beef in one place with Bacon, and in another place with Sage and Parsley cut small. Tye it round with a fillet or Cloth. Bake it in a Pan with a little Water at the bottom to prevent it cracking. The oven should have the same heat as for brown Bread, and six hours will bake it. Let it be covered with a thick coarse paste to keep it from drying.

It is good hot or Cold.

[pp146-147] To cure Beef or Pork \to keep/ many Years to be red & Juicy
Sir C Knowles[83]

Cut up the Beast immediately after being Killed, and sprinkle it all over with Salt pounded fine, made as hot in an oven as the hand can bear. Mix with an Ounce of Salt-petre to every hundredweight of Beef, and lay each piece on a sloping shelf for 24, 36 or 48 hours according to the heat or coldness of the Weather. Wipe each piece well with dry coarse Cloths, and rub it with a quantity of Salt pounded and dried well mixed with half the quantity of best dried Muscovado Sugar, and packed into Casks, or other Vessels for use.

NB Sir C K-- made use of 24 lb weight of Salt, 12 pounds of Sugar, 3 Ounces of Salt petre to three quarters of a hundred of Beef.

---

[83] Sir Charles Knowles, first Baronet (*d.* 1777), naval officer, chief of the surveying branch of the Russian navy 1770-1774 (*ODNB* 'Knowles, Sir Charles (d.1777)'). His method for curing meat can be found in several contemporary printed receipt books. Successful preservation of the meat depended on it being hot (ie very recently slaughtered) when first salted. For a printed version, see, for example, Farley, *London art of cookery* (9th edition, 1800), pp289-90.

[p122] Hamburg Pickle[84]
4 Gallons of Water, 6 pounds of Common Salt, half a pound of Brown Sugar, 4 Ounces of Saltpetre. Boil it well, strain it, and when cold put in the Beef, Mutton, Pork or Tongue. Keep the Meat covered with brine & in 9 or 10 days it will be fit for use, or keep it longer.

It will keep in pickle 2 or 3 Months. The pickle should be boiled up, and skimmed well at the end of six Weeks; and afterwards every Month or three Weeks.

[p90; p160] To pickle Pork or Beef Mrs C'n (?Champion)[85]
Four Gallons of Water, put in one pound of coarse \brown/ Sugar, two Ounces of Salt-Petre, and six pounds of common Bay Salt, boil it & scum it as long as any Scum rises; When cold put in the Meat, which must be quite covered with Liquor.

[p82] To cure Bacon
To a large Flitch of Bacon add 6 Ounces of Salt Petre, rub it well an hour before with common Salt, then keep it a fortnight and turn it and salt it again. Then let it lay a Week and hang it up to dry. After it is dry, keep it in clean Wheat Straw.

[pp47-48] To make a Ham of 16lb weight
Take 3 Ounces of Salt Prunella; half a pound of very coarse Sugar
3 Ditto of Bay salt
All these Ingredients should be rubbed fine in a Mortar

When the Ham is cut off, rub it well with common salt, and let it lay one Night that the Blood may drain out. Then take a small quantity {about half an Ounce} of salt Prunella in fine Powder and opening the knuckle near the Bone, pour it in; then hang it up one Night and having mixed the above Ingredients, rub the Ham well with them, and afterwards add as much common Salt over the Ham as appears necessary. Lay it in a Pan or Dish {skin downwards} for two days; then turn it, and continue to do it for three weeks. Afterwards dry it.

The proportions for Ingredients for the sides, for Pork or Bacon, may be 4 Ounces of salt Prunella, 4 Ounces of Bay salt for each side, which being well rubbed in; Common salt is then used as before directed to brine it. It is supposed

---

[84] In her journal of her visit to Russia Elizabeth recorded that a dinner included a 'Fine piece of Hamburgh Beef', which may be the origin of this receipt (Cross, *An English Lady*, p68).

[85] Receipt on [p160] has no donor.

that the addition of much sugar makes Ham less likely to keep, and more subject to be eaten by Maggots &c.

When made, Ham and Bacon are best kept dry in saw Dust. Salt Prunella is recommended, as the too free use of Common Salt at first renders the Ham and Pork more likely to be hard & salt.

[p125] To cure a Ham
For a Ham of 16 lb weight, take one pound of Bay Salt, half a pound of common Salt; one ounce of Black Pepper, 2 ounces of Salt-petre. After it had lain therein 3 or 4 days, put in one pound of Treacle. Lay it a Month in Pickle; and before it is dressed lay it a ~~Month~~ \Night/ in Water.

[p136] To cure two middle sized Hams
Two Ounces of Salt Petre, a quarter of a pound of Bay Salt, one pound of Sugar.

[p97; p8] An excellent Receipt to cure Ham[86] B
To every Ham use two Ounces of Saltpetre; beat it and rub your Ham well over Night. Next day take a pound of Common Salt, two Ounces of Bay Salt, a pound of coarse Sugar: Mix all well together, and rub it well into the Hams, and put it in a deep Pan, and turn every day, rubbing it well with the Brine for a Month. Then take it out and dry it gradually.

[p147] To cure a Ham
To one of 16 pounds weight add a pound of Bay Salt, ½ a pound of Common Salt, one Ounce of Black Pepper, 2 Ounces of Salt-petre. Having laid in these 4 Days, put on one pound of Treacle. Let it lay one Month in pickle, and one Night in Water before it is dressed.

[p84] To cure Hams Mrs Hall
To a large Ham take a pound of Bay Salt; half a pound of common Salt, two Ounces of Salt-petre and an Ounce of Salt Prunella, pound all these in a Mortar and add to them two Ounces of black Pepper ground. Rub them well into the Ham. Let it lie three days, turning it every day; then pour over it a pound of Treacle, and let it lie three Weeks turning it every day. Then take it out of the pickle and soak it two or three hours in cold spring Water and hang it in a Chimney to dry where a small wood fire is kept for a fortnight or three Weeks.

The same pickle will afterwards do for a tongue or hung Beef.

---

[86] Receipt on [p8] is simply entitled 'To cure Hams'.

[p82] To pickle Hams
Beat the Ham with a rolling Pin: To every Ham add a pound and a half of Bay Salt and three Ounces of Salt Petre. If it is very large four Ounces beat \very/ fine. To every Ham add a pound of Coarse Sugar and a pint of Old Beer. Then rub the Ham twice in a day by the fire for 8 days together. Let it lay three Weeks in the Pickle, turning it once in a day. Then hang it three or four Weeks in a Chimney to dry. You may smoke it if you please.

[p21] To preserve Hams and Bacon
Rub them with Sugar and Salt Petre: One Pound of Salt Petre and Four Pounds of the coarsest brown Sugar is a sufficient quantity for a middling sized Ham. They should be turned every three or four days and lay about a Month. Then take them out, and put them in Bran, & hang them up over Saw-dust smoke for a fortnight or three weeks. The sides for Bacon are rubbed with Saltpetre and Common Salt, and put into the same Brine with the Hams. To be turned every third or fourth day, and for the last Week the Bacon to be laid under the Hams.

Many Persons prefer salting a Hog while warm & fresh Killed.

[p83] An American Receipt for making Hams Mr Nicols
To 250 pounds of Pork mix one Peck of fine Salt, 3 to 4 ounces of Saltpetre, 1¼ pounds of Muscovado Sugar, well together. Let each Ham be well rubbed with the mixture and packed up close, taking care to sprinkle a little coarse Salt between each layer as it is packed up, and keep it close packed up 4 Weeks if mild open Weather, or five Weeks if hard and frosty. Then hang them up to be smoaked. Sometimes the layers are changed, laying the lower ones above, and the upper one below.

It is thought that the smoke from unseasoned Wood is better than that of dry Wood, as it is imagined more Nitre is in it.

The Hams may hang the Winter in the Chimney.

[p90] To make Hams Mrs Champion
Take your Hams, sprinkle them with Salt, let them lay to drain the blood. To each Ham, half a pound of Saltpetre, a quarter of a pound of Bay Salt, one Pound and a half of brown Sugar. Put these into as much Water as will cover the Hams; add as much common Salt as will make your pickle strong enough to bear an Egg. Boil all these together. Scum it when cold, pour it on your Hams. Let them lie five Weeks in the pickle; rub them and turn them every day.

Tongues do this way very well to eat out of the pickle, and will Keep a great while without being Salt.

[pp87-88; p111] To salt Hams[87] See page 111.
Prepare your Hams by rubbing them well with treacle and four Ounces of Salt petre, and one quarter of an Ounce of Black Pepper to each Ham powdered[88] and mixed with the Treacle. Let them lay in this mixture for two days. Then prepare the following pickle: One quart of strong Stale Beer, half a Pound of Common Salt, half a pound of Bay Salt, and half a pound of brown Sugar. Boil these together for a quarter of an hour, and pour the liquor boiling hot on the Ham, which must be turned twice a day.

A small Ham may be two Weeks, large one three Weeks.

Smoke them three days over saw dust. Some use Horse Dung.[89]

When dressed they are to be watered.[90]

[p85] To dry a Leg of Mutton
Take a Leg of Mutton, cut it in the shape of a Ham, salt it in pickle, two parts Salt petre and one part Bay Salt, with some brown Sugar. Let it lay in pickle three Weeks, then take it out and hang it in the Chimney to smoak as Bacon. When it is dry, boil it in Hay in a large Kettle with some Hay Seed in a Bag. To be eat with Fowls as Bacon.

[p63] To pot Partridges
Take the Partridges and season them well with Mace, Salt and a little Pepper, lay them in the Pot with the breast downwards, and to every Partridge put three quarters of a pound of Butter; send them to the Oven; When baked, drain them from the Butter and gravy, and add a little more seasoning. Then put them close in the Pot with the breasts upwards, when cold cover them well with the butter.

Suit the Pot to the Number of Birds in order that it may be full.

You may pot any sort of Game the same way.

[p87] To pickle Pork
Nine pound of Salt, and three quarters of a pound of Salt Petre to a Hog of 20 Stone, rub it well in until it brines under your hand {First cutting it of the size you judge proper}. Put it into your Salting Tub with a layer of Salt at the bottom of your Tub, put it in, the Rind downwards, put over it the Lid, and over that a large Stone or Weight, that the Brine may by that assistance cover it. Look at it

---

87 Receipt on [p111] is entitled 'For salting Hams'.
88 Receipt on [p111] omitted 'one quarter of an Ounce of Black Pepper to each Ham'.
89 On [p111] it says 'Smoke them three days over fresh Horse dung and saw Dust'.
90 On [p111] this line is omitted; it simply says 'See page 87 & 88'.

occasionally and take off the Skin. Do not move the Tub after the Pork is in, as it may cause a fermentation. Pack it down as close as possible.

The legs, the Hocks and Head must be salted with other Salt, as the above is only sufficient for the pickling Pork.

[p34] Pickled Pork
Half a pound of salt Petre, 2 pound of Bay Salt, a Bushel of Common Salt, and three pounds of coarse Sugar. For one Hog.

[p148] To pickle Pork
Half a pound of Salt-Petre, 3 pounds of coarse Sugar, mix them well together, and rub it very well into the Pork, laying one piece on another with the rind downwards. Let it remain 48 hours, then take of Bay Salt and fine Salt an equal quantity, as you think may answer. Mix it very well, and make it as hot as you can bear, and rub your Pork. Then put it in an Earthen Pan, and keep it well covered. In case the Salt does not melt in 3 or 4 Weeks; boil a brine of Salt and Water strong enough to bear an Egg, and when cold put it to the Pork. In a fortnight or three Weeks more pour the Brine off without stirring the Pork. Then boil it & skim it, when cold put it to the Pork \again/. ~~Then boil it and skim it.~~ The Pork should be kept under the brine by a heavy stone or weight.

[p154] To souce a Pig
Cut off the Head; cut it down the back; bone it; strew on it a good deal of Ginger, mace and Salt. Salt it very well, then roll it up very hard with Tape as in Collar of Brawn. Boil it well in Salt Water & Ginger. Take it up and let it stand until cold, put it in the Liquor it was boiled in with some Vinegar. Keep it in it two or three days.

Eat it with Vinegar.

[p136] To cure a Tongue Mrs P'er
Rub the Tongue {if large} with an Ounce of Salt Petre: If of a middle size ¾. Then rub on immediately a pound of common Salt. Wash it with the Brine daily for 3 Weeks, or more. Soak it in Water one Night & boil it full three hours.

[p166] To pickle Tongues Madame de la Combe
Take two Tongues, and sprinkle them with a little Salt. Let them lie one or two hours to drain. Make a pickle with two pounds of common Salt, one pound of common brown Sugar, and a quarter of a pound of Saltpetre. Mix them together and rub the Tongues with the mixture. Let them be a Month in this pickle, and turn them every day. Then take them out and hang them in the Kitchen to dry;

but not against the Wall. When they are quite dry and hard they are fit for use. Lay them in Water two hours before you boil them.

The same pickle with a little addition will do for many Tongues.

[p89] To salt Tongues

The Tongue should be salted two days with common Salt; then add a quarter of an Ounce of Salt Petre, and a little coarse Sugar and common Salt; rub it all in well before the fire. In a Fortnight or three Weeks, it will be fit to dress.

Observe that the Tongue is from a Young Animal.

[p161] Veal Hams

Take the Leg of Veal like a Ham; then take a Pint of Bay Salt; two Ounces of Salt-Petre, and a pound of Common Salt; mix them together with one Ounce of Juniper Berries beat, rub the Ham well and lay it in a hollow Tray with the Skinny side down-wards. Baste it every day with the pickle for a fortnight. It may be boiled, or parboiled and roasted.

In the same pickle two or three Tongues, or a piece of Pork may [be] done.

Chapter XIV: Possets and Gruels[91]

[p80] Barley Water
Add two ounces of Pearl Barley to three Pints of Water. Let it boil a long time gently, put Lemon Peel and Sugar to your taste in a jug, and pour the Barley Water on them.

Some Persons prefer the Barly Water thick & others thin. This will depend on the length of time it is boiling, or on an addition of Water afterwards.

[p20] Beef Tea
Pour two quarts of cold Water on a Pound of lean Beef cut very thin. Let it first boil then simmer for a quarter of an hour. After standing, skim it off and add a little Salt.

Let the Beef be fresh.

[p112] Brandy Posset
A Pint and a half of Brandy, a pint of Sherry, mix them; put in a proportion of Sugar, take 1½ Gallon of Milk, add one quart of Water, boil this last mixture, and pour it on the Former before the Sugar is dissolved.

[p98] Calves Foot Jelly B
A Calf Foot cleaned and cut into pieces, and Ounce of Hartshorn shavings; half an Ounce of Isinglass, three pints of Milk. Bake these in a slow oven until a pint of Milk is consumed. Strain it off; let it stand until cold & then take off all the Fat. Drink a coffee Cup of the Jelly twice in the day.

The Hartshorn shavings may be omitted and it will answer as well. It will Keep in a cold place 2 or 3 days.

[p70] To make Coffee
Always Ground the Coffee fresh when you use it. Put as many Spoonsfull of Coffee as Cups of boiling Water; allowing one full Cup of Water, besides. Let the Pot {of whatever size it may be} be quite full: Let it boil until there is not any scum. The Coffee will then be decreased in quantity. Fill the Pot up with Cold Water, and let it stand by the fire some time to settle.

---

[91] Non-alcoholic drinks, such as coffee, have also been placed in this chapter.

[p70] Café a la Caramêle
Make the Tongs red hot & Take up a large Lump of Sugar with them, and drop it into the Coffee.

[p71] Café a la Crême
Put a Cup ~~filled~~ \full of/ Coffee to two Cups of Cream, and boil them together. Add sugar to your taste.

[pp70-71] Café a la Minuite
Measure how many Cups your Coffee Pot will hold. Put a Cullander in the Pot with a Strainer in it, and lay some Cotton Wool in the Strainer. Put in as many Table Spoonsful of Coffee as you mean to have Cups, lay it upon the Cotton on the Strainer; then pour upon it as many Cups full of boiling Water as you put spoonsful of Coffee, with an allowance of a full Cup over, if you make 5 or 6: But only half a Cup over if you make 2 or 3 Cups. Let it drain, and it will be fit for use; If you pour it through a second time, it will be stronger.

When you heat up this Coffee, let the Pot in which you heat it be quite full. If the next time you make Coffee 'a la Minuite' you boil these dregs in the Water you use; you will save the quantity of Coffee for two Cups; And if the dregs are boiled a third time one Cup may be saved. It is considered material that the Coffee Pot should always be full.

[p13] Egg Caudle +
Fill a large Chocolate Pot with one part of Brandy, or rather more, 3 parts boiling Water. Let it cool a little; then mix by degrees, 2 Yolks of Eggs {some prefer one, thinking two makes it too thick} they should be previously beaten with 2 or 3 Lumps of Sugar or according to taste, then add a little grated Nutmeg. When the whole is well mixed together set it on the fire, and stir it continually untill it simmers. When it is done, then pour it backward and forward from Cup to Cup, untill it is finely frothed. If the liquor is poured on the Egg too hot, it will be apt to curdle, and also if it is suffered to boil when on the fire.

Wine may be used instead of Brandy & Mountain is to be preferred. In that case there is not any occasion for Water, nor will it curdle, either from the heat of the Liquor when mixing, or when on the fire.

Serve it up with toasted Bread or Chocolate.

[p38] Egg Wine Mollands
Boil a pint of Water with a little Cinnamon, beat the Yolk of 5 Eggs with a little of the cold White Wine, and pour it backwards & forwards to froth; then add the

rest of the Bottle of White Wine, and let it boil and mix your Egg with the Wine after it has boiled; let the whole warm together taking care to stir it all the time one way, then pour it into your glasses & serve it warm; sweeten the Wine and Water to your taste, and add a little Nutmeg.

[p119] The best Imperial Mrs B D
One ounce of Cream of Tartar, 3 quarts of Water, about one spoonful Salop. Set it over the fire and keep stirring it until it almost boils. Add the rind of 2 Lemons pared thin. When it has boiled half an hour pour it into a Jug, and sweeten to your taste. The following day pour it into a Bason, or bowl; add the rinds of 2 more Lemons, and the Juice of one Lemon.

[p133] Imperial
A quarter of an Ounce of Cream of Tartar, half the Peel of a Lemon, three Ounces of Sugar, and three quarts of Water boiling hot.

[p87] Imperial Drink
Pour a Gallon of boiling Water on an Ounce of Cream of Tartar, 4 Ounces of Sugar, some slices of Lemon, and the rind of the Lemon. Let it stand 24 hours, stirring it often; then filter it off in Bottles for use.

Where Lemon does not agree, use only the rind.

[p148] Lemonade
1¼ pounds of double refined Sugar, add a pint of cold spring Water. Then pare 6 or 8 large Lemons as thin as possible. Put the Peel to the Sugar & Water; then add two quarts of hot Water, but not boiled. Let it stand covered all Night; then squeeze in the juice of the Lemons, and run it through a Cloth until it is clear.

If it stands a day or two after it is made it will be better.

[p159] Lemonade
Take 12 Lemons; pare the rind of six very thin; put them into a Pan and pour boiling Water on it; cover it close, and let it stand one or two hours: then squeeze the Lemons into a large Pan, and put a kettle of boiling Water to them, and strain the Water from the Peel, and put to it. Clarify a pound and half of double refined Sugar. Mix all well together, and if not sweet enough, make it to your taste. Strain it through a hair Sieve or Jelly Bag.

[p72] Clarified Lemonade Mrs Minet
Pare the rinds of two Lemons as thin as you can; put them into a Jug with the Juice of 6 Lemons, half a pound of Sugar, Half a pint of rich White Wine, and

one quart of boiling Water. Let it stand all Night. In the Morning add half a pint of boiling Milk, then run it through a Jelly Bag, until it is quite clear.

[p18] Milk Punch
Two quarts of Water to one of Milk, half a pint of Lemon Juice, a quart of Brandy and Sugar to your taste; Put the Milk and Water together a little warm, then the Sugar; then the Lemon Juice stirred well together, the Brandy, then stir it again, and run it through a Flannel Bag until its very fine, then bottle it, and it will keep for Years.

[p23] Milk Punch
Take a dozen and a half of Lemons, pare them very fine, steep them in three quarts of Rum for a day or two. Then take them out, and add in the parings. Mash them all together in a Pan with 5 quarts of Water; put Sugar to your taste and two quarts of Milk scalding hot. Strain it through a flannel Bag.

[p24] Milk Punce [*sic*]
Two quarts of Brandy and one of Rum; the rinds of 2 Lemons steeped in it for 12 hours; then strain it off and add to it the Juice of 12 Seville Oranges, three Pints of Milk boiled, two quarts of Spring Water, one pound of fine Lump Sugar. Let it stand 24 hours, then strain it through a Jelly Bag, and bottle it for use.

[pp116-117] Milk Punch Dr Y
One Gallon of Rum, five quarts of Water, 3 pounds of Lump Sugar, 2 Nutmegs grated; 2 dozen of Seville Oranges and 2 dozen of Lemons. Pare the Oranges and Lemons, and steep at least one half of the Peel in a quart of Rum 10 or 12 hours. Put the Sugar into the Water, and squeeze the Oranges and Lemons on it, stirring it all well together, and when the Sugar is dissolved, put in the Rum. Then add two quarts of Milk made pretty hot; stir the mixture well together; and after letting it stand 10 or 12 hours, strain the Punch through a Flannel Bag until it be Fine enough to bottle.

[p52] Mock Asses Milk[92]
Of Great Comfrey Roots 2 Ounces, of Sage one Ounce, of Isinglass & Hartshorn shaving each one Ounce. Boil them in two quarts of Water to one Quart [of

---

[92] Also known as 'snail-water', decoctions such as this usually included crushed snails rather than hartshorn and isinglass. See E Smith, 'An excellent Snail Water' (*Compleat Housewife*, p273). It was used in the treatment of consumptives (*OED*).

canary];[93] then strain it. Take 9 spoonsfull of this Decoction and 3 of New Milk lukewarm early in the morning.

[p75] Negeas
Two spoonsful of Red Wine mixed with Barley Water, Orange Juice and Sugar.

[p48] Oatmeal Jelly Dr R
Put some Grits in a large Pan; pour some Water on them; let it stand 24 hours to ferment; then pour off the sour Water and add some fresh; stir it well, and let it stand a short time to let the Gross part settle. Then pour the Water off into an Iron Pot and boil it. When Cold it will become a Jelly and will Keep a long time.

[p75] Orange Whey
An equal quantity of China Orange Juice and boiled Milk. After standing some time strain off the Curd, and sweeten it.

[p49] Gruel Porridge – Scotch Dr R
Put some Water into a saucepan. Let it boil; Then take a handful of Oatmeal, and drop it gently into it. Let it boil up, observing to stir it well. Then drop in more Oatmeal, and let it boil before you add more, until you find it thick enough for Porridge. You should put a little salt into the Water, before the Oatmeal is mixed. Then put it into a Cup or Bowl, and pour into it as much cold Milk as You choose.

[p49] Water Gruel \Scotch/ Dr R
Put some Oatmeal into a Bason, and pour on it some Cold Water. Let it stand to settle, them pour off the Water and boil it up. This Method makes it lighter than in the common way.

[p182] Sage Wine, for the Head-ache
Four handsful of Red Sage; beat it in a Mortar of Stone to a Sauce. Add to it a quart of Red Wine, and let it stand three or four days close stopped; shaking two or three times, then let it stand to settle.

The next day take of the Sage Wine in the morning 3 Spoonsful & of Water one Spoonful, fasting one or two hours. Use it for some weeks.

---

[93] Smith's receipt uses canary, so presumably that is what ED means.

[p178] Sansparolli[94]
A quart of rectified spirits of Wine, one Ounce of Essence of Bergamot, 2 drams of Musk, half a pint of Water, bottle it.

[p174] Venlo's Syrup from Venlo[95]
22 Ounces of Sarsparilla, boil it in 22 Quarts of Water, until reduced to 7½ Quarts. Then add of Senna leaves, of Chervil leaves, of white Rose leaves, of Carraway seed, each two Ounces. Boil the whole until it is reduced to half the quantity. Then add of Honey and Treacle, a quantity sufficient to form a Syrup.

[p75] Whey
One Glass of White Wine, four Glasses of Milk, a little Orange Juice, a lump or two of Sugar, four or five Glasses of boiling Water poured on the other ingredients. Strain it.

---

[94] Perhaps an imitation of Sarsparilla; see Glossary, definition 2.

[95] According to Henry Beasley, *The Druggist's General Receipt Book* (8th edition, 1886), Venlo's Vegetable Syrup was 'supposed to be a decoction of burdock, mint, dandelion, senna, etc, boiled with sugar, and a small portion of solution of sublimate added'.

Chapter XV: Wines, Catchups and Vinegars

Beer, Brandy, Shrub, Wine, etc

[p171] To recover Beer that is Flat

Take four Gallons out of a Hogshead, and boil it with Five pounds of Honey, scum it and cool it, and put it to the rest. Stop it up close.

[p123] Spruce Beer

12 Gallons of Water just warm; add 8 pounds of Treacle and two Tablespoonsful of Essence of Spruce. Beat up well in a Tub to a Froth, and add to it two spoonsful of good Yeast. Put it in a Barrel. Let it stand two or three days and bottle for use. It will be \fit/ 10 or 12 days.

[p18; p131] To make Cherry Brandy[96] Miss D'

One Gallon of Brandy; four pounds of Morello Cherries slit, 2 pounds of the finest Sugar[97] dissolved in a pint of Water. Half a pint of Apricot Kernels bruised. Let it stand about two Months, refine it through a Flannel Bag.

[p108; p146] Rasberry Brandy

Take some ripe Rasberries, bruise and squeeze them through a coarse Cloth into a Stone Jar. To each quart of juice add a pound of Lump Sugar. Stir it well together, and to a quart of juice add two quarts of Brandy. Let it stand three days, then strain through a flannel Bag. Bottle it, it will be fit to drink in a week.

[p126] The Gloucester Manner of making Cyder

Let your Apples be full ripe when you gather them; Then let them lye on a heap three Weeks or a Month to sweat. Pick out the musty and Rotten Ones; then grind them, and immediately after press them. Put the Juice into a large Tub, and let it stand in it eight or ten days. Then skim off the Head with a Ladle, and rack off the remainder into the Barrel, Keep it open a Fortnight. Then put the Bung gently in; but do not stop it close until the hissing ceases. Let it stand until February and then Rack it From the Lees, and stop it very close. Burn a Brimstone Match in the Cask before you put your Cyder in, which should be done when the Vessel is Full of smoke.

---

[96] Receipt on [p131] has no donor; it is entitled 'To make the Best Cherry Brandy'.

[97] Receipt on [p131] has 'single refined Sugar'.

It is best to Keep your Cask always Full after the Fermentation is over, so that you should always have a reserve of Rich Cyder, to Fill up as there may be occasion.

[p86] Strong Mead
To 20 Gallons of Water add 60 pounds of Honey; boil it and as the scum rises, take it off. Then take a quarter of a pound of Ginger sliced, of Cloves and Mace each a quarter of an Ounce and three Nutmegs sliced. Sew them up in a Bag and put them into a Kettle with a handful of sweet Marjorum, Mint & Balm[98] and a sprig of Rosemary. Let it boil two hours, then strain it into a Tub; let it stand two days, stirring it three times in the day. Then put it into a ~~Gallon~~ Barrel with the Bag of Spice, stopping it close. Keep it at least ½ a year before it is bottled. This proved too good.

[p53] Nectar Dr Ingenhouz[99]
Take two pounds of Raisins of the Sun, one pound of Loaf Sugar, two Lemons sliced with the Peel of one Lemon; Put them into an Earthen pot, pour in two Gallons of boiling Water, having boiled half an hour; stir the mash well twice in a day, let it stand three or Four days, then strain and bottle it. It will be fit for use in a Fortnight.

It will ferment much and is best put into Stone Bottles. Glass Bottles being more liable to break.

[p50] Orgeat[100] Mrs K't
Of Water two Quarts; refined Sugar 4½ pounds; Bitter Almonds half a pound; sweet Almonds ¼ of a pound. The Whites of 5 Eggs well beat. A little Water must be added to the Almonds when beating, and when it is mixed together; it must boil half an Hour and then be strained through a Cheese Cloth. The Water, sugar & Whites of Eggs are to be put in first, and well [*recte* when] they boil, it is to be skimmed.

[p123] Orgeat
One pound of blanc[h]ed Almonds. Beat them in a Mortar with Soft Water by degrees to keep them from oiling, as Fine as a paste. Then add a Gallon of soft

[98] This word has been altered: 'Balm' seems the most likely reading. See Glossary.
[99] See Introduction pp.xxvii-xxviii and Appendix II.
[100] Raffald's similar receipt 'To make Ozyat' uses 'cold seeds' as well as both sweet and bitter almonds (*Experienced English Housekeeper*, p172). According to John Nott, the seeds were melon seeds (Nott, *Cook's and Confectioner's Dictionary*, quoted in *OED*).

Water. Stir it well; let it stand all Night. Then strain it well through a Napkin, very hard. Sweeten it with Loaf Sugar, and add Orange Flower Water to your taste.

[p75] To make Shrub
To every Dozen of Seville Oranges, squeeze three Lemons. To every Gallon of Rum put in one pint of Juice and 2 pound of Sugar pounded very fine. Pare some peel from the White. Mix the juice and Sugar and Rum together with what Peel you like. Cover it close all Night. Have ready some Milk boiled. Let it stand until Cold, put half a pint to every Gallon. Let it stand one hour, stir it well together and run it thro' a Jelly Bag with a piece of Blotting Paper within it, until it is clear.

[p139] Shrub
To one Gallon of Rum or Brandy a Pint and half of the Juice of Lemons & Oranges, one pound and three quarters of the best Lump Sugar, and the peel of two oranges and of 2 Lemons, pared thin and steeped in part of the above Juice a day or two. Squeeze it several times to give it a Flavour. Then mix it with the rest. Shake it several times for a week before it is used.

[p155] Currant Shrub
To one Gallon of Rum or Brandy put two quarts of strained Juice of white Currants, 1½ of Loaf Sugar. Let them stand mixed together in a Pan covered all Night. In the Morning run it through a Jelly Bag, and bottle it for use. If the first part which is run off is not quite fine run it through again.

The Currant juice should be first strained through a Cloth or Sieve.

[p62] White Currant Shrub
Gather your Currants when they are Full ripe, bruise them, drain the Juice; To seven quarts of the Juice put seven pounds of Loaf Sugar, and three Gallons of Rum or Brandy; put the Sugar into the Rum to dissolve, then put in the Juice; mix it well together and run it through a Flannel Bag; then Bottle it for use.

The Currant juice must be passed through a Flannel Bag until it is quite clean before the spirit is added.

[p137] Orange Shrub
Orange juice one Quart; Rum or Brandy 9 Pints; of fine Sugar 2¼ pounds. Put in a Cask and stir it well for two or three days. Then let it stand a Week, and if fine, draw it off in Bottles.

Some of the orange Rinds pared thin may be added, ⅛ of the Rinds will do; but if you prefer it bitter, add more.

[p120] Rum Shrub {Dr Y}
Infuse the Peel of 10 or 12 Seville Oranges into two Gallons of Rum about 5 or 6 hours. Then strain off the Rum, and put to it two Quarts and about half a Pint of Juice of Oranges strained through a Flannel Bag and 3½ pounds of double refined Sugar in powder. Shake the Vessel every day until the Sugar is dissolved, and then let it stand until the Scrub [*sic*] can be drawn off fine for bottling.

[p109] Clara Wine
To 10 gallons of Water put half a Bushel of Clara flowers; but none of the stalks, a quarter of a hundred of fine powdered Sugar, the Whites of 10 Eggs beat a little, put them with the Water and Sugar over the fire, and boil it two hours; skimming it well all the time it boils. Put the Clara into a Cask with a pint of Ale Yeast on it. When the Liquor is no warmer than Milk from the Cow, pour it on the Clara; stir it two or three times in a day until it has done working, then stop it close. It will be fine in about half a Year. Bottle it off. It is the better for Keeping. Rack it off for use.

[p64] Cowslip Wine
Take 8 Gallons of Water {Ale Measure}, 24 pounds of Sugar & the Whites of 6 Eggs well beat. Stir them well together. Let it boil a quarter of an hour, or longer, skim it well, and when cold, put to it 4 Pecks of Cowslip Flowers, the Peels of 18 Lemons & of 4 Oranges, and two spoonsful of thick Yeast. Let it stand 3 days in a Tub, stirring it twice in a day. Then put it into the Cask. Cut the Lemons and put them in at the same time. Squeeze the Lemons and Flowers twice in a day, and in 5 days, or as soon as the fermentation ceases, bung down the Cask, observing that it be quite full.

[p64] Currant Wine
Gather your Currants when they are full ripe, pick the stalks and then wither Currants from them, and then to every quart of Fruit add a quart of Water. Bruise the Currants well with your hands, then put the Water to them, and let them stand two days and two Nights. Then strain the Liquor thru' a hair Sieve, and afterwards, thru' a Flannel Bag, and to every quart of Liquor put a pound of Loaf Sugar. When it is well mixed put in a little new Ale Yeast. Let it ferment one Night & a day. Then put it in a Vessel and do not stop it up until it has done fermenting.

[p83] Currant Wine Mrs K'
Add to the juice of two pecks of Currants squeezed thro' a Bag 17 pounds of Sugar. Mix them well together. Let them stand a whole day; then put it into a five Gallon Cask and fill it up with Water, and when it has corked, add about a quart of Brandy. A Pint of the Juice of Rasberries may be added.

[p155] Currant Wine
To three Gallons of Water, one Gallon and a Pint of white Currant juice, then to every Gallon three pounds of Lump Sugar; put it in a close Tub and stir it well together. Then put it in the Barrel. It will work 16 or 18 days. Keep it filled up once a day, and when it has done fermenting stop it down close. It may stand 8 or 10 Months – the longer the better. It will fine itself fit for bottling.

Try it with a Crane to observe it is fine before it is bottled.

Take the largest White Currants full ripe. Two Bushell of such Currants yeild 20 Gallons Wine Measure.

[p173] Currant Wine Mrs Patmore
Strip the Currants, then bruise them, and strain them through a strong Cloth, a few at a time. To every quart of Juice, add three quarts of Water; and to every Gallon of Liquor, three pounds of Sugar. To every 10 Gallons of Wine put one quart of Rasberry Juice. The Sugar must be dissolved before it is put in the Cask. Lay the Bung hole over, and do not bung it down until it has done hissing. Rack it off the beginning of March; draw off the Fine; and when it begins to run thick, run it through a Bag. Put it again in the Barrel, and add to 10 Gallons, one pound of Sugar pounded, and two pounds of Raisins cut open, and one pint of Brandy. Then bung it up tight.

[p16] Red Currant Wine +
Seven quarts of juice, Seven Quarts of Water, one Pint of Rasberries, 15 pound of Sugar – for a 5 Gallon Cask, and one Quart of Brandy added 2 months after. It had not quite ceased to ferment in the Cask; but soon decreased on adding the Brandy, and was then corked down.

The same proportions for White Wine, omitting the Rasberries.

[p78] Elder flower Wine Miss H' (?Hatton)
To a Gallon of Water allow four pounds of Lump Sugar, boil it together an hour, taking off the Scum; beat the White of 6 Eggs; put half the Whites in, When it is half boiled, and the remainder when it is cold. Let it stand until it is blood warm; Then put in a Pint of Elder flowers dried and picked; A spoonful of Ale Yeast on a toast. Stir it twice a day for three days together; then strain it from the

flowers and put it in the Vessel with a quarter of an Ounce of Isinglass. When it has done fermenting, bung it close for a Year, and then bottle it.

[p127] Elder Flower Wine
Take 6 Gallons of Water, 12 lb of Raisins of the Sun chopped very small & 12 pound of fine Sugar. Boil all these together. Then take the Flower of Elder when in full bloom, rubbed off slightly to the quantity of a Peck. Put them into the Liquor when it is almost Cold. Next day put in six Spoons Full of Syrup of Lemons, and Four Spoons full of Yeast. Let it stand two Days, then put it in your Vessel \straining it through a sieve/.

This will be very like Frontiniac.

[p63] To make Frontiniac wine
Take 6 Gallons of Water; 12 pounds of White Sugar; 6 pounds of Sun Raisins cut small, Boil these together one Hour. Then take about a quarter of a Peck of Elder flowers, when they are falling and will shake off, and put them in the Liquor when it is almost cold. The next day put in 6 spoonsful of Syrup of Lemon & two spoonsful of Ale Yeast. Two days after put in a Vessel. When it has stood a proper time, bottle it. A few Clary Flowers may be added.

[p22] Ginger Wine Wright
To every Gallon of Water add 2½ pounds of Lump Sugar. Boil an hour, scum it well. When the liquor is near cold add the Juice of one large Lemon to every Gallon. Boil the peels with four Ounces of \raw/ Ginger to each Gallon: Cut the Ginger in small pieces & boil it in three pints of soft Water one hour. When it is done put all together in a Tub and work it with a Toast and Yeast: But let it be nearly cold before you put the Yeast in.

When done, put it in the Cask with one Ounce of Isinglass, close it up and let it stand 6 Weeks or more in a cool Place. You may then bottle it. Add a little Brandy to each Bottle.

It is best to boil the Ginger the day before, and then boil it again with the Wine. If you would not have it strong of the Ginger, you may abate the quantity.

[p168] Ginger Wine
Seven Gallons of Water to be boiled until reduced to Six Gallons. Eight pounds of Loaf Sugar, 10 Ounces of Ginger, 8 Lemons and the Peel very thin to be put in \first/ after the former is mixed and taken out of the Cask and the Liquor being again put in, after the Cask has been quite cleaned.

Add Brandy as you like, the quantity to be increased according to the length of time it is intended to be Kept.

[p152] Gooseberry Wine
Take 36 pounds, bruise them and put to them 12 Quarts of boiling Water, and let them stand until next day. Then strain them through a Flannel strainer, and put to the Liquor 2 pounds of Sugar, and let it stand until the next day again, and if the Sugar be melted, strain it again into an Earthen Vessel & let it stand until fine, and then bottle it.

[p6] Green Gooseberry Wine + Brick[en]d[on]
Gather the Gooseberries just before they turn. To every pound of bruised Gooseberries, add one Quart of cold Water; Let it stand six or seven days, stirring it occasionally but not stron[g]ly, then strain it; and to every Gallon of Juice add three or four pounds of refined Sugar, and when in the Cask, to every five Gallons of Liquor add one quart of French Brandy {some also add a Pint of dissolved Isinglass}.

Take care to bruise the Fruit enough to mix with the Water, but not to break the Seed, which would give the Wine an unpleasant flavour. The Brandy is not to be put into the Cask untill the fermen[ta]tion has nearly subsided.

[p61] Green Gooseberry Wine
To every pound of Gooseberries, gathered when green, picked and bruised, put one quart of Water; let it stand 3 days, and stir it twice every day. To every Gallon of Juice when strained, put three pounds of Loaf Sugar. Put it into a Cask and add to every 20 quarts of Liquor one quart of Brandy & a little Isinglass; let it stand nine Months and then bottle it.

Ten quarts of Gooseberries, 15 pounds of Sugar, one quart of Brandy will make 5 Gallons, three quarts and one pint of Wine.

[pp53-54] To make Grape Wine
The juice of the Grapes should be poured from the Grapes when mashed, and Water should be added to it in quantity half that of the Juice, and two \pounds/ of Loaf Sugar should be added to each Gallon.

When this Liquor has been Fermented to a proper degree in the Cask, a pint of Brandy should be added to every eight Gallons, which will check the fermentation. The Cask should be occasionally filled up. If the Wine is on the frot[h], give it vent by a small hole bored near the Bung, and when it is quiet, put the spike into the hole. The Wine will keep better if it is not fined for some Months and when that is done, it should be poured off the Ley into another Cask, and may be best fined by using the Whites of about 2 Eggs to every eight Gallons: Let these be well beat into a thick froth, then add some Wine to them, and having stirred it about with a Stick in one way, put it into the Cask {after having drawn off some of the Wine} stir it well 8 or 10 Minuites, after which fill the Cask and Cork it up.

The Royal Muscadim or Burgundy Grape is the best to make Wine; but the Black Cluster or any other Grape may be used. They should not be too ripe.

[p5] Orange Wine Leaper +

Take three pounds of Lump sugar to a Gallon of Water, boil the sugar and Water together, and clear it with the White of Eggs; when Cold add the Juice of 8 large Seville Oranges to a Gallon; Pare the Oranges thin and put the parings into the Barrel. It must be worked in a Tub by the addition of a sufficient quantity of Yeast, but the Yeast should not be added untill it is nearly cold. When the fermentation has ceased, some Brandy should be added.

[p89; p118] Orange Wine Lady St John[101]

10 Gallons of Spring Water, and 30 pounds of Lump Sugar,[102] boil them together one hour, skimming the Liquor all the time. When it is almost Cold, soak it with the Ale Yeast for three days, beating it up two or three times in the day. Skim off the Yeast before you turn it. You must use the peels and Juice of 50 Seville Oranges, very large, pared as thin as possible. Put the Peel into a quart of Brandy, let them steep all the time the Water and Sugar is working. Next squeeze your Oranges, and having strained them, put the peels, juice and Brandy all into the Barrel. When you turn the Wine, lay Paper over the Bung hole, until it has done working. Then stopping it down close, set it where neither Air nor Sun can get at it. Keep it in the Vessel six Months, then bottle it.

If you prefer it coloured, take two Ounces of Cochineal, beat it, and add it to the Juice, and then to the Wine. You must allow one Gallon for Waste.

[p62] Raisin Wine

Take 400 weight of the best Raisins {⅓ Smyrna and ⅔ Malaga}. Put them into a Barrel to a Hogshead of Water {Wine Measure} & stir them in the Barrel every day for about 3 Weeks or longer if the fermentation continues. Just before you stop up the Barrel put in two quarts of the best Brandy.

[p22] Raisin Wine

Take seven Pounds of good Raisins, pick them from the Stalks, cut them with a Knife. Put them in a Tub with two Gallons of Purest Water. Let them stand three weeks, stirring them two or three times in the day, then squeeze the Plumbs dry

---

101 Receipt on [p118] has no donor.

102 Receipt on [p118] has '30 lb of sixpenny Sugar'.

& put the Liquor into the Cask and lay the Bung on the Hole until you think it fit for stopping up. Then add a handful of Isinglass.

It should stand one Year before it is used.

Or put 60 pound of Raisins to 9 Gallons of Water.

[p156] Raisin Wine

To every 100 Weight of Raisins put 20 Gallons of cold Water. Keep it well stirred in the Tub 5 or 6 Weeks; then press the clear Liquor and put it into Vessels. As it works keep it filled up, and lay something lightly on the Bung hole.

[p156] Smyrna Raisin Wine

Allow six pounds of Raisins to every Gallon of Water {Wine Measure}. Chop the Raisins, but not small. Boil the Water, let it stand to be cold before you add it to the Raisins. Let it stand 14 days, stirring it every day; put a pound of Raisins into the Barrel when you put in the Wine, which must be well squeezed or pressed, and do not stop it up until it has done working.

Let it remaine one year in the Cask.

[p156] A second sort [of Raisin Wine] from the pressings of the Fruit

Put 12 pounds of Fresh Malaga Raisins with seven Gallons of Water for 5 or 6 days. If any Wine is left mix it with it also, when you put it in the Cask. It should not stand more than one Month, or six Weeks; then bottle it for use.

It will not keep long in Bottles; but is a pleasant drink in Summer.

Catchups etc

[p102] Catchup to Keep Many Years

A Gallon of Strong Stale Beer, one pound of Anchovies washed from the Pickle, A pound of Shalots peeled; ½ an Ounce of Mace; half an Ounce of Cloves; a quarter of an Ounce of whole pepper, three or Four large races of Ginger; Two quarts of the Large Mushroom Cups rubbed to pieces. Cover all this Close, and let it simmer until it is half wasted; then strain it through a Flannel Bag. Let it stand until quite cold; then bottle it.

A spoonful of this to a pound of fresh Butter melted makes a fine Fish or gravy sauce.

The Stronger & staler the Beer, the better the Catchup.

[p160] Lemon Catchup

Cut 4 or 5 Lemons {free of Spots} in quarters; throw some Salt over them, put them in a Jar and let them stand before the fire 2 or 3 days, but not too close.

Then boil some of the best Vinegar with some Nutmeg, Cloves, Mace, Ginger, whole Pepper. Pour it on the Lemons, boiling hot. Keep it close covered. It is now fit for use.

[p32] Mushroom liquor and Powder[103]

Wash a Peck of Mushrooms, rub them with a piece of flannel; take out the Gills, but do not peel them. 12 Blades of Mace, 4 Cloves, 4 Bay Leaves, ½ an Ounce of beaten Pepper, one handful of Salt, 8 Onions, a bit of Butter the size of an Egg: Half a pint of Vinegar.[104] Let these stew as quick as they can, stirring it until the Liquor is out of the Mushrooms. Drain them, bottle the liquor and spice when cold. Dry the Mushrooms in an Oven. First in a bread Pan; then in Sieves until they will beat to powder.

This quantity will make 6 or 7 Ounces.[105]

Stop it close in a wide mouthed Bottle.

[p75] To make Walnut Ketchup

When your Walnuts are fit for Pickle, pound and then strain them through a coarse Cloth; Let the Liquor stand to settle. To every pint of clear juice put a pound of Anchovies. Boil them with the juice until they are dissolved, and to every pint; which must be strained after it is boiled, put the following ingredients: One ounce of dried Shalots, half a quarter of an Ounce of Mace. The same of black Pepper and Cloves. Two pints of Ketchup will take near a peck of Walnuts. Cork your Bottles Close.

It makes excellent fish sauce put into Melted Butter.

You must judge of the proper quantity according to your taste.

[p85] [~~*Rice Omelet*~~] Walnut Ketchup

Take 300 Walnuts, pound them well in a Mortar, Let them stand 24 hours; then squeeze the juice out of them, and to every quart of Juice add a pint of Vinegar, a pound of Anchovies, a pound of Ginger, 1½ Ounce of pepper, ½ an Ounce of Cloves, and \one/ Ounce of Mace and a handful of Shalots; boil them together for a quarter of an hour; then strain through a sieve, and let the Liquor stand 24 hours. Then clear it off gently and boil it 5 Minuites. Let it stand until cold, then pour it off gently and put it into Bottle.

---

[103] E Smith, *Compleat Housewife*, gives two receipts for making mushroom powder (pp86 and 121). This receipt is almost the same as that published on p86.

[104] Smith uses 16 blades of mace and a dozen onions; the amount of pepper specified is 'twice as much beaten pepper as will lie on a half crown'.

[105] Smith's receipt 'usually makes about half a pound'.

If a little of this is added to melted Butter, it serves as a sauce for any kind of Fish, Beef Stakes, Mutton Chops &c

[p102] Walnut Catchup {Mr Backhouse}
Half a peck of green Walnuts, slice and beat them in a Mortar; put them into an Earthen Jar with 6 Ounces of Salt; stir them twice in the day with a wooden Spoon for three Weeks, then press out the Juice, and to every quart put Cloves, Mace, Ginger, White and Black Pepper of each half a quarter of an ounce, Shalots half an ounce. Boil them 15 Minuites and cover them in the same Pot for ten days; then strain it off. To a quart of strained Liquor add ¾ of a Pint of Red Port, half a pound of Anchovies. Let these boil one Minuite: when cold, strain, and bottle up for use.

[p103] Walnut Catchup
Take the Walnuts when fit to pickle; beat them in a Mortar and squeeze them through a thin Cloth. Let the Liquor stand & settle. Pour it off clear. To every pint of liquor, add a pound of Anchovies, half an Ounce of Mace, the same of Jamaica Peppers; Boil them together until the Anchovies are dissolved, then strain it and put in half a pint of Vinegar; a good many Shalots and Garlick. Boil all together until tender. Let it stand until cold and bottle it for use.

It makes brown Sauce of a fine Colour & will Keep many Years.

[p131] Walnut Catchup
Take Walnuts when they are ripe for pickling. Beat to pieces in a Stone or wooden Mortar; squeeze the Juice through a Flannel, and to every quart of this Juice put one pint of Vinegar. Let them stand four days, then boil them well over a slow fire until half is consumed; tie up in a Rag one Ounce of Spices consisting of Cloves, Mace, Nutmeg and black pepper. The rind of 2 Seville Oranges and some Garlick; pour the liquor on boiling hot. Let it stand three Weeks or 1 Month. Then bottle it.

[p139] Walnut Catchup
Pound the Walnuts in a Mortar, and squeeze them through a thin Cloth, then let them stand to settle; then pour off clear liquor, and to every pint add a pound of Anchovies. Of Mace, Clove & Jamaica Pepper of each ½ a quarter of an Ounce. Boil all together until the Anchovies are dissolved. Then strain it off and put in a good handful of Shalots & to every quart of this, add half a pint of Vinegar. Boil it up again & let it stand until cool. Then bottle it off, and it will keep good for Years.

[p140] Walnut Catchup
Take a quart of the Juice of Walnuts, one pound of Anchovies & boil it until the Anchovies are dissolved; then strain it off; add ½ a Pint of White Wine Vinegar, a quarter of an Ounce of Mace & ½ an Ounce of Cloves, thirty pepper Corns, eight large Shalots & boil it until the Shalots are tender.

[p146] Walnut Catchup
Beat green Walnuts in a stone Mortar, and to two Quarts of Juice strained through a Flannel Bag add two handsful of Salt; boil it gently until the scum rises, and skim it off until it is pretty clear. Then put to it Mace, Nutmeg, Black Pepper, of each half an Ounce, and ¼ of an Ounce of Cloves finely beaten, and let the whole boil together with a pint of good Vinegar 7 Minuites; then pour it into an Earthen Pan, cover it close, & let it stand until cold. Bottle and Cork it well. Tye a Bladder over it. Set it in a close place, and in 6 Months it will be Fit for use.

The proper time to make it, is when the Walnut is Fit to pickle.

Vinegars

[p86] To make Vinegar
Boil the Water, and when it is quite cold, to every Gallon, put a quart of very ripe Gooseberries bruised, and a pound of the coarsest brown Sugar. Let it stand for five days. Then strain it through a Hair Bag, and put the Liquor into a Vessel, and let it stand in the Sun all the Summer, and in a warm place in the Winter, but not near the fire. The Vessel must be covered. The Vinegar will be fit for use in the April following.

[p39] Vinegar Syrup
For every two pounds and a half of Rasberries a pint of Vinegar and two pounds of Sugar. Put the Rasberries into a Pan with the Vinegar to remain in the Cellar 24 hours, then strain them through Linen, and pass the liquor through a jelly Bag; when the Syrup is made, you must throw the Juice in, which should boil 7 Minuites.

It must <u>not</u> be Corked. A Paper pricked full of holes to be tied over the Bottles.

[p51] Camp Vinegar (Mrs K)
Quarter of an Ounce of Kian Pepper, two large Heads of Garlick, half a dram of Cochineal. 2 Spoonsful of Sugar or Walnut Catchup. 2 spoonsful of Walnut Pickle. Steep them one Month in a quart of good Vinegar, and strain it.

[p53] Gooseberry Vinegar Byd

Take Gooseberries full ripe; bruise them thoroughly; boil the Water and let it stand until cold. To every quart of Gooseberries put three Quarts of Water. Let it stand 24 Hours. Then strain it through a Hair Sieve, and to every Gallon of Liquor, put one pound of brown Sugar, stirring it well. Put it in a Cask and and [*sic*] paste Paper over the Bung: Lay a piece of Flag stone on the Paper, but do not make it too close. If it stands in a warm place it will be ready for use in the Spring.

If a large surface of the Liquor is exposed to the Air, it will be sooner made, and therefore it is better that the Cask should not be full; and if a small quantity of distilled Vinegar is added at the time it is becoming Acid, it will materially forward the making of it.

[p51] Rasberry Vinegar Mrs K

Fill your Jar with Rasberries, and cover them with Vinegar. Let it stand 24 Hours and drain it off and strain it. To every pint add one pound of good Sugar. Put it in a Jar and set the Jar in a pot of Water on the fire until the Vinegar has boiled some Hours. Take care to keep it covered close that no Water from the Pot may get in, and it should be covered with a Bladder whilst in this warm Bath. When taken up and cold, bottle it and cork it very close. When it begins to look tawny it is sufficiently done.

[p146] Rasberry Vinegar

To Two quarts of Rasberries, add one quart of Vinegar. Let it stand before the fire 10 days. Clarify two pounds of fine Sugar. Strain the juice off from the Rasberries. Add the Sugar to it, and boil it untill fine. When cold bottle it in small bottles, and use it as you would Orgeat,[106] mixing it with Water to your taste.

It is pleasant in Fevers.

[p155] Rasberry Vinegar

2 pounds of Rasberries; soak them nine days in one quart of Vinegar. Squeeze the ~~White~~ Whole and add the same quantity of Sugar equal to the weight of the extracted Liquor. Melt the Liquor previously in a small Tumbler of Water. Add to it the White of an Egg with its Shell, which will make the Scum rise. After it is skimmed pour the Syrup into the Liquor which should be boiled 5 or 6 Minuites.

---

[106] See ED's receipt for Orgeat above.

Chapter XVI: Pickling

[p171] Rules for pickling
Use only glazed Stone Jars or Glass for Pickles, and make use of a Wooden Spoon with holes.

[p32] To make Sour Crout
Take some fine hard white Cabages, cut them very small. Have ready a Tub to receive them. Put the Cabage in. To every 4 or 5 ~~Gallons~~ Cabages throw in a han[d]ful of Salt. When they are all put in lay on them a heavy weight, and press them down as flat as possible. Throw a Cloth on them and lay on the Cover. Let them stand a Month. After that they may be used, but they will Keep 12 Months.

The Tub must be always Kept close covered. A few Carraway Seed pounded and thrown in make it eat well.

The way to dress it is with a fine piece of fat Beef or Salt Pork, stewed.

[p110] Coratch[107]
Two heads of Garlick, or 26 Cloves, half an Ounce of common Pepper well bruised, four spoonsful of Soy, 4 spoonsful of Walnut pickle, one pint of Fine Vinegar, one dram of Cochineal; cut the Garlick in slices, and mix all the ingredients, letting it stand 48 hours, then rack it off for use.

[p111] Mandam
A Cucumber chopped very Fine; add one spoonful of Madeira Wine and one of Water, and two of Vinegar, and season to your Palate with onions chopped fine, Cayenne Pepper and Salt.

Better without Water.

[p117] Pickled Cucumbers & Onions[108]
Slice Cucumbers and put them in Salt and Water, in which they should lay two or three days, until the rind is turned Yellow. Then put them on the Fire {Vine leaves should at this time be added} and simmer them until they are green; then take them and drain them. Then boil up some Vinegar with a little Ginger,

---

[107] This receipt is a kind of pickle. In the roll of receipts dating from the reign of Richard II, now known as *The Forme of Cury* , 'Corat' is a dish comprising the chopped and cooked entrails of pigs, cows or sheep, covered in 'a good broth' with chopped young onions, eggs yolks, saffron and salt (*Forme of Cury*, printed edn, London, 1780, p15).

[108] Onions not mentioned in the recipe. Perhaps onions could also be pickled this way?

Mace, Pepper, and Horseradish and pour it on them. As they will be apt to grow mothery; boil them up again in about a fortnight, and after that they should from time to time be looked over.

[p146] Pickle Cucumbers
Take the Cucumbers when gathered, rub them well with Salt and let them lay in it for 24 hours. Then take them out, rub them clean, and put them in a Jar. Then put in a good deal of made Mustard, Garlick, black Pepper, Mace and Horseradish &c.

[p77] To pickle large Cucumbers Mrs Wortham
Scoop out the inside; let it lie 3 or 4 days in Salt and Water; then cut some Horse-radish in pieces, shallots and mustard Seeds, fill the Cucumber with it, then put the piece cut off on and tye it close down, wrap it in vine leaves and put it in a sauce-pan with Vinegar & let it simmer over a slow fire for two days; then boil some Vinegar with Ginger, pepper and Horse radish and pour over it; let it stand to be cold before you tye it down.

The Cucumber must be opened at the side, and not scooped too thin.

[p162] To pickle sliced Cucumbers
Take them when full grown, cut them in slices as thick as a Crown piece. Lay them in a Cullender. Put a row of Cucumbers; then a handful of Salt; then a handful of sliced Onions. Continue doing so until the Cullender is full. Cover them with a Pewter Dish. Let them stand all night, then put them into a Jar. Put in it a blade of Mace, some Ginger and long Pepper & two or three Cloves. Boil the vinegar, skim it well; then put it on and stop them close down to Keep the Steam in. When cold put on a Bladder & Leather, to keep them for use.

[pp121-122] [To mango melons or cucumbers][109]
The exact composition for pickling of Mangoes from a Banyan Manuscript, and serves for Melon or Cucumber.

Take any quantity; Say 50 Cucumbers not over grown, clean them well, scoop out the seed and Pulp. Rub them inside and out with best common Salt, and lay them in a Pan, and strew them over with Salt, employing in the whole

[109] See Glossary under 'mango'. For other receipts where melons or cucumbers are made to resemble mangoes, see, for example, Smith, 'To make Melon Mangoes' and 'To mango Cucumbers' (*Compleat Housewife*, pp104, 107); Raffald , 'To pickle Mango' (*Experienced English Housekeeper*, p178); Rhodes (ed), 'To pickle mangoe' (*In an Eighteenth Century Kitchen*, p41).

one pound and 14 Ounces. Cover them. Let them remain four days, shifting them daily. Then prepare the following Ingredients: 2 lb of peeled Garlick, 1½ pound of Ginger, one pound four Ounces of Mustard seed, one Ounce of Turmeric. Each Clove of the Garlick must be split. The Ginger should be put three Weeks before you use it into an Earthen Pan, strewed with salt to make it tender. It must be cut in small slices and mixed with the Garlick. The Mustard seed should be bruised, but not reduced to powder, The Turmeric pounded. Mix them and add three Ounces of Oil of Mustard Seed & as much strong White Wine Vinegar as will force them into a paste. Tye them close, put them into glazed Jars, and pour on them the best Vinegar boiling hot. The above quantity will take one Gallon. Keep them close covered.

They will be fit to eat in a Month, and will Keep a long time.

[p138] To pickle Cucumbers, or small Melons, to look like Mangoes
Cut off the ends. If the Cucumbers are very long cut them in two. Scoop out the inside. Let them lay in Salt four or five hours, drain them from the Salt, and dry them thoroughly in the Sun. Have ready some bruised white Mustard seed well cleaned and husked [and] Some sliced Ginger. It must be put in Salt and Water, and when it has lain one day or two it will cut in thin slices, which must be well dried before you use it. Some Garlick sliced, a little Salt, a little pounded Turmeric. Mix the ingredients into a Paste with Vinegar. Stuff the insides of the Cucumbers, stick on the ends, rub the pieces with a little sweet Oil and a little of the Paste, and put them into the Jar. As there may not be ends enough for all; stuff them and lay them with the others. Fill the Jar full with the best Vinegar. After a few days fill the Jar again and pour a little sweet Oil on the Top. When they are thoroughly coloured, they are fit to eat.

[pp143-144] To pickle Codlings like Mangoes
Make a brine of Salt and Water strong enough to bear an Egg, into which put a 180 of the fairest and largest Codlings you can get. They should be Full grown; but not Full ripe. Let them lie in the brine 9 or 10 days, shifting the pickle every other day; then dry them and carefully scrape out the core. Take the Stalk so whole that it may Fit in again, and you may leave the Eye in if you do not put the Scoop quite through. Fill it in place of the Core with Ginger and whole Mustard Seed as much as it will hold. Put in the piece, and tye it up tight. Make the pickle of as much white Wine Vinegar as will cover them with sliced Ginger, Cloves of Garlick, and whole Mustard Seeds. Pour this Pickle boiling hot upon them every other day for a fortnight or three weeks.

Stone Jars are best for all sorts of pickle.

This is as good a way as any for middling large Cucumbers, only do not cut them to put \in/ Garlick and Mustard; for they Keep much longer, and eat much more crisp if you let them continue whole.

But neither Cucumbers, Peaches or Melons are comparable to Codlings for imitating the real Mangoe.[110]

[p169] Russia Cucumbers {Smirnove}[111]
Take a very clean \nine/ Gallon Cask, and take out one of the Bottoms; take some sweet scented Thyme, and strew it on the bottom, and some leaves of black Currants; then put a layer of Cucumbers, and over each layer strew some Horse Raddish sliced lengthways into their shreds, and at the same time strew some Dill {or Fennel} Seeds finely pounded; then take for each nine Gallon Cask a bottle of the best Vinegar, and mix it with the necessary quantity of Brine. The Cask must then be closed. The mixture of Brine and Vinegar put on the fire and poured in {through the Bunghole} as soon as it is boiled; Whilst boiling, it must be carefully skimmed.

[p149] Russian salted Cucumbers

For this an[d] other Articles, see *Philosophical Transactions* for 1778 Part 2nd [112]

Put the Cucumbers into a Cask, and as much cold Water as \will/ cover them, with 4 or 5 handsful of Salt, some Oak and black Currant leaves, Dill and Garlick. The Cask is to be then set in a cool place for 48 hours, or untill the Liquor tastes sourish, when it is \to be/ poured off from the Cucumbers into a Pan, and 4 or 5 handsful of Salt are added. Then boil it for 15 Minuites, and when cold return it into the Cask to cover the Cucumbers. The Cask is now to be

[110] See note above regarding pickling fruit and vegetables to resemble mangoes; interestingly at the end of this receipt ED notes that codlings, i.e. apples, produce the best imitations.
[111] For 'Smirnove', see Introduction, p.xxvi and Appendix II.
[112] ED is referring to 'Part of a Letter from Matthew Guthrie, MD, of Petersburgh to Dr Priestley, FRS, on the antiseptic Regimen of the Natives of Russia', read on 30 April 1778, *Philosophical Transactions of the Royal Society*, 68 (1778), pp622-36. This method for salting cucumbers is on p632 and is entitled 'The manner of preparing the Russian salted cucumbers'. Guthrie also included receipts for various kinds of 'quass' ('a liquor which not only serves them for drink but also as sauce for a number of dishes'); 'Russian rye bread'; a kind of porridge made from fermented oat-meal bran; dried horseradish; and preserved turnips. Just over two years later, Elizabeth met Dr Guthrie while she was in Russia (Cross, *An English Lady*, p83).

bunged up for use and placed in a Cellar, where they become crisp and fit to be eaten in 3 or 4 days.

[pp169-170] The process used by the Russians and Germans for perserving [*sic*] Cucumbers during the Winter[113]

Put the Cucumbers into a Cask; pour over them as much Water as will cover them, add four or five handsfull of Salt, some oak and Black Currant leaves, with a little Garlic {if liked} and anise seed. Carry the Cask to a cool place, where it must remain 48 hours until the liquor has acquired a sourish taste; then pour the liquor off from the Cucumbers, and put it into a large earthen Pan; add to it 4 or 5 handsful of Salt, boil this mixture about 15 Minuites, and when cool, pour it over the Cucumbers, which it must cover again; Shut close the Cask, and put it in a Cellar.

These Cucumbers may be eaten in the course of a Few days, or may be preserved a long time if desired.

[p52] To preserve Cucumbers

Take some large and some small Cucumbers; cut the large ones into slices to look like Citron. Let them be of a Fine green, and clear from seed; put them into a strong brine of Salt and Water, & into a straight mouthed Pot, with a Cabbage Leaf over them to keep them down. Tie a Paper over them, and let them stand in a warm place until they begin to turn Yellow; Then take them out, wash them, and set them over the fire in fresh salt and Water to green, with a Cabbage Leaf over them; When they are of a good Colour take them off and keep them in the Water for two days, changing the Water twice in a day, to take out the saltness.

The large ones must be cut, and the seed and soft part should be taken out, before they are put into the Cold Water, then take them out and wipe them dry & put them into a syrup made with double refined Sugar, some Lemon Peel, and a great deal of Ginger, the outside of which must be scraped off before it is put in. Boil the Syrup once in two or three days for about three weeks or as you see occasion, and put it cold to the Cucumbers. They require great attention the first part of the time, after the Syrup is put to them.

[p65] To preserve Cucumbers

Take the largest, greenest and thickest Cucumbers. Put them in ~~a~~ strong Salt and Water, and set them in a warm place. When Yellow, wash them in their own Liquor; put in Fresh Salt and Water ~~and set them in their own liquor; put in fresh salt and Water~~ and Cover them with Vine Leaves. Green them over a slow Fire.

---

[113] This receipt is almost the same as the previous one taken from Dr Guthrie's paper.

When Green, take them off, and let them stand to cool in the same Water. Then cut them open and take out the Seed, wash them, and put them in Fresh Water for two days, changing the Water each day to take out the Saltness. Dry them well in a Cloth and make the Following Syrup: A Pound of fine Sugar to a pint of Water, boil in it some Lemon peel in shreds with a great deal of Ginger scraped & sliced. When the Syrup is cold pour it on the Cucumbers.

[p170] [To make Brine]
The best way of making Brine for the first of these Receipts [on p169], would, I believe, be as follows.

Take one Gallon of Water, put a sufficient quantity of Salt into it to make an Egg swim; then dilute the same with two Gallons more of Water, which will leave the Brine sufficiently strong for salting Cucumbers.

[p17; p163] Mushroom Buttons Mrs Hull[114] +
Wash them in Milk and Water and wipe them with a piece of flannel and throw them into cold Water, drain them and put them in a Saucepan with a little Salt; boil them a Minuite or two, until they are covered with the Liquor, then drain them and spread them on a coarse Cloth and put them in Bottles. Boil the Vinegar, and pour it on cold with a little Mace.

[p12] Mushrooms pickled brown +
Put some Mushrooms in a Saucepan with some Salt, let them stew till quite dry; then put in half Vinegar, half Red Wine and some Mace.

[p16] Mushroom Pickle Mrs Hull Ex[cellent] +
Take the large Mushrooms, break them to pieces, sprinkle them with Salt, let them stand a day or two; squeeze them thro' a coarse Cloth. Let the Liquor stand to settle, pour it clear off and boil it as long as any scum will rise; let it stand until next day, strain it through flannel, then boil it again. When cold put in Ginger, long pepper and allspice to your taste – some prefer boiling the Spice in it.

If you have not a sufficient quantity of Mushrooms at first, you may continue to add more for a Week without any inconveniance.

[p130] To pickle Mushrooms Miss D'
Take your Mushrooms, and cut the inside of the Flap Sacks & peel them, put them into Water, and rub the Buttons with a flannel, cutting off the stalks; Boil

[114] Receipt on [p163] has no donor.

them in a good quantity of Water & Salt, and a bit of Allum; skim them, and when they sink, they are enough; Strain and throw Salt on them; and let them stand until cold, then throw them into cold Vinegar. When you have done your quantity, make your Pickle thus. Put a quarter of a pint of the liquor you boiled the Mushrooms in to a pint and ¼ of White Wine Vinegar, and boil it up with Nutmeg, Mace, and White Pepper; when your Pickle is almost cold, put your Mushrooms in, and do them up very close.

[p133] Mustard +

A quart of the best Mustard Seed well dried, finely beat and sifted, then add 2 parts of White Wine Vinegar, and one of Mountain, also one spoonful of double refined Sugar. Stop it close and it will keep a Year.

This way of making it is preferable to Garlick.

The seed should be good.

[pp39-40] India Pickle[115]

A Pound of raw Ginger and put it in Water one night; then scrape & cut it into slices; sprinkle it with a little Salt, and let it stand in the sun to dry; of long Pepper two Ounces and prepare it as the Ginger; A pound of Garlick cut into thin slices salted and dried as before; a qua[r]ter of a Pound of Mustard Seed bruised and half an Ounce of Turmerick, put these Ingredients, when prepared, into a large Stone, or glass Jar with a Gallon of good White Wine Vinegar; Stir it often for 14 days, then tye it up close.

In this pickle you may put anything, salting it first, and drying it in the Sun.

[p94; p131] India Pickle

One Gallon of Vinegar, one Ounce of Black Peppers, one handful of Salt; boil all together and let them stand, but before it is quite cold, put in one Ounce of Turmerick, boil one pound of Ginger and one Pound of Garlick in Salt Water, and when thoroughly dry put into your Vinegar. The Ginger must be scraped, add a quarter of a Pound of Mustard Seed, and a quarter of a\n/ ~~Pound~~ Ounce of long Pepper.

When the Pickle is once made you may add what you please: Celery, Colliflower, Radishes {scraping them}, French Beans, Asparagus, Cucumbers, Melons, Carrots or Apples, Plumbs, Peaches and Nectarines, or in short

---

[115] This and the following receipts for India Pickle, and the one for 'Yellow Pickle', would later be called 'Piccalilli'.

anything as it comes in Season; Only scalding them in Salt and Water, and observing they are quite dry either by fire or in the Sun.

As the Pickle wastes, fill the vessel up with Vinegar, and it will Keep many Years.

[p160] India Pickle

To a Gallon of Vinegar, one pound of Mustard Seed, one pound of Black Pepper; half a pound of Ginger bruised, Horseradish cut in thin slices. A handful of Shalots, Cayenne Pepper, half an Ounce.

Quere if Turmerick should not be included.

[p63] Yellow Pickle

Take one pound of Ginger, let it lie in Salt and Water one night; then scrape and cut it in slices, and put in a bottle with dry Salt, until the other ingredients are ready. Peel and cut in pieces a pound of Garlick, salt it three days; then wash and put it in the Sun to dry. One Ounce of long Pepper pounded, three Ounces of Turmaric, half a pint of Mustard seed, and one pound of Salt, all dried in the Sun. Put these Ingredients in a large Stone Jar, with one Quart of the best spiced Vinegar, to three quarts of common Vinegar, until the Jar is Full enough. Put in more as you find it wants.

You need never empty the Jar; the Pickle keeps good several Years.

As things are in season put them into the Jar. Take White Cabbages, cut them in quarters, salt them moderately for three days and press out the Water. Collyflowers must be done in the same manner; also Celery & Radishes, which scrape only and leave on the best part. Asparagus and French Beans must be salted only one day: And in the same manner do Melons, Lemons, Apples, Peaches, and Magnum Bonum Plumbs as they are turning Yellow. Cut Carrots very fine into it.

This receipt is proper for all Pickles, except onions, Red Cabbage and Walnuts.

[p135] Quins Pickle[116] Mrs P'-r
One pint of Mushroom Catchup, one pint of Walnut d[itto], 8 Anchovies, 8 Cloves of Garlick, 4 bruised and 4 whole, one teaspoonful of Mushroom Powder and one Teaspoonful of Cayenne Pepper. Let all boil for 10 Minuites, then strain and bottle for use.

[p143] Quin Pickle
Half a pint of Mushroom Catchup, half a pint of Walnut Catchup, 8 Anchovies, 8 Cloves of Garlick, four bruised and four whole; three tea spoonsful of Cayenne pepper, 3 of Mushroom powder; boil them for five Minuites & bottle them when cold.

[p119] Quince[*sic; recte* Quins] Sauce {L[ad]y B'd}
Half a pint of Mushroom pickle, the same quantity of Walnut Pickle, six large Anchovies ~~pounded~~, 6 Cloves of Garlick {3 pounded & 3 whole} two Teaspoonsful of Cayenne Pepper, Two tablespoonsful of ~~Cayenne pepper~~ \Mushroom powder/. Boil all together. Put in a Pot and shake it as you use it.

[p76] To pickle Walnuts
Make a very strong Pickle of Salt and Water, boil and scum it well, pour it over your Walnuts, and let them stand 10 days, changing the Pickle at the end of 5 days. Pour them into a Cullender, and dry them with a coarse Cloth; take good Vinegar with Cloves, Mace, Pepper Corns and sliced Ginger boiled in it; pour it scalding hot on your Walnuts, and let it stay upon them until cold; boil the Vinegar 2 or 3 times to pour upon them hot: When they are cold put in a spoonful of Mustard seed.

You may add some shalots if you like it. A Clove or two of Garlick some think an improvement.

[p119] Pickle Walnuts Mr R'
Lay the Walnuts in cold Water 24 hours, take them out of it, & pour boiling Water over them, and Cover them down close with a Cloth. Repeat this with fresh boiling Water 3 or 4 days, then put them into boiling Water again, and let them lay until thoroughly hot. Take them out, dry them with a Cloth; As you wipe them put them with as much cold Vinegar as will cover them. Let them lay

[116] This and the next two receipts for 'Quin Pickle' and 'Quince Sauce', which are all very similar but not quite the same, do not include quinces; they are savoury sauces. Another slight variation appears in the receipts collected by the Wilshere family of Hitchin; see M Pieris (ed), *Take 6 Carrots*, p42.

in it 24 hours. Take them out and lay one row in the Pot in which they are to be kept. Take 2 or 3 large onions stuck with Cloves, put one at the bottom. St[r]ew in also some Cloves of Garlick and Shalots, some races of Ginger just bruised, and some whole black Pepper and Jamaica Pepper. Then lay the Walnuts in again, and between every 3 or 4 Rows some seasoning {as above} leaving some [room] for Vinegar to cover them. Before you put in the Vinegar to cover them. Before you ~~*illeg*~~ put \in/ the Vinegar, add one Ounce or more of ground Mustard Seed. Then boil up the same Vinegar again adding some fresh to it, and boil and scum it well, and pour it in your Walnuts hot, and tie the pot down close with a thick Cover.

[p103] To pickle Walnuts Green

Take 100 fresh Walnuts before they begin to shell, wrap each in Vine Leaves; put them in a Stone Jar, fill it up with common Vinegar, and put some leaves on the Top to Keep out the Air. Let them stand three weeks; wrap them in fresh Leaves, and pour on the fresh Vinegar. Let them stand three Weeks longer. Wrap them in fresh leaves, which must be washed in Vinegar, and the pickle must be ready to pour on them cold; which must be made as Follows. Six Quarts of the best Vinegar; boil it in common Salt, and bay Salt, of each half a pint; black Pepper and sliced Ginger of each two Ounces; let it stand until cold. Pour the clear liquor and all the spice on the Nuts. Then put an Ounce or more as you like of sliced Garlick and a pint of bruised Mustard seed, and cover them with a handful of Leaves.

[p135] To pickle Walnuts green

Put them into a Jar well lined with Vine leaves, and cover also the Top. Then fill the Jar with common Vinegar, in which two handsful of Salt have been put. Let them stand so until you chuse to pickle. If it is for 5 or 6 Months, they must be covered with Vine Leaves and tyed down close. When you intend to pickle them, take them out one by one and wipe them dry, then put them in a dry close Jar lined with Vine leaves & add as follows:

To each quart of the best White Wine Vinegar, one Ounce of the best flower of Mustard, one large head of Garlick, 2 races of Ginger, one Nutmeg sliced, half a pound of white Pepper, a little Mace, a quarter of an Ounce of long Pepper. Boil them together for about 5 Minuites, and when cold add the Pickle to the Walnuts. Cover them with Vine leaves, and tie them down with a Bladder & leather. They will be fit for use in a Fortnight.

[pp126-127] To pickle Walnuts of an Olive Colour

Tye your Walnuts so close one by one in Vine Leaves; that no Air can come to them. Then put them in a Jar, and cover them with unboiled Vinegar. Let them stand two Weeks; then change the Leaves and Vinegar. Do so three times, and the fourth time put Fresh Leaves and Vinegar, White Mustard seed, Garlick, Horseradish and White Pepper, and tie them down close. They will be fit to eat about January.

It is necessary to chuse Walnuts that are thin shelled when ripe; because they will stay longer before they need pickle them, and then fit to eat will be firmer.

You should also be very careful that none are bruised; for which reason it is best to take your Vine Leaves and Jar with you, and tye them up and put them in under the Tree.

Chapter XVII: Keeping Garden Stuff and Fruit

[p106] To keep Artichoke Bottoms
Boil them as to eat; take off all the Leaves and Choak, take the Buttons[*sic*], and put them in the same [*sic*; *recte* sun], or in an Oven to dry; then put them in Paper Bags. When used, put them in boiling Water.

[p75] To keep French Beans all the year
Put them in an Earthen Pot, and put a layer of Beans and a layer of Salt.

[p152] To Keep French Beans
Put them in stale Beer and a little Salt; and when you want them, boil them with Water that will bear Soap and some Allum. Stop them very close in the boiling, which will make them green.

You must wash them before you boil them.

They will keep all the Year.

[p121] To Keep Green Pease to Christmas
Take fine young Pease, shell them, throw them into a Cullender to drain, lay then on a Cloth 4 or 5 times doubled to drain. Dry them well, bottle them, and Cover them with Mutton Suet. Tye a Bladder over, & set them in a cool place.

Whole Pease buried in the Ground, are said to keep well to February.

[p164] To make Pease Green
Add a little Pot-ash to the Water.

[p4] To Bottle ripe Fruit Daubigny +
You must gather your Cherries or Currants as soon as they are ripe & before they burst. Cut them from the Stalks with a pair of Scizzars, and put them gently into Bottles; Then put the Bottles into a Kettle of cold Water with a little hay. When the Water boils take the Kettle off the fire and leave the bottles to cool in the Water. As soon as the Water is cool, take out the Bottles; Cork and Resin them down, and put them in the Cellar.

The fruit Bottled in this way will keep at least two Years & when boiled up with a little Sugar, or baked in pots will taste perfectly fresh. Care must be taken to gather the fruit in dry Weather, as the least damp prevents their Keeping.

Green pease or young Beans done the same way succeed very well if they are soaked in Milk before they are used and stewed when you send them up they are very good.

Chapter XVIII: Household hints etc[117]

Cosmetics and preparations

[p179] For the Complesion

Take Bean blossoms, red roses, wild tansey and honey suckles; bruise them a little with the Whites of Eggs, and wash with this.

Rosemary Blossoms boiled in White Wine are a great beautifier of the Skin, and sweetens the Breath.

Marrow of Hogs feet, and rose Water mixed with Cowes Milk if applied to the Face lukewarm is a great cleanser of the skin.

Or, Oil of sweet Almonds 2 Ounces; Spermaceti 3 drams; Majesty of Bismuth one dram; Mix together.

[p179] For Spots in the Face

Put a Lemon to the fire, and the Liquor which will run out of it, will clean the face from any redness of Spots.

[p172] To Keep the Hair clean, and preserve it

Two handsful of Rosemary boiled softly in a quart of spring Water until reduced to a pint, covered all the while; then strain them and keep them. Dip a sponge in the Water and rub your hair with it.

[p98] Lady Temple's Hand Paste B

Two pounds of bitter Almonds blanc[h]ed, 2 Ounces of Spermaceti, Two Ounces of Oil of sweet Almonds, 2 Ounces of oil of Tartar, six spoonsful of Brandy. Beat the Almonds in a large Marble Mortar, and mix the other ingredients while they are beating.

[p180] Paste for the Hands

One pound of Almonds; one Ounce of Spermaceti; one dram of Camphor; a Cup of Honey; a Gill of Brandy.

[p180] Another [paste for the Hands]

Half a pound of soft Soap; 2 Ounces of Spermaceti; half an Ounce of Camphor; 3 Spoonsful of oil of Sweet or bitter Almonds which ever you prefer. Put these into a Pan, and the Pan into a Kettle of boiling Water until dissolved.

---

[117] Mrs Raffald did not have any receipts resembling the ones gathered into this final chapter: as they cover a wide variety of subjects, side-headings have been given.

[p178] Honey Water
One quart of rectified Spirits of Wine; 2 drams of Tincture of Musk, half a pint of Water. Filter it, and put it into small Bottles.

[p179; p55] Lavender Water {said to be Smiths}[118]
One and three quarters of an Ounce of English Essence or Oil of Lavender.

A quarter of an Ounce of Ambergris. Three pints and a quarter of rectified Spirits of Wine. Three quarters of a pint of Rose Water, and a few drops of Bergamot. The spirits are to be divided in the first instance and the Rose Water to be put into one half, and the other Ingredients into the other. To stand four days in separate Bottles, to be shook very frequently, and then put together, and filtered through blotting Paper.

[p174] Chopped [*Chapped*] Lips
Bees wax melted, and a little honey mixed.

[p98; p176] Lip Salve
Three Ounces of Spermaceti, three Ounces of White Wax, Seven Ounces of sweet Oil, a quarter of an Ounce of Alkanet Root. Melt these together; but do not let them boil. Put them in China Cups with a little Water at the bottom of each Cup, and when cold turn them out.

[p80] To make Pomade divine[119]
Take of Beef Marrow well picked from the bones and filiments a full pound & half, put it into an Earthen Vessel full of spring Water; change the Water twice in a day for 10 days; then drain it and put a pint of Rose Water to it and let it stand 24 hours; Then strain it through a very thin Cloth, as dry as possible, then add Storax, Benjamin, Cipress, Oriss, of Florence each an Ounce, of Cloves and Nutmegs beat each two Ounces, of Cinnamon half an Ounce; all these must be Finely powdered and extremely well mixed with the Marrow. Then put them in a Pewter Vessel so well closed that nothing can evaporate; suspend the Vessel in a Copper of boiling Water, and let it boil three hours without ceasing. Have more Water ready boiling to replenish that in the Copper, that the Pewter Vessel may be always covered with Water. Then pour if off into Pots.[120]

---

[118] Receipt on [p55] has no attribution. It is not in Smith, *Compleat Housewife*.
[119] See Glossary.
[120] This receipt is virtually the same as that recorded by a member of the Wilshere family of Hitchin. They indicate that 'This Pomade is good for a sore Breast or Bruise & is not the worse for keeping for many years' (M Pieris (ed), *Take 6 Carrots,* p94).

[p180] Marrow Pomatum

One pound of Beef Marrow; put it in a quart of clean Water, change it every day for one Week, then melt it over a slow Fire. Afterwards strain it into a quart of Hot Water. Give it a stir and let it stand 12 hours. Then put the Marrow into a close Pan with half a pint of Oil, & as much essence as you please. Beat it until it is quite cold, and then put it into Pots.

[p85] To make Rose Pomatum

Put as many pounds of Lard as you please into a deep Pan, and to each pound add a large spoonful of Salt; then put as many fresh Rose leaves with the Yellow Stamina [*recte* stamen] of the Roses as you can possibly mix into the Lard. On the next day you will find that a fresh supply of these may be put in, and every succeeding day there will be room for more; continue therefore adding as many as you possibly can for ten days or a fortnight; at the expiration of which time you must tie a bladder over the Pan, and then put it into a Copper or Kettle of cold Water, which must be placed in the fire and made to boil until the Lard, which is standing in it is completely melted. It must be strained and squeezed very dry through a Cloth fit for the purpose. Let it stand to the next day, when you will find it a large Cake of Pomatum; which must be again put into a Jar and melted as before, and again left to drain. This must be repeated until \all/ the fluid is extracted, when you must put the Pomatum into Pots, which must be well covered with Paper, and then put by for some Months, for the older it is, the sweeter it will smell.

Laundry including stain removal

[p167] To make Colours stand in Washing

Put anything coloured in cold Vinegar before it is washed & the colour will stand.

[p171] To recover Black Cloth that is Faded

Take Fig Leaves, boil them in Water and wash the Cloth in it Milk warm; dry it in the Sun.

[p175] To wash Blind Lace

Fold it together and tack it. Soap it well with soft Soap. Sew the parcels which should not be more than 5 Yards long in a white Linen rag [*recte* bag]; put all together in a Sauce-pan of Water; Add a very little Blue, let them boil half an hour, then squeeze them out of that, and put them in some clean Water. Let them only just simmer, squeeze them out of that, and put them in some more Water. They must just simmer. Have ready one Ounce of Isinglass dissolved in a pint of

Water, put a very little blue to it, dip all your bags in it, and squeeze them dry. Then take them out of your Bags, and put them in a folding Sheet, until they are sufficiently dry to Iron, which must be on both sides.

[p176] To clean Silver Lace dry

Two pennyworth of English Talk, and a small piece of Alum, burn them together; sift them through a fine Sieve. Then rub it over the Lace with a fine Brush {soft}. Then rub it with some Crumbs of Stale Bread.

[p179] To get the Gold or Silver out of Lace

Cut the Lace into small pieces, put them into a Cloth, and boil it in an Iron or brass Vessel, with a small quantity of Soap Lees. When you perceive a diminution, which will soon happen unless the quantity of Lace is very great, take out the Cloth, wash it in cold Water, and force out the Soap Lees with a hammer or under your feet. Then untie the Cloth, and you will find the Metal separate.

[p178] To whiten Linen

Wet it well, and lay it on the Grass in a Sunshine day. Cast Water on it wherein Alum has been dissolved and a little Chalk; do this 5 or 6 days, then wash and buck it well; and it will be far whiter and thicker than it was before.

[p171] To take Spots out of Linen

Dissolve some Bay Salt in Water and steep the Linen therein; take the juice of Sorrel, and sharp Vinegar; rub the Spot with them; let it soak in, and the Spot will disappear.

[p173] To take stains out of Muslin, Wine &c

Soft Soap and whiting, lay it on for sometime after rubbing the Muslin.

[p177] [Using Whiting to remove stains]

Whiting and water takes stains out of Buff.
Soft soap and Whiting takes stains of Wine out of Muslin.

[p171] To take out Iron Moulds[121]

Take some Sorrel; bruise it in a Mortar; squeeze it through a Cloth, bottle it, take the juice and boil it over a Lamp; as it boils dip in the iron Mould; do not rub it, only squeeze it. As soon as it is out, put it in cold Water.

---

[121] Almost the same as Glasse, 'To take ironmoulds out of linen' (*Art of Cookery*, p168).

[p171] To clean Ribbons
To be first washed; then boiled in soft Water and Bran for a quarter of an hour. Then wash them in Soap Suds with a few drops of Spirit of Wine. Then rince them well, and dry them in the shade. Iron them with a common Hot Heater.

Scarlet Cloaks will do the same; but they must not be ironed.

[p174] To wash Silk Stockings Miss C[la]y Maid
Cut the Soap in pieces, and pour on it some cold Water. Boil it until the Soap is dissolved. Let it stand until cold. When you wash the Stockings, put some boiling Water to it, so as to be milk warm. Rince them in a strong lather, and fold them wet, and send them to the Mangle.

Care must be taken to mix the red well, tie it in a piece of ~~Cotton~~ rag.

The blue and red to be mixed with the lather.

Sometimes more Soap is required, which may be added.

[p181] To take greasy Spots out of White or Red Silk
Wet the Spot with Spirits of Wine; then rub it over with the White of a New laid Egg. Dry it in the Sun; then wash it with clean Water and press it well.

Dyeing and marking

[p176] To dye Black Lace
Four Ounces of Gum Arabick to half a pint of ~~Milk~~ Ink; put your Lace in it, and let it boil until it is a good Black. Then take it out, and when half dry, pull it out, and wind it round a Bottle.

[p168] To dye Blue
To one pint of Scotts liquid Blue; add three or four Gallons of Water. If you wish to have the Colour bright, put in about a quarter of an Ounce of Vitriol.

Your furniture must be first taken to pieces, washed quite clean, and soaked in cold Water; then rince it, and put in the dye, which should be of a deeper Colour than you intend. The Linen to be dried in <u>a Room</u>, with the Windows & doors shut.

If it is to be calendered, the starch must be put in the Dye.

[p177] Pink Dye
Take the third of a Saucer of the Dye, and mix it well in 6 Quarts of cold Water; dip the Gown into it, and have ready 6 Quarts of boiling water with the Juice of a Lemon squeezed into it. Take the Gown out of the cold Water, and immediately put it into the boiling Water, rince it well until the Water appears

clean at the bottom. Then take it out and hang it upon a Horse upon a Sheet, and hang another Sheet over it. It must not dry near the fire.

Fustick Chips boiled in Water with a piece of Alum, or a Lemon squeezed in when it had boiled, makes a good Yellow.

[p179] To mark Linen

Take of Vermillion as much as will fit on a half Crown piece. Of the Salt of Steel a piece about the size of a small Nutmeg, grind or levigate them well together with Linseed Oil. You may make it thick or thinner as you like.

This will not wash out.

Clothing protection

[p180] ~~A Sweet Bag for Linen~~[122]

A pound of Orrice Root, a pound of sweet Calamus, a pound of Cypress Roots, a pound of dried Lemon peel; a pound of Orange Peel, a Peck of dried Roses. Make these into a gross Powder. Coriander Seeds 4 Ounces, Nutmegs one and half ounces, of Cloves one Ounce, make these into a fine powder and mix with the rest. Add Musk and Ambergrease, 4 handsful of Lavender, A handful of sweet Marjoram, A handful of Orange leaves, a handful of young Walnut leaves. A few Bay Leaves.[123] All dried and rubbed. Mix the whole together, and add some bits of Cotton dipped in Essences. Sew this up in Bags, and put them with your Linen.

[p162] Pot Pouri

Take 3 Pecks of Roses {red} gathered when the Sun shines, that they may be dry. Pick them. Take one and a half pound of Bay-Salt, half an Ounce of Cloves; the same quantity of Nutmegs, Mace and Pimento. Bruise but do not pound the Spices; mix them with the Salt. Then lay the Roses in layers in a Jar, with Salt and Spices sprinkled between each. Cloves, Carnations, Orange Flowers, a small quantity of Lavender or any Flowers that retain their sweetness may be added as they come in Season; always stirring those in the Jar to the bottom of it, when you put in Fresh, which may be done without adding more Spices or Salt.

Damask Roses are preferred, having most Fragrance.

---

[122] Almost the same as Smith, 'To make a sweet Bag for Linen' (*Compleat Housewife*, p235).
[123] Smith omits bay leaves.

[p176] Cloth Balls
Four Ounces of Tobacco pipe Clay, two Ounces of Spirit of Turpentine. Make these into balls with Spirit of Wine, if wanted. Rub the Cloth well, and let it dry on.

[p174] How to render Linen and Cloth impenetrable to Water
Take two Ounces of Turpentine, of pounded Litharge one pound; boil the whole together in two or three pounds of Linseed Oil. With the Mixture do over some of the finest sort of Linen or Lutestring, and let it dry in the Sun, ~~it~~ \which/ by the exposure is rendered harder.

Shoe care

[p130] Blacking
Boil two Ounces of Kid Leather slips in three pints of Small Beer, until reduced to a Quart; then take out the Leather, and put in three Ounces of Sugar Candy, and the quantity of a small Walnut of soft Soap. When about lukewarm, add Four Ounces of Lamp-Black. If too thick add more Beer.

[p130] Or to make Blacking instantly
Beat the Yolk and White of an Egg together, and, with a Stick, stir in as much Lamp or Ivory Black as you judge sufficient. It shines extremely well, and will not soil the ~~neatness~~ neat of Stockings.

[p177] Blacking for shoes {very good} Dr D
Of Ivory Black and brown Sugar, of each, four Ounces. Of Olive Oil One Ounce; of small Beer one pint. Mix the Oil with the Sugar, and a small quantity of the small Beer, add the Ivory Black and the remainder of the Beer, & boil the mixture a Few Minuites.

[p182] To make Shoes Waterproof
One pint of drying Oil; ~~1 pint~~ \2 Ounces/ of Bees Wax, 2 Ounces of Spirits of Turpentine and One Ounce of Burgundy Pitch.

Household paint and varnish etc

[p167] To make a Milk White Paint {*Annales des Artes*}[124]

Of Skim Milk two quarts; fresh slaked Lime eight Ounces; Linseed Oil six Ounces; White Burgundy Pitch two Ounces, Spanish White three Ounces[125]. The Lime is to be slaked in Water, exposed to the Air; mixed in about ¼ of [the] Milk. The Oil in which the pitch is previously dissolved, to be added a little at a time; then the rest of the Milk, and afterwards the Spanish White.

This quantity is sufficient for 27 Square Yards, two Coats; and the price not more than 10 pence.

[p181] To make Yellow Varnish[126]

Take one quart of Spirits of Wine and 7 Ounces of Seed Lace; half an Ounce of Sandrach, a quarter of an Ounce of Gum Anime and one Dram of Mastick. Let these infuse for 40 hours.[127] Strain it off, and keep it for use.

It is good for Table frames, or Chairs, or any wood, black or brown.

Do it on with a Brush three or four times. Nine times at least if you polish it afterwards. A day between every doing. Lay it on very thin the First and second time. Afterwards somewhat thicker.

[p181] White Varnish[128]

To a quart of Spirits of Wine, add 8 Ounces of Sandrach well washed in Spirits of Wine. That Sp[iri]t of Wine will make the Yellow Varnish. Add ¼ of an Ounce of Gum Anime well picked, half an Ounce of Camphor, and a dram of Mastick. Steep this as long as the Yellow Varnish; then strain it out, & keep it for use.

Ink

[p130] Ink

Rain Water, or dead small Beer one Gallon. One pound of Galls grosly bruised. Put them into it, shaking it very often for Four days. Then add 6 Ounces of Green Copperas shaking it well. Four days after add six Ounces of Gum Arabick

---

[124] First published in *Annales des Artes* and reproduced in *The Monthly Magazine, or British Register*, 1 February 1803, p65, in the section 'Literary and Philosophical Intelligence'. Clearly ED obtained this receipt from *The Monthly Magazine*, as she recorded a second receipt from the same page (see below, 'Rancid Oil into Wax').

[125] The original receipt has three *pounds* of Spanish White.

[126] Almost the same as Smith, 'To make yellow Varnish' (*Compleat Housewife*, p366).

[127] Smith has 'thirty six or forty hours'.

[128] Same as Smith, 'To make white Varnish' (*Compleat Housewife*, p366).

Finely powdered, and one Ounce of Allam with four spoonsful of Brandy. It will be fit for use in 12 or 15 days.

To give a blueish Cast infuse some Log-wort [*recte*, Logwood] or Indigo.

[p132] Ink Mr Welford
Galls powdered six Ounces, 3 Pints of Strong Stale Beer, half a pint of Vinegar; let them stand for 3 days, shaking the bottle very often; strain and add green Vitriol, and Gum Arabick both in powder, 4 Ounces, of Sugar Candy and Salt of each ½ an Ounce, 2 ounces of small Spirits of Wine or Brandy.

[pp132-133] Ink Dr Lewis
Galls powdered three Ounces, White Wine vinegar or Fine Beer one quart or if not desired very black, three pints, after standing 3 or 4 days, during which time it should be often stirred. Add one Ounce of Green Vitriol and one Ounce of Lugwood, and one Ounce of Gum Arabick. Let them infuse for about 12 days or 14, shaking the Vessel very often, and then it will be fit for use.

But if it stands still longer, the Ink will be black.

Two ounces of Brandy may be added which will prevent its freezing.

Cleaning etc

[p174] To destroy Bugs
One pint of the Spirit of Turpentine, and one pint of Spirit of Wine, and half a pound of Camphor \que' if not one ounce/, to be mixed all together, and rub the Bedsteads with a Feather dipped in to it.

[p176] To destroy Bugs
Rectified Spirits of Wine, half a pint. New distilled Oil, or Spirits of Turpentine, half a pint; break into it half an Ounce of Camphor. Shake well together, and with a Brush or Sponge dipped in it wet thoroughly every part of the Bed or Furniture.

[p178] To clean Brass
Take a pint of strong Lye; mix with it an Ounce of burnt roach Alum; boil these well together, and then rub the Brass with it. When dry rub it over with Tripoli, and it will not only take away all Spots; but make it look like Gold.

[p178] To clean Silver and give it a fine Polish
Boil it well in Lye, then take it out and smear it over with whiting; let it dry. After that rub it with a warm dry woollen Cloth, and some burnt Alum Powder.

[p175] To clean Mahogany
Three Ounces of Alkanet Root, two Ounces of Rose Pink, one pint of Linseed Oil {cold drawn}. Mix it in an Earthen Pot; let it stand all Night, then rub some of it over the Table with a linen or Woollen Bag, and when it has lain sometime, rub it off with a clean Rag.

[p176] To clean Jewels good
Fine Smalt and Emery, dip a fine Tooth Brush into these Powders mixed together, and rub them with it.

[p178] To refresh Faded Paintings
Take of Tartar and Glass Wort each one Ounce, boil them in a pint of Water, until half is consumed, then strain it. Clean the Painting from Dust with some warm Water & a Sponge, and then pour the strained Liquor over it. This will set a Fine fresh Gloss on it, and make it look as new.

[p171] To prevent the smoaking of Lamp Oil
Steep your Match or Cotton in Vinegar, and dry it well before you use it.

[p171] To take out rust in Iron
Crucible powder, sifted emery, [*no more*]

[p172] [To protect Apple] Trees
Brimstone and Oil destroys the Cochineal in white froth on Apple trees.

[p173] A Paste for holes in Kitchen Utensils
Six parts Yellow Potters Clay, one part of Steel filings, and a sufficient quantity of Linseed Oil, to make it of the consistence of Glaziers Putty.

Poultry Husbandry etc

[p18; p172] To Fat Fowls
Mix Barley Meal with new Milk into a stiff Paste, and make it into long Rolls, large in the middle, small at the ends, wet them in lukewarm Milk; cram the Fowls three times a day. Morn, Noon and Night. They will be fat in a fortnight.

[p25] Fowls to Fatten
Make Barley Meal and Milk it into a Paste, not very thick. Feed them three times in the day, at 8, 1, and 4 o'Clock & give them but little Water each time. Put them up a Fortnight or three Weeks. Fowls at large feed with Barley.
When boiled they should be laid in Milk and Water.

[pp160-161] To fatten Fowls &c

To a quarter of a Peck of Barley Meal, add half a pound of Beef Suet chopped fine. Then make it of the consistence of Paste by adding boiling Milk or Water. Feed the poultry with this Paste three times in the days, between 6 & 7 in the Morning, at Noon & at 5 in the Evening. For drink add to a Quart of Milk a table spoonful of Brandy. This makes them sleep. Cram with the sauce paste, if prefered to Fatten this way.

Turkeys with the same Paste. Ducks the same. Geese with dry Oats without Water. Guinea Fowls with ground Barley, and sometimes Wheat and hard Eggs and Water by itself. Rabbits with dry Oats, and a few Greens, but not Water.

[p177] To feed Fowls with Rice

Boil the Rice to a consistence of paste. One pound will last seven days for one Fowl, when it will be quite Fat. Feed them regularly at 8, 12 and 4 o'Clock, and at the last hour, leave enough for the morning.

[p180] To feed Turkeys

Barley Meal mixed with New Milk made into a Stiff paste. Feed them three times a day & they will be fat in a fortnight.

[p167] Food for Turkeys &c

Barley Meal for Turkeys and Fowls; but half Oatmeal and half Barley Meal is better. Pollard for Duck and breeding Sows, and Young Porkers. Pease for large Hogs.

[p172] [To protect] Poultry

Plant Wormwood or Rue where Poultry is kept. It will keep them free from Vermin.

[p181] To preserve a Henhouse from Vermin

Wormwood and Rue planted near; and boiled Wormwood sprinkled on the floor.

[p181] For the Pip

Put brick dust in the Water. Pull off the Scale with your Nail, and rub the tongue with Salt.

[p172] To keep Eggs
Place them in Chaff, the small end downwards, turning them once a Week. Or in Wood Ashes.

[p172] To chuse Eggs
Place the large end to your Tongue; if it feels warm, it is new, if cold, bad.
Or put an Egg in cold Water, if fresh it will sink; If rotten, it will not sink.

[p172] To chuse Fowls
If a Fowl is young, the Legs will be smooth, if old, rough.

[p173] [To chuse] a Goose
The Bill should be of a pale Yellow, if Young. Both the Bill & feet become red when old.

[p172] [To chuse] a Partridge
If you place the under Bill of a Partridge between your Thumb and finger, and let it ~~hang~~ be suspended, if it is young, the bill will bend \nearly double/ with the weight of the Bird, if old it will not.

[p173] Pigeons
Are red legged when old.

[p172] [To chuse] a Rabbit
If old, the Claws will be long and rough, and grey hairs will be intermixed with the wool. If young the Claws and wool smooth.
\The Ear will also easily slit, if Young./

Other

[pp161-162] The Test of Dr Hardy on the Colic of Poitu[129]
Take one Ounce of Yellow Orpiment, 2 Ounces of Quick Lime; powder them separately and then mix them. Pour on them in a Glass, 12 Ounces of Rain

[129] This is a method for testing for the adulteration of food with lead. James Hardy noted that leaded cider was not only the cause of Devonshire colic, but also of the gout. See James Hardy, *A candid examination of what has been advanced on the colic of Poitou and Devonshire, with remarks on the most probable and experiments intended to ascertain the true causes of the gout. By James Hardy, M D Of Barnstaple, Devonshire* (London, 1778). This test on pp44-45. Hardy states that the original test was prepared by a Doctor De Haen, and gives his Latin text in a footnote.

Water. Having secured the Top of the Glass, digest in a moderate heat 24 hours. When cold and clear, pour it off, and Keep it in a bottle well corked. Boiling it half an hour prepares it equally well.

If a few drops are added to vinegar of Lead or Litharge, and it soon grows black or turbid, the Test is good.[130] It is best kept in small Phials {of an Ounce or half Ounce} as it keeps better.

To try White Wine put a few drops into a Glass half full of White Wine, and if from a Yellow, it becomes of a red Brown or blackish Colour and is also turbid; in proportion as these appearances[131] are more or less apparent; so much[132] the degree of adulteration.

If the Wine is not adulterated, a Milky appearance will only be visible.

[p167] Rancid Oil into Wax M Brugnatelli[133]

Rancid Oil is said to be turned into Wax, Thus. Take 2 parts of Oil, pour in to one part of rectified Spirits of Wine and then another part of Nitric Acid. The rectified Spirits was converted into Ether. The Oil after growing cold and standing undisturbed 12 hours was found changed into a Yellowish White substance, coagulated in a single Mass, insipid, without smell, and of the Nature of Wax.

[p175] To make Mortar impenetrable to moisture[134]

Take of unslaked Lime and fine Sand in the proportion of one part of Lime and three of Sand, as much as a Labourer can carry at once and add Water gradually.

---

130 The method is almost word-for-word to this point; the remainder is partly direct quotation, partly summary.
131 'alterations' rather than 'appearances' in the original.
132 'must' rather than 'much' in the original.
133 Luigi Valentino Brugnatelli (1761-1818) pharmacist, inventor and publisher. His method for converting rancid oil to wax is in *The Monthly Magazine* (1 February 1803), p65. Elizabeth reproduced the method word-for-word, except that she substituted 'rectified spirits of wine' for 'alcohol', which are the same. Since she also copied out the receipt for milk-white paint that occurs on the same page (see above), it is likely that the receipts on page 167 onwards in her book were entered during or after 1803.
134 This method is taken almost word-for-word from Robert Dossie, *Memoirs of Agriculture, and other Oeconomical Arts*, vol II (London, 1771), p22. The title of this chapter (pp20-26), Article III, is 'Account of a Method of making Mortar, which will be impenetrable to Moisture, acquire great Hardness, and be exceedingly durable, presumed to be that used by the Antients'. Dossie states that in 1760 he communicated this method of preparing mortar to the Society for the Encouragement of Arts, Manufactures, and Commerce.

Mix it well together with a Trowel, until it is reduced to the consistence of Mortar. Apply it immediately while it is hot to the purpose, either of Mortar as aliment to Brick or Stone; or of Paister [*recte* Plaster] to the surface of any building. It will then Ferment for some days in drier places and gradually concrete and become hard; But in a moist place it will continue soft for three Weeks or more, although it will at length attain a firm consistence, even if Water should have access to it so as to keep the surface wet the whole time. After this, it will acquire a Stone-like hardness and resist all moisture.

The perfection upon this mixture depends upon the ingredients being thoroughly blended together, and the mixture being applied immediately after to the place where it is wanted. In order to do this, four or five Labourers[135] should be employed for mixing the Mortar to attend the [one] Person who is to apply it.

The Lime should be Stone Lime, and a little bad Cheese improves the mixture; Or it should be made with skimmed Milk, instead of Water.[136]

Dairying

[p163] To make Epping Butter[137]

Put a pint of cold Spring Water to a Gallon of Milk as it comes from the Cow. The Milk Pans must be carefully scalded, and have time to cool before the Milk is set from Cream. The Cream skimmed off at the end of 12 hours, and put into clean Vessels cooled everyday until the Butter is made, which must be twice in a Week. The Cream is then to be shifted into Fresh pots, cleaned as before. From the Milk then skimmed may be taken a second Cream, which will make a good second Broth. The Cream must always be sour before the Butter is made.

In Winter it is necessary to add Vinegar, Lemon Juice, or sour Cream: The two former by being rubbed round the Pot that is to receive the Cream. The Old Cream by preserving a quarter of a pint to add to a quart of new Cream.

In cold weather, the Pot containing the Cream must then be placed in a Large Vessel filled with Water, rather warmer than New Milk: This temperature must be constantly kept up by the addition of more warm Water, until the Cream becomes sour, and thickens to the consistence of a Custard. This operation is to

---

135 Dossie has 'about five labourers'.

136 This last sentence is a very brief summary of Dossie's comments on pp23-6.

137 Epping butter is described in detail by Arthur Young in *General View of the Agriculture of the County of Essex*, vol II (London, 1813), pp278-9. One of the properties of 'Epping butter' was to have a little salt in it. On p283 Young added the comment, attributed to Messrs Griggs, 'Much of the supposed Epping butter comes from the fine dairies in Northamptonshire, and those parts'.

be [per]formed the day after the first Skimming; and the Cream of the following days is to be added to this sour Cream; stirring well after each addition.

In warm Weather, cold Water must be put into the Churn, for the purpose of cooling it, before the Cream is put in; In cold weather a quantity of warm Water for the reverse effect. The Water of course to be let out before the Cream is received.

NB Lemon Juice is better than Vinegar. Half a large Lemon is enough for a quart of Cream

[p176] To make and keep Cheese moist

Put a Plate on it, and lay upon the Plate a double Cloth clipped in small to hang down all round.

[p181] To remove taste from Milk

Dissolve a little Nitre in Water, and put it to new Milk, it will remove any unpleasant taste it may have from the Cows having been fed on Turnips.

[p182] [To prevent a disagreeable taste in Cream or Butter] Curwen's *hints*[138]

The disagreeable taste in Cream or butter from feeding Cows on Green Food is prevented by the following Method.

To every Milk Vessel containing from 6 to 8 Quarts, put on the setting Milk two Tea Spoonsful of the solution of Saltpetre.

The Manner of preparation is as Follows;

Dissolve in Warm Water as much Saltpetre as it will contain, then boil it on a slow fire, until all the Scum which rises on the Surface be taken from it. When cool, strain it off into Bottles for use.[139]

[138] This is copied virtually word-for-word from J C Curwen, *Hints on the Economy of Feeding Stock, and Bettering the Condition of the Poor* (London, 1808), footnote to p144, in the chapter 'On supplying Milk for the Poor'. This entry, the last in Elizabeth's book, must therefore have been made in or after 1808.

[139] In the second edition, the same advice occurs, but with the following instruction added at the end: 'Then of this mixture about 2 teaspoonfuls are to be added to 6 quarts of milk' (J C Curwen, *Hints on Agricultural Subjects, and on the best means of Improving the Condition of the Labouring Classes* (2nd edition, London, 1809), footnote to pp68, 69).

Appendix I: Original order of receipts and their sources

Note: where donors' names were not given in full, those who can be identified have been expanded, those who cannot have been left as they were.

page = page in original manuscript book

chap = chapter in this transcript

page	chap	receipt	donor/source
1	VII	Calves Feet Jelly	Mrs Byde
1	X	Lemon Cream	Mrs Byde
1	X	Almond Cheese Cakes	Mrs Byde
1	X	Almond Cheese Cakes	Mrs Fordham
1	V	Apple Roles	
2	VI	Rice Pudding	
2	III	Pauvre Sauce	
2	IV	Currie	
2	IV	Preparation of the Rice for [Currie]	
2	IV	Mock Turtle	
3	I	Soup Cressé	Daubignée
3	I	Egg Soup	Daubignée
3	I	White Soup	Daubignée
3	I	Crays fish or Lobster Soup	Daubignée
4	II	To Pot Lobsters	Daubigny
4	XII	Maccaroni	Daubigny
4	I	Gravy Soup	Daubigny
4	XVII	To Bottle ripe Fruit	Daubigny
5	XII	Fondool (A Kind of Ramakin)	
5	V	Spanish Puffs	
5	XV	Orange Wine	Leaper
6	VII	A Jelly	Mrs Hads'y
6	XV	Green Gooseberry Wine	Brick[en]d[on]
6	VIII	To preserve Cherries, Currants, Plumbs or other Fruits for Tarts	
6	VI	Imperials	
7	X	Rhenish Cream	
7	VI	Colledge Puddings	
7	XI	A very good plain Cake	Hads'y
7	III	Bread Sauce	

7	XI	Ginger Bread	Jeeves
8	VI	Bath Puddings	
8	XI	Rutland Cakes	Miss Ha't
8	I	Turtle Soup	Mrs Wright
8	XIII	To cure Hams	
9	IV	Mock Turtle	
9	V	Mince Pies	Mrs P' Bengeo Hall
9	VII	Orange Jelly	Mrs ?Mosely
9	XI	A light Cake	Crawly: Hil:
10	IV	Rice for boiled Chickens	
10	II	Haddocks like Pigs Head	
10	II	Oyster Sauce	
10	XII	Norwich Sausages	
10	IV	Bath Receipt for Fricaseeing Tripe	
11	VI	Lemon Pudding	
11	VIII	Hartshorn Jelly	
11	VI	Termin Puffs	
12	I	Brown Pea Soup	Basset
12	XI	Little Cakes (hot) for Tea	
12	XII	To dress Hogs feet and Ears	
12	XVI	Mushrooms pickled brown	
13	III	To roast Sparib of Pork	
13	XIV	Egg Caudle	
13	IV	To stew a Breast of Veal	
14	I	Green Pea Soup without Meat or Water	
14	V	Minced Pyes	Cowell
14	V	Sugar Crust for Tarts	
15	I	Vegetable Soup without Meat or Water	
15	VII	Apple Jelly	
15	II	To stew Eels	
15	II	A rich gravy for Lampreys	
16	XV	Red Currant Wine	
16	IV	Stewed Pigeons	Mrs Harvey
16	XVI	Mushroom Pickle	Mrs Hull
17	XVI	Mushroom Buttons	Mrs Hull
17	III	To Baste a Hare	
17	XII	To make Pease boil Green	

17	IV	A Grilled Breast of Mutton	
17	XI	Buns	Mrs Anderson
18	III	Sauce for Boiled Fowls	Mrs Harvey
18	XVIII	To Fat Fowls	
18	XV	To make Cherry Brandy	Miss D'
18	XIV	Milk Punch	
18	II	Dutch Sauce for Cod or Pike	Mr Y Thomas
18	X	A Custard	Mrs Wright
19	III	Dunstable Larks	
19	IV	A Russian Dish - Chee	
20	X	French Butter	
20	XII	Panada	
20	XIV	Beef Tea	
20	III	Bread Sauce	Cock [*or* Cook] Crawford
20	XII	Stewed Mushrooms	Cock [*or* Cook] Crawford
21	I	Pease Soup	
21	I	Turnips Soup	
21	I	Soup Cressé	
21	XIII	To preserve Ham and Bacon	
22	XV	Ginger Wine	Wright
22	XV	Raisin Wine	
22	IX	Fruit Paste	
23	IX	Fruit Cakes	
23	XI	Bath Buns	
23	XI	Tops and Bottoms	
23	VI	Little Puddings in Cups	
23	XI	Wafer Cakes	
23	XIV	Milk Punch	
24	XIV	Milk Punce [*sic*]	
24	VII	Orange Jelly	Mrs H'
24	VIII	Lemon Jelly	Mrs M'
24	VIII	Orange Sweetmeat	Mrs M't
24	XII	Omlet	?Wiltjie
25	XII	Omlet	Orme
25	II	Dutch Fish Sauce	
25	IV	Fowl a la Tartare	
25	XVIII	Fowls to fatten	

25	III	Sauce for Boiled Fowls	Mrs M
25	IV	Fricandeau	Mrs M
26	XII	Ramakins	Mrs M
26	VI	Orange Pudding	
26	II	Lobster Sauce	Mrs Trail
26	II	To stew Flounders	Sir E Hulse
27	II	The Sussex Sauce for Carp & Tench	
27	II	Dutch Sauce for boiled Turbot or any Flat Fish	
27	II	Cold Sauce for Fish or Flesh	
27	III	To Fry Cucumbers for Mutton Sauce	Racket's Savory Dish
28	II	To stew Lobsters with Pease	
28	IV	To roast a Calfs Head	
28	XII	Sausages	
28	IV	To hash a Calves Head	
29	IV	To Hash a Calves Head White	
29	IV	Garnish for a Calves Head	
29	IV	To make Forced Meat	
30	IV	White Collops	
30	IV	Alamode Beef	
30	IV	Calves Liver Stewed	
30	XII	Stew Pease	
30	XII	French Beans stewed White	
31	II	To pickle Salmon	
31	XII	Beignets a l'Allemande	
31	XII	To stew Cucumbers brown	
31	III	Hashed Mutton	
31	XII	French Beans done Brown	
32	XII	Mushrooms stewed white	
32	XVI	To make Sour Crout	
32	XV	Mushroom liquor and Powder	
32	IV	To fricassee Tripe	
33	I	Curry Soup	Mirzapore
33	IV	Curry	Mirzapore
33	V	Gravy for Meat Pies	
33	V	Gravy for Fish Pyes	
34	XIII	Pickled Pork	
34	XIII	Beef Scarlet	
34	XIII	Hambed Beef	

34	I	Soup Cressé	
35	I	Egg Soup - for 10 Persons	
35	I	White Soup	
35	I	Cray Fish or Lobster Soup	
35	VI	A light Pudding	
35	IV	Pigeons	
35	IV	Pigeons en Compôte	
36	III	Boiled Pigeons	
36	VII	Lemon Syllabub	
36	XI	Savoy Biscuits	
36	X	Potatoe Cream	
36	VII	Orange Jelly	
37	X	Lemon Cream	
37	VI	Carrot Pudding	
37	X	Steeple Cream	
37	VI	Farly Newhavens Receipt for Dutch Puddings	
37	VI	Bushbridge Puddings	
38	V	Biscuit Crusts for Tarts	
38	XI	Maccaroons	
38	XIV	Egg Wine	Mollands
38	XII	Rich Cheese	
38	X	To make abundance of Cream	
39	IX	To preserve Green Leaves	
39	XI	Little Cakes	
39	VII	Dutch Flummery	
39	XV	Vinegar Syrup	
39	XVI	India Pickle	
40	X	Custards or burnt Cream	
40	XII	Calves Feet a la Sainte Manchoult	
40	X	Olivers Biscuits	
40	VIII	Conserve of Quinces	
41	VIII	To preserve Barberries	
41	VIII	To preserve Rasberries	
41	VIII	To preserve Cherries	
41	VIII	To preserve Apricots	
42	VIII	To preserve Green Apricots	
42	VIII	To preserve Currants	
42	VIII	To preserve Quinces, White or Red	

43	IX	To dry Cherries	
43	IX	To dry Plumbs	
43	IX	To dry Apricots	
44	IX	To candy Cherries	
44	IX	To Candy Apricots, Pears, Plumbs &c	
44	IX	To preserve and Candy Orange & Lemon Peel	
45	VIII	Quince Marmalade	
45	VIII	Orange Marmalade	
45	VIII	Peach Marmalade	
45	VIII	Apple Marmalade	
46	VIII	Currant Jelly	
46	X	To make cream of any sort of Fruit	
46	XI	Roles	
46	XII	Petits pois a la Bourgeoise	
47	IV	A Daube	
47	II	To stew Carp	
47	XIII	To make a Ham of 16 lb weight	
48	VI	A Dish of Apples and Rice	Byd
48	XI	Small Tea Cakes	Byd
48	XI	Oatmeal Cakes	Dr R
48	XIV	Oatmeal Jelly	Dr R
49	XIV	Water Gruel \Scotch/	Dr R
49	XIV	Gruel Porridge - Scotch	Dr R
49	XI	Water [*sic*; *recte* Wafer] Cakes	Byd
49	V	Spanish Puffs	Byd
49	III	Sauce Robert	Mrs S
50	III	Sauce Piquants	
50	VIII	To preserve Strawberries whole	
50	IV	Inky Pinky	Mrs K’
50	XV	Orgeat	Mrs K’
51	X	Lemon Sallad	Mrs K’
51	XV	Rasberry Vinegar	Mrs K’
51	IV	Italian Savory Cake	Mrs K’
51	XV	Camp Vinegar	Mrs K’
51	IV	To dress a Cold Fowl	Mrs K’
52	XIV	Mock Asses Milk	
52	XVI	To preserve Cucumbers	

Appendix I: Original order

53	X	A very good Cake and Plain	Had’
53	XV	Gooseberry Vinegar	Byd
53	XV	Nectar	Dr Ingenhouz
53	XV	To make Grape Wine	
54	XII	To drop Caravansera French Beans	
54	IV	Calves Head Brawn	
55	XVIII	Lavender Water	
55	XII	Calves Feet	
56	IV	A Ragout of Veal A small Dish	French Receipt
56	III	A Brown Hash of Chicken &c	
56	IV	Boeuf a la Mode	French Receipt
57	IV	Mutton D'Etruffe	Madame La Combe
57	VI	Veal White	French Receipt
58	III	A Brown Hash of Mutton, Beef or Hare &c	French Receipt
58	IV	A Harrico of Mutton	French Receipt
59	I	Hessian Soup	
59	V	Lemon minced Pies	
59	IV	Veal Ragout	French Receipt
59	VI	An Ommelette a la Pomme	
60	IV	To stew Beef	
60	X	Lemon Cheese Cakes	Miss Clay
60	XI	Sweet Cakes	
61	X	Custards	Miss C’y
61	XV	Green Gooseberry wine	
61	VI	Ground Rice Pudding	
61	VI	Hunting Pudding	
61	VI	Lemon Pudding	
62	XV	White Currant Shrub	
62	XV	Raisin Wine	
62	XII	Stewed Cucumbers	
62	II	To pot Eels like Lampreys	
62	II	To Collar Eels	
63	XIII	To pot Partridges	
63	XVI	Yellow Pickle	
63	XV	To make Frontiniac Wine	
64	XV	Currant Wine	
64	XV	Cowslip Wine	
64	VIII	Currant Jelly	

64	X	Apple Cheese cakes	
65	XVI	To preserve Cucumbers	
65	I	To make a Soup	French Receipt
65	V	A Duck Pye	
66	VIII	Bullace or Damson Cheese	
67	II	To make a Matelote	
67	IV	To stew Beef	Miss C'y
68	X	Lemon Cheese Cakes	
68	XI	A Gateau Fourré	
68	VI	Cream Fritters	(French)
69	IV	To make Brawn	
69	II	To stew Lampreys or Eels	
70	IV	To Cabbage a Hare	
70	II	Carp Sauce	
70	XIV	To make Coffee	
70	XIV	Café a la Caramele	
70	XIV	Café a la Minuite	
71	XIV	Café a la Crème	
71	X	Crème a Petit Pots: Baked Custards	French
71	X	Renish Cream	
71	VI	A light Pudding	
72	X	Lemon Cream	
72	XIV	Clarified Lemonade	Mrs Minet
72	VII	Almond Flummery	
72	VI	Sago Pudding	
73	XI	Little Cakes	
73	VI	German Rice Milk	
73	VI	Firmity	
73	VIII	To preserve Barberries	
73	V	Lemon Minced Pies	
73	XI	Gingerbread	Miss Jeeves
74	VI	Apple Pudding	
74	X	To make German Puffs	
74	X	Apple Cheese Cakes	
74	VI	Paté Royale	
75	XV	To make Shrub	
75	XIV	Orange Whey	
75	XIV	Neagas	
75	XIV	Whey	

75	X	A Triffle	Miss Hatton
75	XV	To make Walnut Ketchup	
75	XVII	To keep French Beans all the year	
76	XVI	To pickle Walnuts	
76	XII	Ramakins	Miss Hatton
76	VI	To make White Puddings	Miss Hatton
76	XI	Wiggs	Miss Hatton
77	XVI	To pickle large Cucumbers	Mrs Wortham
77	VI	Baked Apple Pudding	Miss H' (?Hatton)
77	VI	Rice Omlet	Miss H' (?Hatton)
77	X	Burnt Cream	Miss H' (?Hatton)
77	I	Soup a la Reine	Miss H' (?Hatton)
78	XV	Elder flower Wine	Miss H' (?Hatton)
78	X	Cheese Cakes	Miss H' (?Hatton)
78	II	Fish Sauce	Miss H' (?Hatton)
78	IV	To stew Veal	Miss H' (?Hatton)
79	IV	To make a Curry	Miss H' (?Hatton)
79	VI	College Pudding	Miss H' (?Hatton)
79	XI	Ratafee Cakes	Miss H' (?Hatton)
79	X	Barley Cream	
80	XIV	Barley Water	
80	XVIII	To make Pomade divine	
80	IV	To make Curry	[deleted]
80	XI	Rice Cake	E H
80	I	Root Soup	
80	VI	Rice Omlet	
81	I	Soup a la Reine	
81	XII	Irish Macani	Lord O
81	VI	Potatoe Pudding	
81	XIII	The Peak Receipt	
81	IV	To make Veal Olives	
82	VI	To make a six hours Pudding	
82	XIII	To cure Bacon	
82	XIII	To pickle Hams	
82	VI	Souflée Pudding	Lord O
83	V	Crust of Pastry without flour	Mrs Clitherow
83	XI	A considerable increase by making Bread with Bran Water	
83	XV	Currant Wine	Mrs K

83	XIII	An American Receipt for making Hams	Mr Nicols
84	XIII	To cure Hams	Mrs Hall
84	II	To make a Fricassee of Lobsters	
84	VI	Rice Pudding	
84	XI	Bread with Rice	Mrs Gardiner
85	XVIII	To make Rose Pomatum	
85	XIII	To dry a Leg of Mutton	
85	XV	Walnut Ketchup	
86	XV	To make Vinegar	
86	XV	Strong Mead	
86	XI	Little Seed Cakes	
86	XII	Sausages	
87	IV	To make Forced Meat	
87	I	To make Solid Broth	
87	XIV	Imperial Drink	
87	XIII	To pickle Pork	
87	XIII	To salt Hams	
88	XI	Ginger Bread Cakes	Lady P
88	XII	A very good and cheap Vegetable Hodge Podge	
88	XII	To make Macaroni	Miss Byron
89	XIII	To salt Tongues	
89	XV	Orange Wine	Lady St John
89	V	Potatoe Pastry	
89	VII	Solid Syllaboobs	Mrs Champion
90	VII	Manche Blanche	Mrs Champion
90	XIII	To make Hams	Mrs Champion
90	I	To make a Soup	
90	IV	Harico of Mutton	Mrs Champion
90	XIII	To pickle Pork or Beef	Mrs Champion
91	VII	Calves Feet Jelly	Mrs Byde
91	XI	Small cakes	Mrs Champion
91	V	Meat Mince Pies	Mrs Champion
91	XI	French Bread	
91	VIII	Harlsern [Hartshorn] Jelly	Mrs Byde
92	III	Venison to dress	B. D. Cook
92	III	Poverroy Sauce	
92	VII	To make a very fine Syllabup	

92	III	Sauce for Boiled Fowl	Mrs C'
93	XI	Little Cakes	Mrs Hill of Pelham
93	IV	Ragout of Neck or Breast of Mutton	Mrs C'
93	I	White Soup	Mrs C'
94	X	Lemon Cheese	Mrs C'
94	XI	A Cimmon[*sic*] Cake	Mrs C'
94	XVI	India Pickle	
94	II	To pickle Oysters	Mrs C'
95	VI	To make a quaking Bread Pudding	
95	VI	Rasberry Fritters	
95	VI	Rice Fritters	Mrs C'
96	XII	To dress Macaroni	Mrs C'
96	XII	To make Ramakins	B
96	X	Triffle	B
96	XI	French Rolls	
96	V	Lemon Pies	B
97	V	Mince Pies	B
97	VI	A Rich Plumb Pudding	B
97	VII	Dutch Syllabubs	B
97	IV	Chicken with Rice	B
97	XIII	An excellent Receipt to cure Hams	B
98	VIII	Orange or Lemon Syrup	
98	XVIII	Lady Temple's Hand Paste	B
98	XVIII	Lip Salve	
98	XIV	Calves Foot Jelly	B
98	IV	Mrs Clapham's Mock Turtle	
99	XI	Dr Oliver's Biscuits	
99	XIII	To salt Beef red	Keyser (or, Kuper)
99	X	Almond Cheese Cakes	B
99	VIII	Bullace Cheese	
100	VII	Everlasting Syllabubs	B D
100	X	Sago Cream	
100	X	Raw Lemon Cream	B
100	X	Lemon Cheese Cakes	B D
100	IV	To bake a Calves Head	
101	VI	Plumb Pudding without Eggs	Lady Gould
101	XII	A Ramakin	Mrs D' of Hitchin
101	IV	Bouillée Beef	B D Cook
102	XV	Walnut Catchup	Mr Backhouse

102	IV	Ox Palates Baked	
102	XV	Catchup to Keep Many Years	
102	III	A standing Sauce for a Kitchen	
103	II	Fish Sauce	
103	XV	Walnut Catchup	
103	XVI	To pickle Walnuts Green	
103	III	Shalot Sauce for Roast Fowl	
103	III	Poverry Sauce	
104	III	A good Sauce	
104	V	Welch Pyes	Mrs Fordham
104	XI	Buns	
104	XI	Short Roles	
104	X	To make a Cream of Codlings	
104	XI	Maccaroons	
105	II	To Collar Eels	
105	XIII	To pot Beef	
105	IV	To stew a Breast of Veal	
105	XII	Black Puddings	
105	I	Soup meagre with Pease	
106	V	Paste for Tarts	
106	X	Plain Cheese Cakes	
106	X	Whip Cream	
106	XVII	To keep Artichoke Bottoms	
106	XI	Carraway Bunns	
106	II	Water Souchy	
107	XII	A six Hour Cheese	
107	XII	To dress Calfs Feet	
107	IV	White Sauce for a Fricassee	
107	X	French Cheese	
107	XII	To stew Cucumbers	Duchess of An[caste]r
107	XII	Ramakins	Mrs M'rs
108	V	Spanish Puffs	
108	XI	Thin cakes	
108	VI	Semolina Pudding	Mrs M'y
108	XV	Rasberry Brandy	
109	VI	Curd Puffs	
109	VI	Baked Bread Pudding	
109	III	To boil a Ham	
109	III	To boil a Tongue	

109	II	Lobster Ragoued	
109	XV	Clara wine	
110	XVI	Coratch	
110	IV	Harico of Mutton	
110	III	Celery Sauce	
110	VIII	To preserve Codlings	
110	X	Boiled Custard	
111	XVI	Mandam	
111	XI	Dow Nuts	Mrs Fordham
111	XIII	For salting Hams	
112	XII	Amlet	B D's Cook
112	XIV	Brandy Posset	
112	XII	Loggerhead Cheese	
112	XII	To dress Calve's Brains	
112	XI	Potatoe Bread	
113	II	Stewed Soals	
113	IV	Ragout of Veal	
113	IV	Cuckow and Sauce	B D Cook
114	I	Brown Pea Soup	
114	I	A la Reine Vermicelli or White Soup	B D Cook
115	V	French Pye	B D Cook
115	IV	Ragoued Sweetbread	
115	XII	To do Pigs Ears	
116	X	French Butter	
116	VI	Baked Apple Pudding	
116	II	Dutch Sauce for Cod or Pike	
116	VI	A Twopenny Pudding	
116	XIV	Milk Punch	Dr Y
117	XI	Biscuits	Mrs Fordham
117	X	Almond Cheese Cakes	Mrs Fordham
117	XVI	Pickled Cucumbers & Onions	
117	V	Sugar Crust	
118	X	Boiled Custard	Mrs B
118	VI	Lady Sunderlands Puddings	
118	XV	Orange Wine	
119	XI	French Rolls	
119	XVI	Quince Sauce	L[ad]y B'd
119	XVI	Pickle Walnuts	Mr R'
119	XIV	The best Imperial	Mrs B D

120	XV	Rum Shrub	Dr Y
120	XIII	To salt a Buttock of Beef in a Few hours	Mrs D' H'
120	VI	White Pot	Mr W'd
120	V	A short Paste for Tarts	
121	XIII	To salt Beef	
121	III	To boil a Ham	
121	XVII	To keep Green Pease to Christmas	
121	VII	To Colour Jellies	
121	III	Sauce for cold Fowl or Game	
121	XVI	[To mango melons or cucumbers]	Banyan manuscript
122	XIII	Hamburg Pickle	
122	VI	Plumb Pudding	
122	XII	Oxford Sausages	
122	XI	A Cake	
123	XV	Spruce Beer	
123	XI	Pound Cake	
123	XV	Orgeat	
123	VI	A common Tansey pudding	
123	II	Soals a la Cartolette	
123	VI	A fine baked Pudding	
124	II	A Matelot	
124	XI	Dutch Biscuits	
124	V	Partridge Pye	
124	VII	A floating Island	
125	IV	A Currie	
125	XI	A very light Cake	
125	XIII	To cure a Ham	
125	XI	To make Muffins	
125	VI	Plumb Pudding	as Mrs P'
126	XII	Macaroni	Almacks
126	VII	Flummery	Mrs C't, Albury
126	XV	The Gloucester Manner of making Cyder	
126	XVI	To pickle Walnuts of an Olive Colour	
127	XV	Elder Flower Wine	
127	IV	An excellent Fricassee of Tripe	
127	IX	To make clear Cakes	Mrs B'

127	IX	To dry Cherries	
128	VIII	Cherries Wet	Mrs B’
128	VIII	For preserving Apricots	
128	IX	To dry Apricots	
129	VIII	To preserve Apricots in Syrup	Mrs B’
129	VIII	Apricot Jam	
129	II	To pickle Oysters	
129	VII	Lemon Jelly	Mrs B’
129	VIII	Red Marmalade	Mrs B’
130	XVIII	Ink	
130	XVIII	Blacking	
130	XVIII	Or to make Blacking instantly	
130	VIII	To Clarify Sugar	Mrs B’
130	XVI	To pickle Mushrooms	Miss D’
131	V	Minced Pyes	Mrs B’d
131	XV	To make the Best Cherry Brandy	
131	XVI	To make India Pickle	
131	XV	Walnut Catchup	
132	XI	French Roles	
132	IV	Mock Turtle	
132	XVIII	Ink	Mr Welford
132	XVIII	Ink	Dr Lewis
133	XIV	Imperial	
133	XVI	Mustard	
133	III	A good Sweet Sauce for boiled Mutton &c	
133	XI	Cracknells	
133	VI	Puffs to fry instead of Fritters	
134	II	To dress Sounds and Tongues	
134	II	To stew Carp	
134	XII	To stew Cabbage	
134	XII	Sausages	Lady G’d’
134	I	Brown Pea Soup	
135	III	Essence	
135	V	A short Crust	Mrs P’r
135	XVI	Quins Pickle	Mrs P’r
135	XVI	To pickle Walnuts green	
135	II	Sauce for Fish or Flesh	
136	VI	Princess Amelia’s Pudding	Mrs P’r

136	IV	Stewed Beef Stakes	Mrs P'r
136	V	Seasoning for Meat Pies and Sauce	Mrs P'r
136	XIII	To cure two middle sized Hams	
136	XIII	To cure a Tongue	Mrs P'er
136	II	Salmon Caveach	Ms C'y
136	XI	Little Cakes hot for Tea	[deleted]
137	XV	Orange Shrub	
137	VII	Blanc Mange	
137	VII	Dutch Blanc Mange	
137	II	To stew Carp	
138	XVI	To pickle Cucumbers, or small Melons, to look like Mangoes	
138	IV	To make Curry stuff	Mrs C'
138	VI	Potatoe Pudding	
139	II	To pickle Oysters	
139	XV	Shrub	
139	XV	Walnut Catchup	
139	II	To dress Ling	
139	I	Gravy Soup	
140	II	Pickle Oysters	Mrs L
140	XV	Walnut Catchup	
140	IV	To dress A Duncan Fowl	
140	XI	Plumb Cake	
141	VI	Almond Pudding	
141	X	Lemon Cheese Cakes	
141	X	Cheese Cakes	
141	X	Cheese Cakes	Mrs B
141	XI	Pound Cake (without sugar)	
142	IV	To stew Ox Cheek	
142	VI	Baked Puddings	
142	II	To collar Salmon	
142	XIII	To rough Beef	
143	XVI	Quin Pickle	
143	XII	Sausages	
143	II	To dress Ling	
143	XVI	To pickle Codlings like Mangoes	
144	IV	To stew Tripe brown	Mrs M'w
144	IV	A White Fricassee of Rabbits	
145	VI	Suet Pudding	Mrs G C

145	V	Sea Pye	
145	III	Tongue and Udder	
145	III	Fowls roasted the Scotch way	
146	XV	Rasberry Brandy	
146	XV	Rasberry Vinegar	
146	XV	Walnut Catchup	
146	XVI	Pickle Cucumbers	
146	XIII	To cure Beef or Pork to keep many years to be red & juicy	Sir C Knowles
147	I	Scotch Broth	
147	III	Stewed Chickens	
147	XIII	To cure a Ham	
147	IV	To stew a Leg of Mutton	
148	XIV	Lemonade	
148	VI	A fine Baking Pudding	
148	VI	Sago Pudding	
148	XIII	To pickle Pork	
149	XVI	Russian Salted Cucumbers	Philosophical Society
149	XII	Calves Brains to dress	B D Ck
149	IV	Boeuf a la Daube	
150	II	A Ragout of Oysters	
150	XII	Oyster sausages	
150	XII	Six Hour Cheese	
151	XI	A pound Cake	
151	IV	Bouille Beef	
151	XI	Macaroon Biscuits	
152	XVII	To keep French Beans	
152	XI	A Fine Plumb Cake	
152	XV	Gooseberry Wine	
152	VIII	Hartshorn Jelly	
153	V	Fine paste for Tarts	
153	XI	A Seed Cake	
153	VI	To make Mays Puddings	
153	X	Lemon Cream	
153	X	Orange Cheese Cakes	
154	VI	A Tansey	
154	XIII	To souce a Pig	
154	XIII	Collar Beef	
154	V	Lemon Pies	

155	XV	Rasberry Vinegar	
155	VIII	Currant Jelly	
155	VIII	Rasberry Jam	
155	XV	Currant Shrub	
155	XV	Currant Wine	
156	XV	Smyrna Raisin Wine	
156	XV	A second sort from the pressings of the Fruit	
156	XV	Raisin Wine	
156	VIII	Damson Cheese	
156	IV	Mock Turtle	
157	IV	To make a Pillow, the Indian Way	
157	IV	To boil Rice	
157	IV	A Currey, the Indian Way	
158	VIII	Plumb Cheese	
158	IV	Mrs Clapham's Mock Turtle	
158	XI	Almond Wafers	
158	VI	Custard Pudding	
159	XIV	Lemonade	
159	VI	Millet Pudding	
159	IV	Hodge Podge	B' D
159	V	Crust for a Crocant	
159	VII	Lemon Jelly	
159	XI	Gingerbread	
160	XIII	To pickle Pork or Beef	
160	III	Sauce for a boiled Fowl	
160	XV	Lemon Catchup	
160	XVI	India Pickle	
160	II	To boil Fish firm	
160	XVIII	To fatten Fowls &c	
161	XIII	Veal Hams	
161	XIII	Beef Hams	
161	XVIII	The Test of Dr Hardy on the colic of Poitu	Dr Hardy
162	XVIII	Pot Pouri	
162	XVI	To pickle sliced Cucumbers	
163	XVIII	To make Epping Butter	
163	XVI	Mushroom Buttons	
164	XVII	To make Pease Green	

164	III	Sauce Piquante for roast Veal etc	
164	XII	Colliflower to dress	
164	XII	French Beans	
164	I	Lemon Pickle	Madame De la Combe
165	X	Burnt Cream	
165	X	Burnt Cream another way	Madame De la Combe
165	XI	Macaroon Biscuits	Madame De la Combe
166	IV	Veal Steaks in papers	Madame De la Combe
166	VI	Cream Fritters	Madame De la Combe
166	XIII	To pickle Tongues	Madame De la Combe
167	X	Lemon Cream (without Cream)	Madame De la Combe
167	VI	To answer the purpose of an Egg in a Pudding	
167	XVIII	Food for Turkeys &c	
167	XVIII	To make Colours stand in Washing	
167	XVIII	To make a Milk White Paint	*Annales des Artes*
167	XVIII	Rancid Oil into Wax	M Brugnatelli
168	XVIII	To dye Blue	
168	VI	Custard Pudding	Mrs D' of Hitchin
168	XV	Ginger Wine	
168	XII	Macaroni	Mrs Kennett
169	IV	Minced Veal under the brown raised up	Mrs Kennett
169	VIII	Lemon Jelly	
169	XVI	Russia Cucumbers	Smirnove
169	XVI	Process used by the Russians and Germans for perserving [*sic*] Cucumbers during the Winter	
170	XVI	[To make Brine]	
170	II	Baked Herrings or Sprats	
170	II	Stewed Sprats	
171	XVI	Rules for pickling	
171	XV	To recover Beer that is Flat	
171	XVIII	To take Spots out of Linen	
171	XVIII	To take out Iron Moulds	
171	XVIII	To prevent the smoaking of Lamp Oil	
171	XVIII	To clean Ribbons	
171	XVIII	To recover Black Cloth that is Faded	

171	XVIII	To take out rust in Iron	
172	XVIII	To keep the Hair clean, and preserve it	
172	XVIII	[To protect] Poultry	
172	XVIII	To fat Fowls	
172	XVIII	To chuse Eggs	
172	XVIII	To keep Eggs	
172	XVIII	To chuse Fowls	
172	XVIII	[To chuse] a Partridge	
172	XVIII	[To chuse] a Rabbit	
172	XVIII	[To protect Apple] Trees	
173	XVIII	Pigeons	
173	XVIII	[To chuse] a Goose	
173	III	Meat	
173	III	Chickens, Veal and Lamb	
173	XV	Currant Wine	Mrs Patmore
173	XVIII	To take stains out of Muslin, Wine &c	
173	XVIII	A Paste for holes in Kitchen Utensils	
174	XVIII	To wash Silk Stockings	Miss C[la]y maid
174	XVIII	Chopped Lips	
174	XVIII	To destroy Bugs	
174	XIV	Venlo's Syrup	Venlo
174	XVIII	How to render Linen and Cloth impenetrable to Water	
175	XVIII	To make Mortar impenetrable to moisture	
175	XVIII	To wash Blind Lace	
175	XVIII	To clean Mahogany	
176	XVIII	To clean Jewels	
176	XVIII	Cloth Balls	
176	XVIII	To dye Black Lace	
176	XI	To take the bitter out of Yeast	
176	XVIII	To destroy Bugs	
176	XVIII	To make and Keep Cheese moist	
176	XVIII	To clean Silver Lace dry	
176	XVIII	Lip Salve	
177	XI	To keep Yeast	Mrs H'y
177	XVIII	To feed Fowls with Rice	

177	XVIII	Pink Dye	
177	XVIII	[Using Whiting to remove stains]	
177	XVIII	Blacking for Shoes	Dr D
177	VIII	To preserve Oranges whole or in halves	B D
178	XVIII	To whiten Linen	
178	XVIII	To refresh Faded Paintings	
178	XVIII	To clean Silver and give it a fine Polish	
178	XVIII	To clean Brass	
178	XIV	Sansparolli	
178	XVIII	Honey Water	
179	XVIII	For the Complesion	
179	XVIII	Lavender Water	said to be Smiths
179	XVIII	For Spots in the Face	
179	XVIII	To mark Linen	
179	XVIII	To get the Gold or Silver out of Lace	
180	XVIII	Marrow Pomatum	
180	XVIII	Paste for the Hands	
180	XVIII	Another [paste for the hands]	
180	XVIII	A Sweet Bag for Linen	
180	XVIII	To feed Turkeys	
181	XVIII	To make Yellow Varnish	
181	XVIII	White Varnish	
181	XVIII	To take greasy Spots out of White or Red Silk	
181	XVIII	To remove taste from Milk	
181	XVIII	To preserve a Henhouse from Vermin	
181	XVIII	For the Pip	
182	XVIII	To make Shoes Waterproof	
182	XIV	Sage Wine, for the Head-ache	
182	XVIII	[To prevent a disagreeable taste in Cream or Butter]	Curwen's *hints*

Appendix II: Donors of receipts

Notes:
The people listed here were known to Elizabeth Dimsdale; in cases where receipts had a person's name in its title, the source is described in a footnote.

Family relationships come from a family tree in the possession of the Dimsdale family unless otherwise stated.

Spellings of Christian names have been standardised, eg Ann for Ann, Anne etc; Susanna for Susanna, Susannah etc.

Sources:
In addition to papers in the Dimsdale Family Archive (DFA) (in private hands), the following items have been consulted (for full details, see Bibliography):

Accounts	G Sheldrick (ed), *The Accounts of Thomas Green, 1742-1790*
Burke's	L G Pine (ed), *Burke's Peerage Baronetage and Knightage,*
Crisp	F A Crisp (ed), *Visitation of England and Wales, Notes,* vol 13
Cross	A G Cross, *By the Banks of the Thames. Russians in Eighteenth-Century Britain.*
Cussans, I	J E Cussans, *History of Hertfordshire*, vol I, *Braughing Hundred …*
Cussans, II	J E Cussans, *History of Hertfordshire*, vol II, *Hertford Hundred*
HALS,DE/X3	Hertfordshire Archives and Local Studies, the diaries of John Carrington, farmer of Bramfield
HALS, HBR	Hertfordshire Archives and Local Studies, Hertford Borough Records
Herts 1731-1800	A Jones (ed), *Hertfordshire 1731-1800 as recorded in* The Gentleman's Magazine
ODNB	*Oxford Dictionary of National Biography*, online version (subject and their dates given)
VCH	W Page (ed), *Victoria History of the Counties of England: A History of the County of Hertford*, 4 vols

Mrs. Anderson: William Anderson voted for Baker and Calvert in the 1784 Hertford Borough election (HALS, HBR, vol 24, p90).

Duchess of Ancaster: either, Mary, second wife of the 3rd Duke of Ancaster, daughter of Thomas Panton, married 27 November 1750, died 19 October 1793; or, Mary Ann, second wife of the 5th Duke of Ancaster, daughter of Major Layard, married 2 January 1769, died 13 January 1804. In August 1782 and January 1783, Thomas Green was paid by the housekeeper of the Duchess of Ancaster for tuning a harpsichord at Sacombe Park. John Carrington, farmer of Bramfield, recorded in his diary the funeral cortege of Duchess Mary Ann stopping, on 23 January 1804, at the Red Lion, Woolmer Green to refresh the horses on their way to Lincolnshire (*Accounts*, pp58, 59; *Burke's*, p57; HALS, DE/X3/7, entry dated 23 Jan. 1804).

Mr Backhouse: member of a Quaker family

Basset[t]: members of the Bassett family lived in Hertford up until at least the middle of the eighteenth century. In his diary John Carrington mentioned a Joseph Bassett mainly in connection with the sale or purchase of timber (HALS, DE/X3, *passim*).

Brickendon: *see* Lady Gould below

Mrs Byde (Byd'; B'; B'e; By'e): probably Eleanor, wife of Thomas Plumer Byde, MP, of Ware Park. She died at Wigmore Street, Cavendish Square, 23 March 1794. Byde was one of Thomas Dimsdale's first banking partners from 1769 - and possibly earlier - until at least 1774. Thomas Green frequently tuned instruments at Ware Park for the Byde family (*Accounts*, *passim*; Cussans, I, p141; DFA, Thomas Dimsdale junior, Memoranda).

Miss Byron: probably one of the daughters of Richard and Ann Byron (daughter of John Iles of Hertford, and niece of Thomas Dimsdale's second wife Ann) and sisters of Thomas Byron of Bayford.

Mrs C---t Albury: probably Ann Calvert (née Byron), wife of Edward Calvert of Albury; her grandfather, John Iles of Hertford, was one of the elder brothers of Ann, second wife of Thomas, 1st Baron Dimsdale. Thomas's grandmother was Susanna Bowyer, eldest daughter of Felix Calvert, purchaser of the Furneaux Pelham estate (DFA, Thomas Dimsdale junior, Memoranda).

Mrs Champion: probably Susanna, the daughter of Thomas Dimsdale's younger brother Joseph, who married George Champion of Bristol. She was a beneficiary of Elizabeth's will (see Appendix 3).

Mrs Clapham: John Carrington often dined with 'Clapham'. Carrington's daughter, Mary Ann, married James Clapham (HALS, DE/X3, *passim*).

Miss Clay (C---y): probably a cousin of the Dimsdales. The Clays were connected to them through Felix Calvert. Elizabeth Clay (née Calvert) was Felix's third child; Susanna, Thomas Dimsdale's grandmother, was the eldest (DFA, Thomas Dimsdale junior, Memoranda).

Mrs Clitherow: the Clitherow family's seat was at Bird's Place, Essendon; Thomas Green tuned instruments for both Mr and Mrs Clitherow on several occasions (*Accounts*, pp51, 53, 54, 60; *VCH*, III, pp458-9).

Cowell: possibly connected with Dr Cowell, a Quaker who served with Thomas Dimsdale in the English army 1745 and who obtained a post at St Thomas's Hospital in 1749. No known later connection with the Dimsdales (William Wadd, *Mems. Maxims, and Memoirs* (1827), p281).

Crawly: Hil: a John Crawley voted for Dimsdale and Calvert in the 1784 Hertford Borough election (HALS, HBR, vol 24, p89).

Baron Dimsdale: presumably Thomas, 1st Baron Dimsdale, 1712-1800.

Dr D: possibly Dr John Dimsdale of Hitchin and later Hertford, one of Elizabeth's brothers.

Mrs D(imsdale) of Hitchin: presumably Elizabeth Dimsdale's sister-in-law, Priscilla (née Pitts), wife of Elizabeth's brother, John Dimsdale of Hitchin; she was born 1749, married 1773. She was a beneficiary of Elizabeth's will.

Miss D(imsdale): possibly Priscilla Dimsdale, Elizabeth Dimsdale's niece, and daughter of John Dimsdale of Hitchin and his wife Priscilla. Close to Elizabeth and Thomas in the 1790s in Hertford, when they were living at Cowbridge House. Born 1779, married a Gosselin. She was a beneficiary of Elizabeth's will.

Mrs Fordham: there were Fordhams at Royston, Sandon and Therfield. Edward Fordham of Therfield (1721-1778) and his wife Mary (née Carter) had four sons, each of whom married. 'Mrs Fordham' could be any of these five ladies. John Fordham of Royston (1748-1830), banker and brewer married Mary Newling; Edward King Fordham of Royston (1750-1847) married Sarah Chantrey; George Fordham of Sandon and Odsey (1752-1838) married Elizabeth Fordham; and William Fordham of Sandon (1756-1829) married Sarah Newling (J Fordham, *Memoirs and Family History*).

Mrs Gardiner: most likely one of the Mrs Gardiners of Thundridge Bury. The Gardiner family owned the manor of Thundridge from 1543 to 1811 (*VCH*, III, pp378-9).

Lady Gould: possibly Jane, wife Sir Charles Gould, who took his wife's surname of Morgan on inheriting the property of her relations. This may imply a connection with Brickendonbury. (Cussans, II, pp67-68; *ODNB*, 'Morgan [formerly Gould], Charles, (1726-1806)'). Or, possibly Elizabeth, wife of Sir Henry Gould and daughter of Dr Walker, Archdeacon of Wells. Sir Henry died at his house in Lincoln's Inn Fields, London, on 5 March 1794, not far from the Dimsdales' London House at Red Lion Square (*ODNB*, 'Gould, Sir Henry, (1710-1794)').

Mrs Hadsley (Hads'y; Hads'): perhaps the wife of Jeremiah Rayment-Hadsley of Ware Priory; she was formerly Miss Goodwyn of St Paul's Churchyard. Mr Hadsley died in 1777. Thomas Green taught music to Miss Hadsley of Ware and purchased a harpsichord either for or from Mrs Hadsley in 1788/9 (*Accounts*, pp84, 92, 140, 141; Cussans, I, p 154; *Herts 1731-1800*, p156).

Mrs Hall: possibly Sarah Hall, died 24 June 1804, aged 64; wife of Richard Hall, a Director of the East India Company, who died 23 November 1786, aged 56 (Cussans, II, pp79-80).

Miss Hatton: a Robert Hatton voted for Baker and Calvert in the 1784 Hertford Borough election. In April 1803 John Carrington collected taxes from Miss Hatton of Broadoak End, near Hertford. Elizabeth Ann Hatton was one of the witnesses to Elizabeth's will. (HALS, HBR, vol. 24, p98; HALS, DE/X3/6, entry dated 30 April 1803)

Mrs Hill of Pelham: presumably a resident of either Brent, Furneux or Stocking Pelham.

Sir E Hulse: either, Sir Edward Hulse, 2nd baronet, died 1800; or, Sir Edward Hulse, 3rd baronet, died 1816. The latter's wife's maiden name was Lethieullier and she was therefore connected to the Dimsdales through Bethiate Fryer, the first wife of Nathaniel Brassey, father of Thomas's first wife Mary Brassey.

Ingenhouz: Jan Ingen Housz, 1730-99. Friend of Thomas and Elizabeth Dimsdale; taken by Thomas early in 1768 to assist with an emergency general inoculation of Little Berkhamsted and Bayford villages. Inoculated members of the Habsburg family at Vienna at the same time as Thomas was inoculating in St Petersburg and Moscow. First describer of photo-synthesis; conducted experiments with fertilizer in the garden of Cowbridge House. Maintained at Bowood by the Marquess of Lansdowne; buried at Calne, Wiltshire (DFA; personal communication between Robert Dimsdale and Norman and Elaine Beale). See also Introduction, pp.xxvii-xxviii.

Jeeves: a Jeeves family lived opposite Cowbridge House, Hertford, home of Thomas and Elizabeth from 1790 until 1800. Mr Jeeves transcribed Elizabeth's Journal. He had two unmarried sisters. Thomas Jeeves voted for Dimsdale and Calvert in the 1784 Hertford Borough Election (DFA, 1854 letter of Joseph Dimsdale, ref. D16; HALS, HBR, vol 24, p98).

Mrs Kennett: either, Hannah, the wife of Alderman Kennett, Lord Mayor of London 1780 during Gordon Riots, a vintner (d.1782). In 1788, she married George Hankin of Hertfordshire. (*Herts 1731-1800*, p.162; *ODNB*, 'Kennett, Brackley (c.1713-1782)') Or, Sarah, his daughter in law, who, in 1774, married his son Revd Mr Brackley Kennett, morning preacher at Berkeley Chapel. She was the daughter of [*blank*] Mahew, esq, of Hertford (*Herts 1731-1800*, p156).

Mrs Minet: presumably Rebekah Minet, died 18 April 1819, aged 76; wife of Daniel Minet, FRS, died 25 February 1790, aged 61; memorial in St. Leonard's, Bengeo (Cussans, vol II, p38).

Mr Nicols: possibly Henry Nicols, friend and correspondent of Thomas Dimsdale; Russia Company member (DFA).

Orme: in about January 1781, the Hon Mrs Orme, wife to Robert Orme, esq, MP, daughter of the late Viscount Townshend, died at Hertford; Robert Orme died in June 1790; and their eldest daughter, Audrey, died in 1791. Robert Orme junior was the vicar of All Saints, Hertford, 1786-1843, and was also long time rector of Bayford and Essendon (Cussans, II, p88; *Herts 1731-1800*, pp200, 222, 224).

Mrs Patmore: two men named William Patmore voted for Baker and Calvert in the 1784 Hertford Borough election (HALS, HBR, vol 24, p88).

Mrs P... Beng[e]o Hall: the Proctor family lived at Bengeo Hall (*Herts 1731-1800*, p160).

Smirnove: Iakov Ivanovich Smirnov (1754-1840); Ukrainian chaplain to the Russian Church in London from 1782 to 1837; also diplomat and agricultural specialist (Cross, *passim*).

Lady St John: either, Susanna Louisa, wife of John, 11th Baron St John of Bletso, of Bletsoe, Bedfordshire; she was daughter of Peter Simond, a French Huguenot merchant in London; she died in 1805, aged 80, at Bath. Or, her daughter-in-law, Emma Maria Elizabeth, wife of Henry 12th Baron St John; she was the second daughter of Samuel Whitbread the elder of Cardington, Bedfordshire (*Burke's*, p1856).

Mrs Wortham: possibly Ann, wife of Hale Young Wortham of Aspenden, and daughter of Thomas Proctor of Bengeo Hall; she died 2 June 1824, aged 62 (*Herts 1731-1800*, p160).

Mrs Wright: possibly another Brent Pelham and Calvert connection. Honour Wright, daughter of William Wright of Beaches, near Brent Pelham, and his wife Margaret, one of the daughters of Felix Calvert (*d.* 1698). Baron Thomas's maternal grandmother was the eldest of Felix Calvert's children (DFA, Thomas Dimsdale junior, Memoranda).

Dr Y: perhaps William Yeates. Mentioned in vestry book of St Andrew's, Hertford, 1777-1779: doctor's account paid; churchwarden 11 February 1779; petitioner for a peal of bells 22 October 1781. He voted for Dimsdale and Baker in the 1784 Hertford Borough election (HALS DP/49/8/2; HALS, HBR, vol 24, p89).

Appendix III

TNA, PROB11/1538/279, the will and codicils of Elizabeth, Baroness Dimsdale[1]

[*margin*] The Honourable Elizabeth Baroness Dimsdale

I Elizabeth Dimsdale, of the Parish of Saint John in the town of Hertford in the County of Hertford, Widow of Thomas Baron Dimsdale deceased, do make this my last Will and Testament in manner and form following, hoping the Lord will receive my Soul and desiring my body may be buried in a plain private manner by the side of my dear husband the said late Baron Dimsdale at Stortford. Of my temporal affairs I dispose as followeth.

First I give and bequeath to my brother in law Stephen Hagger[2] the sum of one hundred pounds of lawful money of Great Britain.

Also I give and devise all that my estate at Butchery Green in the Town of Hertford aforesaid, which was left me by Richard Iles,[3] \lately/ in the occupation of the widow Hart, with all appurtenances thereto belonging, unto my nephew Doctor William Dimsdale, son of my brother John Dimsdale, his heirs and assigns forever. And I give and bequeath unto the said Doctor William Dimsdale the sum of thirty pounds of lawful money of Great Britain. Also my Journal to and from Russia in a black box, and all that is in it, my book of pictures of the Russian People in the Russian Empire and the five volumes of \the/ Account of Russia.

Also I give and bequeath to my niece Elizabeth Hagger[4] of Hertford fifty pounds of the like money.

Also I give and bequeath to my nephew John Dimsdale, son of my said brother John Dimsdale, thirty pounds of like money.

---

[1] Punctuation and paragraphs added; common abbreviations extended silently.

[2] Stephen Hagger's deceased wife was Susanna, Elizabeth's sister. The will of Stephen Hagger, mealman, of Hertford, was proved on 5 May 1814. He appointed as one of his four executors 'my Sister Elizabeth Dimsdale widow of the late Thomas Baron Dimsdale' but in the event she predeceased him (TNA, PROB11/1556/2405). A transcript of Stephen's will and information about the Hagger family were kindly supplied by Martin Hagger. See also the family tree in the endpapers.

[3] Presumably a relative of Ann Dimsdale, née Iles, Baron Thomas's second wife; Elizabeth's stepson Richard Iles Dimsdale died in 1812, after this will was written.

[4] Daughter of Susanna and Stephen Hagger.

And I give and bequeath to my nephew Joseph Dimsdale, son of my said brother John Dimsdale, thirty pounds of like money.

Also I give and bequeath to my niece Priscilla Dimsdale, daughter of my said brother John Dimsdale, fifty pounds of like money and my cabinet which stands in my chamber and \all/ that it contains, the Glass Case of Shell Flowers which were my cousin Bells, the glass case of stuffed birds given to me by Mistress Plumer, and all the pictures that are in the china room.

Also I give and bequeath to my sister Priscilla Dimsdale, wife of my said brother John Dimsdale, all my china (except the eleven china dishes and turin that Baron John Dimsdale[5] gave me which I desire may be offered to him for his Acceptance).

The silver turin which was my said late husbands I give & bequeath to Nathaniel Baron Dimsdale.[6]

And understanding that I have a power to give to any of the said late Baron's children the plate that was his and of which I am to have the use only for my life, I therefore give and bequeath the same plate (except the silver turin), an account or inventory of which signed by me is in the possession of the said Nathaniel Baron Dimsdale, unto my daughter Ann Dimsdale[7] for her own sole and absolute use as it has ~~happened~~ \appeared/ to me rather a hardship she was excluded from having any of the other plate of her late father.

Also I give and bequeath unto my nephews Thomas Hagger and Stephen Hagger[8] twenty pounds apiece, unto Mistress Susannah Champion[9] the sum of thirty pounds of like lawful money, unto Thomas Neatby Hagger (Grandson of my said brother in law Stephen Hagger)[10] and to Hannah Downes his Sister[11] the sum of ten pounds apiece of like lawful money. Also I give unto my Servant John Tott, if he shall be living in my service at my decease, the sum of ten pounds of like money

[5] Thomas' eldest son, who inherited his father's Russian title.

[6] Thomas's second son, who received his Russian title of Baron in his own right from Catherine the Great for his medical services.

[7] Thomas's younger daughter.

[8] Sons of Susannah and Stephen Hagger.

[9] Daughter of Thomas Dimsdale's younger brother Joseph; Susannah had married George Champion of Bristol.

[10] Grandson of Stephen Hagger, son of his son Joseph. Joseph was believed to be abroad at the time of his father's death.

[11] Wife of Robert Downes and granddaughter of Stephen Hagger, daughter of his son Joseph.

All which several legacies I desire may be paid and delivered by my executor within six months next after my decease.

Also I do hereby give and forgive unto my brother Doctor Robert Dimsdale all the interest already due or hereafter to become due during his natural life for and in respect of a mortgage by him made to my said brother John Dimsdale of a messuage or tenement cottage and other hereditaments in Stortford for securing the payment of five hundred pounds with interest, which said Principal Sum and all Interest due for the same amounting together to the sum of six hundred and fifty pounds I have lately paid off and have taken an assignment of the said premises to myself. And from and after the decease of the said Doctor Robert Dimsdale I give and bequeath the said sum of six hundred and fifty pounds and all my estate, Interest, Claim and demand in and to the said mortgaged premises unto his son William Dimsdale, his executors administrators and assigns for his and their own use and benefit.

And after payment of my just debts, legacies, funeral and testamentary charges and expenses I give and bequeath all my monies in the public funds and all monies that may be owing to me, except the aforesaid Principal sum and interest, and also all my household furniture of every kind, liquors in the cellars and all my effects whatsoever (except such things as are mentioned in a paper addressed to my said brother John and my Sister Priscilla Dimsdale) unto my said brother John Dimsdale, his executors, administrators and assigns for his and their own use and benefit.

And I do hereby constitute and appoint my said brother John Dimsdale sole executor of this my last Will and Testament. In witness whereof I have hereunto set my hand and Seal this second day of September in the year of our Lord one thousand eight hundred and eight ~ E Dimsdale *[12] ~

Signed, sealed, published and declared by the said Elizabeth Dimsdale the testatrix as and for her last will and testament in the presence of us who have hereunto subscribed our names as Witnesses: Elizabeth Ann Hatton - Thomas Nicholson – William King.

17th Nov 1803[13]
My dear brother John and Sister Priscilla Dimsdale. It is my desire and Particular request that when it shall please Almighty God to take me out of this world that I be not buried for nine or ten days but remain until there appears marks of decay, then carried to Bishop Stortford and buried by my dear husband in the most private manner.

---

[12] A mark to indicate that the original will was sealed.
[13] This *is* the correct date – see below for verification of this 'codicil'.

I desire my brother Dr Robert Dimsdale may have, if he is alive at the time of my death, three pair of common sheets and three pair of Pillow bears three ditto table cloths and ditto six Napkins. And my daughter Mary Dimsdale of Bristol[14] to have the best shawl and my Sister Priscilla Dimsdale the other as there is two.

My desire is that my nephew Joseph Dimsdale may have my box of coins and medals, the two five guinea pieces, my book of old letters of my great grandfather and grandmother, in short all it contains. My desire is at my death that my brother John Dimsdale give my nephew John Dimsdale one of my books, to make it equal between John and Joseph as my regard to them both is the same and I should be sorry to act with partiality to either of them.

One of my large bibles it is my desire my niece Elizabeth Hagger may have - they were my Aunt Sarah Bowyers and it was her request to me to give her one at my death. The gold watch and gold case it was the Barons desire my daughter Ann Dimsdale might have at my death. It is my particular request my niece Elizabeth Hagger may have some of my clothes and linen which is proper for her to wear. And I likewise desire my maid living with me, if she continues to behave well, to have some of my inferior clothes and linen. I recollect my Sister Priscilla Dimsdale did say she should like to have my manuscript book which I give her, it contains serious religious Anecdotes.

In regard to the diamond solitaire the Great Dutchess, now Empress, of Russia gave me but not the diamonds, It was the Barons desire it might remain in ~~the~~ \his/ family. I desire it may be given to my Son Baron John Dimsdale at my death.

These particular requests I have not a doubt but my brother John and Priscilla Dimsdale will most strictly observe and comply with, and I trust and believe we shall at last meet and know each other in a state of happiness, for the goodness and care of an Almighty God who has attended me all through my life will never forsake \me/, and my heart overflows with gratitude and praises which cannot be expressed in words, and remember how much I wish you and all your family health and happiness. Adieu for ever in this world

E. Dimsdale

I desire Baron John Dimsdale may have the china turin & dishes which he gave me returned to him if he wishes to have them.[15]

---

[14] Mary Champion married Thomas's son Joseph in Bristol in 1776; Joseph died there in 1784.

[15] In the probate register, this bequest is added after ED's signature but the affirmations below suggest that it was incorporated in the main body of this first codicil.

At my death I desire that my nephew William Dimsdale son of Doctor Robert Dimsdale of Bishops Stortford may have twenty pounds. \If/ I have not in a former Paper given my maidservant Betty Squires twenty pounds, I wish her to have it at my death, should she then live with me. The twenty pounds which I have left in my will to Stephen Hagger Junior I wish to be divided between his children.[16] I desire that the Cook & housemaid now living with me may have five pounds each at my death, should they then continue in the family. The housemaid Mary Warren is the servant of my sister.

E. Dimsdale – 21 June 1812

[*affirmation by John Dimsdale*]
I John Dimsdale of Hertford, in the County of Hertford, Esquire, do hereby solemnly, sincerely and truly affirm and declare that I am one of the dissenters from the church of England commonly called quakers and that I am the natural and lawful brother of Elizabeth Dimsdale, late of the Parish of Saint John in the Town of Hertford in the said county of Hertford, Widow, deceased, who departed this life on or about the sixteenth day of the month of October last, and that being at the house of the said deceased at Hertford aforesaid and on examining the said deceased's Papers he found in a bureau, and in which the said deceased usually deposited her papers of moment and concern, the papers writing [*sic*] hereunto annexed purporting to \be/ and contain the last will and Testament with two codicils annexed of the said deceased enclosed in an envelope or cover sealed up ~~in~~, the said will beginning thus "I Elizabeth Dimsdale of the Parish of Saint John in the Town of Hertford in the county of Hertford widow of Thomas Baron Dimsdale deceased", ending thus "In witness whereof I have hereunto set my hand and seal this second day of September in the year of our Lord One thousand eight hundred and eight", and thus subscribed "E Dimsdale"; the first Codicil or testamentary Schedule beginning thus "17th Nov 1803. My dear brother John and Sister Priscilla Dimsdale it is my desire and particular request that when it shall please Almighty God to take me out of this troublesome world", ending thus "And remember how much I wish you and all your family health and happiness Adieu forever in this world", and thus subscribed "E Dimsdale"; the second Codicil beginning thus "At my death I desire that my nephew William Dimsdale son of Doctor Robert Dimsdale of Bishops Storford [*sic*] may have twenty pounds", ending thus "The housemaid Mary Warren is the servant of my sister", and thus subscribed "E Dimsdale".

[16] Stephen Hagger, son of Elizabeth's brother-in-law Stephen, had died on 29 August 1810. His children were named Susanna, Letitia, Elizabeth, Hannah and William.

And that on then viewing and carefully perusing the said will beginning and ending as aforesaid he particularly observed the words thirty and thirty written on an erasure in the twenty second and twenty \fourth/ lines of the said will to be computed from the top thereof, and that also viewing and carefully perusing that first codicil or testamentary schedule of the said deceased beginning and ending as aforesaid, he particularly observed the Obliterations in the 12th, 13th, 14th & 15th lines of the first side of the said codicil to be also computed from the top thereof and also the obliterations in the fourth [*sic*], fifteenth, sixteenth and seventeenth lines of the second side of the said codicil, and that the said will and codicil are now in every respect in the same plight and condition as when he found the same deposited or enclosed in the said envelope or cover in the said deceased's bureau as aforesaid, save the *Jurate* appearing written thereon.

And he, lastly, affirms and declares that he doth verily and in his conscience believe that the said second codicil or testamentary schedule bearing date the said seventeenth day of November 1803[17] beginning, ending and subscribed as aforesaid to be the very Paper referred to in and by the last will and Testament of the said deceased. ~ John Dimsdale ~ The 6th Day of November in the year of our Lord 1812.

The said John Dimsdale made and subscribed the aforegoing declaration or affirmation according to Act of Parliament before me, C Coote Sur[rogate] ~ Pst[18] William Brown Not[ary] Pub[lic].

[*affirmation by William Pitts Dimsdale and Joseph Dimsdale*]
I William Pitts Dimsdale of Cornhill, London, Banker,[19] and Joseph Dimsdale of Saint Johns Street West Smithfield, in the county of Middlesex, Druggist,[20] do hereby solemnly, sincerely and truly affirm and declare that we are two of the dissenters from the church of England commonly called quakers and that we knew and were well acquainted with Elizabeth Dimsdale, late of the parish of Saint John in the town of Hertford in the said county of Hertford, widow, deceased, for some time before and down to the time of her death which

[17] Earlier in the affidavit, this codicil, dated 17 November 1803, is actually referred to as the first codicil or testamentary schedule.
[18] Perhaps abbreviation short for 'present', ie witness?
[19] William Pitts Dimsdale was the eldest son of Elizabeth's brother John; 'Pitts' was the maiden name of his mother, Priscilla. In her will Elizabeth referred to 'my nephew Doctor William Dimsdale, son of my brother John Dimsdale': here William stated that he was a banker.
[20] Joseph and William were brothers; Joseph was the youngest son of John Dimsdale.

happened on or about the sixteenth day of the month of October last, and also with her manner and character of handwriting, having often seen her write and subscribe her name. And now viewing and carefully perusing the papers writing [*sic*] hereunto annexed, purporting to be and contain that last will and testament with two codicils thereunto annexed, the said will beginning thus "I Elizabeth Dimsdale of the parish of Saint John in the town of Hertford in the county of Hertford Widow of Thomas Baron Dimsdale deceased", ending thus "In witness whereof I have hereunto set my hand and seal this second day of September in the year of Our Lord one thousand eight hundred and eight", and thus subscribed "E Dimsdale"; the first codicil or testamentary schedule beginning thus "17 Nov 1803 my dear brother John and sister Priscilla Dimsdale It is my desire and particular request that that [*sic*] when it shall please Almighty God to take me out of this world", ending thus "And remember how much I wish you and all your family health and happiness. Adieu forever in this world", and thus subscribed "E Dimsdale"; the second Codicil beginning thus "At my death I desire that my nephew William Dimsdale son of Doctor Robert Dimsdale of Bishop Stor[t]ford may have twenty pounds", ending thus "The housemaid Mary Warren is the "servant of my Sister", and thus subscribed "E Dimsdale", they do verily and in their conscience believe the whole body, series and contents of the said second codicil or testamentary schedule of the said deceased, beginning, ending and subscribed as aforesaid, together with the several interlineations appearing therein, as also the memorandum, in the words following, appearing on the back thereof "I desire Baron John Dimsdale may ~~may~~ have the china turin and dishes which he gave me returned to him if he wishes to have them", And the said names "E Dimsdale" appearing, set and subscribed thereto, and the said names "E Dimsdale" appearing, set and subscribed to the said second codicil beginning and ending as aforesaid, to be all the Proper handwriting and subscription of the said Elizabeth Dimsdale Widow deceased ~ W P Dimsdale ~ Joseph Dimsdale.

The sixth day of November in the Year of our Lord 1812, the said William Pitts Dimsdale and Joseph Dimsdale made and duly subscribed the aforegoing declaration or affirmation according to Act of Parliament before me ~ C Coote Sur[rogate] ~ Pst Wm Brown N P.

Proved at London, with two Codicils, 11th November 1812, before the Worshipful Charles Coote Doctor of Law and Surrogate by John Dimsdale, the brother and sole Executor, to whom Admon' was granted by having first made a solemn and sincere declaration or Affirmation according to act of Parliament duly to adm[inister].

Glossary

Abbreviations used in the Glossary (for full details, see Bibliography):

Glasse	Prospect Books, 'Glossary and Notes' in Hannah Glasse, *Art of Cookery* (1995 facsimile edition), pp173-204
ED	Elizabeth Dimsdale
Ellis	William Ellis, *Country Housewife's Family Companion* (2000 edition)
Jaine	Tom Jaine, personal communication
Mason	Laura Mason, *Sugar-Plums and Sherbet*
Nott	John Nott, *Cook's and Confectioner's Dictionary* (1980 reprint)
OED	*Oxford English Dictionary* (online edition)
Prospect glossary	Glossary on website of Prospect Books https://prospectbooks.co.uk/glossary/
Raffald	Elizabeth Raffald, *The Experienced English Housekeeper* (1997 edition)
Rhodes	D Rhodes (ed), *In an Eighteenth Century Kitchen*
Wilson	C Anne Wilson, *Food and Drink in Britain*

[ ] = ED's spelling

ale-yeast: *see* barm

alkanet root: southern European plant, *Alkanna tinctoria*, has blue flowers and a blackish root; from the latter red dye is obtained; also called dyer's bugloss, orcanet; various uses, including food colouring (*OED*).

allspice [all Spice]: an aromatic spice, also called Jamaica Pepper or Pimento, *see* pimento.

almonds, Jordan: not from the country of that name but a corruption of 'jardin', the Spanish word for garden (Glasse, p174). See Wilson (pp333, 335-7) for the use of almonds in England from medieval times.

alum [allam; allum; roach alum]: a whitish transparent mineral salt, very astringent; used in dyeing, tawing skins, and medicine, also for sizing paper, and making materials fire-proof . (*OED*) According to *Encyclopedia Britannica* (vol 1, 1769) 'what we commonly call roche or rock alum' was 'prepared from stones cut from the rocks of the quarry; and stands contradistinguished from the common alum, or that prepared from earths' (quoted in Glasse, p196).

ambergris [ambergrease]: a wax-like substance of marbled ashy colour, found floating in tropical seas, and as a morbid secretion in the intestines of the sperm-whale. It is odoriferous and now used in perfumery; formerly in cookery. (*OED*) ED uses it in a lemon cream and Lavender water.

anchovy: Lamb (1726) says that anchovies 'are a small Sea-Fish, that being pickled in Salt, are brought to us in little Barrels'. They were imported from the Mediterranean (quoted in Glasse, p174).

anise seeds: aniseed.

apples, Rennets: any of a large class of dessert apples of French origin, of which the most popular varieties are round or flattish in shape, small- or medium-sized, firm-fleshed, with good keeping properties (*OED*). See Glasse, p174, for more details.

artichoke bottoms: refers to the globe artichoke.

bain-marie [Baine Marie]: '"Bain-Marie" is a flat vessel containing boiling water; you put all your stewpans into the water, and keep that water always very hot, but it must not boil.' (*OED* quoting W Kitchiner, *Cook's Oracle*, (1882) p398; this is the earliest dated usage in *OED*) ED's much earlier receipt for 'Créme a Petit Pots: Baked Custards' explains how to make a bain-marie.

balm: name of some fragrant garden herbs (family Labiatæ); the chief are Balm Gentle or Balm-mint (*Melissa officinalis*) and Bastard Balm (*Melittis melissophyllum*) (*OED*).

Banyan manuscript: a Banyan was a Hindu trader, especially one from the province of Gujarat, so by extension this was a manuscript from that province of India.

barberries: small translucent red fruit of *berberis vulgaris*, an ornamental garden shrub. Much used for their decorative qualities and for their pleasant sweet-sour flavour. The fresh berries in bunches were scattered over cooked meats, and, as can be seen in Nott's recipes (B 16-25) they were also candied, pickled, and made into jellies and syrups.

barley, French: 'French Barley is skinned, and has the Ends ground off; the Pearl Barley is reduced by a longer Grinding to a little round white Lump' (J Hill, *Useful Family Herbal* (1754), p25, quoted in *OED*).

barley, pearl: *see* barley, French.

barm: ale-yeast, or barm, was the form of yeast used in baking until the mid-nineteenth century; it was the frothy mass produced on top of ale during its fermentation (Glasse, p173).

bay salt: made by natural evaporation in the sun in southern Europe. It is large and coarse-grained and was thought stronger than common salt but in fact it is a better material for use in salting meats, etc, because it is slower in dissolving (Ellis, p483).

beet leaves: the Romans introduced beet into Britain for the sake of their leaves, which were boiled in pottages; in the early modern period they were largely abandoned in favour of spinach (Wilson, pp196, 216).

beet [beat] leaves, white: a plant or genus of plants (family *Chenopodiaceæ*), having, in cultivation, a succulent root much used for food, and also for yielding sugar. There are two species, the Common or Red Beet (*Beta vulgaris*), found wild on the British coasts, and cultivated in several varieties, both as an esculent, and as an ornamental foliage plant, and the White Beet (*Beta cicla*), chiefly used in the production of sugar (*OED*).

Benjamin: Gum benzoin from the tree *Styrax benzoin* (*OED*).

bergamot: fragrant oil prepared from the rind of the fruit of the tree *Citrus bergamia* (*OED*).

bismuth, majesty of, [magistery of bismuth]: the subnitrate or basic nitrate of bismuth, used as a paint and cosmetic under the name of Pearl White or Pearl Powder (*OED*).

bladder: used for covering preserves and pickles; sometimes used in conjunction with a piece of leather. The combination is explained thus: 'The bladder, being thin, would stretch well and give a tight seal; but it would be porous when wet and not very strong. The leather, fastened over it, being thicker, would not provide a good seal but would give greater protections against mice, insects etc' (Glasse, p177).

blancmange: this changed in content over the centuries, by ED's time it was a kind of jelly, coloured with milk, cream or egg whites. See Wilson, pp206-8, 225-6.

blood-warm: as warm as blood; of the normal temperature of blood in the body (*OED*).

blue: a blue powder used to combat yellowing, and hence preserve the whiteness of garments and fabrics in laundering, by adding a slight tint of blue (*OED*).

bread, fine: made from finely bolted wheat flour (Glasse, p177).

bread, household: made from coarsely bolted wheat flour (Glasse, pp177-8).

brimstone: vernacular name for sulphur (*OED*).

brimstone match: a match or splinter of wood with its end dipped in brimstone.

briscuit of beef: brisket of beef.

buck, to: (in laundry) to steep or boil in an alkaline lye as a first process in buck-washing, or bleaching (*OED*).

buff: (buff-leather): properly, leather made of buffalo hide; but usually applied to a very stout kind of leather made of ox-hide, dressed with oil, and having a fuzzy surface, and a dull whitish-yellow colour (*OED*).

bullace: a small plum, still common in English cottage gardens (Glasse, p178).

calamus, sweet: some eastern aromatic plant or plants; but also applied by some English herbalists to the native Sweet Flag or Sweet Rush (*Acorus Calamus*) (*OED*).

calendered, to be: to press (cloth, paper, etc) between rollers, for the purpose of smoothing, glazing, etc (*OED*).

camphor: a whitish translucent crystalline volatile substance, belonging chemically to the vegetable oils, and having a bitter aromatic taste and a strong characteristic smell; prepared by distillation and sublimation from various species of *camphora* trees found in the Far East (*OED*).

canary (wine): a light sweet wine from the Canary Islands (*OED*).

candy, boil to a: sugar, mixed with a little water, boiled until it fizzled, thickened and candied (Wilson, p303).

candyheight, boil to: In 'To boil sugar Candy height', Raffald gives the following instructions (p124): 'Put a pound of sugar into a clean tossing pan with half a pint of water. Set it over a very clear slow fire, take off the scum as it rises, boil it till it looks fine and clear, then take out a little with a silver spoon. When it is cold, if it will draw a thread from your spoon, it is boiled high enough for any kind of sweetmeat. Then boil your syrup, and when it begins to candy round the edge of your pan it is candy height. NB It is a great fault to put any kind of sweetmeats into too thick a syrup, especially at the first, for it withers your fruit and takes off the beauty and flavour'. See also Rhodes, p8: 'when Sugar is boiled to a Candy height it will draw between your Fingers in great Flackes like berdlime & So you may use it as you please'. *See also* casting height.

capers: buds of the shrub *Capparis spinosa* gathered for pickling. The plant grows like the common bramble, abundant on walls and rocky places in the South of Europe (*OED*).

capsicum [capiscum]: *see* cayenne.

Captains' Biscuits: a hard variety of fancy biscuit (*OED*).

caravansera: 'To drop Caravansera: French Beans'. French, kidney, or haricot beans (*Phaseolus vulgaris*) came from South America, and were not known in Europe till after the time of the Spanish explorers (*OED*). The reference to 'caravansera' which was a kind of inn in Eastern countries where caravans put up, being a large quadrangular building with a spacious court in the middle (*OED*) is obscure.

carraway comfits: caraway seeds coated many times with boiling sugar to produce small white 'comfits' (Glasse, p179). See Wilson, p302, for details of comfit making.

carrouch: as this cannot be identified, Tom Jaine suggests that ED may mean 'caveach', the liquid used to pickle fish (see below).

casting height: one of the accepted descriptions of sugar temperature. Margaret Savile (1683) advised that to test whether sugar is at casting height 'stirre itt sometimes with a stick or a spoone, & when you stirre itt swing your stick from you and when itt is att a casting heigth[*sic*], your Sugar will flie from your stick, in great flakes of snow, or like Feathers flying in the aire' (Mason, p55). See also Rhodes, p8: 'when it is boiled to a Casting height it will draw between your Fingers in great Flackes like Fethers or like great Flackes of Snow Flying in the Ayre'.

catchup, *or* ketchup: a sauce made from the juice of mushrooms, walnuts, tomatoes, etc., and used as a condiment with meat, fish, or the like. Often with qualification, as *mushroom ketchup*, etc (*OED*; first mentioned 1711).

caveach: term found in many languages, always meaning the pickling of cooked fish. *OED* gives the term 'caveach' (1822) a Spanish derivation; in fact its use in English goes back further. Mary Kettilby (1714) had a recipe for 'Caveached Mackerel' and there are seventeenth-century examples. The origin of 'caveach' seems to be the Persian 'sikbaj' (sometimes rendered 'sakbay'), meaning 'vinegar stew'. It would have entered the European vocabulary through the Arabs, via Spain (Glasse, p179).

cayenne [chian; chyan; kian]: cayenne pepper. A very pungent powder obtained from the dried and ground pods and seeds of various species of capsicum, of South America; used as a condiment in cookery and as a stimulant in medicine; formerly called Guinea pepper (*OED*; first mentioned 1756). See Wilson, p293.

celery head: celery stalks.

celery roots: perhaps celeriac, a turnip-rooted variety of garden celery (*OED*; known from at least 1743).

chalot: shallot

chaff: collective term for the husks of corn or other grain separated by threshing or winnowing; and also, cut hay and straw used for feeding cattle (*OED*).

chaffing dish of coals: a portable brazier to hold burning coals or charcoal and designed to be set on a metal stand. Dishes could thus be finished or reheated away from the fierce heat of the hearth (Glasse, p179).

cherries, Carnation: variety of cherry no longer available, said to be 'a most delicate Fruit either for the Table or Conservatory' (Glasse, p178).

chervil: garden pot-herb, the young leaves of which are used to impart an aromatic flavour to soups, stews, salads, etc (*OED*).

chian: *see* cayenne.

China orange: *see* orange, China.

chocolate mill: whisking mill, known also as a molinette, was used to whisk chocolate drinks (Glasse, p180, where it is pictured).

chocolate pot: pot for chocolate.

chyan: *see* cayenne.

Cipress: *see* cypress.

citron: juicy pale yellow fruit, which is larger, less acid, and has a thicker rind than the lemon (*OED*).

clary flowers [clara flowers]: the herb *Salvia sclarea* (Glasse, p180).

cloves, powder of: ground/powdered cloves.

cochineal: dye-stuff consisting of the dried bodies of the insect *Coccus cacti*, which is found on several species of cactus in Mexico and elsewhere; it was at first commonly supposed to be the berry or grain of a plant (*OED*). Used as food colouring.

cockcombs: crest of a cock or cockerel, often used as a decorative garnish (Glasse, p181).

codling [codlin]: variety of apple, elongated in shape. The name 'codling' seems to have been applied to a hard kind of apple, not suitable to be eaten raw; hence to any immature or half-grown apple. In the beginning of the seventeenth century it was applied to a variety suitable to be cooked while still unripe (*OED*).

codling jelly: jelly made from codling apples.

coffins: *see* paper.

colander [cullender]: vessel, usually of metal, closely perforated at the bottom with small holes, and used as a sieve or strainer in cookery (*OED*).

corundum: a crystallized mineral belonging to the same species as the sapphire and ruby, but opaque or merely translucent, and varying in colour from light blue to smoky grey, brown, and black (*OED*).

Cos[s] lettuce: variety of lettuce introduced from the Greek island of Cos (*OED*).

crane: (to see if wine is fine) a bent tube, used to draw liquor out of a vessel; a siphon (*OED*).

crayfish [crays fish]: although 'crayfish' were small freshwater creatures, in eighteenth-century cookery books the term 'crayfish' was often used for the spiny lobster, a larger creature which lives in the sea (Glasse, p182). In ED's receipt 'Crays fish or Lobster Soup' it definitely means lobster.

cream of Tartar: purified and crystallized bitartrate of potassium, used in medicine and for various technical purposes (*OED*). *See also* tartar.
croquette: a ball or mass of rice, potato, or finely minced meat or fish, seasoned and fried crisp (*OED*).
crown: coin to the value of 5 shillings.
crucible powder: powder used for refining metals (*OED*).
crust: pastry case; pastry crust.
cullender: *see* colander.
cumming seed: cumin.
curry: preparation of meat, fish, fruit, or vegetables, cooked with a quantity of bruised spices and turmeric, and used as a relish or flavouring, especially for dishes composed of, or served with, rice. Hence, a curry was a dish or stew (of rice, meat, etc) flavoured with this preparation (or with curry-powder) (*OED*; first mentioned 1598).
curry powder: ED's receipt 'A Currie' uses 'Currie Powder' and says where it can be purchased. The first mention of 'curry powder' in *OED* is given as 1810, so this is earlier. ED's 'To make Curry stuff' is a receipt for curry powder.
cypress [Cipress]: (in pomade) perhaps an extract from the Cypress tree or its leaves (not in *OED*); 'chypre' was not known until the late nineteenth century (*OED*).

drudge: dredge, sprinkle with
Dutch oven: a large pot heated by surrounding it with fuel, and placing hot coals on the lid; also, a cooking utensil made of sheet-metal, placed in front of a grate and heated by radiation and by reflection from the back of the chamber (*OED*).

emery (for cleaning): coarse variety of corundum (*q v*), used for polishing metals, stones, and glass (*OED*).
eschalots: shallots

faggot of sweet herbs: bundle.
fenugreek [Founigreak]: a leguminous plant (*Trigonella Fœnum Græcum*) cultivated for its seeds (*OED*).
fine: (of liquids): free from turbidity or impurity, clear (*OED*).
firmity: *see* frumenty.
flannel (bag): an open woollen stuff, of various degrees of fineness, usually without a nap (*OED*).
flitch: side of a hog/pig, salted and cured; a 'side' of bacon (*OED*).

flour, Lammas: Lammas-wheat was winter wheat (*OED*), so presumably Lammas flour was made from winter wheat.

forced: stuffed.

Founigreak seed: *see* fenugreek

French roll: an enriched bread. ED has various receipts.

fricassee: a seventeenth-century definition of this was 'varieties of Meat boiled together in a Broth'. But the word developed a wider meaning and could refer to slices of meat fried or stewed; also to a dish of sliced, hard-boiled eggs, of chicken, rabbit, fish, etc. Originally, the preparation was always started by frying the chopped-up ingredients in butter, then adding liquid and thickening with eggs or flour (Glasse, p185).

Frontignac [Frontiniac]: muscat wine made at Frontignan, in the department of Hérault, France (*OED*). ED's receipt 'To make Frontiniac wine' provides an imitation.

frumenty [firmity]: a dish made of hulled wheat boiled in milk, and seasoned with cinnamon, sugar, etc (*OED*).

fustic [fustick]: two kinds of wood, both used for dyeing yellow: a) the wood of the Venetian sumach (*Rhus Cotinus*), now only with defining word, *young* or *Zante fustic*; b) the wood of the *Cladrastis* (*Chlorophora*, *Maclura*) *tinctoria* of America and the West Indies, sometimes called for distinction *old fustic* (*OED*). Used cut into chips.

galipot: *see* pitch, White Burgundy.

gall: an excrescence produced on trees, especially oak, by the action of insects, chiefly of the genus *Cynips*. Oak-galls are largely used in the manufacture of ink and tannin, as well as in dyeing and in medicine (*OED*).

gallipot: a small earthen glazed pot, mostly used by apothecaries for storing drugs and ointments, also by artists for mixing colours (Glasse, p185). Used by ED for storing Damson cheese.

ginger, flour of: dried ginger. Most ginger used in the receipts is what we would call 'root ginger'.

ginger, races of: rhizomes of ginger, often referred to roots of ginger although this is not botanically correct (Glasse, p195).

girdle: a circular plate of iron which is suspended over the fire and upon which cakes are baked or toasted (*OED*).

girkins: gherkins.

glass wort: name for certain plants containing a large amount of alkali, and so were formerly used in the manufacture of glass (*OED*).

glazier's putty: stiff, malleable greyish-yellow paste composed of finely powdered chalk mixed with raw linseed oil (or occasionally other ingredients) (*OED*).

Gloucester, single: various stories exist concerning the difference between Double and Single Gloucester cheeses. Was it due to the double skimming required of milk from Gloucester cows (cream rose slowly therefore had to be done twice)? Double had cream added taken from the morning' milk and added to the evening milk for making, whereas Single Gloucester used to be made from the partially skimmed milk remaining. Singles were typically the same diameter as Doubles (20" wide) but about half the height (2½" rather than 5). Whereas the Double Gloucester was a prized cheese comparable in quality to the best Cheddar or Cheshire, and was exported out of the County, Single Gloucester tended to be consumed within the County. (http://www.britishcheese.com/doublegloucester)

grape, Black cluster: could be grown in England (Glasse, p186).

grape, royal Muscadim: Muscadine grape; the white muscadine grape could be grown in England (Glasse, p186).

gravy beef: a part of the leg of beef cooked for the sake of its gravy (*OED*).

gravy, white: chicken, rabbit or veal gravy.

green copperas: the proto-sulphate of iron or ferrous sulphate ($Fe\ SO_4$), also called green vitriol, used in dyeing, tanning, and making ink (*OED*).

green vitriol: same as green copperas.

gridiron: cooking utensil formed of parallel bars of iron or other metal in a frame, usually supported on short legs; used for broiling flesh or fish over a fire (*OED*).

grists, grits: corn that is to be ground (*OED*).

Guinea, colour of: presumably golden.

gum anime: name given to various resins; the original, obtained from a West Indian tree (*Hymenœa Courbaril*), much used in making varnish; the others from Africa (*OED*).

gum arabic [gum arabick]: resin exuded by certain species of Acacia (*OED*).

gum dragon: *see also* sandrach. Alternative name for gum tragacanth, a mucilaginous substance obtained from shrubs of the genus *Astralagus* (Glasse, p186).

hair sieve: sieve with the bottom made of hair finely woven; usually for straining liquid (*OED*).

harrico [of mutton]: a ragout (originally of mutton, now sometimes of other meat) (*OED*).

hartshorn: deerhorn, used as a source of gelatine (Ellis, p487).

hasty pudding: simple, quickly-made pudding; usually of oatmeal or flour boiled in milk or water to produce a kind of thick batter (Glasse, p187).
hogshead: liquid measure.

ice: cover in a meringue mixture. See receipt 'Sugar crust for tarts' (p47).
imperial: imperial drink (formerly imperial water), a drink made of cream of tartar flavoured with lemons and sweetened (*OED*).
incle, inkle: kind of linen tape (*OED*).
indigo: substance obtained as a blue powder from plants of the genus *Indigofera*, N.O. Leguminosæ, and largely used as a blue dye (*OED*).
iron-mould: spot or discoloration on cloth, etc, caused by iron-rust or an ink-stain (*OED*).
isinglass: derived from sturgeons' sounds; originally brought by Dutch traders from Russia to Britain (Wilson, p45).
ivory black: a fine soft black pigment, obtained by calcining ivory in a closed vessel; sometimes loosely applied to bone-black (*OED*).

jagging iron: an instrument used for ornamenting pastry, etc, now made in the form of a wheel with teeth, set in a handle (*OED*).
Jamaica pepper: another name for allspice, *see also* pimento.
jelly bag: a bag for straining jelly through (*OED*; first mentioned c1600).
Jordan almonds: *see* almonds, Jordan.

kernel: (relating to a buttock of beef) a bundle of fat before the shoulder (W Marshall, *Rural Economy of the Midland Counties,* II, 439, quoted in *OED*).
ketchup: *see* catchup.
kettle: a vessel, commonly of metal, for boiling water or other liquids over a fire; a pot or caldron (*OED*).
kian: *see* cayenne.
kid leather slips: *see* slips.

Lammas flour: *see* flour, Lammas.
lamp-black: a pigment consisting of almost pure carbon; made by collecting the soot produced by burning oil or (now usually) gas (*OED*).
lamprey: a fish of the genus *Petromyzon*, resembling an eel in shape and in having no scales. It has a mouth like a sucker, pouch-like gills, seven spiracles or apertures on each side of the head, and a fistula or opening on the top of the head (*OED*).
laurel leaf: probably a leaf of the bay-laurel, ie a bayleaf. See *OED sub* 'bay' and 'laurel'. Laurel leaves are toxic but were used occasionally in

cooking if a bitter almond flavour was required. They were added to boiled milk and then removed again quickly (Glasse, p189).

lawn: fine linen.

lead, vinegar of: another name for litharge.

leather, piece of: *see* bladder.

lemon thyme: a cultivated variety of *Thymus Serpyllum*, having a scent like that of lemons (often called *T. citriodorus*) (*OED*). In several receipts ED says 'Lemon, thyme' suggesting lemon *and* thyme, but she may mean 'lemon thyme'.

lemon, syrup of: Nott, L 39, 'To make Syrup of Lemons': 'Pare your Lemons, slice them thin, lay in a Bason a Layer of Sugar beaten fine, and a Layer of Slices of Lemon, so continuing 'till you have laid all in; then let it stand all Night. The next Day pour off the Juice that runs from the Fruit through a Tiffany-Strainer, and put it into Glasses.'

lettuce, cabbage: the common, round, hearted lettuce.

levigate: to reduce to a fine smooth powder; to rub down; to make a smooth paste of (*with* some liquid) (*OED*).

ley: lees [of wine]

ling: a long slender gadoid fish, *Molva vulgaris* or *Lota molva*, inhabiting the seas of northern Europe. It is largely used for food (usually either salted, or split and dried) (*OED*).

linseed oil: oil extracted from the seed of flax (*OED*).

Lisbon wine: white wine produced in the province of Estremadura in Portugal and imported from Lisbon (*OED*).

litharge: protoxide of lead (PbO) prepared by exposing melted lead to a current of air (*OED*).

loaf, penny: in theory the weight varied according to the price of wheat, but Elizabeth David (1977) provides a note of 'The Penny White Loaf of the Cookery Books'. Her main point is that cooks would know what was meant in the recipe. White penny loaves weighed 6-8 ounces; an ordinary penny loaf (of coarse flour) weighed about twice as much (cited in Glasse, p178).

logwood [lug-wort; lugwood]: the heartwood of an American tree (*Hæmatoxylon Campechianum*) used in dyeing (*OED*). Used for colouring - from dark green to black (Jaine).

long pepper: *see* pepper, long.

lozenge, cut to shape of: a lozenge was 'a small cake or tablet, originally diamond-shaped …' (*OED*).

lugwood: *see* logwood.

lustring [lutestring]: a glossy silk fabric; a dress or a ribbon of this material (*OED*).

lye: alkalized water, primarily made by the lixiviation of vegetable ashes, but also applied (especially with prefixed word as in soap-lye, soda-lye) to any strong alkaline solution, especially one used for washing (*OED*).

mac[c]aroni: a variety of pasta formed in short, narrow tubes, usually boiled and served with a sauce, especially in Italian cookery; a dish consisting of this (*OED*; first mentioned 1673).

Maderia [wine]: a fortified wine produced on the island of Madeira; produced in dry, medium, and sweet varieties, the sweet being well known as a dessert wine. In colour Madeira characteristically has an amber tint, in shades ranging variously from light to dark. Until the turn of the eighteenth century, Madeira - like its cousins, port and sherry - was exported as an unfortified beverage wine (*OED*).

mango: jars of pickled mangoes reached Britain in the second half of the seventeenth century, and 'were copied with the aid of home-grown cucumbers or melons, and even onions or peaches'; hence various receipts 'to mango cucumbers' etc (Wilson, p295).

Manus Christi [height]: a particular stage in the boiling of sugar to make candies. 'To know when sugar is boiled to a Manus Christie Heighte It will then draw between your Fingers like a Small thread & So you may use it as you please' (Rhodes, p8). During the seventeenth century recipes referred to sugar boiled to 'candy height', the point at which it fizzled, thickened and candied. Sugar brought to this stage was used to make various suckets including the sweetmeat 'manus Christi' (Wilson, p303).

mastic[k]: an aromatic gum or resin which exudes from the bark of the lentisk or mastic tree; used chiefly in making varnishes (*OED*).

matting: a fabric composed of a coarse material (such as coir, bast, hemp, or grass), used as a covering for floors (*OED*). Here used for tying up, so presumably a string or cord of such material.

meat spoonful: used as a measure.

milk warm: as warm as milk newly drawn from the cow (*OED*).

mitonage: *mitonner la soupe* means to let soup simmer; so presumably here mitonage means soup.

molasses: thick, brown, uncrystallized syrup drained from raw sugar; later also concentrated syrup obtained from sugar during the process of refining (*OED*).

morel [morelle]: any of various edible fungi (discomycetes) of the genus *Morchella* (family *Morchellaceae*), mainly of temperate regions. In England, especially *M. esculenta*, found in grass and open woodland in spring ('common morel'); also called 'sponge mushroom' (*OED*). See *truffles* for further information.

Morello [Morella] cherry: a dark variety of sour cherry, used chiefly in cooking (*OED*).

mothery: mouldy (*OED*).

mountain wine: a type of wine formerly produced in Malaga, Spain. (*OED*)

musk: a reddish brown substance with a strong, persistent odour secreted by a gland of the male musk deer; highly prized in perfumery (*OED*).

mushroom powder: dried and pounded mushrooms. See ED's receipt 'Mushroom liquor and Powder'.

muslin: a lightweight cotton fabric in a plain weave (*OED*).

mustard, flour [flower] of: mustard powder, made from the crushed seeds of certain plants of the family *Brassicaceae* (*Cruciferae*), used in cookery for its pungency (*OED*).

Naples biscuits: a kind of biscuit flavoured with rose water (*OED*). Elizabeth David has described them as 'the original sponge fingers' (Glasse, p191).

neat: (of stockings) meaning here not clear; perhaps 'neatness'.

nitre: *see* saltpetre.

oil of mustard seed: an oil obtained from pressed mustard seeds (*OED*).

oil of Tartar: a saturated solution of potassium carbonate (*OED*).

oil, sweet: an oil of pleasant or mild taste, such as olive oil (*OED*).

orange, China: (*or*, sweet orange) the fruit of *Citrus sinensis* and its varieties, which has a pleasantly acid pulp and is used for eating and making juice (OED; see Glasse, p192).

orange, Seville: (or, bitter orange) the fruit of *Citrus aurantium*, whose pulp is bitter and which is now used chiefly for making marmalade (*OED*; see Glasse, p192).

orange chips: a slice of orange peel prepared for eating, usually by being dried or candied (*OED*).

orange flower water: an aqueous solution of orange flowers; the fragrant watery distillate left over in the preparation of neroli oil and used for culinary purposes and in perfumery (*OED*).

orgeat: a syrup or cooling drink made from barley or almonds and orange-flower water (*OED*).
oriss of Florence: any of various irises grown for their fragrant rhizomes; (more fully Florentine orris) the whitish-flowered *I. germanica var. florentina* (*OED*).
orpiment, yellow: arsenic trisulphide, As_2S_3; a bright yellow mineral of the monoclinic system which occurs naturally as prismatic crystals or massive deposits; formerly used as a dye or artist's pigment; also called *yellow arsenic* and (as a pigment) *king's yellow* (*OED*).
oyster liquor: both the liquor in which pickled oysters were kept (see 'To stew Carp'); and, the liquor that comes out of oysters when they are first opened (see 'A Ragout of Oysters').

pack-thread [packthread]: strong cord or twine used for sewing or tying up packs or bundles (*OED*).
palate: the palate is the roof of the mouth; the softer parts, to the rear, were those used in cookery (Prospect glossary).
pap, as thick as: semi-liquid food, such as that considered suitable for babies or invalids, usually made from bread, meal, etc, moistened with water or milk (*OED*).
Parmesan cheese: a hard, dry cheese made in Parma and elsewhere in northern Italy (*OED*; first mentioned in English 1519).
paper coffin: paper case (*OED*).
paste: pastry.
paste, puff: puff pastry.
patty pan [patties]: a small tin or pan, frequently fluted, in which patties are baked (*OED*; first mentioned 1660).
peas, split: 'husked peas, split for making pease-soup or pease-puddings' (P L Simmonds, *Dictionary of Trade Products* (1858), quoted in *OED*).
peel [piel]: a pole with a broad flat disc at one end, used to place loaves, etc., in an oven, and to withdraw them when baked (*OED*).
pennyroyal [Penny Royal]: a small-leaved, creeping mint, *Mentha pulegium*, native to damp heaths and similar places in Europe and western Asia; also, the fresh or dried leaves of this plant, formerly used medicinally and as a herb in cooking (*OED*).
pennyworth: as much as could be bought for a penny.
pepper, Jamaica: same as allspice, *see also* pimento.
pepper, lying or long: a condiment prepared from the immature fruit-spikes of the allied plants *Piper* (*Chavica*) *officinarum* and *P. longum* (*C.*

Roxburghii), formerly supposed to be the flowers or unripe fruits of *P. nigrum* (*OED*).

pepper, red: *see* cayenne.

Petit Patties [Pa't'ies]: small pasties used as garnish. Glasse, p60, has a receipt for 'Petit Patties for Garnishing of Dishes'.

piel: *see* peel.

pimento: allspice; the dried aromatic berries of the pimento tree, or a preparation made from them (*OED*).

pip, the: any of various respiratory diseases of birds, especially poultry, when accompanied by a white scale or horny patch on the tip of the tongue (*OED*).

pitch, White Burgundy: also known as galipot, 'a concrete resinous juice, of a yellowish white colour and strong smell … comes from Guienne, where it is afforded by two species of pine', quoted in *OED*.

plums, *magnum bonum*: any of several varieties of large cooking plum (*OED*).

poivrade, poivrade sauce [pauvre, poverroy]: 'A Poivrade Sauce, made as follows: Take Water, Vinegar, and White Wine, of each a like Quantity, put in some Pepper, Salt, and Shallot, threadfine, with some Lemon, and a little Anchovey; boil all together and strain it' (J Thacker, *The Art of Cookery* (Newcastle, 1758), p69, quoted in *OED*).

pollard: pollard wheat. 'Of wheat there are two different species cultivated in this kingdom; namely the smooth or polled wheat, and that with a rough or bearded ear' (J Banister, *Synopsis of Husbandry*, II:I, p56 (1799), quoted in *OED*).

pomade divine: a healing salve made from various ingredients, usually including lard and some scented essence (as almond, vanilla, etc) (*OED*).

pomatum: an ointment for the skin or hair (*OED*); same as pomade, which was originally a scented grease or ointment applied to the skin as a perfume, cosmetic, or salve. In later use a scented ointment or oil used to dress the hair (*OED*).

posset: a drink made from hot milk curdled with ale, wine, or other liquor, flavoured with sugar, herbs, spices, etc, and often drunk for medicinal purposes; a kind of syllabub made from similar ingredients (*OED*).

potash [pot ash]: potassium carbonate as used in the manufacture of glass (*OED*); here used to make peas green.

pot herbs: aromatic herbs used for flavouring pottage. See Wilson, Chapter 6, 'Cereals, potherbs and pottage'.

potato flour: *OED* first mentioned 1792.

potato starch: *OED* first mentioned 1801.

potter's clay: particular type of clay most suitable for making pottery.

poverroy sauce, poverry sauce: *see* poivrade.
powder vinegar: *see* vinegar, powder.
purple rensale: perhaps purple groundsel, which is the same as purple ragwort (*OED*).

quick lime: lime which has not yet been slaked; calcium oxide, CaO (*OED*).

race of ginger: *see* ginger, race of.
ragout: a highly seasoned dish, usually consisting of meat cut into small pieces and stewed with vegetables (*OED*).
raisins of the sun: sun-dried grapes, ie raisins, as distinct from raisins of Corinth, ie currants.
raisins, Malaga: raisins made from a grape grown in Malaga, Spain (probably chiefly the variety Muscat of Alexandria) (*OED*).
raisins, Smyrna: raisins produced in the vicinity of Smyrna, the chief port in Asia Minor (now Izmir in modern Turkey) (*OED*). A distinction was made between 'Smyrna raisins' and 'raisins', see the advertisement in the *South Carolina Gazette* 24-31 March 1735: 'To be sold by William Kellaway … Smyrna Raisins, and Raisins in the Sun' (*OED*).
rasp: grate.
raspings [raspins]: fine dry breadcrumbs produced by grating the crust of baked or stale bread (*OED*).
raspberry [rasberry], white: different fruit from red raspberry. Raffald, p105, has receipt for White Raspberry Jam.
ratafia [ratafie]: (liquid): a liqueur made by steeping nuts, kernels, fruits, or herbs in any sweetened spirit (*OED*).
ratafia [ratafie] cakes/biscuits: a kind of cake or biscuit flavoured with ratafia essence (*OED*).
ratafia essence: an essence used as a flavouring for food and drink, typically extracted from almonds or the kernels of cherries, apricots, and peaches (*OED*).
rennet: the digestive juice secreted in the stomach bag, or vell, of several mammals; used in cheese making. See Wilson, p151.
Rhenish Wine [Renish]: wine from the Rhine region.
roll, penny [penny role]: 'Tis fancied the streets are paved with penny rolls, the houses tiled with pancakes …' (B Franklin in *London Chronicle*, 29 Nov 1766, 524/1, quoted in *OED*). Contemporaries would know the size. See Glasse, p178, for 'penny loaf'.

rose pink: a pinkish pigment made by colouring whiting or chalk with a decoction of Brazil wood or other coloured wood (*OED*).
rose water: water distilled from roses or scented with essence of roses, used as a perfume or flavouring, or in medicinal preparations, etc (*OED*).
royal muscadim: *see* grape
rue: any of various southern European dwarf shrubs constituting the genus *Ruta* (family Rutaceae), especially (more fully **common or garden rue**) *R. graveolens*, which has yellow flowers and bitter, strongly scented feathery leaves, and was formerly much used for medicinal purposes (*OED*).
rusk: originally bread or cake broken into small pieces and hardened by rebaking, especially for use as ship's stores; in later use, plain or sweet bread which has been baked twice until it is dry and crisp (*OED*).

sack: a dry, amber wine imported from Spain and the Canaries (Glasse, p197).
sago: a species of starch prepared from the 'pith' of the trunks of several palms and cycads; chiefly used as an article of food (*OED*).
salamander: a circular iron plate which is heated and placed over a pudding or other dish to brown it (*OED*; first mentioned 1755: Glasse, 'Put it in the Oven to brown, or do it with a Salamander').
salep [salop]: the pulverized root of plants of the orchid family, *Orchis latifolia*, *O. mascula* and related species, which grow in parts of Europe and in Asia. Salep was supposed to have great nutritional powers (Glasse, p198).
salt, common: sodium chloride.
salt of steel: usually, iron chloride (but used also for the sulphate or other salts of iron) (*OED*).
saltpetre: sodium nitrate; sometimes potassium nitrate. Saltpetre is a white crystalline substance having a saline taste; it is the chief constituent of gunpowder, and is used medicinally (*OED*). Also known as nitre. ED uses it in curing hams & pork. See also Glasse, pp197-8.
sal-prunella [salt prunella]: not the same as saltpetre, despite Dr Johnson's assertion to the contrary. Sal-prunella is saltpetre that has been burned on charcoal to become a nitrite. The use of nitrites in preserving produces a red colour and is attended by greater risks than the use of nitrates (Glasse, pp197-8).
salt, white: prepared from seawater on the east coast of England and Scotland and from brine springs in Worcestershire and Cheshire. The Cheshire salt mines were started in 1670, when deposits of rock salt were discovered near Northwich. The salt produced there was sent to the west coast to be heated and dissolved in brine and recrystallized, thus making what was called 'salt upon salt' (Glasse, p198).

samphire: a herb which grows by the sea, eg on cliffs, and which used to be pickled as a standard relish for meat, fish or salads (Glasse, p198).
sandrach/sandract: probably Sandragon ('dragon's blood'). A bright red gum or resin, an exudation upon the fruit of a palm, *Calamus Draco*; formerly applied also to the inspissated juice of the dragon-tree, *Dracœna Draco*, and to exudations from *Pterocarpus Draco*, *Croton Draco*, and other plants (*OED*).
sarsaparilla: 1) the dried roots of plants of the various species of *Smilaceœ*; especially *Jamaica sarsaparilla*, *Smilax officinalis*; 2) a medicinal preparation of the root used as an alterative and tonic. The early mentions often relate to the supposed efficacy of the drug in the treatment of syphilis (*OED*).
savory, winter: *Satureja montana*, a hardy evergreen undershrub (*OED*).
Savoy biscuit: a kind of sponge-biscuit, made of finger-shaped pieces of paste covered with sifted sugar which, when baked, are joined together in pairs (*OED*; first mentioned in Nott, 1723 edition).
Savoy [cabbage]: a rough-leaved hardy variety of the common cabbage, much grown for winter use (*OED*).
savry: the herb 'savory'.
scotch: to make an incision or incisions in (especially the flesh); to cut, score, gash (*OED*).
Scott's liquid blue: a colour used in bookbinding. Its preparation is described in John Hannett, *Bibliopegia, or the Art of Book-binding, in All Its Branches* (Cambridge, 1836) pp67-68 (*OED*).
scum it: skim off the scum.
Sea or Captains' Biscuit: probably the same as 'ship's biscuit': hard biscuit prepared for use on board ship (*OED*).
seed-lac [seed lace]: also gum-lac. The dark-red resinous incrustation produced on certain trees by the puncture of an insect (*Coccus* or *Carteria lacca*); used in the East as a scarlet dye. The incrusted twigs are called stick-lac; the resin broken off the twigs and triturated with water to remove the colour is called seed-lac; melted, strained, and formed into irregular thin plates, it is known as shell-lac (*OED*).
semolina: 'The commercial name for the fine hard parts of wheat rounded by attrition in the millstones, imported chiefly from Italy' (quoted in *OED*; first mentioned in 1784).
senna: a shrub of the genus *Cassia*, native in tropical regions, bearing yellow flowers and flat greenish pods (*OED*).
Seville oranges: *see* oranges, Seville.

shallot: a small onion, native in Syria and cultivated for use as a flavouring ingredient for salads, sauces, etc (*OED*).
shivers: fragments, small pieces (*OED*).
shrub [scrub]: a prepared drink made with the juice of orange or lemon (or other acid fruit), sugar, and rum (or other spirit) (*OED*).
sieve, lawn: a fine sieve, made of lawn (or silk), used in cookery, porcelain-manufacture, etc (*OED*).
Single Gloucester: *see* Gloucester, Single
sippets [sippits]: small sops of fried or toasted bread used to garnish broths, soups, gravy or meat (Glasse, p200).
sives: chives (*OED*).
skellet: skillet, a shallow frying pan.
skimmer: a shallow utensil, usually perforated, used to skim liquids (*OED*).
slips, kid leather: perhaps 'long and relatively thin and narrow pieces or strips' (*OED*).
small-beer yeast: yeast liquor for making inferior quality beer. *See also*, barm.
smalt: a species of glass, usually coloured a deep blue by oxide of cobalt, etc, and after cooling finely pulverized for use as a pigment or colouring matter (*OED*).
snow water: perhaps water from an ice house, ie very cold water.
soap lees: spent soap-lye (*OED*).
soap, soft: a smeary, semi-liquid soap, made with potash lye; potash soap (*OED*).
sop: a piece of bread or the like dipped or steeped in water, wine, etc, before being eaten or cooked (*OED*).
sorrel: one or other of certain small perennial plants belonging to the genus *Rumex*, characterized by a sour taste, and to some extent cultivated for culinary purposes (*OED*). ED uses it in receipts for removing stains.
sound[s]: swimming bladder of certain fish, especially of cod or sturgeon (*OED*).
soy [of butter]: a sauce prepared chiefly in Japan, China, and India, from soybeans, and eaten with fish, etc (*OED*; first mentioned 1696).
Spanish white: *see* white, Spanish.
spermaceti: a fatty substance, which in a purified state has the form of a soft white scaly mass, found in the head (and to some extent in other parts) of the sperm-whale and some other whales and dolphins; used largely in various medicinal preparations, and in the manufacture of candles (*OED*).
spice of all sorts: perhaps allspice.
spinage juce: the juice of spinach. Presumably the liquid drained off after spinach has been cooked in a closely covered pan.

spirit of wine; rectified spirits of wine: (pure) alcohol; rectified spirit (*OED*).
spruce, essence of : 'The black spruce is used only for beer ... Of this spruce, is made the essence, which is as well known in Europe as in America (J Belknap, *History of New Hampshire* (1792), III, p110, quoted in *OED*).
Spruce beer: the adjective 'Spruce' refers to Prussia. *OED* gives the first mention of spruce beer in 1741, but the name appears to refer to the ingredient essence of spruce, from a tree, rather than precisely from Prussia. See previous entry.
steel, salt of: *see* salt of steel.
stocking piece [of beef]: the receipt implies a cut suitable for making a stock or gravy (not in *OED*).
storax: a fragrant gum-resin described by ancient writers; in early modern use applied to the resin of the tree *Styrax officinalis* (*OED*).
sugar, brown: unrefined or partially refined sugar as opposed to crystallized or loaf-sugar (*OED*).
sugar, candy: the name candy sugar, from 'khanda', the Sanskrit word for 'a piece', applied to large crystalline pieces of sugar grown on threads suspended in a saturated solution of refined sugar (Glasse, p201).
sugar, clarified: to clarify sugar it was boiled with water and eggs and then skimmed (Nott, S166, 'To clarify Sugar').
sugar, coarse: unrefined (but partially purified) sugar; *see* sugar, Lisbon.
sugar, double refined: *see* sugar, treble refined.
sugar, fine: *see* powdered.
sugar, heights of: *see* candyheight; casting height; Manus Christi [height].
sugar, Lisbon: clay was used to prepare the raw sugar that was shipped from the West Indies, often via Lisbon, to the refineries. 'Clayed sugar' or 'Lisbon sugar' meant the same thing - an unrefined, yet somewhat purified, sugar (Glasse, p201).
sugar, loaf: sugar normally came in a conical 'loaf' (Glasse, p200).
sugar, lump: 'lump sugar' was just lumps broken off the loaf (Glasse, p201).
sugar, moist: unrefined or partially refined sugar (*OED*).
sugar, Muscavado: raw or unrefined sugar obtained from the juice of the sugar cane by evaporating it and draining off the molasses (*OED*).
sugar, powdered: fine or powdered sugar grated from the loaf (Glasse, p201).
sugar, single refined: refined/single refined was 'ordinary' refined sugar, which was likely to be yellow (Glasse, p200).
sugar, sixpenny: another name for lump sugar. See the two identical receipts for 'Orange Wine' except one has 30 lbs of 'sixpenny sugar' and the other 30 lbs of 'lump sugar'.

sugar, treble refined: during its production process, sugar was boiled in water and then filtered, ie, refined. Ordinary refined sugar was usually yellow; double-refined sugar, which had been reboiled, recrystallized and refined again, was off-white; triple refined (or treble refined, or royal sugar) was more expensive and whiter (Glasse, p201).
sweetbread: the pancreas, or the thymus gland, of an animal, especially as used for food (distinguished respectively as heart sweetbread, stomach sweetbread, or belly sweetbread, and throat sweetbread, gullet sweetbread, or neck sweetbread); considered a delicacy (*OED*).
sweet herbs: parsley, thyme, etc. 'Sweet' was specified to exclude bitter herbs, which were more in use then than now (Glasse, p201).
sweet oil: *see* oil, sweet.
sweetmeats: this term, as used in the eighteenth century, referred to a wide variety of edibles: preserved, candied fruits; sugared seeds and nuts; sugared cakes and pastries; sugar boiled with pulp of various fruits, or flavourings, and fashioned into little flat cakes, lozenges, drops, etc (Glasse, p201).

talc [talk]: a hydrated silicate of magnesium (*OED*).
tammy soup strainer: tammy = strainer (*OED*).
tansy [tansey]: a mediaeval tansy was a fried mixture of eggs flavoured with the bitter juice of tansy leaves, eaten at Easter in remembrance of the 'bitter herbs' of Passover. Wilson (p145) states that early in the seventeenth century the traditional tansy was thickened with breadcrumbs, cream and spices, and served with sugar scattered over it. Gradually, as more crumbs, Naples biscuit, and sugar were added, it became a sweet pudding, baked or boiled, still including chopped tansy, but now coloured green with spinach juice (Glasse, p202).
tartar: Bitartrate of potash (acid potassium tartrate), present in grape juice, deposited in a crude form in the process of fermentation, and adhering to the sides of wine-casks in the form of a hard crust, also called *argal* or *argol*, which in the crude state varies from pale pink to dark red, but when purified forms white crystals, which are cream of tartar (*OED*).
tasser: not in *OED*. Perhaps 'tarrass', which was a waterproof mortar made of a sort of pumice imported from Germany. (Ellis, p491)
teaspoonful: a teaspoon seems to have been a larger measure in the eighteenth century than the standard teaspoon of today; its main use was for measuring rather than stirring. (Glasse, p190)
tincture: a solution, usually in alcohol, of some principle (resin or extract) (*OED*). Here 'tincture of Musk' is used in making 'Honey Water'.

tossing pan [tos pan]: pan for tossing food in cooking (*OED*).
treacle: the uncrystallized syrup produced in the process of refining sugar (*OED*). ED may be referring to molasses (see above).
Tripoli: a fine earth used as a polishing-powder, consisting mainly of decomposed siliceous matter, especially that formed of the shells of diatoms; called also *infusorial earth* or *rotten-stone* (*OED*).
truffles [trouffles]: often with morels. Any one of various underground fungi of the family *Tuberaceæ* (*OED*). The species of truffle found in England was not the same as either of the two principal edible species found in France and Italy, although still worth eating (Glasse, p203). In his *Dictionarium Botanicum* (1728) Richard Bradley says 'I have taken some Pains to search for them in England, and have found them in many Places, in Woods especially, in Surrey, Middlesex, Kent, Essex, in Hertfordshire, and Northamptonshire, and I guess, we have very few old Woods in England without them' (quoted in Glasse, p202). Bradley observed that truffles and morels tended to occur together.
tun: to put into or store in a tun, being a large cask or barrel, usually for liquids, especially wine, ale, or beer, or for various provisions (*OED*).
turpentine: a term applied originally (as in Greek and Latin) to the semifluid resin of the terebinth tree, *Pistacia Terebinthus* (Chian or Cyprian turpentine); now chiefly to the various oleoresins which exude from coniferous trees, consisting of more or less viscid solutions of resin in a volatile oil (*OED*).
turpentine, spirit of: commonly called oil of turpentine. A volatile oil, contained in the wood, bark, leaves, and other parts of coniferous trees, and usually prepared by distilling crude turpentine (*OED*).

verjuice: the acid juice of green or unripe grapes, crab-apples, or other sour fruit, expressed and formed into a liquor (*OED*).
vermicelli: a kind of pasta made in the form of long, slender, hard threads (*OED*). Glasse (p155) has 'To make Vermicella'.
vermillion: cinnabar or red crystalline mercuric sulphide, much valued on account of its brilliant scarlet colour; largely used as a pigment (*OED*).
vinegar, elder: perhaps vinegar flavoured with elder berries. Raffald (p176) provides a recipe for elder-flower vinegar. *OED* includes elder-vinegar but without a definition.
vinegar powder: vinegar in a dry form (*OED*).
vitriol: *see* green vitriol.

wafers, wafer paper: a preparation of paste in thin sheets, used in cookery and pharmacy (*OED*). The modern equivalent is rice paper.

walnut, green: when used in walnut catchup, 'green walnuts' are those that are picked before the shell is formed. (See Raffald, p174). ED has a receipt 'To pickle Walnuts Green', in which vine leaves are used to keep the walnuts green; see also 'To pickle Walnuts of an Olive Colour'.

whey: 1) the watery part of milk which remains after the separation of the curd by coagulation, especially in the manufacture of cheese (*OED*); 2) a medicinal drink.

whip syllabub: ED does not say how to make this. Raffald (p102) uses sweetened thin cream, lemon juice and Maderia or brandy, milled (whipped) to a froth with a chocolate mill; the froth is placed on a hair sieve to drain.

white, Spanish: finely powdered chalk used as a pigment or for its cleansing properties (*OED*).

whiting: a preparation of finely powdered chalk, used for whitewashing, cleaning plate, and various other purposes (*OED*).

winter savory: *see* savory, winter

wormwood: the plant *Artemisia Absinthium*, proverbial for its bitter taste. The leaves and tops are used in medicine as a tonic and vermifuge, and for making vermouth and absinthe; formerly also to protect clothes and bedding from moths and fleas, and in brewing ale. It yields a dark green oil (*OED*).

yeast, ale: yeast produced in the brewing of ale (*OED*); *see also*, barm.

Bibliography

Manuscripts

The National Archives

PROB11/737/441, will of Joseph Dimsdale, surgeon, of Bishops Stortford, proved 18 February 1744/5

PROB 11/1352/110, will of the right honourable Thomas Dimsdale, Baron of the Russian Empire, proved 17 January 1801

PROB11/1538/279, will and codicils of Elizabeth Dimsdale, dated 2 September 1808, 17 November 1803 and 21 June 1812

PROB11/1556/240, will and codicils of Stephen Hagger, mealman, of Hertford, proved 5 May 1814

PROB11/1801/465, will of Miss Ann Dimsdale, spinster of Hertford, proved 29 June 1832

RG6/1337, Society of Friends' Registers, Notes and Certificates of Births, Marriages and Burials, Bedfordshire and Hertfordshire, register of Monthly Meeting of Hertford,

Essex Record Office

D/Z 15/1, Minutes of the Benevolent Medical Society for the United Counties of Essex and Hertford

Hertfordshire Archives and Local Studies

D/EHx/T3, volume of draft and abbreviated copies of title deeds relating to miscellaneous and unspecified Hertfordshire properties, 1750-1793

D/EX 363/Z2, verses by Dr John Carr

DE/D/1172, Inventory of household goods at Cowbridge House, Hertford, late Miss Ann Dimsdale's

DE/R/F211/13, Receipted bill from Dr [John] Dimsdale for medical attendance and the supply of medicines (1776)

DE/R/F212/12, Bill for medical services from Dr [John] Dimsdale (1779)

HBR, Hertford Borough records, various volumes

NQ2/1A/15, Hertford Monthly Meeting Minutes, 1728-1741

Temp Acc 35, the receipt book of Elizabeth Dimsdale

University of Nottingham Library

PwF 230/1, letter from William Baker to the third Duke of Portland, 8 November 1792

Manuscript receipt books now in print

Baines, A and Imray, J, (eds), *Elizabeth Serrell of Wells, Her Recipes and Remedies: An Eighteenth Century Kitchen Commonplace Book* (Wells, 1986)

Grant, B, (ed), *The Receipt Book of Elizabeth Raper, and a portion of her Cipher Journal, written 1756-1770 and never before printed* (London, 1924)

Hess, K (ed), *Martha Washington's Booke of Cookery and booke of sweetmeats; being a family manuscript, curiously copied by an unknown hand sometime in the 17th Century* (Columbia, 1981)

Masson, M, (ed), *The Compleat Cook* (London, 1974) (manuscript cookery receipts of Rebecca Price)

O'Donoghue, V F, and O'Donoghue, P N, (eds), *Georgian Cookery; Recipes and Remedies from 18th century Totteridge* (New Barnet, 2007)

Pieris, M, (ed), *Take 6 Carrots, 4 Heads of Celery, 8 Large Onions ... The Receipts of a Hertfordshire Family* (Hitchin, 1994)

Prochaska, F, and Prochaska, A, (eds), *Margaretta Acworth's Georgina Cookery Book* (London, 1987) (a partial transcript)

Rhodes, D, (ed), *In an Eighteenth Century Kitchen: A Receipt Book of Cookery 1698* (London, 1968)

Spurling, Hilary, *Elinor Fettiplace's Receipt Book* (Harmondsworth, 1986)

Primary printed sources

Beasley, Henry, *The Druggist's General Receipt Book* (8th edition, 1886)

Cross, A G, (ed), *An English Lady at the Court of Catherine the Great* (Cambridge, 1989)

Curwen, J C, *Hints on the Economy of Feeding Stock, and Bettering the Condition of the Poor* (London, 1808)

Curwen, J C, *Hints on Agricultural Subjects, and on the best means of Improving the Condition of the Labouring Classes* (2nd edition, London, 1809)

Dossie, Robert, *Memoirs of Agriculture, and other Oeconomical Arts*, vol II (London, 1771)

Ellis, William, *The Country Housewife's Family Companion* (London and Salisbury, 1750; reprinted Totnes, 2000)

Guthrie, M, 'Part of a Letter from Matthew Guthrie, MD, of Petersburgh to Dr Priestley, FRS, on the antiseptic Regimen of the Natives of Russia', read on 30 April 1778, *Philosophical Transactions of the Royal Society*, 68 (1778), pp622-36

Farley, John, *The London art of cookery. and housekeeper's complete assistant* ... (9th edition, London, 1800)

(Glasse, Hannah), *The Art of Cookery made plain and easy* (London, 1747) (facsimile edition, Totnes, 1995, reprinted in paperback, 2004).

Hardy, James, *A candid examination of what has been advanced on the colic of Poitou and Devonshire, with remarks on the most probable and experiments intended to ascertain the true causes of the gout. By James Hardy, M D Of Barnstaple, Devonshire* (London, 1778)

Kirkpatrick, H., *An account of the manner in which potatoes are cultivated and preserved, and the uses to which they are applied in the counties of Lancaster and Chester* (Warrington, 1796)

'Memoirs of Baron Dimsdale', *Monthly Magazine, or, British Register*, 11:74 (July 1801), pp.511-13

Moxon, Elizabeth, *English Housewifry* (1764 edition; web edition published by eBooks@Adelaide)

Nott, John, *Cook's and Confectioner's Dictionary* (London, 1726; reprinted by L. Rivington with a glossary by E. David, London, 1980)

Philosophical Transactions of the Royal Society, 68 (1778)

Raffald, Elizabeth, *The Experienced English Housekeeper* (Manchester, 1769), edited by Ann Bagnall, and with an Introduction by Roy Shipperbottom, (reprinted, Lewes, 1997).

Sheldrick, G, (ed), *The Accounts of Thomas Green, 1742-1790* (HRS, vol VIII, 1992)

Smith, (E), *The Compleat Housewife: or, Accomplished Gentlewoman's Companion* (16th edition, London, 1758; facsimile, Oxford, 1983)

Stirling, A M W, (ed), *The Letter-Bag of Lady Elizabeth Spencer-Stanhope* (online version; Project Gutenberg ref 7253)

The A to Z of Georgian London, with introductory notes by Ralph Hyde (adaptation of John Rocque's survey of mid-eighteenth century London) (London, 1982)

The A to Z of Regency London, with introduction by Paul Laxton (facsimile of Richard Horwood's 1813 map of London) (London, 1985)

The ladies' library: or, encyclopedia of female knowledge, in every branch of domestic economy: comprehending, in alphabetical arrangement, distinct treatises on every practical subject, ... In which is included a vast fund of miscellaneous information, ... In two volumes. ... vol 2 (London, 1790)

The Monthly Magazine, or British Register, 1 February 1803, no. 97 (no. 1 of vol15)

Walker, J, (ed), *Datchworth Tithe Accounts* (HRS, vol XXV, 2009)

Young, Arthur, *General View of the Agriculture of the County of Essex*, vol II (London, 1813)

Secondary sources

Beale, N, and Beale, E, *Echoes of Ingen Housz* (Salisbury, 2011)

Bishop, W J, 'Thomas Dimsdale, MD, FRS (1712-1800) and the inoculation of Catherine the Great of Russia', *Annals of Medical History*, IV, no. 4 (July 1932), pp311-338

Clendenning, P H, 'Dr Thomas Dimsdale and Smallpox Inoculation in Russia', *Journal of the History of Medicine and Allied Sciences*, XXVIII, no. 2 (April 1973), pp109-125

Connell, B, *Portrait of a Whig Peer* (London, 1957)

Crisp, F A, (ed), *Visitation of England and Wales, Notes,* vol 13 (London, 1919)

Cross, A G, *By the banks of the Neva: chapters from the lives and careers of the British in eighteenth-century Russia* (Cambridge, 1997)

Cross, A G, *'By the banks of the Thames': Russians in eighteenth-century Britain* (Newtonville, Mass., 1980)

Cussans, J E, *History of Hertfordshire*, vol I, *Braughing Hundred …* (London and Hertford, 1870-73)

Cussans, J E, *History of Hertfordshire*, vol II, *Hertford Hundred* (London and Hertford, 1874-78)

Fordham, J, *Memoirs and Family History* (privately printed, 2004)

Graham, I M, 'Two Hertfordshire Doctors', *East Herts Archaeological Society Transactions*, XIII, part 1 (1950-51), pp44, 46-54

Jones, A, (ed), *Hertfordshire as recorded in* The Gentleman's Magazine (Hatfield, 1993)

Kebbel, T E, 'Dimsdale, Thomas (1712–1800)', rev. Andrea Rusnock, *Oxford Dictionary of National Biography* (Oxford University Press, 2004) [http://www.oxforddnb.com/view/article/7675, accessed 14 Feb 2008]

Krondl, M, 'A Hertfordshire culinary history query', *Herts Past & Present*, 3rd series, 21 (Spring 2013), p10

Lehmann, G, *The British Housewife: Cookery Books, Cooking and Society in eighteenth-century Britain* (Totnes, 2003)

Mason, L, *Sugar-Plums and Sherbet: the pre-history of sweets* (Totnes, 1998)

Munby, L, 'True Quakers? The Dimsdale family and the rise of the medical profession 1600-1800', in L Munby, *The Common People are not Nothing: Conflict in Religion and Politics in Hertfordshire 1575-1780* (Hatfield, 1995), pp155-166

Namier, L B, and Brooke, J, (eds), *The House of Commons, 1754-1790*, vol II, *Members A-J* (London, 1964)

Oxford Dictionary of National Biography (online version)

Page, W, (ed), *The Victoria History of the Counties of England: Hertfordshire*, 4 vols (London, 1908-12)

Pine, L G, (ed), *Burke's Peerage Baronetage and Knightage,* (100th edn; London, 1953)

Razzell, P, *The Conquest of Smallpox: The Impact of Inoculation on Smallpox Mortality in Eighteenth Century Britain* (London, 1977)

Salman, R N, *The History and Social Influence of the Potato* (Cambridge, 1949)

Sotheby's, *Books for Cooks: catalogue of the collection of* Stanley J. Seger (London, 2010)

Stead, J, 'Quizzing Glasse: or Hannah scrutinized', in (Hannah Glasse), *The Art of Cookery made plain and easy* (London, 1747) (facsimile edition, Totnes, 1995, reprinted in paperback, 2004), pp.xv-xxxiv

Weatherill, L, *Consumer Behaviour and Material Culture in Britain 1660-1760* (2nd edition, London, 1996)

Wienreb, B, and Hibbert, C, *The London Encyclopaedia* (London, 1983)

Wilson, C A, *Food and drink in Britain* (paperback edition, London, 1991)

Yost, G, 'The Compleat Housewife or Accomplish'd gentlewoman's Companion: A Bibliographical Study', *William and Mary College Quarterly*, 18:4 (October 1938), pp419-35

Zupko, R E, *British Weights and Measures: A History from Antiquity to the Seventeenth Century* (Wisconsin, 1977)

The Hertfordshire Record Society

The Hertfordshire Record Society exists to make Hertfordshire's historical records of all kinds more readily available to the general reader. Since 1985 a regular series of texts has been published.

Membership enquiries and orders for previous publications to the Hon. Treasurer, 50 Sollershott Hall, Sollershott East, Letchworth SG6 3PW

Annual Subscription (2013-2014) £17.50

Previous publications:

I: *Tudor Churchwardens' Accounts*. Edited by Anthony Palmer (1985) O/P

II: *Early Stuart Household Accounts*. Edited by Lionel M Munby (1986) O/P

III: *'A Professional Hertfordshire Tramp' John Edwin Cussans, Historian of Hertfordshire*. Edited by Audrey Deacon and Peter Walne (1987) O/P

IV: *The Salisbury-Balfour Correspondence, 1869-1892*. Edited by Robin Harcourt Williams (1988) O/P

V: *The Parish Register & Tithing Book of Thomas Hassall of Amwell* [Registers 1599-1657; Tithing Book 1633-35]. Edited by Stephen G Doree (1989) Price £6.00

VI: *Cheshunt College: The Early Years*. Edited by Edwin Welch (1990) O/P

VII: *St Albans Quarter Sessions Rolls, 1784-1820*. Edited by David Dean (1991) O/P

VIII: *The Accounts of Thomas Green, 1742-1790*. Edited by Gillian Sheldrick (1992) O/P

IX: *St Albans Wills, 1471-1500*. Edited by Susan Flood (1993) O/P

X: *Early Churchwardens' Accounts of Bishops Stortford, 1431-1538*. Edited by Stephen G Doree (1994) Price £6.00

XI: *Religion in Hertfordshire, 1847-1851*. Edited by Judith Burg (1995) Price £6.00

XII: *Muster Books for North & East Hertfordshire, 1580-1605*. Edited by Ann J King (1996) O/P

XIII: *Lifestyle & Culture in Hertford: Wills and Inventories, 1660-1725*. Edited by Beverly Adams (1997) Price £6.00

XIV: *Hertfordshire Lay Subsidy Rolls, 1307 and 1334*. Edited by Janice Brooker and Susan Flood; introduction by Mark Bailey (1998) Price £6.00

XV: *Observations of Weather': The Weather Diary of Sir John Wittewronge of Rothamsted, 1684-1689*. Edited by Margaret Harcourt Williams and John Stevenson (1999) Price £19.00 (£15.00)

XVI: *Survey of the Royal Manor of Hitchin, c1676*. Edited by Bridget Howlett (2000) Price £6.00

XVII: *Garden-Making and the Freeman family A Memoir of Hamels, 1713-1733*. Edited by Anne Rowe (2001) Price £18.50 (£15.00)

XVIII: *Two Nineteenth Century Hertfordshire Diaries, 1822-1849*. Edited by Judith Knight and Susan Flood (2002) Price £19.50 (£15.00)

XIX: *"This little commonwealth": Layston parish memorandum book, 1607-c1650 & 1704-c1747*. Edited by Heather Falvey and Steve Hindle (2003) Price £21.00 (£15.00)

XX: *Julian Grenfell, soldier and poet: letters and diaries, 1910-1915*. Edited by Kate Thompson (2004) Price £20.00 (£15.00)

XXI: *The Hellard Almshouses and other Stevenage Charities, 1482-2005*. Edited by Margaret Ashby (2005) Price £21.00 (£15.00)

XXII: *A Victorian Teenager's Diary: the Diary of Lady Adela Capel of Cassiobury, 1841-1842*. Edited by Marian Strachan (2006) Price paperback £9.99

XXIII: *The Impact of the First Civil War on Hertfordshire, 1642-1647.* Edited by Alan Thomson (2007) Price £22.00 (£17.50)

XXIV: *The Diary of Benjamin Woodcock Master of the Barnet Union Workhouse, 1836-1838.* Edited by Gillian Gear (2008) Price £22.00 (£17.50)

XXV: *Datchworth Tithe Accounts, 1711-1747.* Edited by Jane Walker (2009) Price £22.00 (£17.50)

XXVI: *John Carrington's Diary*, I, *1798-1804*. Edited by Susan Flood (not yet published)

XXVII: *Humphry Repton's Red Books of Panshanger and Tewin Water, 1799-1800.* With an Introduction by Twigs Way (2011) Price £30.00 (£17.50)

Maps:

The County of Hertford From Actual Survey by A Bryant In the Years 1820 and 1821 (2003; reprinted 2012) Price £8.50 (£7.50)

A Topographical Map of Hartford-Shire by Andrew Dury and John Andrews, 1766 (2004) Price £9.50 (£8.50)

For more information visit www.hrsociety.org.uk

Index of Persons

Christian names have been standardised; * = more than one occurrence; initials refer to donors of receipts. People of the same name have not necessarily been differentiated except for members of the Dimsdale family who were directly related to ED,

Index of Places

Unless well-known or otherwise stated, all places are in Hertfordshire; modern counties and countries given.

Index of Receipts

Receipts have been indexed by title and/or by chief ingredient, for example 'raisin wine' and 'wine, raisin'. Methods have been indexed separately, for example, 'pickle, to, hams' and 'pickle, mushroom'.

Index of Subjects

Cooking utensils and kitchen equipment have been indexed but ingredients have not. Unusual weights and measures such as 'dram' and 'handful' have been indexed but common ones, such as 'pound' and 'gallon', have not.

THE DIMSDALE FAMILY

ROBERT [Th
d 1713

JOHN [Theydon Garnon] = Susanna Bowyer (1700)
1675-1730 1682-1754

ROBERT [Theydon Gamon]
1705-65

Baron THOMAS, MD [Hertford] = (1) Mary Brassey (1739)
1712-1800
d 1744
= (2) Ann Iles (1746)
d 1779
= (3) ELIZABETH DIMSDALE (1779
1732-1812

JOHN
1747-1820
Banker
2nd Baron

NATHANIEL, MD
1748-1811
MP; Baron

SUSANNA
b 1749
d young

THOMAS
b 1750
d young

JOSEPH, MD
1751-84
= Mary Champion

RICHARD ILES
1753-1812
= Mary Haylett

ANN
1755-1832

THOMAS
b 1756
d young

ROBERT
1756-1825
3rd Baron
= Finetta Py

ANN
d 1837

THOMAS ROBERT
d 1865
4th Baron

CH